# HITLER, STALIN, AND MUSSOLINI

## TOTALITARIANISM IN THE TWENTIETH CENTURY

### THIRD EDITION

BRUCE F. PAULEY

UNIVERSITY OF CENTRAL FLORIDA

HARLAN DAVIDSON, INC.

WHEELING, ILLINOIS 60090-6000

**Visit us on the World Wide Web at www.harlandavidson.com.**

Library of Congress Cataloging-in-Publication Data

Pauley, Bruce F.
Hitler, Stalin, and Mussolini : totalitarianism in the twentieth century / Bruce F. Pauley.—3rd ed.
    p. cm. — (The European history series)
    ISBN 978-0-88295-269-7 (pbk.)
    1. Europe—Politics and government—20th century. 2. Hitler, Adolf, 1889–1945. 3. Stalin, Joseph, 1879–1953. 4. Mussolini, Benito, 1883–1945. 5. Totalitarianism—History—20th century. I. Title.
D445.P38 2008
940.5—dc22                                              2008036441

Cover: Details from photos of Hitler, Stalin, and Mussolini. The Hitler portrait shows him addressing the German Reichstag in Berlin on September 1, 1939, when he issued his declaration of war against Poland, thus starting World War II. The highly stylized version of a photograph, which was used for Nazi propaganda and appeared on the front pages of German newspapers, shows a calm but determined and confident leader dressed in a simple uniform, prepared to lead his country into a presumably certain victory. For information on the other photos, see the photoessay.

Manufactured in the United States of America
11 10 09 08 1 2 3 4 5  6 7 8 VP

*THE EUROPEAN HISTORY SERIES*
*SERIES EDITOR*
*KEITH EUBANK*

1

*FOR MY GRANDCHILDREN*
*ALENA, BEN, AND WILL PAULEY*
*MAY THEY LIVE IN A WORLD*
*FREE FROM TERROR*
*AND ENVIRONMENTAL DEGRADATION*

# FOREWORD

Now more than ever there is a need for books dealing with significant themes in European history, books offering fresh interpretations of events which continue to affect Europe and the world. The end of the Cold War has changed Europe, and to understand the changes, a knowledge of European history is vital. Although there is no shortage of newspaper stories and television reports about politics and life in Europe today, there is a need for interpretation of these developments as well as background information that neither television nor newspapers can provide. At the same time, scholarly interpretations of European history itself are changing.

To understand European history is also to better understand much of the American past because many of America's deepest roots are in Europe. And in these days of increasingly global economic activity, more American men and women visit Europe for business as well as personal travel. In both respects, knowledge of European history can deepen one's understanding, experience, and effectiveness.

The European History Series introduces readers to the excitement of European history through concise books about the great events, issues, and personalities of Europe's past. Here are accounts of the powerful political and religious movements which shaped European life in the past and which have influenced events in Europe today. Colorful stories of rogues and heroines, tyrants, rebels, fanatics, generals, statesmen, kings, queens, emperors, and ordinary people are contained in these concise studies of major themes and problems in European history.

Each volume in the series examines an issue, event, or era which posed a problem of interpretation for historians. The chosen topics are neither obscure nor narrow. These books are neither historiographical essays, nor substitutes for textbooks, nor monographs with endless numbers of footnotes. Much thought and care have been given to their writing style to avoid academic jargon and overspecialized focus. Authors of the European History Series have been selected not only for their recognized scholarship but also for their ability to write for the general reader. Using primary and secondary sources in their writing, these authors bring alive the great moments in European history rather than simply cram factual material into the pages of their books. The authors combine more in-depth interpretation than is found in the usual survey accounts with synthesis of the finest scholarly works, but, above all, they seek to write absorbing historical narrative.

Each volume contains a bibliographical essay which introduces readers to the most significant works dealing with their subject. These are works that are generally available in American public and college libraries. It is hoped that the bibliographical essays will enable readers to follow their interests in further reading about particular pieces of the fascinating European past described in this series.

*Keith Eubank*
*Series Editor*

# CONTENTS

*Illustrations*

*Maps:*

# PREFACE

With each edition of this book the specter of totalitarianism has taken on new perspectives. When *Hitler, Stalin, and Mussolini* was first published in 1997 it had been only six years since the collapse of the Soviet Union and eight since the fall of its empire in East Central Europe. Books and articles based on recently opened Soviet archives were just beginning to appear, and Russia, the core of the old Soviet Union, was in turmoil with its political and economic future very much in doubt. When the second edition appeared six years later, the Taliban regime in Afghanistan, which in many ways had intruded into the personal lives of Afghans in even more repressive ways than the three dictatorships featured in this book, had just been overthrown by U.S. and Afghan opposition forces. The democratic but largely ineffective regime of Boris Yeltsin had recently been replaced by the more sober and pragmatic rule of President Vladimir Putin, one of whose first acts was to ruthlessly suppress a rebellion in the southern province of Chechnya.

Still more dramatic events related to totalitarianism have occurred since the publication of the second edition of this book in early 2003. The brutal and undoubtedly totalitarian regime of Saddam Hussein in Iraq was removed from power by U.S. and Allied forces in the spring of that year. What will take its place, however, is still very much in doubt more than five years later. Far from following the example of post–World War II Germany and Japan, as expected by President George W. Bush, it has remained divided between rival ethnic and religious factions, much like Yugoslavia in the 1990s following the collapse of other Communist regimes throughout East Central Europe. The establishment of a stable Western-style democracy in Iraq is still, in 2008, a very questionable outcome of the Second Gulf War. In the meantime, elements of the Taliban have reappeared in the southern part of Afghanistan while the government of President Hamid Karzai in Kabul has little real authority outside the capital city and is not safe from attack even there.

Totalitarian and posttotalitarian regimes are not limited to Europe and the Middle East. In the Far East, North Korea remains the purest remaining example of Stalinism. On the other hand, China and Vietnam have abandoned economic Communism with its hopelessly unproductive collectivized farms and government-owned and controlled industries in favor of private farms and free industrial enterprises. These changes have produced spectacular results: Vietnam has increased its output of rice four to six times since 1986 making it the world's second biggest exporter of rice while China has become an industrial powerhouse. Both countries are still governed by Communist parties which tolerate no other organized parties. However, their control of the press appears at present to be loosening and both countries welcome foreign tourists and do not restrict foreign travel by their own citizens in sharp contrast to the Soviet Union and its satellites. Whether their Communist parties will be able to maintain their monopoly on power when economic downturns inevitably occur is anyone's guess.

In the meantime, new dictatorial regimes have appeared in Myanmar (formerly known as Burma) in Southeast Asia and Zimbabwe in southern Africa. The control they exercise over their populations is limited only by their primitive means of communication. The Myanmar military junta has not hesitated to crush protesting Buddhist monks and has prevented foreign journalists from reporting to the world on the desperate conditions of a quarter of the country's population which was devastated by a typhoon in the spring of 2008. In Zimbabwe, the President-dictator, Robert Mugabe, has driven out the white owners of highly productive farms in order to reward his followers with land, even though the result has been massive unemployment and critical food shortages. Russia clearly returned to a much more authoritarian style of government under President Putin. Whether Putin remains the country's de facto ruler in his new role as prime minister is so far unknown. Even Italians are looking for a far stronger government with the recent re-election of Silvio Berlusconi. The common denominator in all these countries, plus most of the former Communist countries of East Central Europe, whether they are present or recent totalitarian dictatorships, is enormous corruption which is made all the worse by the absence or at least limitations on freedom of the press which might otherwise expose misdeeds.

With so many totalitarian or near-totalitarian regimes remaining in the world today or struggling to emerge from the shadows of totalitarianism, it is clear that the examples of totalitarian dictatorships discussed in this book cannot be dismissed as mere intellectual curiosities with no relevance to the present.

This third edition of *Hitler, Stalin, and Mussolini* contains new facts found in the reading of nearly forty more books, most of which have been published since 2002. Thirty of these titles have been added to the Bibliographical Essay. Fascinating new details have been added to every chapter, but the largest additions have been made in Chapter 7 on terror, in Chapter 9 on Stalin's lack of preparedness for war in 1941, in Chapter 10 on the attempted reforms of Nikita Khrushchev and Mikhail Gorbachev, and most of all in Chapter 11, which highlights changes that have taken place in the former dictatorships since the turn of this century. This new edition also includes several new pictures, which illuminate issues raised in the text, three entirely new maps, and a much expanded index. None of the information in this book derived from the most recent literature on totalitarianism has persuaded me to revise my original thesis: the totalitarian regimes were moderately successful when following pragmatic policies; however, the pursuit of their utopian objectives led to disaster in each of the three totalitarian states.

Once again, I would like to thank a number of friends and colleagues who in one fashion or another have helped me with this third edition and with understanding the concept of totalitarianism in general. I have profited from several conversations with my colleague, Vladimir Solonari, of the University of Central Florida who had the misfortune of growing to maturity in the Soviet Union. Another colleague at UCF, Hong Zhang, provided me with some useful information about Communism in her native China. Two stints as a guest professor at the University of Nebraska-Lincoln in 2002 and 2006 gave me numerous opportunities to discuss Nazism with Alan Steinweis, who is currently working on a book on *Kristallnacht,* and Lloyd Ambrosius, who offered me some useful insights into American foreign policy as it related to the dictatorships. In addition, I wish to thank him as well as the Chair of the History Department at UNL, Kenneth Winkle, for supporting the annual Carroll R. Pauley Memorial Lecture Series.

My knowledge of history in general and the history of totalitarianism in particular has been enormously enhanced by twenty-two research and study trips to Europe and the Near East and two more to the Far East between 1954 and 2008. Over half of the thirty-two illustrations in this book are photographs taken by me during these trips which took me to the Soviet Union as well as to all of the East Bloc countries of Europe prior to the fall of the Berlin Wall in 1989. In addition I have visited several former Nazi concentration camps and numerous monuments and buildings associated with Mussolini in Italy and on the Greek island of Rhodes, once an Italian possession. Like other historians, I have found that there is no substitute for visiting sites where important historical events occurred.

Two long-time and close Austrian friends were particularly helpful during three of these journeys. My junior-year-abroad roommate in Vienna in 1957–58, Dr. Walter Siegl, twice invited me to visit him in Moscow, the first time in 1980 when he was the chargé d'affaires at the Austrian embassy, and the second time in 1996, when he was the Austrian ambassador to Russia. Both visits were absolutely fascinating and were particularly useful in exposing me to conditions in the Soviet Union when it was at the height of its power, and later when Russia was struggling to adjust to posttotalitarian conditions. My other Austrian friend, Dr. Helmut Sohmen, the chairman of the BW Group (formerly the World Wide Shipping Company) in Hong Kong, has been a long and faithful correspondent on historical issues and current events and has been a gracious host in both Austria and Hong Kong. All of these friends and colleagues have added prodigiously to my understanding and love of history over my forty-four-year career.

# PREFACE
# TO THE SECOND EDITION

When the first edition of this book was published in 1997, readers
had the luxury of believing that totalitarianism was purely a product
of the twentieth century and a never-to-be-repeated phenomenon.
The people of the United States and Canada could also imagine
that mass murder and terror were things that only occurred on other
continents and certainly not in North America. The suicide attacks
on the World Trade Center in New York City and the Pentagon in
Washington as well as the existence of the Taliban regime and its al-
Qaeda allies in Afghanistan have shattered these illusions. What the
world has learned since September 11, 2001, is that totalitarianism
and terror are still realities and cannot be relegated to the status of
historical curiosities.

The Taliban regime surpassed any of the regimes described in this
book in the extent to which it attempted to control every facet of the
lives of the Afghan people. Its Ministry for the Promotion of Virtue
and the Prevention of Vice regulated daily life in ways undreamed of
by Hitler, Stalin, or Mussolini. Laughter, music, and dancing, as well
as modern inventions such as television were all prohibited. The total
repression of women made the reactionary philosophy and policies
of even Nazi Germany look downright progressive by comparison. If
in some respects the fascists of Germany and Italy wanted to return
to the bucolic days of the nineteenth century when a woman's place
was in the home, the Taliban wanted to return to the seventh century
when Islamic women were presumably totally veiled and never seen
in public. Whereas the totalitarian states of the twentieth century
humiliated, imprisoned, and tortured their internal enemies out of
the public's view, the Taliban conducted very public executions in a
former soccer stadium. If both the Axis powers and even the Allies
sometimes resorted to attacking civilians to achieve their goals during
the Second World War, civilians were the primary victims of the al-
Qaeda organization. If fascism and Communism were secular religions
that sometimes borrowed the terminology and rituals of traditional
religions, the Taliban was openly and fanatically committed to the

most extreme and reactionary form of Islam. Like new religions, the Taliban and the three totalitarian regimes discussed in this book were all utopian. All four regimes tried to create a new, and in their eyes, perfect society. Those who rejected this brave new world were dealt with as enemies who had to be suppressed for the common good.

One of the fascinating revelations about extreme Muslim fundamentalism is the similarity it bears to extreme anti-Semitism from the late nineteenth century to the end of the Second World War. Anti-Semites in Germany and Austria as well as other European countries blamed the Jews for all the allegedly undesirable aspects of modernization. Jews were seen as having enormous influence around the world and were held responsible for capitalism, socialism, urbanization, secularism, materialism, liberalism in journalism, atonal music, and a host of other supposed modern evils. Because a few prominent Jews could be found in all of these areas the allegations of the anti-Semites seemed plausible to people who wanted to believe them and who had been economically hurt by modern developments.

Now, at the turn of the twenty-first century Americans have assumed the role that Jews played a century ago. It is now Americans who are the people with tremendous international influence. Americans are the modernizers when it comes to such things as the emancipation of women, consumerism, secularism, and popular music. The Taliban and the al-Qaeda have sought to counter such modernization with religious totalitarianism that would turn the clock of history back by twelve hundred years.

This second edition of *Hitler, Stalin, and Mussolini* incorporates new information found in over seventy books I have read since the publication of the first edition. About forty-five of these titles have been added to the bibliographical essay. Every chapter contains new information. However, chapters 6 through 10 in particular have been expanded with new facts concerning health care, diplomacy, and the Second World War. None of the new information contradicts the central thesis of the first edition, namely that the totalitarian regimes were moderately successful when they pursued pragmatic policies, but self-destructed when they implemented their more extreme ideological objectives. Certainly these regimes were all far more pragmatic than the Taliban in Afghanistan, which went so far as to dismiss all female teachers and physicians. The second edition also includes numerous new photographs that will help to illustrate important points in the text and three new maps.

I wish to thank the many scholars who sent me useful suggestions regarding the first edition. Likewise, Darlene Willis, the interlibrary loan librarian at Windsor-Severance public library in Windsor, Colorado, did yeoman work in providing me with numerous books critical to the second edition of this book. I would also like to extend my thanks to Gary Hollingsworth and Michelle Harm for allowing me to use copies of the Hollingsworth collection of Soviet posters. Institutions wishing to see this fascinating collection in its entirety should contact Hollingsworth Fine Arts at 407-422-4242.

# PREFACE
## TO THE FIRST EDITION

"Totalitarianism" is one of the most controversial terms of the twentieth century. First used by Italy's democratic critics in the mid-1920s to describe the new Fascist regime, it gained currency in Anglo-Saxon countries during the 1930s in reference to Nazi Germany and the Soviet Union as well. It became extremely popular between the signing of the Nazi-Soviet Non-Aggression Pact in August 1939 and the German invasion of the Soviet Union in June 1941, a time when the two dictatorships were virtual allies. However, once the Soviets became enemies of the Nazis, and especially after the American intervention into the war in December 1941, the term suddenly became a political embarrassment and disappeared from public discourse. With the opening of the Cold War in the late 1940s and 1950s, following the Soviet occupation of East Central Europe, the term reached a new peak of popularity only to fall into disfavor during subsequent decades when relations between the Soviet Union and the West improved.

Fading memories of Adolf Hitler, Joseph Stalin, and Benito Mussolini made "totalitarianism" an anachronism at best, and a polemic at worst, loosely applied only to a country's most diabolical enemies. Scholars from the 1960s to the 1980s were particularly loath to use a term that could label them as unreconstructed cold warriors and preferred the term "authoritarian" to describe the Soviet Union of their day. Members of President Ronald Reagan's administration, however, were eager to revive the term after his election in 1980. The biggest catalysts for changed thinking, however, resulted from the opening of the Berlin Wall and the collapse of the Soviet Empire in Eastern Europe in 1989 and the disintegration of the Soviet Union itself in 1991. Interestingly enough, those people who had actually lived in totalitarian states were not the least reluctant about using the term once they were finally free to do so.

Whatever they may be called, the dictatorships of Germany, the Soviet Union, and Italy were breakthroughs in the physical and intellectual control of their own populations, and the dictators of Communist Russia and Nazi Germany slaughtered more people than any other rulers in the history of the world, ancient or modern, with the probable exception of their fellow totalitarian ruler Mao Tse-tung in Communist China.

All of the totalitarian dictators are remarkable both for what they intentionally accomplished and for what they achieved despite themselves. Mussolini greatly enlarged Italy's colonial empire but wound up losing it all. He concentrated more power in his hands than any of his predecessors; but in the process he created such revulsion that a postwar constitution established a premiership so weak that Italy has experienced new government heads an average of once a year for the last half century. No one since Alexander the Great changed so large a portion of the world as much in just twelve years as did Hitler. He wanted to build a great continental empire and managed instead to lose a quarter of Germany's pre-1937 territory and to leave his country, as well as the Continent, divided. He carried the concepts of nationalism, racism, and dictatorship to unheard of heights, but in so doing he created a backlash that thoroughly discredited all three ideas, most of all his favorite doctrine of racism. Lenin and Stalin wanted to eliminate deeply ingrained Russian habits of slackness and inefficiency, as well as their country's economic backwardness. They succeeded instead in discouraging creativity, polluting the environment, and leaving the Soviet Union still far behind its rivals in the West.

In the pantheon of historical monsters, Adolf Hitler has long held pride of place for most students of history. His evil reputation is well deserved, but his placement in a special category apart from Stalin is probably due to the far greater documentation of his crimes than to the objective facts. The total collapse of Nazi Germany, the postwar Nuremberg Trials, and the early access to Nazi archives have provided historians with a bonanza of raw historical materials that even now have by no means been fully exhausted. The Soviet Union, on the other hand, remained comparatively sealed off to Western historians until its downfall in 1991; its archives are only now beginning to open up, revealing contents far uglier than even the most ardent anti-Communists had imagined. Fascist Italy, by comparison, has often received an almost benevolent treatment from historians, when they have considered it at all. Mussolini and Italian Fascism have frequently been depicted as either slightly comical or relatively harmless. This reputation is undeserved. That the Fascists inflicted only moderate destruction on foreign states can be attributed to Italy's lack of human and natural resources and the backward state of its economy, not to a tolerant leader or even to a peace-loving population. Losing wars is seldom popular, and Italy began losing almost as soon as it entered World War II.

All of the dictatorships, but again especially those of the Soviet Union and Germany, succeeded in deporting, imprisoning, and killing their most productive workers and intellectuals, thus contributing to their own ultimate demise. Hitler eliminated by one means or another most of the half-million Jews who had lived in Germany when he came to power in 1933, even though the Jewish community had produced half the country's Nobel Prize winners. The destruction of the German Jewish community was merely the beginning of the Holocaust which eventually claimed the lives of 5 million to 6 million European Jews and nearly as many non-Jews. Stalin actually managed to outdo Hitler to become by far the biggest mass murderer in history by slaughtering at least 20 million people. All of them, unlike Hitler's victims, were citizens of his own country and killed in peacetime; often they were his nation's most productive inhabitants. All of these deaths, one should hasten to add, represent only those people whose murder can be directly attributed to the three dictators. They do not include the tens of millions of soldiers and civilians who died as a result of Hitler's launching of World War II or Stalin's disastrous military tactics.

This book does not purport to be a complete history of Europe's three twentieth-century totalitarian dictatorships. Such a work would require many volumes and, if based on original research, would be far beyond the capacity of any one historian. My goal in these pages is much more modest, but nevertheless important. It is to evaluate some of the many theories historians have proposed as to why the totalitarian movements arose and seized power, how they utilized their unprecedented authority, and why they ultimately failed. For well over half a century, the subject has produced endless controversies, only a few of which can be alluded to herein.

The destructiveness and indeed self-destructiveness of the regimes is patently obvious. If any system of government deserves to be called evil, it is surely totalitarianism. And yet if totalitarianism had been nothing more than terror and nihilism, one would be at a loss to explain its popularity with a substantial part of the subject populations. There is no question that short-term apparent achievements usually disguised long-term baneful goals. But to be fair to the people who lived under totalitarianism, students of history must be ever mindful that those people did not enjoy the benefit of hindsight. To understand totalitarianism, or indeed any historical subject, one must begin at the beginning, not at the end.

This work has benefited enormously from classroom discussions I have had with students at the University of Central Florida over the past twenty-five years. In addition, several of my colleagues at UCF, including Carole Adams, Charles Killinger, Edmund Kallina, and John Evans, graciously consented to read all or portions of the manuscript. I received much moral and material support from my chairman, Richard Crepeau, as well as from Dean Kathryn Seidel, Provost Gary Whitehouse, and President John Hitt. UCF also greatly facilitated the writing of this book by providing me with a sabbatical leave. My thanks also go to Charles F. Delzell, emeritus professor at Vanderbilt University, Professor Gilbert McArthur of the College of William and Mary, and George M. Kren of Kansas State University for reading the manuscript and offering excellent suggestions. I gained valuable insights into East German totalitarianism at a summer seminar in 1993 at Yale University sponsored by the National Endowment for the Humanities and directed by Professor Henry Ashby Turner, Jr. A special debt of gratitude is owed to the editor of The European History Series, Professor Keith Eubank, who invited me to contribute to it and saved me from making many errors of fact and judgment. I alone, of course, remain responsible for any mistakes that may remain in this book. My wife, Marianne, whom I met in a class on totalitarianism, once again patiently sacrificed many outings so that the writing of this book could be brought to a timely conclusion.

# 1 / *THE IDEOLOGICAL FOUNDATIONS*

## *DEFINITIONS OF TOTALITARIANISM*

Surprisingly, there has been a greater agreement among historians about how to define *totalitarianism* than there has been about whether the definition actually fits any of the states usually described as totalitarian. Advocates of the term stress: (1) the extraordinary powers of the leader; (2) the importance of an exclusionist ideology; (3) the existence of a single mass party; (4) a secret police prepared to use terror to eradicate all domestic opposition; (5) a monopoly of the communications media as well as over the educational systems; (6) a determination to change basic social, artistic, and literary values; and (7) an insistence that the welfare of the state be placed above the welfare of its citizens.

Much less agreement can be found among historians about the importance of purges to totalitarianism, the role of state economic planning, and the degree to which citizens of totalitarian states were able to maintain some sort of private life. Scholars who object to the term altogether note that even in the Soviet Union and Germany, where the governments were the most powerful, many individuals maintained private lives comparatively free of authoritarian controls. In the Soviet Union there were competing factions, interest groups, and bureaucratic networks that could defy government decrees. And, industrial and military leaders in Germany as well as the monarchy and the Roman Catholic Church in Italy all retained considerable autonomy. Proponents of the totalitarian concept, on the other hand, assert that it was an ideal, which, like all ideals, could never be perfectly achieved.

The argument between ideals and practices is an old one, and it has been applied to any number of political, historical, and even artistic terms. Was the United States really a democracy in the eighteenth and nineteenth centuries when slavery was legal and women were denied the franchise? Has there ever been a perfect democracy, even in fifth-century B.C. Athens? Is there even a definition of "democracy" that would apply to all states claiming such status? For that matter, are there universally accepted definitions of "freedom" or "class"? Obviously, to insist on the perfect implementation of political ideals would make all classifications impossible.

The totalitarian dictators did not in fact control every facet of their respective country's existence. They were free, however, to reach major decisions without consulting or by ignoring the advice of other individuals or institutions. They were not bound by any laws or customs and were unlikely to be affected by appeals to conscience, sentiment, or pity. They were not even restrained by official ideology because they alone decided what the ideology du jour should be; they did not hesitate to reverse previously held ideological positions however much they might deny it.

In many ways, totalitarianism was a secularized religion complete with charismatic leaders, sacred books (with old and new testaments), prophets, martyrs, saints, disciples, heretics, hymns, ceremonies, processions, and concepts of heaven and hell. True believers claimed to be in possession of the one revealed truth that could not be disputed on the basis of rational arguments. There were chosen people who belonged to the "right" class or race and nonbelievers and nonfavored groups who had to be eradicated from the righteous community by instruments of inquisition. The young were to be thoroughly indoctrinated in the new "religion" so that it would be perpetuated indefinitely. It is no wonder, therefore, that many traditional religious leaders soon realized that they were competing with the totalitarian leaders and parties for the very soul of the people.

Comparisons between democratic and totalitarian ideals help in the understanding of both. Surprisingly, there are some superficial similarities. Totalitarian regimes, like democracies, claimed to rule on behalf of the governed but were "unhindered" by the "divisiveness" of parliamentary states. Hitler and Mussolini (though not Stalin) also resembled democratic leaders in wanting to be photographed mingling with the "masses." They had elections or at least plebiscites (in the case of Nazi Germany). Both systems even had constitutions. The similarities, however, are far more apparent than real. Totalitarian regimes were ultrapaternalistic. They decided what was in the best interest of their citizens, not the citizens themselves, whose willingness or ability to do the right thing was very much in doubt. Elections consisted only of unopposed candidates selected by the totalitarian party. Constitutions, if not ignored as in the case of Nazi Germany, existed to protect the government, not ensure rights of individuals against the government, as in democracies. Most important, democracies are characterized by an optimistic philosophy of human nature; in the tradition of late seventeenth- and eighteenth-century English and French enlightened philosophers, humans are thought to be by nature rational. As such they are capable of managing their own affairs with only minimal assistance from a government. Totalitarian philosophy, on the other hand, holds that humans are by nature either too irrational or too ignorant to be entrusted with self-government.

Another way of understanding twentieth-century totalitarian dictatorships is to compare them with their nontotalitarian predecessors. Arbitrary, authoritarian, and brutal forms of government, which censor all forms of literature and minimize individual rights, are as old as civilization itself. The first Napoleonic regime in the early nineteenth century also resembled the totalitarian dictatorships in its charismatic leadership. But these other forms of despotism depended on the tolerance of the army, church, or business interests. Moreover, they allowed considerable freedom of expression so long as it did not threaten the regime. Their leaders were often constrained by customs or a sense of responsibility to God. The totalitarian dictatorships, on the other hand, were not satisfied with the mere absence of opposition; they demanded positive support, especially from the shapers of public opinion: journalists, teachers, authors, and artists. The lack of rapid and mass forms of communications, together with high illiteracy rates, made it impossible for pre-twentieth-century regimes to control their subjects physically and intellectually. Finally, as alluded to above, earlier dictatorships usually lacked the religious zeal and desire to completely transform society.

The totalitarian dictatorships of the twentieth century had at their disposal mass-circulation newspapers, mass-produced posters, telegraph machines, telephones, automobiles, railroads, airplanes, cinemas, radios (and more recently television sets), and mandatory-attendance public schools. Orders from dictators could be transmitted to the lowliest government, party, and military officials instantly. No village was too remote to be outside the reach of the regime's instruments of propaganda.

## MARXISM-LENINISM-STALINISM

Although most scholars believe that there were important common denominators between the regimes of Communist Russia, Fascist Italy, and Nazi Germany, none would argue that they were without major differences in their beliefs and practices.

The Soviet dictators, Lenin, Stalin, and their successors, like their fellow autocrats in Italy and Germany, claimed to follow an immutable and indeed scientific ideology. The works of the nineteenth-century German economic philosopher Karl Marx were supposed to be the foundation of the Communist ideology. In reality, first Lenin and then Stalin changed Marx's ideas almost beyond recognition. (See figure 1.) Marx, especially in his famous work *Das Kapital,* argued that a class struggle had existed throughout history and would soon produce an international revolution of industrial workers. Marx, however, had no blueprint for the future Communist utopia beyond saying that the means of production would be owned in common, thus preventing any further exploitation of one class by another. Even Lenin, prior to his seizure of power in the fall of 1917, had no practical plans for postrevolutionary government beyond vague concepts: nationalization of industries; large-scale and communal farming; and central economic planning.

Lenin and also Stalin inherited from Marx unverifiable beliefs about the behavior of various social groups, which were given the status of scientific laws and were hence beyond dispute or public opinion. They also inherited from the master an unscrupulous attitude toward anyone whom they perceived as impeding the development and consolidation of the revolution.

Lenin, however, unlike Marx and his more orthodox followers in Russia known as Mensheviks, was unwilling to wait for the Industrial Revolution to follow its natural course in Russia, which was by far the most economically backward of the major European states at the beginning of the twentieth century. By promising to turn over confiscated noble lands to peasants, Lenin believed he could gain at least the temporary support of peasants—for whom Marx had had nothing but contempt—and thus carry out an early revolution. Nor did he believe that the proletariat was capable of organizing any kind of revolution on its own. It needed instead to be led by a small group of dedicated professional revolutionaries over which he would exercise dictatorial control. Thus, Lenin quickly abandoned Marx's idea of majority rule. His creed was out of step with contemporary developments in Marxism in western Europe, but it was very much in the tradition of Russian authoritarianism and secret conspiracy. Lenin's drastic alteration of Marxism was to have ominous consequences for the future. Unlike the regimes of Italy and Germany, which came to power by at least pseudoconstitutional means, in the Soviet Union the Communists were able to achieve power only through the use of force and were never able to depend thereafter on popular support.

Lenin, however, though intolerant of overt opposition, was at least willing to put up with discussions within the Bolshevik party, which he founded in 1903. Dissidents might be demoted, or even expelled from the party, but they were not killed. Stalin moved one step beyond Lenin. Under the former, meaningful discussion within what by then was called the Communist party soon came to an end. The use of terror was no longer confined to non-Communists, but was now also directed against those within the party itself.

Lenin and Stalin did at least resemble Marx in foreseeing a much greater role for the postrevolutionary state in the economic life of Russia than did Mussolini in Italy or Hitler in Germany. To some degree they had little choice because the Russian bourgeoisie was so weak. Not only would all the factories and other means of industrial production be owned by the state, but so too would all the agricultural land, which would be cultivated on large collective farms. Uprooting 120 million peasants from their ancestral homes would require far more force than the relatively modest economic plans envisaged by Mussolini and Hitler. Indeed, it required a veritable civil war in which there were literally millions of casualties. It also required a bureaucracy and police apparatus far larger than those of the other two dictatorships. Excess became the very essence of what became Stalinism. At the height of the Stalinist terror in the 1930s, an estimated one of every eight Soviet men, women, and children was shot to death or sent to a labor camp in which many died.

## FASCISM AND NAZISM

Whereas Soviet Communists saw their movement as an instrument of progress for all humanity, fascists and Nazis made little attempt to appeal to other nationalities, believing that alien races could never be assimilated. Superficially, the ideology of the Fascists in Italy was almost diametrically opposed to Communism. In fact, both Fascists and Nazis (often generically lumped together as "fascists" with a small "f") made anti-Communism or anti-Marxism (to include social democratic parties) a major part of their programs. Here, chronology is important. By the time the Fascist and Nazi parties were born in 1919, the Communists had already seized power in Russia, were engaged in a brutal civil war, and had attempted to carry their revolution deep into Poland.

Consequently, fascism in both Italy and Germany arose in an atmosphere of anti-Communist hysteria. If the Communists were international in their outlook and appeal (though they were frequently nationalistic in practice), fascists were militantly nationalistic. If the Communists favored the industrial working class and sought to destroy private property along with the middle and upper classes, the fascists (at least in Germany) called for a classless "people's community" (in German, *Volksgemeinschaft*) and the protection of private property. If the Communists were outspoken atheists, fascists and Nazis, on the whole, pretended, at least, to be the defenders of Christianity. If Marxists in theory wished to emancipate women, fascists would protect them from the evils of politics and glorify their traditional roles as homemakers and prolific mothers. Despite these apparently diametrically opposed views, however, the practices of Communists and fascists turned out, in many cases, to be remarkably similar.

Fascism in both Italy and Germany was more than simply anti-Communism. It was also passionately opposed to the liberal, democratic, parliamentarian values of the Western democracies, which dated back to the eighteenth-century Enlightenment and the French Revolution. Fascists believed that they had exalted the rights of individuals at the expense of the community. In the words of a Nazi slogan, *"Gemeinnutz geht vor Eigennutz"* (the common good comes before the good of the individual). Although unwilling to go nearly as far as the Communists in outlawing private property, they were equally intolerant of diversity, and just as filled with hatreds and resentments.

Like the Communists they saw violence as unavoidable. The fascists promoted considerably more control of their economies than was acceptable in the West, at least prior to World War II. Capitalists were allowed to prosper in the fascist states, but only if they cooperated with the aims of the political authorities.

The two fascist states, however, differed significantly from each other as well as from Communist Russia and the democratic West. Mussolini was very much interested in pursuing old-fashioned colonialism in Africa and creating a new, albeit smaller, Roman Empire around the Mediterranean Sea in places like Albania, Greece, Tunisia, Nice, and Corsica. His glorification of warfare as an exalting and purifying experience found no echo in the Soviet Union and even went beyond the public pronouncements of Hitler, at least before World War II. However, whereas Mussolini was constantly touting the virtues of war, his preparations for combat were woefully inadequate. Hitler, on the other hand, professed his love of peace, until at least 1938, while accelerating the rearmament of Germany. Finally, Fascism and Nazism differed sharply on the subject of race. Racism and anti-Semitism were not part of Fascist ideology until 1938, and, when finally introduced, were unpopular with many Italians.

For Adolf Hitler, race was as central to the understanding of history as the class struggle was for Marxists. To him it was even more important than nationalism, although throughout the 1920s and 1930s he liked to pose as a traditional nationalist who wanted nothing more than to reunite all nearby ethnic Germans into his Third Reich. Hitler borrowed his philosophy heavily from nineteenth-century racists. (However, he admitted being indebted only to the anti-Semitic composer, Richard Wagner.) Hitler was anxious to show that his racist ideas were thoroughly grounded in German history, but unlike the Communists, neither he nor Mussolini claimed to have an infallible ideological founding father, apart from himself.

The Nazis believed that there was a definite racial hierarchy among humans: they and other "Nordics" (a term often used interchangeably with "Aryans") such as the Scandinavians, Dutch, and Anglo-Saxons of Britain and the United States, were at the top. Mediterranean people such as the Italians and French came next, followed by the Slavs (Russians, Poles, etc.); and finally Africans, Gypsies, and Jews, who were definitely at the bottom. The Jews, however, differed from other "inferior races" because, far from being "lazy" or "stupid," they were hard working and diabolically clever in their businesses and professional practices. Worse, they were conspiring to take over the world and were therefore the mortal enemies of unsuspecting Aryans. Asians, particularly Japanese, did not easily fit into the Nazis' racial hierarchy. The problem was solved when Japan became a German ally, after which the Japanese were dubbed "honorary Aryans."

Racism, as will become readily apparent in the pages that follow, was fundamental both to the domestic and foreign policies of Hitler's Germany. It led directly to the discrimination, segregation, deportation, and finally extermination of the German-Jewish population and later to the slaughter of Jews in other European countries. It was also behind the Nazis' euthanasia program that resulted in the murder of tens of thousands of other groups of "racial inferiors," including the mentally ill, the physically handicapped, and homosexuals. Finally, it was racism that tempted Hitler to invade the Soviet Union because he became convinced that it was dominated by Jews who could not hope to build or run a state capable of stopping the German army.

Hitler's expansionist plans were much more ambitious than Mussolini's, although both dictators were influenced by nineteenth-century ideas about living space or *Lebensraum*. For Hitler, however, this space could only be acquired in Europe, in areas that Germans themselves would be willing to colonize. Ukraine seemed to be the perfect place to colonize because of its fertile soil, relatively low density of population (or so Hitler imagined), and tolerable climate. Such an area, which was larger than Germany itself, would enable the Reich's population to grow to 250 million in a century, but this German and Germanized population would be economically independent. Ukraine would not necessarily have been Hitler's final conquest, however. According to the Nazi leader, a healthy population was one which was always increasing and which, in turn, would continuously require new land in order to grow its food. He had no confidence in Germany's ability to increase its agricultural productivity and probably would have been astonished to learn that West Germany, prior to German reunification, had been able to provide most of its own agricultural needs with little more than half the territory of Hitler's Germany. In any event, for Hitler there were only two possibilities: limitless expansion or utter ruin.

It should be noted, however, that Hitler's own racist and expansionist ideas were a form of contemporary Social Darwinism. Charles

Darwin was a nineteenth-century English biologist who explained biological evolution, or namely his theory of natural selection, in *The Origins of Species*, published in 1859. According to Darwin, only those individuals of each species in the animal and plant kingdoms that had characteristics best suited to their environment would live long enough to reproduce and thereby pass those "successful" characteristics on to their offspring. Thus, only the fittest of each species would survive the struggle for existence. An English social scientist named Herbert Spencer extrapolated what Darwin had written and then applied a similar notion to human society, in which he saw individuals, nations, and even entire races all competing for survival. Spencer's "Social Darwinist" ideas were at the height of their popularity when Hitler was growing up around the turn of the twentieth century, and they permeate Hitler's famous book, *Mein Kampf,* which he wrote in the middle of the 1920s. Hitler took the ideology of Social Darwinism literally, frequently assigning the same task to two different people on the theory that the fitter of the two would perform the job better. At the end of his life he also reached the logical conclusion (for him) that the Slavic Russians, having defeated the Germans, must be racially superior and more fit to survive.

Some historians have regarded Nazi Germany as backward looking in contrast to Fascist Italy, which they view as forward looking. It is true that the Nazis had a soft place in their hearts for peasants and the simple rural life and even attempted to create a back-to-the-farm movement. They also hated modern music and art and even frowned on some modern medical practices. By contrast, Mussolini was committed to modern architecture and technology, often bragging about his air force setting new speed records. The differences in the outlooks of the two regimes, however, were superficial and not unique. A-back-to-the-farm movement also existed in the United States during the 1930s, and many Americans, even to this day, tend to view life on farms and in small towns as being more virtuous than life in big cities. In any event, many historians have pointed out that Hitler's foreign policy could only be achieved by a modern, mechanized army, not by peasants carrying pitchforks.

Neither Fascist Italy nor Nazi Germany can be easily categorized as either revolutionary or reactionary, traditional or modernistic, backward looking or forward looking. Both clearly contained all of these elements. Even Communist Russia cannot be easily pigeon-holed. Though it denounced everything about the tsars, it became profoundly conservative during and after the reign of Stalin.

The dictators of all three totalitarian states took their ideologies very seriously even though they were willing to change them for tactical purposes whenever it suited their fancy. All three of them spoke of creating a new utopia based on national renewal and rebirth which would be implemented by a single totalitarian party. Ironically, they enjoyed their greatest successes when they were not driven by ideological considerations and met their greatest catastrophes precisely at those times when they sought to put their most extreme ideological concepts into practice.

# 2 / *THE SEIZURE OF POWER*

Totalitarian dictatorships were established in Russia, Italy, and Germany in part because of long-term authoritarian traditions that already existed in all three countries, and in part because of more immediate political and economic crises. Otherwise, however, the circumstances in which the three totalitarian parties came to power varied substantially. The Bolsheviks (as they were still called until 1918) took over the most backward great power of Europe, in the middle of a disastrous war. The Fascists attained power in 1922, three years after the end of World War I, in what was only a partially industrialized country. The Nazis took the reins of power in one of the most industrially and educationally advanced countries in the world, but not until 1933 when Germany was in the throes of the Great Depression. In each case the totalitarian party was in a minority when it attained power but faced an opposition that was too divided to stop its ascent.

## RUSSIA ON THE EVE OF THE REVOLUTION

Although it was not totalitarian, because it did not seek to mobilize the masses prior to the World War, tsarist Russia was very definitely autocratic. Under the tsars Russia had never experienced the liberating influences of the Renaissance, the Reformation, or (for the most part) the Enlightenment, which had so deeply altered the political, cultural, social, intellectual, and religious life of Western and Central Europe. Until 1864, there was no local self-government in Russia and no national parliament until 1906. The state had dominated the Russian Orthodox Church since the reign of Peter the Great in the early eighteenth century. The government also censored the press and limited the right of assembly. The state was typically totalitarian in being supported by a huge bureaucracy, a powerful army, and a secret police. The main limitations on its power were not constitutional but technical. It simply lacked efficient means of thought control due to its own technological backwardness.

The tsarist government was also the state's largest employer and initiated the industrialization of the country in the 1880s. Although this government-directed modernization was necessary to prevent Russia from falling even further behind the West, it had some distinct drawbacks. The already deep divisions between the minority of rich and majority of poor grew still larger, as did differences between industrialists and workers, workers and peasants, the highly educated few and the 55 percent who were still illiterate. Even differences between the majority of ethnic Russians and non-Russians grew, as the national minorities became more aware of their own identities.

Increased education in the second half of the nineteenth century meant that those with advanced educations, especially if they had had an opportunity to travel in the West, became increasingly embarrassed by their country's backwardness. With no democratic means of bringing about meaningful changes, violent revolution seemed to be the only viable alternative. Such a revolutionary opportunity came in 1905, following Russia's humiliating defeat at the hands of Japan. However, the Revolution of 1905 failed to satisfy either democrats or the more radical revolutionaries.

Marxist historians long argued that a proletarian revolution had been inevitable in Russia with or without the coming of World War I. Western scholars have long been divided on that issue. In any event, it is safe to say that Russia's entry into the war made a national revolution far more likely. Its defeat at the hands of Britain and France in the Crimean War in the 1850s revealed Russia's backwardness and soon led to the emancipation of the serfs, as a means of promoting modernization through social mobility. The consequences of its defeat by Japan have already been noted. But it was World War I that proved fatal to the Russian monarchy. Although Russian losses between 1914 and the overthrow of the Tsar in 1917 were proportionately smaller than those of Britain and France, they were still huge in absolute terms—6 million people. Moreover, Russia's World War I casualties were often the result of poor leadership or the lack of weapons and ammunition, which Russian industries could not produce in adequate numbers.

On the eve of the revolution, and in the middle of World War I, Russia remained the only belligerent country with no system of food rationing, so that during the conflict the poor were desperately hungry while the rich remained well fed. Ultimately, it was this shortage of food which led women, tired of standing in long lines, to riot in the capital of Petrograd (earlier and again today known as St. Petersburg). By this time even the army, the police, the civil servants, the landed gentry, and the leading figures of business and finance—the groups upon which the Romanovs had long depended—had become disgusted with the Tsar's incompetence and his reliance upon the advice of his German-born wife and the peasant faith healer-turned-courtier, Grigori Rasputin whose last name in Russian means "debauchee." The bread riots, which occurred in March 1917, set in motion a chain of events that brought down the 300-year-old Romanov dynasty within a week and led to the establishment of a middle class, democratic Provisional Government out of the remnants of the Duma. A revolutionary conspiracy had long sought to overthrow the regime, but in the end it was disgruntled housewives who took the lead.

Meanwhile the revolutionary Lenin had been biding his time in Swiss exile. Born Vladimir Ulianov in 1870, his maternal grandfather was a baptized Jew, a fact that was carefully hidden from the public. But unlike the other totalitarian dictators, Lenin showed no evidence of harboring a racial anti-Semitism. He also differed from the other dictators in that he came from a loving, prosperous family and had a happy childhood. His father, a school teacher, was a loyal tsarist official, and his mother taught him the rudiments of German, English, and French. He went on to earn a law degree with honors at the University of St. Petersburg.

A defining moment in Lenin's life came at the age of seventeen when his older brother, Alexander, was executed for planning to assassinate Tsar Alexander III. Lenin's path to respectability was now barred, and an unbridgeable gulf had opened between him and the regime that had taken his brother's life. He began reading Marx when he was eighteen years old and formed a Marxist group a year later. In 1895, he was arrested for trying to publish an underground Marxist newspaper. After fourteen months in a St. Petersburg prison he was sent to Siberia for three more years of imprisonment, during which he had plenty of time to read and write.

Much of the time between 1900 and 1917 Lenin spent in exile in Switzerland reading history, economics, and philosophy and writing revolutionary tracts. However, by 1914 he had begun to doubt that another Russian revolution would occur in his lifetime. The outbreak of World War I changed his mind, however, as he immediately recognized its revolutionary potential. Shortly after the Tsar's overthrow, the German High Command facilitated Lenin's return to Russia (by rail), in the hope that the revolutionary would create such havoc in his native land that Germany could soon end the fighting on the Eastern Front.

Though the Bolsheviks were much too weak to seize power on their own when Lenin arrived in Petrograd, they quickly gained popularity thanks to Lenin's demagogic "April Theses" calling for "Bread, Land, and Peace." Specifically, he demanded an immediate end to the war, the transfer of factories and industries from capitalists to committees of workers (called *soviets*), and the redistribution of the lands of noble estates to the peasants, even though the Bolsheviks were adamantly opposed to private ownership of the land. The Provisional Government could not accede to any of these demands without alienating its own supporters and its Western allies or violating its own legalistic principles. A Russian summer offensive soon turned into a rout, leaving the government essentially defenseless.

Lenin, ignoring the Bolshevik party's minority status (except in Petrograd and Moscow), and refusing to form alliances, even with other socialist parties, overcame heated opposition within his own party to an early revolution by threatening to resign and by appealing to the rank and file as well as to the masses. (See figure 2.) Lenin's view ultimately prevailed, and the Bolsheviks overthrew the Provisional Government housed in the tsar's Winter Palace in November. (See figure 3.) Thus the capital of the largest country in the world fell to a handful of fighters in little more than a day with the loss of just six lives. A week later, Moscow was taken after only a few hundred people had been killed. Lenin's energy, organizational skills, speaking ability, and ruthless will to power had finally paid off. However, millions more would die before the Bolsheviks were fully entrenched in power.

### THE ESTABLISHMENT
### OF THE SOVIET DICTATORSHIP

Within days the Bolsheviks had managed to alienate large numbers of would-be supporters. Private citizens lost control of their property, which was now claimed by the state. Banks became a state monopoly and only small withdrawals were permitted. Private trade, even for small shopkeepers, was forbidden. Peasants were required to sell grain to the government at whatever price the government chose to pay. Having long demanded the election of a Constituent Assembly, in which every party would be represented proportionately, the Bolsheviks did permit the election to take place a few days after they came to power. But the freest election in Russian history resulted in their party coming in a poor second, garnering only 9.8 million votes of 41.7 million cast. Consequently, the Bolsheviks broke up the assembly with the use of two hundred pro-Bolshevik sailors and outlawed future meetings of the body following its first and only meeting in January 1918.

The Bolshevik coup was also followed by the systematic elimination of all competing political institutions. The liberal press was suppressed; the entire judicial system, including the supreme court, or Senate, was replaced by "people's courts." Local governments were abolished; opposition parties were outlawed; and provincial governments, universities, learned societies, and clubs were all Bolshevized in a matter of eight months.

So precarious was Lenin's grip on power that survival of the regime quickly replaced world revolution on his list of priorities. In order to concentrate exclusively on domestic affairs, Lenin overrode the objections of other Bolsheviks and authorized the separate Treaty of Brest-Litovsk of March 1918 with Germany and its allies. Russia thereby lost 1.3 million square miles and 62 million people. Most of the territory acquired during the previous two centuries, from Finland to Ukraine and the Caucasus, was surrendered, at least temporarily. Lenin thought the sacrifice was justified since he expected proletarian revolutions would soon occur in those regions. The treaty was unpopular with Russian nationalists, however. Other Russians objected to the terror of the secret police, to continued food shortages, and to the governmental confiscations of peasant foodstuffs. By May 1918, the Bolsheviks had provoked a full-scale civil war that lasted for nearly three years.

The Bolsheviks, who officially changed their name to Communists in March—the same month in which they moved the nation's capital to Moscow—were opposed by a tremendous number of groups collectively known as the "Whites." The Whites were supported by the Russian Orthodox Church, which acted virtually as their propaganda arm; reactionary monarchists, big landowners, the middle class, some peasants, nationalists seeking self-determination for their people, and even moderate socialists like the Mensheviks. However, even though these groups were numerous, they were very divergent, lacked a clear-cut program, especially with regard to agricultural land, and were not always willing to cooperate with each other. The Communists or the "Reds," on the other hand, were highly organized and homogenous, controlled the major industrial centers, and held interior lines of communications, especially between Moscow and Petrograd, which facilitated the shifting of troops to endangered fronts. Support given by big landowners and monarchists to the Whites alienated most of the peasantry, which feared losing the land that it recently had confiscated. Additionally, the interventionist aid given to the Whites by the British, French, Americans, and Japanese proved more beneficial to Bolshevik propaganda than to the Reds' opposition.

By the beginning of 1921, 9 million people had been killed in the Civil War itself and another 5 million, mostly peasants, had died as a result of a famine caused by the government's requisitioning of crops. To these figures can be added the 6 million Russian soldiers who died in World War I. Finland, the Baltic States, and Poland had been lost by 1921. However, Ukraine and the states in the Caucasus had been reincorporated into what after 1922 was called the Union of Soviet Socialist Republics, or Soviet Union. Nonetheless, the Communists were now firmly in power.

Although they had gained power, the Communists had alienated an enormous number of people in the process. The opponents included the nobility, who lost their estates; the bourgeoisie, who lost their businesses; the peasantry, who had had their crops confiscated or purchased at artificially low prices; and even the industrial workers, who had their trade unions abolished. Between 14,000 and 20,000 church officials and active laymen were shot during Lenin's regime and ecclesiastical land was confiscated by the officially atheistic authorities. Tens of thousands of scientists, writers, doctors, and agronomists were deported or fled the nation, as did all of the nobility. Altogether, around 3 million Russians had left Russia by the end of the Civil War. Moreover, foreign governments were outraged by the Communists' indifference to international law and normal diplomatic relations. They were particularly incensed by Soviet attempts to incite Communist revolutions on their territory.

The creation of these domestic and foreign enemies created a kind of siege mentality within the Communist party. Now, nothing could be done that might weaken the party. Only through strict party discipline, terror, and massive armaments could the regime survive, or so it appeared. This policy was strongly espoused by the regime until

Stalin's death in 1953 and to a lesser extent almost to the end of the Soviet Union in 1991. (See figure 4.) Only the nature of the threat, real or imagined, changed from decade to decade.

By early 1921, the total area under cultivation was less than 60 percent of the prewar level, and the agricultural yield was less than half of what it had been. Marketable surpluses had decreased even more because of the replacement of relatively efficient, large noble estates with small farms. The output of heavy industry in 1920 was only 13 percent of the prewar level. When previously loyal sailors mutinied on Kronstadt Island near Petrograd in March 1921, Lenin finally realized that his radical socialist program called "war communism," which had nationalized industries and requisitioned peasant foodstuffs, had gone too far. To consolidate Communist power and restore the economy he introduced a breathing spell called the New Economic Policy (NEP), which ended grain requisitioning and permitted peasants to sell their grain on the open market and allowed the operation of small-scale retail businesses with fewer than twenty employees. Larger businesses, transportation, and banking, however, remained government monopolies. By 1927, industrial production was back to its prewar level. Pragmatism had triumphed over ideology, but only temporarily.

When Lenin launched his NEP in the spring of 1921, he had little more than a year left before suffering the first of three crippling strokes, the last of which killed him in January 1924. Historians have long debated his legacy. Had totalitarianism already been fully established before his death or was it merely a possibility? Had Communist ideology ceased to evolve? Did Stalinism in effect exist before Stalin?

There are in fact some excuses for Lenin's often ruthless words and actions, at least between 1917 and 1921. The Communists were engaged in a desperate struggle for survival against what were often seemingly insurmountable odds. Revolutions and civil wars are not noted for their moderation and toleration. It is possible that Lenin regarded the Communist dictatorship as only temporary because according to Communist theory the state would eventually "wither away." It can also be conceded that, unlike Stalin, he was neither a sadist nor paranoid. Yet most of Lenin's political philosophy and tactics, even if intended for the unusual circumstances in which he lived, were perpetuated and even vastly intensified after his death. Lenin, perhaps trusting his own charisma to control the Communist party, denounced "factionalism" and abolished the internal democracy that had marked the organization's early years, probably because he distrusted the party's rank and file.

In short, Lenin provided no safeguards against a dictatorship. Trained as a lawyer, he did not uphold the law either in practice or as an ideal. He did not allow free elections because he could not rely on their outcome. Recognizing the unwillingness of the Soviet people to follow the policies of the Communist party voluntarily, he was dependent on terror and centralization even though the Bolsheviks had denounced the tsar's autocracy and (relatively mild) secret police before the revolution. Under such circumstances, no genuine constitutionalism was possible. After intraparty democracy was abolished, the party's dictatorial control over the country attracted careerists and fortune hunters. Perhaps worst of all, he established concentration camps and authorized the killing of 200,000 Russians by the party's secret police, which he referred to as "our brave Cheka." By comparison, only 14,000 Russians had been executed in the last half century of Romanov rule. By the time of his death in 1924 the foundations, at least, of the Soviet brand of totalitarianism had been established: a bureaucratic society; a monopolistic ideology which included militant atheism; a terrorist secret police; the exploitation of labor; and a tireless search for new enemies.

During the last year or so of his life, when Lenin was suffering from cerebral arteriosclerosis, he began to realize that the party leadership he had brought together to fight the Tsar, carry out the revolution, and win the Civil War, was a group of thugs. In his Political Testament, which was not published in the Soviet Union until 1956 (although it was published abroad earlier), he urged that he be replaced by a collective leadership so that the defects of certain individuals would be compensated by the merits of others. He had become particularly suspicious of the party's general secretary, Josif Vissarionovich Dzhugashvili, better known since 1912 by his pseudonym, Joseph Stalin, or "man of steel."

Stalin had been a useful ally of Lenin's before and after the revolution. Lenin admired Stalin's toughness, his ability to get things done, which included robbing banks to replenish the party's coffers, his indifference to long-winded arguments about ideology, and his apparently blind loyalty. In April 1922, Lenin rewarded Stalin by making him the party's general secretary (to help maintain party discipline). Lenin soon had reason to rue that decision, however. Stalin had made it virtually impossible for Lenin to communicate with the other party leaders during his last illness and had been especially rude to Lenin's wife. In the Testament, Lenin suggested that Stalin be removed from the party's Central Committee altogether. However, Lenin was so critical of all members of the Committee in his Testament that it suppressed the document and ignored Lenin's recommendation about Stalin.

The long and tortuous struggle for power that began well before Lenin's death and did not end until December 1927 need not detain the reader for long. Stalin's biggest asset was the same as Hitler's a few years later: his opponents were divided and underestimated him. Of all the famous Bolshevik revolutionaries, he was the only one who had only briefly been in the West, had demonstrated no skills as an ideologue, and was a poor public speaker.

In any event, next to Lenin's most likely successor, Leon Trotsky, the flamboyant but not very amiable organizer of the Red Army during the Civil War, the colorless personality of Stalin seemed almost reassuring to other Communists. And unlike Trotsky, Stalin had never publicly opposed Lenin, the founder of Bolshevism, whose body, mummified like an Orthodox saint, was now on permanent display in a huge mausoleum on Red Square in Moscow, the new capital. Stalin also stood aside while his more moderate rivals, all of whom were Jewish, fought among themselves. Biographers have also noted how Stalin's position as general secretary enabled him to appoint trusted people to influential positions while purging his rivals. Thus, he built a personal following upon which he could rely at party congresses. Stalin's opponents, who had always supported a one-party dictatorship and had joined Lenin in rejecting factionalism, were in no position to argue when they were outvoted. The party congress, once regarded as the sovereign body of the Communist party, became a mere platform where Stalin announced his policies.

Despite his reputation as an intellectual dullard, Stalin enunciated in December 1924 the theory of "Socialism in One Country," skillfully contrasting it with what he alleged was Trotsky's theory of "Permanent Revolution." Actually, Lenin himself, Stalin's claims not withstanding, had never abandoned the idea of fomenting international revolutions, and Trotsky did not favor offensive measures regardless of the circumstances. But to party and nonparty members, weary of revolution and war and anxious for stability, Stalin's slogan sounded more cautious and patriotic. It implied that Russians could not only initiate a socialist revolution in their own country, but could also complete it without having to wait for developments in other countries. Stalin thus made himself look like a moderate who would not engage in dangerous foreign adventurism or attempt any more radical social or economic measures, such as the rapid collectivization of peasant lands.

By the close of 1927, Stalin's dictatorship was fully established. Henceforth he could be expelled only by force. The Politburo, the party's leading organ, had become his rubber stamp. Now, at last, he no longer had to play the role of a moderate.

## THE FAILURE OF LIBERAL ITALY

Italy, prior to World War I, although a constitutional monarchy, lacked a strong democratic tradition among its masses. Its constitution, inherited from the Kingdom of Sardinia-Piedmont, had been handed down by King Charles Albert in 1848, rather than having been drafted by a popularly elected assembly. It allowed the king to choose the prime minister if no party in the Lower House of the Parliament, the Chamber of Deputies, had an absolute majority. No such majority ever existed either before or after the unification of Italy. The king also appointed the members of the Senate, and the members of the Chamber of Deputies were elected on a very narrow franchise until 1912.

During this time the Italian standard of living, though generally higher than Russia's, especially in northern Italy, was far behind that of Western and Central Europe. The Industrial Revolution was slow to reach Italy because of its shortage of natural resources, its isolation from the rest of Europe, and its difficulties in domestic communications due to its elongated shape, mountainous terrain, numerous islands, and, especially, its sharp political divisions prior to 1860. Northern cities like Milan, Turin, and Genoa were on an industrial par with the more advanced parts of Europe, while most of southern Italy, which had an illiteracy rate of 80 percent in 1900, would be referred to as a Third World region today.

Unlike Russia, Italy was not a quarrelsome multinational state. However, owing to the lateness of Italy's unification, in the early twentieth century regional antagonisms were still quite severe. Only after three wars, fought between 1859 and 1870, were the dozen or so Italian states united into a single kingdom. Though the relative speed of unification, after a millennium and a half of disunity, seemed almost miraculous, many problems were left unresolved, and for that matter have not been fully resolved to this day. Differences between the relatively industrialized, secular, and well-educated north, and the agricultural, illiterate, clerical, and crime-infested south, remained as strong as ever in pre–World War I Italy. There were a bewildering number of political parties, but none had a nationwide constituency, which might have helped bridge local differences. Regional politics was dominated by single parties, which inhibited political competition and invited corruption.

Even the manner in which Italy was unified, especially in retrospect, proved to be highly unsatisfactory. It was achieved over the objections of the Papacy, which lost its lands in central Italy. And it required the help of foreign intervention. French and Prussian victories over Austria in 1859 and 1866 drove the Austrians out of northern Italy, and the Prussian invasion of France in 1870 forced Napoleon III to withdraw his troops from Rome, where they had been protecting the pope since 1849. At no time did Italian troops themselves defeat the Austrians. Postunification efforts to appease nationalistic ambitions by colonizing Ethiopia only ended in disaster when Italian troops were humiliated by the Africans in 1887 and 1896.

Democracy itself failed to sink deep roots in Italy in the half century preceding World War I. Universal manhood suffrage was finally instituted in 1912, raising the electorate from 1.8 to over 5 million voters (of whom 3 million were illiterate). However, the expansion of the franchise came too late to give the Italian masses significant experience in politics prior to the advent of Fascism. The elections of 1913 produced victories for both conservative and Marxist extremists. The rich were mainly interested in keeping the poor politically impotent, and the middle classes were more interested in the welfare of their own cities than that of the country as a whole.

World War I only aggravated Italy's many political and economic problems. Staunchly Catholic Italians opposed intervention against their coreligionists in Austria-Hungary; most Socialists favored neutrality; most businesspeople, and the majority of peasants, were indifferent. On the other side, some big industrialists, such as steel makers and shipbuilders, as well as intellectuals, university students, the king and his court, Nationalists, the liberal press, and the army all favored intervention, even though collectively they were undoubtedly the minority. Most of the Italian Parliament at first opposed intervention, but its members had been kept in the dark about the government's negotiations leading to an alliance with the Entente Powers. In May 1915, Parliament was finally intimidated into voting for war by the vociferous mobs in larger cities such as Milan (where Mussolini led interventionists). Thus, Italy was the only belligerent to enter the war with a badly divided populace, a schism that would only worsen following the long and bloody conflict.

The interventionists assumed that the Italian army would be instrumental in ending the war in just six months because a stalemate had developed between the Entente Powers—Britain, France, and Russia—and the Central Powers, primarily Germany and Austria-Hungary. Incredibly, however, they had failed to consider how they would penetrate the Alps, which provided Austria-Hungary with an almost impregnable natural defense along its southwestern border with Italy. Ultimately, 650,000 Italian soldiers lost their lives and another million were wounded in order to annex 750,000 Italian-speaking Austrians, 400,000 of whom would have been surrendered to Italy if it had merely remained neutral.

Extravagant promises made by Italian politicians during the war were almost certain to be unfulfilled by its outcome. Indeed, the Paris Peace Conference of 1919 did not cede Italy all the territories it had been promised in the secret Treaty of London, which the Entente had used as bait to encourage Italian intervention. Italy received nearly all the former Austro-Italians, along with three-quarters of a million difficult-to-assimilate ethnic Germans (see figure 5) and South Slavs from the now defunct Austro-Hungarian Monarchy. Nevertheless, Mussolini and other disgruntled Italian nationalists angrily referred to the Treaty of St. Germain with Austria as the "mutilated peace," symbolic of a spirit that contributed mightily to the birth and growth of the Fascist party. Italy, though technically victorious, now joined the ranks of defeated states like Germany, Austria, and Hungary, which wanted to overturn what they felt to be an unsatisfactory peace settlement.

The first postwar years saw the Italian economy deteriorate. Loans from Italy's wartime allies, which had kept its armament factories producing, now ceased, causing massive unemployment. Joblessness worsened with the return of over 3 million war veterans who helped drive up unemployment to 2 million by the end of 1919. Meanwhile, the currency collapsed and the cost of living skyrocketed.

These economic problems need not have been insurmountable if the major political parties had been able to agree on a common course of action. The Socialists were probably in the best position to help resolve the crisis. They became the largest party in Parliament after the elections of November 1919—which were based on a new system of proportional representation—holding 156 of 506 seats in a fractured Parliament. However, the party was badly divided, refused to collaborate with other parties, and obstructed the passage of progressive legislation in Parliament. Its left wing seceded in January 1921 to form the Italian Communist party which wanted to make the crisis worse, not better. The resulting chaos would enable the party to carry out an immediate revolution in order to establish a dictatorship of the proletariat along the lines of the Russian Bolsheviks. Even moderate Socialists were now torn between reformism and Leninism and refused to cooperate with other political parties. A new Catholic Popular party lacked internal cohesion and could agree only on its opposition to anticlericalism. The middle-class Liberal party was led by the elderly Giovanni Giolitti, who as prime minister for much of the early postwar period had lacked sufficient popular support and was able to form governments only by default.

Thus, the government would have been unable to take strong actions even if so inclined; but Giolitti thought the problems would resolve themselves if left alone. Consequently, runaway inflation and class antagonisms went largely unchecked. Some peasants seized lands, others refused to pay rents, and 1 million of them even went on strike in 1920. Socialist leaders added to the chaos, which peaked between December 1919 and the end of 1920, by organizing numerous strikes that led to violence between the strikers and the police. All of these conditions frightened the conservative middle and upper classes and created enormous, albeit highly exaggerated, fears of a Bolshevik revolution erupting in Italy.

## THE BIRTH AND TRIUMPH OF FASCISM

It was in the midst of this hysteria that the *Fasci di Combattimento,* or Fascists, were founded by Benito Mussolini on March 23, 1919, five days after a huge Socialist demonstration in Milan. Until 1915, Mussolini had been a radical left-wing Socialist and editor of the party's official newspaper, *Avanti.* Soon after the outbreak of World War I, however, he broke with the party over its policy of nonintervention. After helping in a minor way (which he later claimed was crucial) to persuade the government to enter the war, he served seventeen months in the army. He had engaged in violent behavior as an adolescent, and now he worshipped violence because he felt it eliminated the weak. Mussolini's prowar philosophy proved popular with veterans, who initially made up the bulk of his new movement at a time when recent memories of war were still distasteful to most Italians. Although Mussolini's military views were remote from Marxist orthodoxy, he continued to preach the antimonarchism, anticlericalism, and anticapitalism that he had propounded while still a Socialist. He advocated workers' representation in industrial management and higher inheritance taxes and managed thereby to attract a few dissident Socialists. He even concluded a pact with the non-Communist left but was forced by local Fascist leaders to abandon it in favor of courting business interests and Nationalists. Here was a rare example of a future totalitarian leader giving in to other officials within the movement over a question of tactics.

The Fascists began growing rapidly in May 1920, after a series of Socialist strikes. By February 1921, they had 100,000 members, and by October 1922, when they seized power, they had 300,000 members and perhaps 1 million sympathizers. Veterans were now joined by white-collar workers such as teachers, lawyers, shopkeepers in provincial towns, and rural middle-class landowners who were eager to destroy the peasants' Socialist affiliations. Unlike the Nazis, however, few Fascist party members came from the peasantry or industrial working class. In the meantime, the Fascists officially became a political party and won 35 seats in the parliamentary elections of November 1921. Now they emphasized nationalism, dropped their antimonarchism to appease the king and the regular army, and attracted young people seeking thrills and adventure by their use of violence against Socialists.

By October 1922, the Fascists and their Nationalist allies still had only 50 deputies in Parliament, but the opposition was so divided that Mussolini decided it was time to take power. He organized between 17,000 and 26,000 of his paramilitary "Blackshirts"—the formation and operations of which the government had done little or nothing to control—in northern Italy for a so-called March on Rome, which began on the 27th. The men were not well trained or well equipped. The army certainly could have prevented them from occupying local government buildings, police and railway stations, and telephone and telegraph offices if Prime Minister Luigi Facta and King Victor Emmanuel III had stayed firm. Instead, the king took the unprecedented step of refusing Facta's request for the imposition of martial law.

The king's motivations have been the topic of great controversy, but apparently he was concerned about the loyalty of the army and to a lesser degree was influenced by rumors that there were actually 100,000 Blackshirts underway. He was also aware of implicit Vatican support of Fascism, possibly feared an all-out civil war, and was cognizant that all leading politicians believed it was necessary for Mussolini to enter the government. On October 30, he invited Mussolini—who had remained in Milan safely near the Swiss border during the march—to form a new government in what was technically, but not morally, a constitutional move. The government had capitulated to intimidation, and Mussolini, at the age of thirty-nine, became the youngest prime minister in Italian history.

What were the underlying reasons the Fascists managed to come to power little more than three and a half years after their founding? Clearly, much of the explanation has to do with middle-class fears—deliberately inflamed by the Fascists themselves, but also given a certain credibility by the words and actions of Italian Socialists and Communists—that what was transpiring in the Soviet Union could very well occur next in Italy. A successful revolution had never been a serious possibility, and, in any event, Socialist radicalism was very much in decline in 1922 when the economy was improving. There is often a gap, however, between reality and perception. Hence, the middle and upper classes were still frightened by Marxist radicalism and disgusted by the inactivity of liberalism and parliamentarianism in the face of the evident danger. Fascism presented itself as a third course, one that was neither liberal nor Marxist, but nationalistic and authoritarian instead. Traditionalists hoped that the Fascists would reinforce the existing social order. Even many liberals thought that Fascism was an inevitable, if only temporary, solution to a system that was unable to cope with Italy's problems. The Roman Catholic Church was unwilling to oppose the Fascists because the latter were anti-Marxist and favored aid to parochial schools. Nearly all non-Socialists believed, often unenthusiastically, that Mussolini was the only realistic alternative to socialism, violence, anarchy, and parliamentary stalemate. The Fascists' promise that they would actively solve Italy's many economic, political, and social problems also contrasted well with the passivity of Liberal Italy. (Fascist activism would soon find an admirer in none other than Adolf Hitler.)

To attain power Mussolini had changed nearly all of his principles (if he ever had any), or at any rate his policies. He had begun his career as a radical Socialist, sharply at odds with the bourgeoisie, and came to power at the head of a revolt of younger members of the bourgeoisie who feared Marxism. He switched from being an antimonarchist to a royalist. He gave up his (early) antimilitarism to flatter the army. He exchanged internationalism for rabid nationalism. He changed from being the defender of civil liberties to their suppressor. He disavowed his early anticlericalism in order to curry favor with the church. He abandoned the idea of breaking up large landed estates even though just 13 percent of the rural population owned 87 percent of the land. Of Mussolini's early leftist ideology only some rhetoric remained. He proclaimed the advent of a new society but left the privileged classes untouched. But like other true believers, he discovered the most difficult thing to do was to convert from fanaticism to moderation. Depending on one's point of view, Mussolini can be described as an unprincipled, unscrupulous opportunist or as a clever politician who knew how to adapt his policies to the shifting winds of public opinion.

Mussolini was far from being a totalitarian dictator when he formed a government in 1922. In his first cabinet only four ministers out of fourteen were Fascists. The others were members of the Catholic Popular party: an admiral, a Nationalist, and a liberal philosopher. Of the major parties, only Socialists and Communists were not represented. It is true that Mussolini's position in this new government was quite strong; in addition to being prime minister, he was foreign minister, and minister of the interior. However, only the third ministry was extraordinary for an Italian head of government. The Italian Parliament gave Mussolini's government a big vote of confidence along with special emergency powers for one year. This new government also pleased the armed forces and most academicians, whereas other people adopted a wait-and-see attitude. The Italian and foreign press (especially in the United States, but also that of Britain, France, and Norway), soon became favorably disposed toward Mussolini and assumed that almost anything would be better than the preceding five postwar governments.

Mussolini was enormously fortunate, as was Hitler a decade later, in coming to power just before the beginning of a general upturn in the European economy. During the first three years of Mussolini's rule unemployment declined by 73 percent. Controls and taxes on industries were cut and the national budget was balanced. At a time when the government was still a hybrid between authoritarianism and parliamentarianism, Mussolini created an atmosphere of efficiency, of which the punctuality of trains became a famous (if exaggerated) symbol. Strikes were also ended and social peace was restored. In general, Italians were given a sense of renewal. Among the few people who were not happy with Mussolini's first year in power were the Fascist party's most militant members, a situation that would be repeated in Germany shortly after Hitler's takeover of power. Even in this early phase of Mussolini's rule, however, he was gradually limiting civil liberties, replacing police chiefs and key positions in the civil service with Fascists, and eliminating all non-Fascist paramilitary groups. The Blackshirts, meanwhile, were transformed into a national militia paid by the state.

This transitional period ended with the kidnapping and murder of Giacomo Matteotti, a long-time opponent of Mussolini and his Blackshirts. The murder caused a national uproar in the still predominantly free press. Following so soon after the violence of the election, it contradicted the common-sense assumption that Fascism would moderate with the responsibilities of power. Mussolini's prestige and popularity, which had appeared unassailable a few days before, now hit an all-time low. The problem was that for non-Fascists nothing had changed since Mussolini's appointment in 1922. Liberals, Catholics in the *Popolare* party, and Socialists all still glared at each other with ill-disguised contempt. The Catholic Church even warned the *Popolari* against collaborating with the Socialists. Worst of all, there was no one to take the place of Matteotti as a courageous and outspoken opponent of the regime.

At the end of 1924, local Fascist leaders finally jarred Mussolini out of his stupor by demanding that he either reassert Fascism by a return to the use of force, or resign. Mussolini himself became convinced that even partially free institutions could not exist side by side with Fascist ones. He feared that a free press, a vocal parliamentary opposition, and a partially independent judiciary might someday topple the regime. Consequently, he began to tighten censorship of the press as early as July 1924. The real change, however, came after a speech he gave to Parliament on January 3, 1925, when he disclaimed any complicity in Matteotti's murder, but defiantly accepted moral responsibility for it. Henceforth, he proclaimed, Italy would be a totalitarian state and all opposition parties would be disbanded. He dismissed all non-Fascists from his cabinet. During the next few months independent labor unions, the free press, and all rival social organizations were eliminated. In 1926, elected local governments were replaced by appointed officials. Local governments were henceforth carefully regimented, and the police and civil service were purged of anti-Fascists. A Special Tribunal for political trials, from which there was no appeal, was created, and a secret police was also established. The Italian Parliament continued to exist, and even had a minority of non-Fascist members; but Mussolini was no longer responsible to it. Instead, he was responsible only to the king. However, the sympathetic Victor Emmanuel III was more a potential than an actual threat to Mussolini's authority prior to 1943.

Mussolini's slogan now became: "Everything within the State. Nothing outside the State. Nothing against the State." This assertion was actually more a boast than a reality because the Roman Catholic Church, the army, high civil servants, and big business, in addition to the king, were never completely eliminated by Mussolini as independent forces. But what little overt, as opposed to theoretical, opposition remained after 1926 was repressed by the secret police, special courts, and the policy of the imprisonment of citizens without trial. This elimination of all antiregime institutions, what the Nazis would call *Gleichschaltung* (or coordination) eight years later, was substantially completed by the end of 1928. These changes had not come about by some preconceived plan. Mussolini had simply responded to events, like four assassination attempts against his life in 1925–26, and moved with great tactical skill and some luck to turn them to his advantage.

Like Stalin, and Hitler a few years later, Mussolini was as much the dictator of his ruling party as he was the dictator of the state. Even his Blackshirts, who were so crucial in his coming to power, became an anachronism with the disappearance of a serious political opposition after 1926, although this elimination was actively promoted by Mussolini, who was seeking diplomatic acceptance. Now the party did not formulate policies, it merely implemented them. This does not mean that belonging to the party was without advantages for its 1 million

members in 1932 or its 2.6 million members in 1939. These membership totals (which do not include another 20 million memberships in
subsidiary organizations) are not only a reflection of the party's political influence, but also of the privileges that membership entailed. In
fact, official party membership was advisable for one wishing to enter
a profession, speak or write publicly, or engage in various cultural
activities. After 1935, it was mandatory for all civil servants, including
schoolteachers. Starting in 1940, it was required for advancement in
any career as it was in Nazi Germany and the Soviet Union. On the
other hand, few peasants joined the party even though they comprised
about half the country's population. Likewise, urban workers remained
grossly underrepresented in the party's rank and file.

## GERMANY AND THE IMPACT OF WORLD WAR I

In many ways the history of Germany prior to the triumph of totalitarianism is remarkably similar to that of Italy. Both became unified
nation-states only during the third quarter of the nineteenth century
after failed attempts during the Revolutions of 1848–49. Consequently,
regionalism was still strong in both countries well into the twentieth
century. Both states produced strong nationalists in the late nineteenth
and early twentieth centuries that sought to overcome regionalism
by pursuing aggressive foreign policies and acquiring colonies. Both
had strong authoritarian traditions that inhibited the development
of democratic institutions. Both had rapidly growing populations,
with large numbers of people emigrating to the Western Hemisphere,
especially between 1870 and 1914. Both had burgeoning Marxist
parties in the early twentieth century, which terrified the propertied
bourgeoisie.

Of course, there were also substantial differences between the two
countries. The Industrial Revolution reached Germany nearly a half-
century earlier than Italy, in part because of Germany's plentiful supply of coal, navigable rivers, central location (on the Continent), and
the Prussian-led customs union, which facilitated trade and enlarged
markets. On the other hand, Germany's lack of natural defenses exposed it time after time to invasions from neighboring France and Russia, thus encouraging the growth of a national militarism, something
which never really took hold in Italy.

It is important, however, not to see the emergence of totalitarian-ism as an inevitable product of remote historical events or geography. Nationalism and imperialism were hardly unique to Germany and Italy around the turn of the twentieth century. It would be difficult, for example, to find a more aggressive exponent of nationalism at this time than Theodore Roosevelt in the United States. And the colonial empires of Germany and Italy on the eve of World War I were mod-est compared to those of Britain and France or even Belgium and the Netherlands. Although the Industrial Revolution had caused social hardships in Germany, the government did more to ease them than did the British government in the eighteenth and early nineteenth centuries. It is true that racism was growing in popularity in late nine-teenth-century Germany, but so too was it in many other countries including France and the United States. Only World War I, postwar political and economic developments, and the unique personalities of Mussolini and Hitler, combined with older historical and intellectual traditions, were capable of producing totalitarian dictatorships.

The most important common denominator for the rise of the to-talitarianism in all three states was the First World War, known at the time as the "Great War." Killing, thanks to new weapons such as the machine gun, had become industrialized—leading to the death of around 10 million men. European society in all the belligerent countries had been radically transformed by the enormous increase in the power of national governments even in democratic states such as Britain and the United States. Governmental lying and censorship had become an integral part of war propaganda. National resources were fully mobilized and rationed. Where democratic traditions were weak, as in Russia, Italy, and Germany, totalitarian controls appeared to be a natural and familiar way of dealing with postwar crises.

Even though both Germans and Italians emerged from World War I feeling frustrated and cheated, their experiences during the war had been quite different. As already noted, Italy had entered the war late and had done so voluntarily—albeit with a badly divided popula-tion—hoping to pick up huge chunks of territory with relatively little effort. But the effort turned out to be far from small and the annexa-tions much more modest than anticipated. Germany, on the other hand, entered the war at its onset, believing itself compelled to do so because of Russia's early and secret mobilization. The German army responded by implementing its infamous Schlieffen Plan (named for an earlier chief of the general staff) which called for the quick defeat

**Boundary Changes After the First World War**

of France, within an expected six weeks, before the Russian mobilization could be completed. The plan seemed fully justified in the eyes of
most Germans because it was the only apparent way to avoid fighting
a dreaded two-front war. However, its early implementation, before
all diplomatic means of avoiding the war had been exhausted, and
its violation of Belgian neutrality, to which Prussia (the core of the
later German Empire) had agreed in 1839, made Germany look like
the aggressor. This belief was especially strong among non-Germans
who were unaware of the significance (to Germany) of the Russian
mobilization.

Not only did World War I begin with a huge controversy, but it also
ended ambiguously, which again led to enormous arguments between
the victors and the vanquished. Traditionally, wars have concluded
with the victors firmly in control of the enemy's capital or its strategic
fortresses and territories, the defeated power no longer capable of
putting up an effective resistance. The armistice of November 11,
1918, took place under very different circumstances. In the east, both
Russia and Rumania had signed separate treaties with the victorious
Central Powers, which now dominated vast territories stretching from
Finland through the Baltic States and Poland to Ukraine, an empire
which later inspired Hitler.

In the west, the German army had been slowly retreating since
July, but seemingly in good order. By November, the front was still in
France and Belgium. Historians have long known that the situation
for Germany was much worse than it appeared on the map. Its army
was exhausted and demoralized and no longer capable of replacing
its losses, many of which were now due to desertions. No one was
more aware of the precarious situation than the chief of the general
staff, Erich von Ludendorff, who in late September 1918 insisted that
Emperor Wilhelm II bring the fighting to an early end before the
army collapsed altogether. Ludendorff also urged the formation of a
new and more popular government that would be responsible to the
*Reichstag* or Parliament, thus creating a true democracy. Such a government, he maintained, would be more likely to negotiate a moderate
peace and would enable the authoritarian imperial government to
avoid responsibility for the defeat.

All of these facts are now well known to scholars. Unfortunately,
they were not known at the time to the German people, who had
been told by a very effective propaganda machine for four years that
the German army was winning or at worst was making only minor

strategic withdrawals. The German public was not fully aware of the growing disparity of strength on the Western Front or the significance of the collapse of the Balkan Front following the withdrawal of Bulgaria from the war in late September 1918. The sudden end to the fighting, which should have been called a surrender rather than an armistice, and, later, the unfavorable Treaty of Versailles, appeared inexplicable. Thus was born the "stab-in-the-back" legend promoted by a wide variety of conservative nationalists: the German army had not been defeated in the field, but had been "sold out" by traitors, mostly Jews and Socialists, who had meekly capitulated to a hate-filled enemy bent on destroying Germany.

The Treaty of Versailles was another subject of historical debate that was to prove useful to rising German demagogues. The treaty that was signed in Louis XIV's palace outside of Paris on June 28, 1919, required Germany to surrender 13 percent of its national territory, all of its colonies, 26 percent of its coal reserves, 75 percent of its iron ore, and to pay an unspecified amount of reparations. The sum was later set at $33 billion (equal to at least fifteen times that amount in the currency of the 2000s) and was indeed intended to cripple Germany's already exhausted economy for decades. The victors justified the enormous reparations on the grounds that Germany and its allies had committed aggression in 1914. The treaty also reduced the German army to 100,000 officers and men, a level too small even to maintain domestic order against strikes and possible Communist uprisings. At the time, the victors, for the most part, regarded the treaty as just if not indeed generous. Virtually all Germans were equally convinced that it was an instrument to suppress, exploit, and permanently humiliate Germany. They also regarded the treaty as a betrayal of the armistice terms, the famous Fourteen Points of President Woodrow Wilson. Furthermore, the secret inter-Allied negotiations leading to Versailles flatly contradicted one of the Points that had stipulated that treaties ought to be "openly arrived at."

The controversy over Versailles, which lasted throughout the entire interwar period on both the scholarly and popular levels, arose because the treaty directly linked alleged German aggression to reparations and because the Germans were never willing to admit that they had been defeated militarily. In their eyes they had been cheated rather than defeated. They believed that they had put down their arms voluntarily on the basis of a compromise agreement that had later been betrayed. Ultimately, not a few historians and even statesmen in the

West, especially in Britain and the United States, came to accept the German position and argued that their legitimate grievances should be rectified.

## THE WEIMAR REPUBLIC AND THE RISE OF THE NAZI MOVEMENT

Knowledge of the origins of World War I, the circumstances surrounding its conclusion, and especially the controversy over the Treaty of Versailles is absolutely essential to understanding the fate of the new German Republic and the rise to power of Adolf Hitler. The Versailles treaty was not harsh enough to render Germany militarily impotent forever. Ironically, its implementation, particularly with regard to disarmament clauses, required German cooperation. On the other hand, what came to be known unofficially as the "war guilt clause" (Article 231), was bitterly resented by Germans, and reparations were blamed, often unjustly, for every failure of the postwar German economy. What the German people failed to understand was that the direct economic consequences of the war were far more responsible for Germany's economic plight in the 1920s than the Treaty of Versailles. To cite just one example, the economy was burdened in 1923 by the 4.5 million permanently disabled veterans, war widows, and children orphaned by the war who collectively consumed over 18 percent of federal expenditures.

The new German state, commonly known as the "Weimar Republic" for the city in central Germany where its constitution was drawn up in 1919, was truly crippled, though not mortally wounded, from birth. Besides being made to bear the millstone of Versailles, the republic was handicapped by its constitution. Although historians have sometimes exaggerated this document's inherent flaws, they were still substantial. Foremost among them was its apparatus for proportional representation. Designed to assure representation in the Reichstag for every shade of public opinion, it assigned one parliamentary seat to every party that could garner 60,000 popular votes, no matter how geographically scattered those votes might be. On the other hand, the Weimar constitution mandated that party secretaries, not the voters, would decide which politicians actually sat in Parliament.

Proportional representation produced a bewildering number of parties. Often around thirty parties appeared on each ballot, a dozen or so of which gained parliamentary seats. Consequently, no party ever came close to winning an absolute majority, making every government formed a coalition of at least three parties—there were twenty such coalitions in just fourteen years. Decisive action, especially during crises, was next to impossible. Small, often extremist parties like the National Socialists found it easy to gain representation, and their parliamentary deputies enjoyed handsome salaries paid by the state, free travel on trains, and immunity from arrest, all huge advantages for a poor, young party struggling for recognition.

Historians have sometimes overemphasized the significance of proportional representation in the ultimate failure of the Weimar government. It has worked successfully in other countries including Switzerland and the Scandinavian states although it has created serious problems in Israel. Moreover, proportional representation was more a reflection of the deep political and social divisions in German society than the cause of such divisions. Other defects in the Weimar constitution, such as the president's right to appoint anyone chancellor in the absence of a parliamentary majority, and the right of the president to grant a chancellor dictatorial powers in an emergency, were designed to deal with a presumably temporary crisis such as a Communist coup. No one could have anticipated in 1919 that these measures would eventually enable Adolf Hitler to come to power legally and then rule by decree.

Once established, the Weimar Republic was never able to sink deep democratic roots. It might have been able to overcome all the problems associated with the Treaty of Versailles and the constitution if only it had enjoyed a decent amount of prosperity. However, between its founding in November 1918 and its demise in January 1933, it experienced at most five years of modest prosperity, from the middle of 1924 to the middle of 1929. Real income in 1928, the best year of the Weimar Republic, was only 3 percent higher than it had been in 1913. Meanwhile it had grown by 70 percent in the United States and 38 percent in France. An inflation, the worst in the history of the Western world, culminated in November 1923 and reduced the German mark to one trillionth of its prewar value. Some speculators made fortunes, but most people, especially in the traditionally thrifty middle class, saw their lifetime savings evaporate—and blamed the government.

Economic insecurity, as well as lingering anger over the Treaty of Versailles, were perfect ingredients for both right-wing and left-wing extremism in the Weimar Republic. Karl Marx had always considered his native Germany the logical starting point for the proletarian revolution. Lenin also had high hopes that German workers would rise up during or after the war. His expectations seemed justified when a small group of Communists seized power in Bavaria in April 1919. Though their rule lasted only three weeks, the hysterical reaction to it on the part of the bourgeoisie lasted for over a decade.

It was in this setting of anti-Communist paranoia, bitterness over the Treaty of Versailles, and growing inflation, that Hitler got his start in politics. In 1919, Hitler was an absolute political nobody. He had been born in the Upper Austrian town of Braunau am Inn in 1889. His father died in 1903, and his mother, much to Hitler's distress, died four years later. After dropping out of secondary school at the age of sixteen he spent six years painting picture postcards in Vienna before moving to Munich in 1913. When World War I broke out he volunteered for the military, serving with some distinction as a courier. But when the war came to a sudden end he was right back where he had been in 1914, with no close family members or home and about to face unemployment. How Hitler transformed himself virtually overnight from a lazy outsider with no future into a heroic leader is one of the greatest mysteries of world history.

In September 1919, while still in the army, Hitler was given the task of investigating what his superior officers thought was a political party with a suspicious-sounding name: the German Workers' party, or DAP. The DAP (which was one of seventy-three similar groups in Germany) turned out to be insignificant in size and right wing rather than left wing in its orientation, and the army soon lost interest in it. After giving an impromptu speech, during his initial contact with the party, Hitler was asked to join the party's executive committee in charge of recruiting and propaganda. Hitler had finally found a home and a profession. A young, unknown, poorly educated foreigner like Hitler could have only made his mark in a small party.

Thanks to Hitler's speaking ability and his recruitment of people who would be loyal to him, the DAP grew rapidly. By July 1921 he had become so indispensable to the organization that he was able to become its dictator, or *Führer* (literally "leader" or "guide"), and eliminate the party's internal democracy merely by threatening to resign (much as Lenin had done within the Bolshevik party). (By contrast, Mussolini did not gain dictatorial power over the Fascist party until he became prime minister of Italy.) Hitler also added the words "National Socialist" to "German Workers' Party"—NSDAP or *Nazi* party for short (a combination of letters from the German name NAtional SoZIalist)—in an attempt to increase the party's appeal to both nationalists and socialists. Little more than two years later, Hitler, inspired by the Fascists' successful March on Rome, believed he was ready to seize power.

The infamous "Beer Hall Putsch" in which he participated (but did not solely lead), turned out to be a fiasco, however, largely because local Bavarian police and government authorities, unlike their counterparts in Italy, did not remain passive during this attempted coup. Instead of seizing power in Munich and using it as a base for a march on Berlin, as he had planned, Hitler found himself in prison. In a normal state the failure of the putsch should have marked the end of Hitler's political career. For Hitler, however, the putsch and his highly publicized trial for treason a few months later turned out to be his moment in the sun. Far from denying his responsibility for the move, he exaggerated it. And far from throwing himself on the mercy of the court, he used what had become a national forum to denounce the "November criminals" who had signed the armistice and the Treaty of Versailles. It was impossible, he argued, to commit treason against traitors. Hitler was convicted but given the lightest possible sentence—five years, of which he served only thirteen months.

Hitler's imprisonment during 1924 and part of 1925, along with his being legally forbidden to make public speeches until 1927, gave him time to reflect on his failed tactics. This he did in a two-volume work published in 1925 and 1927 called *Mein Kampf* or "My Battle." The book gave him an opportunity to answer embarrassing questions about his youth, describe how the Nazi party should be organized, make insightful remarks about the power of propaganda, and generally outline his ideology and domestic and foreign policy goals. The book itself has long been controversial, mostly because of the assumption that Hitler laid out his political blueprint in the book, which was then ignored both at home and abroad.

*Mein Kampf* is indeed remarkably frank; its advocacy of war and murder is probably unsurpassed among major political works for its sheer brutality. A blueprint, however, it was definitely not. It does reveal Hitler's virulent anti-Semitism, but that hardly made him unique in Germany (or in Europe) at the time, and it is silent about the eventual fate of the German Jews beyond the need to deny them citizenship. It says nothing about eradicating rival political parties, destroying trade unions, or crippling churches. It does discuss the necessity for ample living space, but, aside from Ukraine, does not specify where it should be obtained. Finally, in *Mein Kampf* Hitler pontificates about the inevitability and indeed desirability of war, but he does not say when or how this war will take place. The two volumes were so long—nearly 700 pages—and so diverse in subject matter, that readers, even Nazis, tended to take from the book what they wanted and dismiss the rest. The problem was not, as so many people have argued since, that no one including foreign statesmen read it. The problem was whether anyone should have taken it seriously.

By the time Hitler was released from prison in February 1925, a great deal had changed in Germany since November 1923. A new and stable currency had replaced the inflated one, and unemployment was declining, as was political extremism. In the same year, a conservative monarchist and war hero, Paul von Hindenburg, was elected president by a popular vote. His administration was both a help and hindrance to the Weimar Republic. On the one hand, conservatives were a little more willing to tolerate the republic if Hindenburg could do so. On the other hand, Hindenburg was already seventy-eight years old when he was elected to his first seven-year term. He was on the verge of senility in 1932 when he was elected to a second term, the most critical moment in all of German history.

Hitler realized in 1925 that a second coup attempt was out of the question. He would have to come to power legally or not at all. This was a remarkable change in tactics for someone who, in the popular mind, was capable of acting only out of rage and impulse. In fact, Hitler's biggest accomplishment between his release from prison in 1925 and his rise to power in 1933 was probably his ability to restrain his over-anxious supporters. After coming to power in 1933 his primary task was to calm down zealous ethnic Germans in neighboring countries who were all too eager to be annexed by an insufficiently rearmed Germany. Hitler was remarkably successful in both instances, up to at least 1939, proving that he was perfectly capable of acting rationally.

Nonetheless, from February 1925, when the Nazi party was refounded, until the middle of 1929, its growth was so slow that had that rate continued, Hitler probably would have died of old age before the party had become a major force in German politics. Whereas it had 55,000 members on the eve of the Beer Hall Putsch, it had only 35,000 in 1926 and 60,000 in 1928. Partly due to Hitler's being forbidden to speak publicly, party revenues were severely limited. If success breeds success, failure breeds apathy. In the parliamentary elections of May 1928, the Nazi party was able to garner only 2.6 percent of the vote, less than half of what it had won under a pseudonym four years earlier.

Hitler, nevertheless, did not let these lean years go to waste. Nazis founded, renamed, or enlarged various subsidiary organizations including the *Sturmabteilung* (SA) or Storm Troopers, the Hitler Youth, the School Children's League, the Student League for university students, and various other organizations for lawyers, physicians, women, peasants, and industrial workers. By appealing to so many different demographic groups the party was becoming not only totalitarian, but also a state within a state. Hitler wanted to make it clear that there was a place for virtually everyone in the party or one of its subsidiaries with the major exception of Jews. To a considerable extent he succeeded.

Unlike the German Communist party (*Kommunistiche Partei Deutschlands* or KPD), which appealed in practice only to industrial workers, and the Fascists, whose attraction was limited almost exclusively to the middle class and the wealthy, the Nazis became a truly mass movement, especially after 1930. Although often described as a lower middle-class movement, attractive to artisans, clerks, small shopkeepers, elementary school teachers, and other low-level civil servants, a higher percentage of upper middle-class professionals eventually joined the Nazi party. Industrial workers were underrepresented, but still about one-quarter of them had joined by 1932, especially those who were unemployed. The Nazi party, in fact, was the only party in Germany, apart from the Catholic Center party, to appeal to voters across class lines. The two things that held most of their heterogeneous following together were their dislike of the Weimar Republic and their attraction to Adolf Hitler.

## THE GREAT DEPRESSION
## AND THE NAZI TAKEOVER

Nazi party membership began to explode in the middle of 1929 with the onslaught of the Great Depression, which came earlier to Germany than to the United States. Nearly 1.4 million Germans were unemployed by that time, or more than double the figure for the previous year. In 1930, unemployment more than doubled again, finally reaching a peak in mid-1932 of 6.2 million, or about one-third of all the nation's workers. Even these figures are misleading because they do not include part-time workers and workers who were no longer receiving unemployment benefits. Although unemployed workers did not necessarily flee to the Nazis—many joined the Communists instead—there is no doubt that the growth of Nazi party membership closely paralleled the rising unemployment, caused as much by the fear of unemployment, especially within the middle class, as unemployment itself. As party membership grew, so too did the Nazi vote. In the relatively prosperous year of 1928, they gained only 810,000 votes in Reichstag elections. That number skyrocketed after the onset of the Depression to 6.4 million or 18.3 percent in September 1930 and to 13.7 million or 37.4 percent in July 1932, when the Depression was at its worst.

Political parties with radical and simplistic solutions tend to do well during times of political and economic turmoil. The Communists in Russia and the Fascists in Italy had proven this in 1917 and 1921–22. On the other hand, they do poorly during times of prosperity and political stability, as the Nazis had discovered in the second half of the 1920s; but the Great Depression gave the Nazis a second chance. Hitler had said that the recent relative prosperity was only temporary, and he had been proven right. The German Reichstag and government were no more able to cope with the economic crisis than the Duma in Russia and the Chamber of Deputies in Italy had been able to deal with their respective crises.

Hitler's campaign rhetoric was highly effective. Instead of merely making material promises, he spoke in semireligious terms about renewing German unity, pride, indeed greatness. He promised the German people a whole new system of government, not just a change in government, of which there had been far too many already. He appeared to fulfill the need for heroic leadership at a time when the nation desperately wanted some. He also enjoyed the distinct advantage, as did Lenin and Mussolini before him, of not having held power during times of political and economic disasters. Far from glorifying war, "National Socialism means peace" was the party slogan in 1932, when five major elections were held. Even anti-Semitism was toned down in Hitler's speeches. During the campaigns all of these messages were promoted in Nazi party rallies, which were more numerous than those of all other parties combined. Nevertheless, as the charismatic head of a heterogeneous protest movement Hitler needed to come to power quickly or he likely would not come to power at all.

Ironically, Marxists, both in Germany and in the Soviet Union, were of great help in Hitler's acquisition of power. The German government had helped smuggle Lenin into Russia in 1917. Now it was time for Stalin and German Marxists to return the favor. German Social Democrats, who were moderate and democratic in practice, maintained their radical Marxist rhetoric during the entire Weimar Republic, which alienated the bourgeoisie. The Socialists, in fact, lacked a real program both when they were in the government and when they dropped out of the government, as they did in 1930 when their collaboration was needed most. They were more concerned with appeasing their constituents than in offering practical proposals for solving the economic crisis.

If the crimes of the German Socialists were ones of omission, those of the German Communists and their wire-puller in the Kremlin, Joseph Stalin, were ones of commission. Among students of history, Stalin's aims are disputed. He may have wanted to promote a Hitlerian Germany that would go to war against the capitalist West, after which the Soviet Union would be able to pick up the pieces. On the other hand, he may have hoped that a Hitler dictatorship would force the German Socialists to combine with the KPD in a proletarian revolution. However, still other historians believe that Stalin feared a Communist Germany might replace the Soviet Union as the leader of the international Communist movement called the Comintern. In any event, the Soviet dictator forbade any collaboration between the German Communists and what they liked to call the "Social Fascists," the Social Democrats. On the other hand, he ordered the KPD to vote with the Nazis in the Reichstag on a number of issues.

Both the SPD and the KPD, in good orthodox Marxist tradition, were convinced that Hitler was the "tool" of capitalists. In reality, Hitler was no more an agent of capitalism in 1932–33 than Lenin was a German agent in 1917. Both men were happy to accept aid from any source foolish enough to offer it to them, but they felt no sense of obligation in return. Although Hitler did receive some financial assistance from German industrialists, as numerous Marxist historians have asserted, it was minor compared to the revenues the Nazis were able to raise through party membership dues and rallies.

The German Communists were also useful to the Nazis as bogeymen. The KPD benefited from the Depression almost as much as had the Nazis themselves. They had won only 3.26 million votes in 1928, but 4.5 million in 1930 and 5.28 million in July 1932. Most alarming for conservatives, however, was the addition of 700,000 votes in November, giving the Communists nearly 17 percent of the vote at the very time the Nazis' vote dropped by over 2 million or 4.3 percent. Together with the Socialists, the two Marxist parties drew 37.4 percent of the votes compared to 33.1 percent for the Nazis. The Nazis were now able to argue, with at least some plausibility, that the German people had only two choices: themselves or the Marxists. At the same time, conservative politicians, like former chancellor Franz von Papen, assumed that the Nazis were now in trouble and therefore more open to compromise. He imagined that if he could persuade Hindenburg to name Hitler chancellor with himself as vice chancellor, Hitler and his legions would be captives of conservative interests. He would then help them establish an authoritarian but not dictatorial regime.

These delusions, a virulent fear of Communism within the middle and upper classes, and a feeling among many Germans that Hitler ought to at least be given a chance to show what he could do, were just three reasons behind Hitler's appointment as chancellor by President Hindenburg on January 30, 1933. Ironically they were all reminiscent of Mussolini's takeover of power a little over a decade earlier. Both appointments were constitutional, but morally reprehensible. Mussolini's appointment had been accompanied by the threat of violence, which at least was not overt or immediate in the case of Hitler. However, Hitler had made no secret of his desire to become a dictator and throw out the Weimar constitution. On the other hand, Hitler could rightly claim to lead what was now by far the largest party in the Reichstag, something Mussolini could not argue in 1922. However, neither man commanded anything like a majority in their respective parliaments; both were able to come to power only because of their opponents' bitter divisions. In both cases, wealthy conservatives and nationalists imagined they could control "their" men once they were in power. The self-deception was particularly grotesque in Hitler's case. The Nazis turned out to be just as destructive of conservative values as they were of Marxist ideals. Little did the conservatives know that once Hitler was allowed to get his foot in the door of power he would soon smash the door down and totally ransack the conservatives' household.

However, Hitler was no more a dictator the moment he came to power in 1933 than Mussolini was in 1922 or Lenin in 1917. Hitler, however, like Lenin (but perhaps not like Mussolini), fully intended somehow to gain total power as soon as possible. Hitler, like Mussolini, at first headed a cabinet in which his own party was in a minority; Nazis held just four of fourteen seats. Despite earlier promises to von Papen that there would be no more campaigning, Hitler immediately announced that there would be one last election five weeks later. He was confident that incumbency and the Nazis' control of the police would give the party an absolute majority and enable him to override the constraints of both the Reichstag and the president.

A week before the election a mysterious fire gutted the Reichstag building. The Nazis immediately claimed that it was part of a Communist conspiracy. Historians have long debated how the fire actually started, but what matters most is that Hitler was able to persuade the eighty-five-year-old president to grant him emergency powers. Hitler was thereby able to revoke all civil liberties guaranteed in the Weimar constitution, outlaw the Communist party, and rule by decree. As it turned out, the "emergency" lasted for twelve years, to the very end of Hitler's rule. The Nazi vote of 43.9 percent still fell short of their goal, but together with their Nationalist allies they controlled 52 percent of the Reichstag deputies. The Reichstag, minus its Communist deputies, but with the approval of the Catholic Center party, now passed the "Enabling Law," which gave the Nazis four years to rule without its interference.

During the next six months the Nazis carried out their *Gleichschaltung.* They eliminated all other political parties, censored the mass media, and imprisoned political opponents. They outlawed independent trade unions. They also robbed the thirty-five German states of their autonomy, purged the civil service (particularly at the upper levels) of Jews and anti-Nazis, and destroyed the independence of the judiciary. In five months Hitler had accomplished as much as Mussolini had in five years.

Still beyond Hitler's control was the army, to some extent the churches, the four-million-man SA, and the president of the republic. The Gleichschaltung of the army and churches had to wait, but the

SA and the president were taken care of in 1934. The leaders and rank-and-file of the SA felt that their sacrifices during the *Kampfzeit* (fighting time) prior to Hitler's takeover, had not been fully appreciated or duly rewarded. Hitler had needed the SA to intimidate his opponents and Jews. But once his power was secure the SA was an embarrassment and a threat to his goal of restoring stability. When the SA leadership made vague threats about a "second revolution," Hitler decided to act. On the night of June 30, 1934, he had fifty of its leaders executed (along with at least thirty-five other Nazi enemies) on the pretext that members of the SA had been plotting a putsch and practicing homosexuality. Most Germans were more relieved than outraged because the SA members had been regarded as hoodlums. President Hindenburg proved to be even less of a problem. He obligingly died on August 2, 1934. Hitler then merged the offices of president and chancellor, though he never used the former title. Hitler also automatically replaced Hindenburg as the commander-in-chief of the army and the day after the president's death required all German soldiers to swear an oath of allegiance to him. Hitler, unlike Mussolini, was now alone at the top, being both the head of government and the head of state.

It is obvious that there were strong similarities in how the three totalitarian parties seized and consolidated power. Rather than following a script to power they all took advantage of domestic crises and the divisions of their enemies. They all consolidated their power in stages. There was one big difference, however. Both the Fascists and the Nazis came to power legally, at least superficially. However much they might be disliked by many elements of their respective country's population, few people doubted the legitimacy of the fascist governments. This simple fact made it easier for the Fascists and Nazis to remain in power. The Communists, on the other hand, never overcame the stigma of illegitimacy.

# 3 / PERSONALITIES
# AND POLICIES
# OF THE DICTATORS

The impact the totalitarian dictators had on the world is all the more remarkable considering their humble beginnings. Only Lenin came from a cultivated family, and he was also the only one who had earned an advanced degree. In earlier and more stable times it is highly unlikely that the dictators would have gained anything like the prominence they eventually achieved. Ironically, they were all beneficiaries of the democratic atmosphere of post–World War I Europe; monarchs and diplomats were in disgrace and the recently enfranchised masses were eager to accept the leadership of one of their own. Stalin, Mussolini, and Hitler all recognized this mood and made a virtue of necessity by boasting of their humble origins.

## STALIN'S YOUTH AND EARLY CAREER

In the department of modest beginnings, Joseph Stalin outdid his counterparts. Born and raised in poverty, he died the most powerful and feared man in the world. Stalin's nationality was also the most ambiguous of the dictators. He was born in the town of Gori in the Caucasian state of Georgia and did not start learning Russian until he was eight or nine. He never lost his Georgian accent and occasionally mumbled Russian case endings because he was unsure of their accuracy. Nevertheless, he was anything but pro-Georgian, often treating his native land with brutality and contempt. On the other hand, Stalin never felt himself fully Russian either. His class background was equally ambiguous. He was neither a worker nor an intellectual.

Little is known about Stalin's childhood in large part because as dictator Stalin destroyed all the papers that could have shed light on his early life along with the people who knew him in his early years as a revolutionary. Informants often gave contradictory accounts of the man. Much of what we have been told has come from individuals who were trying to remember events that had occurred forty to sixty years earlier; they also had reasons, conscious or unconscious, to distort their stories. According to recently discovered documents, Stalin was born in 1878, not 1879 as previously believed. His parents were desperately poor ex-serfs who were at best semiliterate. His birthplace was a one-room hut with wooden walls and a brick floor that smelled of foul water and unwashed bodies. His father was a self-employed shoemaker who drank heavily and regularly thrashed the young Stalin until his eyes were black and his body was covered with bruises. Such beatings were not unusual at that time and place and did not mean that a child would inevitably grow up to be a monster. But it is entirely possible that Stalin's treatment as a child may have destroyed good relations both with his father and with all other human beings. It may also have been the beatings that made him hard and without compassion.

Stalin's mother had a more positive influence on the young Joseph's life than his father. She had married at fifteen and lost her first two children at birth; not surprisingly she became overindulgent with her first surviving child. She was a quiet, pious woman whose only pleasure was attending the local Russian Orthodox Church. Her fondest ambition was for her son to become first a choirboy, which he did, and then a priest. She defended him against his father and encouraged him to attend a seminary, but Stalin showed little appreciation in return. As an adult he rarely visited her although he did write her regularly. He failed to attend her funeral in 1936, but this may have been due to his fear of assassins in his native Georgia where he was especially hated.

The seminary helped Stalin develop a phenomenal memory, an asset he shared with the other totalitarian dictators, and also with Napoleon. Moreover, the seminary helped make him dogmatic, which later made Marxist absolutism all the easier for him to accept. Stalin was likewise indebted to the institution for the repetitive, declamatory, and liturgical style of speaking he used effectively in his public speeches. Stalin did very well in his first year at the seminary, getting high marks for both his conduct and work. He also read widely outside the prescribed curriculum. During his second year, however, he became angry when other students tried to lead a discussion, and he bitterly resented the atmosphere of petty espionage used by the seminary's authorities to discover breaches of rules and the reading of forbidden literature. His involvement in revolutionary activity finally led to his expulsion in 1896, leaving him with no qualifications for a conventional career.

By this time, Stalin had reached his full height of only five feet, four inches. Moreover, his face was pitted from smallpox at the age of five, he had a partially crippled arm, and deformed toes on his left foot. After he became the Russian dictator he wore elevator shoes; at parades he usually stood on a slightly raised platform. Almost certainly his short stature, ugly face, and lower-class social origins gave him an inferiority complex, which made him touchy, vindictive, and suspicious throughout his whole life. His poor physical appearance also made Stalin want to avoid being shown close-up in films and newsreels (see figure 6), in sharp contrast to Hitler and Mussolini.

We have no knowledge of what Stalin did between his expulsion from the seminary and 1899. We know only that in December of the latter year he got his first and only regular job working in a weather observatory recording temperatures. By this time, he had joined the Russian Social Democratic party. As noted above, during and after the Revolution of 1905, he led bandit squads that robbed banks to finance the Bolsheviks. In 1912, he was also briefly an editor of the party newspaper, *Pravda*. However, he spent most of the pre-Revolutionary years in prison or in exile in Vienna. In all, he was arrested seven times, sent to Siberia six times, beginning in 1903, and escaped five times. Between 1908 and 1917 he was a free man for only a year and a half. However, prison and Siberian exile in tsarist Russia were far cries from what they became under Stalin. For Stalin and other revolutionaries of the nineteenth and early twentieth centuries, prison and exile provided an opportunity for an advanced education in radical literature and a chance for discussions with fellow revolutionaries, who were often experienced teachers.

Stalin took no part in World War I and was also not one of the leaders of the Bolshevik Revolution. He was no doubt relieved when tsarist officials rejected him for military service in December 1916 because of his weak left arm. Official Soviet accounts claimed he had been rejected because he was considered "too dangerous." His minor role in the events of 1917, especially compared with those of Lenin and Trotsky, later became an embarrassment to Stalin. After his rise to dictatorial power he took care of that little problem by simply altering records, suppressing memoirs, and forcing editors, historians, artists, and film makers to create an imaginary account of the Revolution. Trotsky's role was expunged, and Stalin became the equal of Lenin, the man who had never left Russia and was there to greet Lenin upon his return from exile.

The future dictator's role as a husband and father was no more impressive than his role in the Bolshevik Revolution. Information about his first wife, Ekaterina "Keke" Svanidze is as sketchy as most other aspects of Stalin's early life. By some accounts they married in 1902 and she died in 1908; other sources place their marriage in 1905 and her death in 1907. All accounts seem to agree that she was no revolutionary and was, in fact, a devout Christian and believer in traditional Georgian values: a woman's place was in the home; she should dress modestly and submit to her husband's authority in all things. Fortunately for her these values coincided with Stalin's philosophy of male dominance. Stalin treated all women the same—whether they were his wives, daughter, or mother—much as his father had treated him. He was a foul-mouthed bully, disrespectful and capable of exacting physical abuse. Ekaterina died shortly after giving birth to a son, Yakov. Stalin's grief at her passing, however, was genuine.

Stalin married his second wife, Nadezhda Alliluyeva, in 1919. Also a Georgian, she had been his secretary and was only sixteen, twenty-two years his junior, when they married. Apparently he married her for companionship. Being a semi-intellectual himself, he hated women, and for that matter men who were genuine intellectuals. Nadezhda bore him two children, Vasily, in 1921, and Svetlana, in 1926. They had a modest but comfortable life with a two-room town apartment in the Kremlin, the old government quarter in the center of Moscow, and a fine home in the country, which Stalin, with his interest in architecture, changed from a gloomy rural house into an airy villa. Stalin was affectionate with Svetlana, except when she wore short skirts and tight sweaters. In general, however, his marriage was not happy. Nadezhda did not hesitate to give her husband tongue lashings when he richly deserved them, and he retaliated by embarrassing her in public. It was evidently after one such episode, in 1932, that she went home and shot herself. Stalin kept the nature of her death a state secret and thereafter did not allow other top Communist party members to bring their wives to his social functions.

## STALIN THE DEMIGOD

Stalin was vain and easily offended and could also be rude to his colleagues, not to mention brutal and vengeful. What is remarkable, however, especially in light of the millions of murders for which he was responsible, is that Stalin could and often did give the impression of being benign toward his colleagues and the general public. In meetings, at least early in his career, he had the good sense not to say anything before everyone else had had his say, even encouraging them to explain their positions. Then he would repeat the conclusion toward which the discussion had been moving. His brevity as well as his attention to details gave the impression of wisdom and self-confidence. Once firmly ensconced in power he allowed his underlings to bicker so that he alone could arbitrate. (See figure 7.) He could be amazingly patient and an ideal listener, especially with some low-level provincial official; in the process he often gained another client. When he wished, Stalin could also exude a simple, folksy charm, which some of his interviewers found completely disarming. In the early 1930s, he began giving interviews to highly selected journalists and people of distinction. On these occasions he seemed like a modest disciple of Lenin. The German journalist, Emil Ludwig, was so taken in that he said he would willingly turn over the education of his children to the Soviet leader. The American ambassador to the Soviet Union from 1936 to 1938, Joseph E. Davies, said that Stalin appeared to have "a strong mind which is composed and wise. His brown eye is exceedingly kindly and gentle. A child would like to sit in his lap and a dog would sidle up to him."[1] On the other hand, Stalin could be extraordinarily rude and coarse in debates and would break up meetings with crude heckling. Like Hitler, he encouraged personal conflicts between his colleagues and then assumed the role of arbiter.

Like many dictators he was utterly conceited about his general knowledge. Markings in his personal library indicate that he did do some reading in Russian history, past rulers' techniques of absolute rule (he was especially attracted to Peter the Great and Ivan the Terrible), and the history of warfare. But Stalin went far beyond these readings to imagine that he could judge things better than professionals in all sorts of fields including military science, linguistics, economics, physics, and biology. His ultimate intellectual claim, of course, was

1 Quoted in T. H. Rigby, ed., *Stalin* (Englewood Cliffs, NJ, 1966), 78.

to be an interpreter of Marxism and Leninism. Every one of Stalin's theoretical words had to be treated as sacred dogma even though in most areas Stalin's knowledge was at best that of an amateur, if not that of an outright ignoramus.

The idea that Stalin was all wise was part of what historians have called the "cult of personality." The cult can be traced back to Stalin's eulogy to Lenin at the latter's funeral in 1924. The eulogy, much like the liturgies Stalin had heard in seminary, was filled with ecclesiastical rhetoric. Stalin helped make the anniversary of Lenin's death a national day of mourning. Petrograd was renamed Leningrad. Lenin's works were published in many languages and his every word acquired the status of Holy Writ. (This task was made much easier by Stalin's absolute control over access to Lenin's manuscripts.) Finally, Lenin's body was mummified and placed in a huge mausoleum in Moscow. This cult of personality, which Lenin himself found repugnant, was thus begun by Stalin, who also claimed the status as Lenin's most trusted and faithful disciple, his chosen successor who alone was capable of interpreting the master's often contradictory writings. By bestowing on Lenin the stature of a superhuman, Stalin was laying the foundations for "Leninism" and, more important, for his demigod status as well. (See figure 8.) His own status as a cult figure dates at least in part to the celebration of his (alleged) fiftieth birthday in 1929 when the Soviet press printed hundreds of letters written "spontaneously" by people from all walks of life praising Stalin.

Like God, Stalin was not only all knowing, but also all good, all just, and all powerful. The national anthem mentioned him by name, something that even Hitler and Mussolini dared not demand. Stalin himself raised his cult to a new height by publishing a book in 1938 entitled *History of the All-Union Communist Party: Short Course*. Better known simply by its subtitle, it became the bible of High Stalinism. It was absolutely breathtaking in its distortion of history. In its pages, all of Stalin's opponents were shown to be agents of imperialism. Stalin was credited with organizing the Revolution, establishing a productive and prosperous agriculture, smashing treason, and leading the world's proletariat. To make sure that the masses got the point, Stalin also carefully monitored fictionalized films. Paintings depicted Stalin leading strikes before the Revolution and advising a complaisant Lenin. Almost every office and private home was adorned with an idealized portrait of the great leader.

The degree to which the general public accepted the Stalin cult is difficult to determine, as indeed are all aspects of public opinion in a totalitarian dictatorship. There is some evidence, however, that the deified image of Stalin was widely believed by millions of Soviet people of all incomes and occupations. This conviction must have been common among people belonging to the enormous state apparatus, who owed their jobs directly to the dictator. In any event, his deification made it impossible for the Communist party to control him and justified in advance everything Stalin did.

Not surprisingly, this great man, with unlimited power, could set his own work schedule and entertain himself as he pleased. His working day was eccentric and unhealthy to say the least. He arose around noon, went to his office and worked for six or seven hours, and then had dinner around ten o'clock with his cronies (a schedule which the entire ruling elite was forced to follow, even Communist leaders in foreign countries, because Stalin might call them at any hour of the night). The evening meal would be the occasion for rambling stories told repeatedly by Stalin, and practical jokes—played on others, of course. Stalin would puff contentedly on his pipe or on cigarettes while watching his guests sit on tomatoes or cakes. He especially enjoyed watching his guests get drunk hoping to loosen their tongues; no one dared refuse a drink that had been offered to him by Stalin. Dinner would then be followed by one to three movies; those featuring Charlie Chaplin, cowboys, or Tarzan being among Stalin's favorites. He also liked grand opera, never missing a performance of *Boris Godunov*; *Aïda* was another favorite. Finally, like many Russians, Stalin enjoyed playing chess. His opponents were wise if they did not try to win.

## MUSSOLINI: THE YOUNG SOCIALIST

Benito Mussolini's childhood was in some ways similar to Stalin's, although one should not push the analogy too far. He was born in the village of Predappio in the Romagna—a region with a history of class violence and radicalism—in east-central Italy in 1883, five years later than the Soviet dictator. Mussolini's family was of modest means, but his later claims notwithstanding, it was by no means poverty stricken. There were plenty of books in the house and even some domestic help. The fathers of both Stalin and Mussolini were artisans. Mussolini's father, Alessandro, was a blacksmith, who was active in the local Socialist party and as such was an atheist. He drank heavily and was prone to womanizing. Mussolini later admitted that he had been strongly influenced by his father. His mother, Rosa, like Stalin's, was religious. However, she differed from Stalin's mother in being well educated, which enabled her to teach elementary school. The adult Mussolini and the Fascist party tried to reconcile these two disparate influences in Mussolini's upbringing.

As a child Benito was stubborn, sullen, and incapable of real affection even toward his parents, sister, and younger brother. He taught himself to read but did not talk much, preferring to fight instead. He was a gang leader in his boarding school and loved to lead other children in acts of vandalism. In his second year, in 1893, the ten-year-old Benito led a revolt to protest the institution's food. Once he was even expelled for stabbing another boy.

Thanks no doubt to his mother, the only person he ever genuinely loved (like Hitler), the young Benito remained in school until he earned his diploma at the age of eighteen, thereby surpassing both Stalin and Hitler. However, like the other two dictators, he was sensitive about his lack of advanced education and disliked intellectuals. In school he learned what he wanted to rather than the prescribed curriculum. He had a preference for the history of ancient Rome, which continued to fascinate him as an adult. He developed an almost religious veneration for Julius Caesar in particular.

By the time Mussolini's formal education was complete he had reached his full height of five feet, six inches. He has often been described as short, but actually his height would have been close to average for his time and place. Nevertheless, like Stalin, he seems to have been self-conscious about his size because photographs of him were almost always taken at a high tilt, looking up. He loved to be seen next to King Victor Emmanuel III, who was even shorter than he was. (See figure 9.) He also preferred ministers who were shorter than himself. To compensate for his size he stood ramrod straight, pushed out his lower lip and jaw, and tilted his head backwards so that he seemed to be looking down. What Mussolini lacked in stature he made up for with his barrel chest, which he inherited from his father. To show it off he was frequently photographed stripped to the waist, helping peasants bring in the harvest or posing among bathers. Hitler, who lacked Mussolini's physique, thought such pictures were unbecoming of a head of government.

Mussolini, like the other dictators, including Lenin, rarely had a regular job outside politics. He disliked hard work and lacked the will to hold a nonpolitical job. After he had completed his education he taught as a substitute teacher in an elementary school for a year, a common means in those days of raising one-self socially. However, he probably never intended to make teaching a career and, in any case, was unable to have his teaching contract renewed.

Between 1902 and 1904, Mussolini went to Switzerland, perhaps to escape conscription into the Italian army, perhaps to run away from his parents, or possibly to escape debts. He became a common laborer for a short time and even begged. He slept in a crate and was arrested for vagrancy. He worked for as little as $4 a week and felt exploited. This experience, along with his father's politics, led the young Mussolini to socialism. In 1904, he associated with a number of exiled Italian and Russian revolutionary socialists. While still in Switzerland he began making public speeches to Italian Socialists, in which he attacked religion and militarism, which eventually led to his arrest and deportation. While in multilingual Switzerland he learned French and some German, which would prove useful to him in his career.

At the end of 1904, Mussolini took advantage of a decree that amnestied draft evaders and returned to Italy to serve in the army, after which he returned briefly to elementary school teaching. In 1909, he moved to Trent in the Italian-speaking portion of the Tyrol, at that time still part of the Austrian Empire. He entered Socialist politics and became the editor of an Italian-language newspaper. His experience in multinational Austria may have aroused his Italian nationalism, but he was eventually expelled because of his violent anticlericalism.

In 1912, after a stormy tenure in socialist journalism and serving a prison term for inciting insurrection, Mussolini became a major figure in national politics when he became the editor of the Socialist party's official newspaper, *Avanti*. He was highly successful in this new role, raising the paper's circulation in just two years from 28,000 to 94,000 with his slashing, vitriolic articles. His creed of revolutionary violence, antipatriotism, anticlericalism, and antimilitarism put him squarely in the party's left wing. A year earlier, in 1911, he had denounced the Libyan War as a "mad adventure," for which he was jailed for five months.

The outbreak of World War I proved to be a major turning point in Mussolini's life and political philosophy. For several weeks he was not sure what his attitude toward the war should be and adhered to the orthodox Socialist policy of neutrality. By October, however, he asked the party's executive to change its policy. He thought great historic events were taking place and that Italy's neutrality was shameful, an attitude he would retain a quarter century later. However, his efforts to influence the party were a total failure. He remained almost alone and resigned from *Avanti*. He was later expelled from the party altogether. In December 1914, he founded a new newspaper, *Popolo d'Italia*, in which he agitated for intervention on the Entente side, against Austria, and violently attacked neutralists. Rumors had it—now confirmed by uncovered documents—that he was being subsidized in this effort by both the French government and some Italian industrialists.

From September 1915 to January 1917, Mussolini served as a draftee in the Italian army, but he was on the front for only one-third of that time. He gradually came to like life in the trenches. Somehow it gave him a sense of physical well being. He was a conscientious but not outstanding soldier. Like Hitler, he rose to the rank of corporal and eventually to sergeant, but unlike Hitler, he received no prestigious decorations for bravery. The only serious wounds he suffered (in the buttocks) were unrelated to combat. He did resemble Hitler, however, in believing that winning was a matter of willpower.

Mussolini's views toward marriage began evolving about the same time his political opinions underwent a radical change. In 1910, Rachele Guidi, the daughter of his father's mistress, became his common-law wife. In 1916, shortly after leaving the Socialist party, many of whose members regarded marriage as a strictly bourgeois institution, he formally married Rachele in a civil ceremony. By 1925, when Mussolini was courting the respectable middle class and the Roman Catholic Church, he renounced his former anticlericalism and had a church wedding. Rachele was an unpretentious country woman who stayed out of politics by continuing to live in Milan for several years while her husband was in Rome. Between 1910 and 1929, she bore him three boys and two girls; he had a sentimental attachment to his children but spent little time with them. They, in turn, had a hard time living up to his high expectations.

Mussolini's living arrangement, with himself in Rome and his family in Milan, made it all the easier for him to bring a succession of literally hundreds of mistresses into his office at the Palazzo Venezia. (See figure 10.) This living arrangement was especially attractive for

Mussolini because he was hen-pecked by his wife. Innumerable women would visit him, either at his initiative or under some pretense. They arrived at a private back entrance of the palace and usually spent as little as fifteen minutes with him, but never spent the night. Ordinary Italians seemed pleased with this practice because his mistresses and two illegitimate children made Mussolini seem more human and virile. If his infidelities did not cause any political damage, they did hurt him physically, for he contracted syphilis as early as 1907 and apparently retained it much of his life.

Besides his mother, mistresses, and perhaps his younger brother, Arnaldo, Mussolini was also fond of music: Palestrina, Vivaldi, Verdi, and Wagner were his favorite composers; triumphal marches, great symphonies and, later in his life, grand opera were his favorite forms of music. In his early days he had also appreciated cartoons and satires, but later he regarded Fascism as too sacred to be ridiculed. Somewhat surprisingly, perhaps, expensive material possessions did not appeal to him. Like the other totalitarian dictators, he was far more interested in power than wealth.

## THE DUCE: STRENGTHS AND WEAKNESSES

Although Mussolini could be both brutal and domineering, he did have a number of characteristics that not only enabled him to come to power but also to become, for a time, the most popular ruler in Italian history. Like his counterparts, Stalin and Hitler, he could turn on the charm whenever he wished. His vitality, quick wit, courtesy, and intelligence impressed even his critics. His presence could be exciting, disturbing, and commanding, so that many people voluntarily felt compelled to obey him. If he was a dramatic actor in public, Mussolini, the former journalist, knew how to impress and flatter his many interviewers, especially foreigners. Whereas Hitler carried on monologues with his visitors, Mussolini questioned them and always learned something new. Americans regarded him as self made and a man of action. Even the future British prime minister, Winston Churchill, who met the Duce, admitted that if he had lived in Italy in the 1920s he would have been a Fascist.

Mussolini's skills as a propagandist have never been doubted. He succeeded so well in convincing others of his point of view that he also fooled himself. When speaking publicly his voice was both powerful and flexible; his tone could be solemn, prophetic, imperative, or exalting. In addition, he was a talented actor, could appear wholly dedicated to a cause, and was adept at perceiving the mood of a crowd.

Unfortunately, Mussolini's negative characteristics far outweighed his positive ones, although this fact was by no means immediately apparent. He was, first of all, a terrible administrator. Although he had an excellent memory for facts and was hard working, he lacked the patience for making careful decisions or pursuing a long-term strategy. Instead, he had an inexhaustible capacity to retain trivial details. His impulsiveness was uncontrollable, and he was constantly changing his mind. He surrounded himself with job seekers but had an absolute gift for giving jobs to the wrong people. He deeply distrusted his own subordinates and removed without warning most of his ministers. Frequently, these changes meant that unqualified nonentities replaced capable ministers. He probably had an inferiority complex, which made him feel threatened by men who were either too competent or too zealous. He did not want to hear bad news and was therefore frequently poorly informed about domestic and foreign affairs. He hated to have his authority questioned and rarely listened to advice, but when he did it tended to be the advice of the last person with whom he had spoken. Like all the dictators, he was vain and loved flattery. And like the others he had no intimate friends.

None of the above negative characteristics would have necessarily been disastrous if Mussolini had been a mere figurehead, or if he had been good at delegating authority. He was neither. He jealously gathered more and more authority into his own hands. As early as 1926, he personally held the offices of prime minister, president of the Fascist Council, foreign minister, minister of the interior, minister for corporations, minister for all three armed services, and commander-in-chief of the Fascist Militia. At other times he was also minister for colonies and minister for public works. Obviously he could not keep up with all of these jobs, so he dispersed power to undersecretaries who did not dare act on their own, even on small matters.

From all of the above, it is obvious that a cult of personality existed for Mussolini, especially when he was at the height of his popularity in the early 1930s. The cult was nearly as powerful as Stalin's and surpassed that of Hitler. Even before his appointment as prime minister he was known as IL DUCE—always spelled in block letters—or "the leader" of Fascism. He had come from the people, but was infinitely above them. Like Hitler, he was downright contemptuous of the "mob," which he compared to women who liked strong men. Propaganda portrayed him as a savior to a population that had lost sight of its aims, that lacked faith in itself, and that was suffering from a mass inferiority complex. He saw to it that he was given credit for every public benefit attributable to the regime: making the trains run on time; ridding farming regions of snakes; and raising Italy's international prestige. Corrupt or incompetent party officials might at times deceive Mussolini, but he would eventually root out these betrayers of his vision. Just as the pope was regarded as the infallible leader of Roman Catholicism, Mussolini, as the slogan said, "was always right." Even people who did not consider themselves Fascists subscribed to "Mussolinismo." According to the myth, the Italian people would become more heroic, disciplined, prepared to make sacrifices for the common good, more serious, and more hard working.

## THE YOUNG HITLER

Adolf Hitler has been the subject of more books and articles than any other political figure in history, yet much about his life, especially his youth, remains a mystery because of the scarcity of reliable sources. He had few good friends as a child and committed as little to paper as possible as an adult. Although his book, *Mein Kampf*, is partly autobiographical, it leaves much out, and that which is included is often deliberately misleading. Hitler attempted to portray what was mostly an idle and self-indulgent youth as a time when he overcame poverty, suffering, and loneliness to build the "granite foundations" of his Nazi ideology.

Hitler, like Stalin, was something of an outsider, not being a native, in the full sense, of the country he came to rule. Born in Austria in 1889, he did not become a citizen of Germany until 1931. Like Stalin, Hitler was not proud of his heritage and as chancellor humiliated his homeland. His birthplace of Braunau am Inn was in a rather poor and remote corner of the Empire on the German border. His ancestors had been peasants, but not serfs. His father, Alois, was the first in his family to rise up the social ladder. Unlike the fathers of Stalin and Mussolini, Alois's position at the top of the Imperial and Royal Customs Service made him very much part of the respectable middle class. Much has been made, especially during Hitler's lifetime, of Alois being the illegitimate son of a poor peasant girl named Schicklgruber. But in 1876, when Alois was forty years old, he unofficially changed his surname to Hitler. So Hitler was Adolf's legal surname from birth, which was fortunate for him, because it is difficult to imagine frenzied crowds shouting "Heil Schicklgruber." It has also been alleged that Alois's father may have been a Jew. The allegation is almost certainly false, but Hitler himself may have had doubts about his "racial" makeup that could be atoned only by persecuting Jews. Interestingly enough, the Nazi racial laws of 1935 would have excluded Hitler from the elite SS, since he could not have proven that all four of his grandparents were Aryan.

Hitler's mother, Klara, was his father's third wife and second cousin and was twenty-three years his junior. Three babies died in infancy before Adolf's birth (compared to two for Stalin), a fact that probably caused his mother to be just as overprotective of her son as was Stalin's mother. The family moved a great deal when Adolf was a boy until his father retired in the provincial capital of Linz in 1895. Until he died in 1903, the domineering father was around the household much of the time. Then, at thirteen, and for the next four years, Hitler's only parent was his doting mother who catered to his every whim. He grew up spoiled, immature, and with a strong aversion to systematic work—perhaps a reaction to his father's extreme punctuality.

Although Hitler did moderately well in elementary school, where there was no serious competition, his grades began to fall when he entered secondary school, mainly because he lacked discipline. He claimed that he had led his class in geography and history, but even there his grades were just "adequate" and "satisfactory." Only in drawing and gymnastics were his marks above average. One teacher called him uncontrolled, dogmatic, hot-tempered, lacking in perseverance, and despotic. He did at least become a choirboy, like Stalin, and was deeply impressed by the splendor and solemnity of the Roman Catholic services. At one time he even wanted to be an abbot.

During his teenage years Hitler had only one good friend, a fellow Linzer named August Kubizek. The boys shared an enthusiasm for the music of Richard Wagner, but otherwise it was an unequal relationship. Hitler did nearly all the talking while Kubizek was a passive listener. Hitler did not want Kubizek to have any other friends, a despotic attitude that Kubizek tolerated because he found his friend so serious and fascinating.

After dropping out of school at the age of sixteen, Hitler went off to Vienna in 1907 to enter the Academy of Fine Arts. His dreams were shattered, however, when his admission was rejected. For the next six years he lived a mostly comfortable but lazy life thanks to an orphan's pension and an inheritance from an aunt. He filled his days sleeping late, studying the architecture of the Habsburg capital by day and attending the opera in the evening. Like Stalin and Mussolini, he hated regular work, especially manual labor. At most he would consent to paint picture postcards of Viennese landmarks for tourists.

By his own admission in *Mein Kampf*, Viennese politics made a strong impression on the young Hitler. The Austrian capital was one of the most anti-Jewish cities in the world. Its coffee shops, which Hitler loved to frequent, were filled with anti-Semitic newspapers. Between 1897 and 1911, the city's mayor, Karl Lueger, was the first politician in the world to be elected on the basis of a specifically anti-Semitic program. Lueger, however, as Hitler pointed out in *Mein Kampf*, was only a cultural and religious anti-Semite, not a racial one, a character "flaw" not suffered by another of Hitler's early heroes, Georg von Schönerer. The latter, however, made the critical error, in Hitler's view, of attacking the Roman Catholic Church, thus alienating millions of potential followers. Hitler also mentioned the Austrian Social Democrats in *Mein Kampf*. He could not abide their Marxist internationalism and Jewish leadership, but he did admire their elaborate organizational structure and mass propaganda. Hitler was also impressed in a negative way by the Austrian Parliament, whose sessions he occasionally attended. This was a time when the ten or so Austrian nationalities were represented proportionately, and the leaders of each nationalistic party tried to outdo the others in their chauvinism and demagoguery. The consequence was that not much was accomplished in Parliament and the emperor-king, Franz Joseph, often had to rule by decree. For Hitler, the undignified shouting matches, bargaining, and compromises that he witnessed were the very essence of democracy and parliamentarianism.

The only mentors Hitler was willing to acknowledge in *Mein Kampf* were dead men whose political philosophies contained grave errors. He said not a word about Austria's "German [meaning ethnic German] Workers' party," or DAP, which was founded in 1903 and became the forerunner of the Austrian Nazi party. The organization combined Lueger's cultural anti-Semitism with Schönerer's racial anti-Semitism and, like the post–World War I German Nazis, tried to appeal to both nationalists and workers. In the summer of 1918, the party emphasized that point by changing its name to the German National Socialist Workers' party. Almost certainly Hitler did not want to give the Austrian Nazis credit for ideas that he later appropriated.

Hitler claimed in *Mein Kampf* that by the time he left Vienna in May 1912 (actually it was 1913) "the granite foundations" of his political philosophy had already been laid, including his anti-Semitism. This contention is doubtful. Hitler may have already developed a distaste for parliamentarianism. And it is likely that he had acquired the vocabulary of anti-Semitism from Lueger and Schönerer as well as from numerous anti-Semitic newspapers. On the other hand, he voiced no anti-Semitic opinions while in the Austrian capital and retained a good professional relationship with Jewish art dealers. He also enjoyed the music of Felix Mendelssohn and Gustav Mahler, two composers with Jewish ancestors.

Hitler left Vienna for Munich to evade service in the Austro-Hungarian army, an institution he hated because of its multinational character. After the Austrian criminal police tracked him down in Munich, a physical examination declared him unfit for service. He was now twenty-four years old and still without regular employment, a home of his own, or a family. He almost certainly had picked up many of the political ideas that would later compose his National Socialist ideology. However, there was no evidence that he was destined for political prominence.

During his first year in Munich, Hitler continued to live the life of a vagabond artist. Then everything changed. On August 1, 1914, Germany declared war on Russia and France and World War I was underway. He later wrote that on that day he "fell down on [his] knees and thanked Heaven from an overflowing heart for granting [him] the good fortune of being permitted to live at this time."[2] Two days later, Hitler volunteered for the army. He later claimed the war was the happiest time in his life. It was a thrilling, liberating experience. Now at last, he had a regular job, a purpose in life, and comrades. He was the only one of the totalitarian dictators to serve in the armed forces with some distinction, winning the Iron Cross First and Second Class, which were rarely awarded to enlisted men. He never abandoned a wounded comrade or pretended to be sick in order to avoid a perilous

2 Adolf Hitler, *Mein Kampf* (Boston, 1943), 61.

mission. He even refused to take a leave. When the war ended, Hitler was in eastern Germany recovering from a British gas attack. He claimed in *Mein Kampf* that the German army had not been defeated but had been undermined by Jews and Socialists on the home front. For him this myth was a satisfying explanation, at least politically, for why his world had suddenly come crashing down. (Interestingly enough he rejected the stabbed-in-the-back theory in a private dinner conversation during World War II.)

Several things deeply impressed Hitler about the war. One was his mere survival; he was among the 25 percent in his regiment to do so. Over time he became more and more convinced that he led a charmed life. He also expressed in *Mein Kampf* his admiration for the ferocity and one-sidedness of Entente propaganda. (See figure 19.) Likewise, the British naval blockade demonstrated Germany's lack of self-sufficiency. At the same time, however, Germany's conquest of Russia's western territories provided Hitler with a model of how this deficiency could be overcome.

## HITLER: THE CHAOTIC DICTATOR

No one who knew Hitler in Vienna, Munich, or the trenches of France could have guessed that he was a monster in the making. Although his childhood was disrupted by several moves, the early death of his father, and career disappointments, there was nothing so extraordinary about his youth that would have marked him as a likely candidate to become a totalitarian dictator. On the contrary, just to become the chancellor of Germany he had to overcome daunting handicaps: his foreign birth; his lack of a university education; and his comparative youth. At forty-three he became, like Mussolini in Italy, the youngest government head in German history.

If Hitler's youth did not point directly to a spectacular career as a politician, he did retain many of his youthful traits after he became chancellor, at least until the middle of World War II. He still hated routine work and did as little of it as possible, often preferring to spend his time concentrating on nonpolitical subjects like architecture, automobiles, or highways. (Unlike Stalin, he traveled widely throughout his adopted country.) He was content with laying down general and often vague lines of policy although he would interfere in anything he chose especially when it came to Jews, foreign policy, or war. He would postpone decisions until the last minute, if indeed he did not avoid making them altogether. Likewise, he frequently arrived late, if at all, for appointments. He either gave long monologues or sat in sullen silence. He rejected working with others and frequently refused to accept the advice of experts. When he deliberated it was only with himself. The despotic and ill-tempered nature that one of his early teachers had noted flourished as he grew older. His rages and stubbornness were those of an uncontrolled child who had never learned to become a part of a give-and-take adult world. He had few friends, and one of them, Ernst Röhm, the leader of the SA, he had killed during the purge of June 1934.

Other characteristics became apparent only after Hitler became chancellor. He was frequently absent from Berlin, preferring his mountain retreat at Berchtesgaden, thus making himself inaccessible to important ministers. He did not believe in informing officials of their tasks until the last minute, when they were told only the absolute essentials. He retained the power to reject or confirm any legislation, but was unconcerned with its preparation. He allowed the government to proliferate into numerous departments and ministries working largely independently of each other. Nazi propaganda to the contrary notwithstanding, this system created a bloated bureaucracy and enormous inefficiencies. Further chaos and duplication was caused by Hitler not giving written or explicit orders and, as mentioned, sometimes giving the same task to two different people. He would test and defend diametrically opposed points of view with different people, making it even more difficult for contemporaries and historians to determine what his real opinions were on a given issue. He was hypersensitive toward any attempt to impose the slightest institutional or legal restriction on his authority. Like Stalin and Mussolini, he relied on others based on their personal loyalty to him, which he placed far above competence.

Hitler's unbureaucratic style of ruling created a huge void in documentation. (He did not even make marginal comments on documents.) Historians to this day are puzzled about whether there was method in his madness or whether his management style was simply the result of laziness being erratic. It could easily have been all three. By creating or allowing chaos he made himself all the more indispensable as the one person who could untangle confused lines of authority. He was the ultimate arbiter in a heterogeneous party and the only source of unity in a disorderly government. Even the Nazi party deteriorated after Hitler came to power, as did the Communists and Fascists in Russia and Italy. The NSDAP was incapable of surviving on its own or producing a new leader, and Hitler like Stalin and Mussolini, made no realistic arrangements for a successor fearing that such a person might try to replace him prematurely. Unlike Italy, there was no Grand Council or monarch who could theoretically depose the Führer.

Fortunately for Hitler, the public, both domestic and foreign, was almost entirely unaware of the chaotic and inefficient nature of the Nazi government. By remaining aloof from rough and tumble political infighting, and especially from most controversial decisions and actions, Hitler retained his popularity; anger was deflected to the Nazi party, the popularity of which steadily declined after 1933. He never so much as attended an execution let alone large-scale repressions. This separation of Hitler from the party and unpopular decisions was reinforced by a carefully cultivated Führer myth that depicted Hitler as a wise and moderate leader who was opposed to radical elements in his own party. He was a God-fearing and deeply religious man who would protect the country from atheistic Communism. Consequently, even those people who had never subscribed to Nazi ideology could, in good conscience, continue to support the chancellor. (See figure 11.) There was, in fact, far more rapport between Hitler and the German people than there had been between Emperor Wilhelm II and his subjects. Only a few people remained immune to the Fuhrer cult: dedicated Marxists; some highly religious people; a few exceptional intellectuals; and some members of the upper middle class.

To protect his image, Hitler never appeared in public wearing glasses, preferring instead to read from large "Führer" typescript. He hated physical exercise except for downhill walks to a waiting car. His only physical prowess was his ability to hold out his right arm for hours giving the Nazi salute during parades, the result of using a chest expander. (See figure 12.) He never engaged in sports because they might make him look undignified or inferior. For the same reason he never posed for photographs while laughing or smiling. After his first few months in office he was rarely photographed in civilian clothing. The Führer myth was also reinforced by some of Hitler's personality traits. Many people, from secretaries to foreign statesmen, have testified to his ability to be amiable, cordial, extraordinarily charming, and persuasive. He joked and laughed readily—as long as the joke or the camera was not on him. He was magnanimous toward someone who committed a faux pas in his presence. His private mode of living was modest and unassuming. His villa in Berchtesgaden was comfortable, but not grandiose before 1935. He even waived his chancellor's salary, although this was not as great a sacrifice as it appeared because his royalties from *Mein Kampf*, which was eventually translated into sixteen languages, sold upwards of 10 million copies, and netted him some 8 million marks. He was not financially corrupt but did not hesitate to corrupt his generals with monetary bribes.

Even foreigners who were not taken in by the Führer myth saw Hitler as more foolish than dangerous. This attitude is perhaps best exemplified by a letter that Charlie Chaplin sent to Hitler in October 1933. The star of silent movies wrote that he could forgive Hitler for stealing his mustache and appearing in more films than he did. He could never forgive Hitler, however, for getting more laughs.

If Hitler could have maintained some degree of objectivity toward himself, the Führer myth might have remained a fairly harmless way of compensating for the regime's lack of ideological unity and clarity and could have been the cement which held the party together. Instead, by 1936 at the latest, he fell victim to the idea that he was infallible. He intimated that his insights were God-given and that he was an instrument of Providence. By definition, a mistake was something that did not agree with his dogmatic opinion. The words "I don't know" never escaped his lips. Ultimately, this characteristic impaired his judgment and led to his downfall. The Führer cult inevitably resulted in Hitler being surrounded by flatterers and sycophants who would not dream of criticizing him or engaging him in rational debate. As with Stalin and Mussolini, the most banal platitudes that came from his lips were accepted as the words of a genius.

## HITLER'S PRIVATE LIFE
## AND RELATIONS WITH WOMEN

Hitler's appearance and private life frequently fell far short of his heroic image. Physically, he did not match the Nordic ideal of a tall, blond-haired superman. On the other hand, contrary to the view of anti-Nazi propaganda and even that of many historians, Hitler was not short. At five feet, nine inches he was, if anything, slightly taller than the norm for his place and generation. Although he is best remembered for his mustache and brown hair, which constantly fell down over his eyes, contemporaries who met him were most impressed with his light, piercing blue eyes. Hitler was not muscular, but he did succeed in avoiding a middle-age paunch. Much less impressive was his body odor and bad breath.

Hitler posed as a great lover of the arts, and in fact did show more interest in the arts than any German ruler since the "mad" king, Ludwig II of Bavaria, in the nineteenth century. Actually, his tastes were those of the German and Austrian middle class around the turn of the century. He retained his youthful enthusiasm for the operas of Richard Wagner, almost certainly because they appealed to his love of the grandiloquent and bombastic. Otherwise, however, he showed little interest in music, except for Verdi's *Aïda* and Viennese operettas with Franz Lehar's, *The Merry Widow*, being his favorite musical composition. He ignored symphonic works and chamber music.

Like Stalin, Hitler loved movies, one or two of which he would see every evening along with a newsreel, until the habit was broken in the middle of World War II. He preferred westerns, adventure movies, and light musicals with lots of legs as opposed to movies with tragic plots or travelogues. His two favorite movies were *Snow White and the Seven Dwarfs* and *King Kong*. He was also fond of Mickey Mouse cartoons. In addition, he had a taste for imported pornographic movies, even though they were proscribed for the general public. He saw some movies ten times, but would never invite a famous pianist to perform or a scholar to speak to him and his guests. Again like Stalin, his social evenings lasted far into the night; he usually would not retire until two o'clock in the morning or later.

To the outside world Hitler appeared to lead an austere and celibate life. Some people have speculated that he was a homosexual, and Mussolini once referred to him as a "horrible sexual pervert." In fact, however, Hitler enjoyed women even though, or perhaps because, he regarded them as intellectually inferior. (See figure 13.) At the suggestion of his propaganda minister, Josef Goebbels, he refrained from marriage until the last day of his life so that he could maintain the image of being devoted solely to the welfare of the Reich. Nevertheless, unbeknownst to the German public, he had a number of mistresses. What is interesting about these women is that they were all around twenty years younger than he was, about the same age differential as that between his parents. All of them, moreover, eventually committed suicide or at least tried to do so. Eva Braun, his last and best-known girlfriend, was born twenty-three years after Hitler. Despite his low opinion of women, he gave them the impression they were beautiful and worthy of his admiration. He never became cross with his secretaries. Women were able to say blunt things to him that would have cost men their freedom at the very least.

There were obviously numerous and even striking similarities between the three totalitarian dictators. All of them had modest social origins, which they exploited to prove that they understood the grievances of the "common man." They also had domineering fathers, nurturing mothers, and weak formal educations, handicaps which certainly would have precluded them from attaining power under the far more stable social and political conditions of prewar Europe. They did have excellent memories but almost certainly had inferiority complexes. All of them were schoolyard bullies. None of them had many friends as children and not any as adults. Foreign travel was very limited both before and during their dictatorships. None of them held a regular job for any length of time prior to launching his political career nor did they have the training for any other profession. All of them regarded women as intellectually inferior and merely good for sexual gratification and domestic entertainment. None of them was a successful husband or father. They all dressed modestly and none had an impressive physical appearance; they were all touchy about how they were depicted in photographs. They all had rather plebeian interests when it came to the fine arts and entertainment. None of them had what could be described as a normal personality, but neither were they clinically insane. All of them encouraged the creation of a cult of personality which even foreigners could not always resist. The management styles of Hitler and Mussolini were similarly chaotic. Stalin, on the other hand, was more of a "hands on" ruler. If Hitler and Mussolini were actors who frequently appeared in newsreels, Stalin was a puppeteer. They were all more interested in power than wealth but did not see themselves as tyrants. Rather they were leaders sacrificially devoted to historic missions. They all had only a small capacity for love, but an unbounded capacity for hate. All of them had an unquenchable belief in themselves.

Among the few people the dictators respected were each other. Hitler regarded only Mussolini and Stalin as his equals. Despite Hitler's later disillusionment with Italy's poor performance in World War II, he never betrayed his friend. His feelings of comradeship with the Duce were genuine, which he demonstrated on a number of occasions. Stalin also considered Hitler a "very able man" who, like himself, had risen from lowly origins to become a world historic figure. He was especially impressed with Hitler's purge of the SA in June 1934. For his part, Hitler thought that Stalin was one of the most extraordinary figures in world history and that the Soviet Union would disintegrate without him. After his victory in the Second World War he planned to spare Stalin and exile him to a spa whereas he intended to have President Roosevelt and Prime Minister Churchill hanged. Stalin also had positive feelings toward Mussolini, and there is some evidence that those feelings were reciprocated. Mussolini's Italy, for example, recognized the new Communist regime in the Soviet Union in 1924, the first Western country to do so. Good diplomatic and even cultural relations were thereafter maintained between the two countries, that is, until World War II.

# 4 / TOTALITARIAN ECONOMIES

Nothing differentiated the Soviet Union from the other two totalitarian dictatorships more than its economic policies. Except for that of German Jews, private property in the fascist states was not adversely affected by totalitarianism. The policy of the Communist government of Russia, on the other hand, was nothing less than to own and control almost all property, from agricultural land to factories, transportation systems, and natural resources although it did not extend to personal possessions like clothing and home furnishings. This policy alone meant that the Soviet regime had to be far more totalitarian in its authority and to intervene more intimately in the lives of its citizens than either the Nazis or the Fascists. What Stalin attempted to do, no absolute ruler before him would have dared. It amounted to changing a whole country's way of life. It is no wonder, then, that Stalin's First Five-Year Plan, launched in 1928, is sometimes called the Second Bolshevik Revolution. To carry it out, Stalin virtually declared war on his own country and reduced its real per capita income by half.

## THE END OF THE NEW ECONOMIC POLICY

The Russian economy recovered fairly quickly from the devastation wrought by three years of world war and three more of civil war. In many cases, all that was needed to resume agricultural production was the return of peasant soldiers to their fields. Industries could often restore production as soon as machines were repaired and the transportation systems functioned normally again. In neither case were huge investments of time or money necessary. By 1928, the process of recovery was largely complete. Actual progress however, was likely to be much slower and more expensive because it required building new and more modern farms and factories, not merely restoring old ones.

The Achilles heel of the Soviet economy was always agriculture. For Lenin and other Communists, allowing peasants to confiscate the lands of noble estates and a few wealthier peasants had never been more than a temporary expedient. Productivity actually declined during the 1920s compared to prewar years because small peasant farms were less efficient than noble estates had been, and peasants were happy to consume more of their own produce. As compared to the last prewar years, only one-third as much food was available in the cities. In 1913, 12 million tons of grain had been exported. During Lenin's New Economic Policy the figure almost never reached 3 million tons. Production was also held down by the widespread use of primitive farming implements such as horse-drawn wooden plows. Because marketable food was reduced both urbanization and industrialization were slowed. However, in retrospect, at least, the NEP was a golden age for peasants—a time when they owned more land and had a higher standard of living than ever before or for many decades thereafter. They had regarded the NEP as a welcome and permanent arrangement, not a temporary tactic.

For the party faithful, however, the NEP had always been an embarrassing compromise with the evil forces of capitalism. The Communist leaders were not rational economists, although they liked to portray themselves as such to the West. Instead, they were advocates of a millenarian utopia based on the elimination of private property. Once this new economic system was achieved a superior society would emerge. By 1924, however, some Communists had accepted the NEP as legitimate. Even Stalin, at this time, posed as a moderate and supported the NEP.

Things began to change as early as 1926–27, when the more prosperous peasants known as kulaks saw the price of their produce arbitrarily cut by 20 percent by the government. Not surprisingly, the most efficient farmers lost their incentive to produce. Had the government planned to create a food shortage it could hardly have done a better job. By 1928, prices paid to peasants did not even cover the cost of production. The party had created its own agricultural crisis.

The refusal of peasants to sell or grow more food gave Stalin the pretext for which he had been waiting. The collectivization of 25 million mostly small Russian farms into a relatively small number of large-scale and presumably more efficient farms had been a goal of the Communists since before the Bolshevik Revolution. The move would ensure that crops would remain under the party's control, from planting to consumption. Peasants would no longer be able to defy the regime by withholding a portion or all of their crops from the market. Now the government could buy produce at artificially low prices and sell surpluses to foreign countries. Huge profits from these sales would finance the country's industrialization and obviate the need for borrowing from abroad.

Stalin had no inhibitions about the use of force and no patience for education. He decided to use such ferocity against the kulaks that poorer peasants would be terrorized into joining collectivized farms. Even though the idea that kulaks were the objects of hatred and jealousy on the part of poorer peasants was almost pure fantasy, by encouraging attacks on the more enterprising peasants, Stalin removed any would-be natural leaders who might have put up the greatest resistance to collectivization. Stalin wanted to hit the peasants so hard and so massively that they would have no opportunity to organize resistance. By the late 1920s, his power was nearly absolute and his remaining opponents could no longer put up effective resistance. He dismissed the grave fears expressed by moderates as groundless.

In his desire to modernize the Soviet Union, Stalin wanted to control all aspects of the Soviet economy and the lives of every citizen; he also needed to provide food for the burgeoning cities. These ambitious goals blinded him to economic realities. It is unlikely that he foresaw the economic disaster wrought by collectivization. He was convinced that a socialist transformation of the countryside would bring great progress, and no amount of evidence to the contrary would dissuade him from this view. Collectivization, moreover, was at least as much political as it was economic. Two hundred and fifty thousand large collective farms, each monitored carefully by Communist party agents, would be much easier to control than 25 million privately owned farms. Stalin's claim that collectivization had mass peasant support was pure nonsense. Collectivization was strictly a revolution imposed from above.

## STALIN'S WAR AGAINST THE PEASANTS

The First Five-Year Plan initially called for the collectivization of only 15 to 20 percent of all peasant holdings. When the people on these lands resisted, however, force was used against them and the whole process was accelerated. Collectivization turned out to be one of the greatest atrocities and nonmilitary, man-made disasters in the twentieth century, comparable only to Mao Tse-tung's collectivization in China and Hitler's slaughter of Jews.

Like the Jews of Germany, Soviet peasants, especially the "wealthier" ones, were the objects of years of hostile propaganda describing them as the embodiment of social evil. They, along with "bourgeois specialists," were the loathsome and repulsive "enemies of the people." The kulaks were not even given a chance to join the collective farms. Officials in charge of "dekulakization" were told to rid themselves of "rotten liberalism" and "bourgeois humanitarianism"[1] in order to eliminate the decayed remnants of capitalist farming. All the kulaks' possessions were confiscated and declared state property. In the middle of the winter they were robbed of their warm clothes including underwear and boots. Those who were not killed immediately were arrested and herded, fifty at a time, into freight cars and sent to labor camps in northern Russia or Siberia. An estimated 10 to 12 million were deported in this fashion, of whom about one-third died of cold and hunger by 1935. If their children happened to survive they carried the social stigma, written in their identity papers, of belonging to a hated class and as such were denied education and jobs and were liable for arrest.

Like Jews a few years later, kulaks were considered guilty, not because of anything they had done, but because of who they were. Even if they gave away all their property, they remained kulaks in the eyes of the government. The biggest difference between the Jewish Holocaust and the one taking place in the Soviet Union was that the latter involved an indigenous population in peacetime. It is also much less known to this day because it affected primarily illiterate and semiliterate peasants who rarely were in a position to make their plight known to the world.

By the end of 1931, a massive famine broke out, especially in Ukraine and the northern part of the Caucasus isthmus. The harvests of 1931–32 were not in themselves small enough to cause starvation. Rather it resulted from grain being taken from peasants in order to finance the unrealistic goals of industrial development. In the still fairly normal harvest of 1930, 85.5 million tons of grain were harvested; 22

1 Quoted in Robert Conquest, *The Harvest of Sorrow: Soviet Collectivization and the Terror-Famine* (New York, 1986), 147.

million tons were extracted from the peasants, and 5.5 million tons were exported. In 1931, the harvest dropped to 69.5 million tons, 28.8 million tons were taken from peasants, and 4.5 million tons were exported. In the middle of the famine, in 1932, 29.5 million tons were procured from the peasants.

Peasants were reduced to eating rotten food, which pigs would refuse, such as potatoes, beets, and other root vegetables. They also ate weeds, leaves, bark from trees, frogs and snails, the meat of diseased horses and cattle, mice, rats, sparrows, ants, earthworms, the leather soles from shoes, and, in some cases, even human flesh. Not surprisingly, many died of food poisoning before they could starve to death. At the end of 1932, the Soviet government introduced domestic passports but denied them to peasants in order prevent them from moving to the cities. No person without a passport could live or work in a city or obtain food rations. Ukrainians were told that there were "bourgeois nationalists" in their midst who were responsible for food shortages. Communist officials said that those who had died were lazy and had refused to work on the collective farms. When famine struck the Soviet Union in 1921, Lenin successfully had appealed to the world for help. Stalin's response to the current crisis was to deny that there even was a famine. People who mentioned it were accused of making anti-Soviet propaganda and given three to five years in prison. Stalin would not even tolerate party officials giving him confidential reports on the famine. To admit that there was a famine would have undermined the government's claim that collectivization had been a huge success.

The West received only contradictory and therefore seemingly inconclusive reports about the systematic brutality and famine being suffered by the Soviet peasantry. The main reason for the lack of accurate information was that foreign visitors, who were treated like royalty, were allowed to see only model collective farms, where peasants were well housed and fed and raised cattle that were in good condition. Foreign journalists, who after 1933 were kept out of famine areas altogether, had to file their reports with Soviet authorities before sending them to their editors, and the journalists would lose their visas if their dispatches discussed the famine. The International Red Cross was also prevented from investigating the famine. The French Radical leader and two-time prime minister Edouard Herriot was able to spend five days in Ukraine in 1933, but he was permitted to see Kiev only after its streets had been cleaned of homeless children, beggars, and starving people. The U.S. State Department, which was kept well informed of the famine by the American consulate in Riga, Latvia, refused to make any information available to the American public for fear it would damage U.S.-Soviet relations. President Roosevelt was trying at this time to cultivate good relations in order to counteract the growing danger presented by Germany and Japan. The famine could not, however, be kept entirely secret from the Soviet people, who could see starving peasants from trains. The Soviet government explained this phenomenon by saying that some malnutrition had resulted when peasants had refused to sow or reap properly.

One of the few people who did finally expose the truth about the famine was a man who, fearing reprisals, used the pseudonym Miron Dolot. Dolot tells a horrifying tale about the ordeal in his village. It began with the most prominent villagers—the teacher, legal clerk, and store owner—being arrested and deported by Communist agents, part of a legion of 100,000 fanatical urban party activists who invaded the countryside to impose collectivization. With their leaders gone, the remaining farmers were defenseless. The village church, the pride of the community, was destroyed in a few minutes. Graves were looted for jewelry and other valuables. The villagers' livestock was expropriated for the collective farms before proper housing and forage for the animals had even been prepared. The horses were turned loose and died of disease before tractors could replace them. A "Bread Procurement Commission" continued to search for hidden food in the middle of the famine and confiscated whatever foodstuffs it could find.

Estimates of how many people died in the famine and in the whole process of dekulakization vary widely; 4 to 6 million peasants died during the famine of 1932–33, nearly half of them children; another 3.5 million eventually perished in forced labor camps as result of collectivization. Estimates of all deaths from unnatural causes between 1930 and 1937, including starvation, beatings, or overwork in labor camps, range as high as 14 million. Altogether, no fewer than 120 million peasants were affected in one fashion or another. Of the 20 to 25 million Ukrainian peasants, about one-fourth to one-fifth died. Rural mortality was twice as high in Ukraine as it was in the Russian Federation because food relief was not permitted to cross the border from Russia into Ukraine. The attack on Ukrainian peasants had been preceded by an assault on the Ukrainian intelligentsia. Of approximately 240 authors who wrote in the Ukrainian language, about 200 were killed during the 1930s.

Tens of millions of peasants who survived still found themselves forced from their ancestral homes. About 17.7 million peasants successfully moved into the rapidly industrializing cities, many of them secretly and illegally, but millions of others were prevented from relocating because they could not obtain internal passports in 1932. The luckiest peasants were able to stay in their homes, but they had to surrender their carts, farm implements, horses, and livestock.

Historians can make only rough estimates of the human losses due to collectivization because no figures were ever published by the Soviet government. It was much more forthcoming, however, about animal losses. Rather than see their livestock driven into the collective farms peasants slaughtered them. Other farm animals simply died from neglect because urban party members who had no knowledge of animal husbandry often ran the collective farms. Consequently, between 1928 and 1934, the number of horses in the country declined from 32 to 15.5 million. The number of cattle dropped from 60 to 33.5 million head, pigs from 22 to 11.5 million. Sheep and goats declined by 65.1 percent. Overall, livestock fell from an index of 100 in 1928 to 44 in 1933, while grain production declined from 100 to 81.5, even though the Five-Year Plan called for it to increase to 155. Even these figures probably understated the reality. This was a disaster from which Soviet agriculture did not recover for twenty-five years.

Stalin's role in collectivization is more controversial than one might suppose given the fact that he initiated the process in December 1929, when he ordered the kulaks wiped out as a class. And it was he who finally decided to end the killing and enforced starvation. Some historians have pointed out, however, that like Hitler's role in the Jewish Holocaust, no one has ever found a document in which Stalin ordered the deliberate starving of peasants. Other historians have also noted that once begun, collectivization developed a momentum of its own. Victims of the repression were not necessarily always kulaks, even by the wide and flexible standards of the Communist party. They were often economically marginal people who were considered a burden on the community. Another favorite target was women who had violated the sexual mores of the countryside. Other hostilities were directed against the village political, social, and economic elite, especially outsiders. Any social antagonisms that already existed in cities were intensified by the famine. Not until the spring of 1933 did the government make any attempt to alleviate the suffering.

Even if every atrocity connected with collectivization cannot be attributed to Stalin, it is interesting to see how easy it was for him to interrupt the process and then resume it. After just four months of "voluntary" collectivization, so much chaos had been created that even Stalin apparently realized that a breathing spell was necessary. Instead of admitting his miscalculations, however, on March 2, 1930, he accused local party officials of creating the disorder because they were "dizzy with success." Peasants would now be free, if they wished, to return to their own farms. Consequently, in just two months the number of collectivized farms shrank from 50.3 percent to 23 percent of all farms and continued to decline until the fall. The reversal, however, turned out to be only temporary and collectivization soon resumed. By the end of 1934, 90 percent of the sown acreage in the Soviet Union was on 240,000 collectivized farms.

From the beginning, the collectivized farms were failures. No advanced plans had been worked out for their organization, their size, or even how the peasant hands should be paid. The most hard-working and enterprising peasants, the kulaks, were now either dead or in work camps and were therefore unavailable for work on the new farms. The Soviet Union's industrial base was still simply too small to provide the necessary machinery. The autonomy of the farms' management was severely limited, which prevented them from taking initiatives and adapting themselves to local circumstances. Confronted by inadequate resources, unrealistic quotas, and hostile peasants, the managers of farms made a show of success by simply inventing production figures, a common practice in factories as well. As much as possible they ignored government orders. Ironically, the only successful aspect of the farms was the small private plots that Stalin permitted as a concession to the peasants' traditional way of life, even though he had opposed such an idea in 1929. Families were allowed one cow and a few pigs and sheep on about one acre of land. Even though they made up only 3.8 percent of the nation's cultivated land in 1938, these plots were responsible for not less than 21.5 percent of the country's farm produce. In 1950, they produced over half of all the Soviet Union's food.

By the late 1930s, when collectivization was complete and the new giant farms were well established, the average Soviet citizen's diet was much worse than it had been in 1928. He ate about the same amount of bread, but less of everything else, especially meat and dairy products. Nor did conditions improve in later decades despite huge sums of money spent on Soviet agriculture. As late as the 1980s, twenty-five Soviet peasants were still needed to do the work of four farmers in the United States. The farms continued to be run, in many cases, by incompetents who had to deal with a huge bureaucracy and the intrusion of ignorant and distant central planners. As for the Soviet peasants, they regarded their new status as worse than the serfdom from which they had escaped in 1861. They were ruthlessly exploited and deprived of any control over their own lives. Not until 1975 were they permitted internal passports, without which they had been unable to leave their villages.

## THE FIRST FIVE-YEAR PLAN AND INDUSTRIALIZATION

Originally, collectivization was merely supposed to be part of the First Five-Year Plan, and not a very big part at that. The Plan, despite its name, was not the beginning of economic planning in the Soviet Union. Production had been planned each year during the NEP. Even during the first and subsequent five-year plans, planning was adjusted annually and was subject to immediate revision. Given these facts it is legitimate to ask what was unique about the five-year plans. Essentially their purpose was psychological or propagandistic. The First Five-Year Plan called for gross industrial output to increase by 235.9 percent and labor productivity to rise by 110 percent. These pseudo-scientific figures, however, were purely for show. The plans were much less a rational method for fulfilling human needs, or even the demands of the regime, than they were a method of inspiring or at least intimidating the Soviet people to work harder. The five-year time span was long enough to make huge gains seem possible, but short enough to make the sacrifices look temporary. The regime did not even expect the goals of the plans to be fulfilled.

The psychological purpose behind the First Five-Year Plan appears to have succeeded, at least for a time. There was much genuine enthusiasm in the cities and among party activists in the countryside and an understanding of the need for belt tightening. The spirits of the party faithful were revived after having been depressed by the compromises of the New Economic Policy. Enthusiasm was kindled by the frequent use of military terms such as "agricultural front," "militant discipline," and "shock brigades."

A number of gimmicks were used to increase industrial production along with coercion. Trade unions lost their independence including the right to strike—which was now called "sabotage"—and to collective bargaining. They became mere government agencies to enforce policies and to spread technical education. The early Bolshevik idea of workers managing factories was abandoned. Shock brigade groups were organized in 1928 to set spectacular examples for other workers. Needless to say they were not popular and some members were actually killed by other workers. (See figure 14.) Relief payments for able-bodied workers ended in October 1930. Now, on-the-job discipline was enforced by terror. In November 1932, workers guilty of one day's unexcused absence from their job were subject to dismissal. In January 1939, this "permissive" law was changed to stipulate that an employee would be fired if more than twenty minutes late for work. In 1940, so-called industrial commissariat chiefs were given the authority to transfer workers and their families from place to place to fill different factories' work-force needs.

When it came to wages, however, Stalin in an early example of his off-and-on pragmatism, preferred an almost capitalistic carrot to a dictatorial stick. "Wage equalization," which had been retained in state industries by Lenin, was denounced by Stalin in 1931 and replaced by payments for piecework in most industries. He also called for clear distinctions of wages (paid by the factories but dictated by the state) for skilled and unskilled labor, which did not differ significantly from those used in the West.

The best thing that can be said about industrialization during the First Five-Year Plan was that it was not as bad as collectivization. Nevertheless, extreme haste created chaos and inefficiency. Many problems arose before 1930 from the dismissal of numerous "bourgeois specialists," especially engineers, although Stalin by the end of 1936 reversed himself on this issue. Then there were factories built for which no machinery was available. And some machines were delivered to plants unable to house them. Labor was hastily recruited and untrained in one place while skilled workers sat idle in another. Much of the labor, including the slave labor of political prisoners and kulaks, was wasted on nearly useless projects such as the White Sea-Baltic Canal. Stalin's battle cry to "overfulfill quotas" was pure nonsense, because factories could not increase production without using up more supplies than had been allotted them by the Plan.

Stalin hailed the First Five-Year Plan as a "success" in 1932, one year ahead of schedule. The Second Five-Year Plan began immediately and called for the consolidation of gains made in the first plan and a restoration of quality of manufactured goods. (See figure 15.) Extravagant claims of industrial progress for the first and subsequent plans were made for both domestic and foreign consumption, and for a long time they were believed, even in the West. Most of the figures were simply falsified. Instead of the fivefold increase in industrial production for the years 1929 to 1941, claimed by Stalin at the time, the true figure was closer to one and one-half times, about equal to the rate experienced by Germany during the same period and less per year than what the Soviets themselves had achieved during the NEP.

The standard of living for urban workers in early 1941 was no higher than it had been in 1928 or 1913 even though the gross national product (GNP) was 71 percent higher in 1937 than it had been in 1928. Housing was desperately overcrowded and unsanitary and could not keep up with the rapid pace of industrialization. The closing of many private workshops at the end of the NEP had reduced the availability of consumer goods that the state was unable and unwilling to provide. Clothing and shoes in particular were in shorter supply. However, many people in the isolated Soviet Union thought that living conditions in Depression-stricken Europe were even worse than theirs. The misery of everyday life was also occasionally interrupted by various celebrations when food and drink were plentiful. Meanwhile, the only people to see a real improvement in their living standards were the new managerial elite, favored writers, and artists who supported the modernization effort in their works, as well as members of the secret police. This elite had fine houses, were driven about in limousines, and sent their children to special schools; their servants shopped in stores that were closed to the general public. These privileges were even proudly announced in the Soviet press.

Apologists for Stalin have argued that as chaotic as industrialization was it had been necessary to meet the challenge of Nazi Germany. The only problem with that argument is that when the First Five-Year Plan began in 1928, Adolf Hitler was a virtually unknown figure even in Germany. No one inside or outside Germany took the Nazi movement seriously until the Reichstag elections of September 1930, when most of the worst aspects of industrialization and collectivization had already become apparent. Hitler did not come to power until 1933 when the First Five-Year Plan had already been completed. Apologists also make the doubtful assumption that the pace of industrialization achieved by Stalin could have been made only by the brutal and wasteful methods he employed. Nevertheless it is true that some form of rapid industrialization was a prerequisite for the Soviet victory in World War II. (See figure 16.)

## THE FASCIST ECONOMY

Compared with the massive and truly totalitarian intervention of the Soviet state into the Russian economy, the role of the state in the economic affairs of both Italy and Germany seems almost trivial. Much of the reason for this difference is the simple fact that neither Mussolini nor Hitler cared very much about the fundamental aspects of economic matters, although they did care about the propaganda value of massive economic projects. Even though anticapitalism was an important aspect of Fascist and Nazi propaganda, especially in the early years of both movements, private enterprise continued in the fascist states. There was little nationalization of private property, property belonging to Jews being the one important exception. Nevertheless, both states attempted to control their economies to some extent in order to solve particular problems and especially to prepare for war. This could be done through giving certain sectors of the economy credits or direct government subsidies. Production in particular industries was regulated as were distribution, foreign trade, prices, and wages. The more important the industry, the greater the government's intervention when it felt that private initiative was inadequate. Only rarely, however, did this lead to direct government control of industries.

Despite the striking differences between Communist and fascist economies, however, there were some important similarities. All three totalitarian states supported heavy or basic industries like steel, electricity, and chemicals over consumer-oriented industries. Across the board, weak consumer demand for goods was perpetuated by low wages. Nevertheless, these tendencies were far stronger in the Soviet Union than in Italy or Germany where, by comparison, consumer goods were abundant.

The Fascist regime in Italy never created a complete and integrated economic program, but switched back and forth between differing policies. In general, the long-term achievements of the government, if perhaps not always the intentions of the government, were minor corrections in the private enterprise system. Even direct state investment in industry began merely as an emergency measure during the Great Depression.

All three of the totalitarian dictatorships had a penchant for spectacular public works projects that would be of great propagandistic value to the regime. In the Soviet Union it was canals (now used in large part by foreign tourists), huge dams, large factories and the Moscow subway. In Italy and Germany super highways were probably the most publicized state-financed works. Unique to totalitarian Italy was the excavation of the ancient forum and other ruins in and around Rome. These projects gratified Mussolini's long-time interest in Roman history, put a good many people to work, and aroused pride in Italy's long and glorious history. To emphasize the point, four huge maps displaying the growth of the ancient Roman Empire were attached to a wall of one of the ruins, where they can be seen to this day. Mussolini also ordered the construction of a broad avenue above and through the forum connecting the ancient Coliseum with the monument to Victor Emmanuel II, the unifier of Italy. (See figure 17.) The avenue served as an ideal staging point for numerous colorful parades during the Fascist era, which were in part designed to provide workers with a sense of community and identity with the regime. Other public works projects included clearing and improving ports and harbors, building hydroelectric works, electrifying railways, draining land, and building aqueducts.

Trade unions in both Italy and Germany in many respects served about the same purpose as those in the Soviet Union. They were not designed to protect workers from exploitation by management, but were instruments of government control. In both Italy and Germany, however, they did help to reduce the industrial workers' sense of social and cultural isolation by generating a feeling of belonging to the national community. In both Italy and Germany unions handled social security benefits, claims for severance pay, and sometimes negotiated contracts that were beneficial to the workers. Primarily, however, they were a source of employment for lower middle-class bureaucrats.

The Great Depression that began in 1929 caused both fascist states to adopt policies of autarky or self-sufficiency. It is really going too far, however, to describe autarky as a specifically "fascist" economic policy. In reality, during the 1930s all the industrialized countries, including the United States, foolishly tried to protect existing domestic industries from foreign competition and create new ones by exacting protectionist tariffs that were so high that they virtually barred imported goods. At most, Italy and Germany carried this policy somewhat further than the democracies because they were trying to prepare for war. The policy was generally counterproductive because new domestic enterprises were often less efficient than foreign ones. In Italy, for example, the increase of wheat production reduced the need to import inexpensive American and Canadian grain, but also reduced the acreage available for vegetables, olives, and fruit, for which Italy was well suited. The result was an overall increase in the cost of food for Italian consumers.

Ruralization, that is the attempt to get city folk to return to the small towns and villages from which they came, was also not unique to Italy and Germany. In Italy the government supported sharecropping contracts and the homesteading of land-reclamation areas and virtually prohibited migration from rural locales to towns and cities. The Fascist regime also tried to "return to traditions" by praising artisan culture featuring peasants in traditional dress in folklore festivals, all part of an unsuccessful attempt to create a particularly Fascist mass culture. In the United States the Roosevelt administration tried to discourage rural migration to cities where there was high unemployment and even attempted to get poor farmers in the Upper Midwest to homestead land in the Matanuska Valley north of Anchorage, Alaska. In Germany, marriage loans were made available to farm laborers who promised to remain on the land, and new farm housing was exempt from taxation. At best, however, these efforts only retarded the urbanization that had been underway for over a century.

One way in which Fascist economics did differ from that of both Nazism and Communism, at least superficially, was corporativism. It initially evolved from the struggle among industrialists, unions, the party, and the state and was designed to settle occasional concrete problems arising from dissatisfied workers in industry. Later, however, the idea was broadened into a high-sounding answer to the harsh individualism of liberal capitalism and the class warfare of Marxism. In 1934, employees and management in related industries were brought together in twenty-two corporations where their interests could be harmonized under the joint auspices of labor courts, which would settle disputes without resorting to strikes. Each corporation was to act as a small parliament with nominal powers to set wages and conditions of employment. It was supposed to be a reversion to medieval guilds, which had comprehended all classes within a single vocation. In each corporation there were Fascist officials from the Ministry of Corporations who sat with the representatives of labor and management.

The corporative goal of social harmony was admirable, but the big industrialists prevented any meaningful implementation of the program. In practice, corporativism turned out to be an elaborate and expensive fraud because the corporations had little authority and no autonomy. Their meetings therefore had an academic or theoretical character. Any rules they drew up were obligatory only if approved by Mussolini. The big beneficiaries were Fascist party members for whom a great many jobs were created, and businesspeople and landlords who continued to make their own decisions and who no longer had to fear strikes, which had so plagued pre-Fascist Italy. Even class antagonisms were not reduced; they were merely driven underground. After the Chamber of Deputies—the Lower House of the Italian Parliament—was abolished in 1938, it was replaced by a Chamber of Fasces and Corporations in 1939. Eight hundred members represented the twenty-two corporations. But they could only make proposals to Mussolini, not pass legislation.

No basic improvements were made in the already miserable plight of peasants during the Fascist era. The average size of land holdings declined under Mussolini until more than 87 percent of the total farm population owned little more than 13 percent of the land. The biggest proprietors, who made up only one-half of 1 percent of the total rural population, owned nearly 42 percent of the land. Agricultural income, already bad before the Depression, only worsened after 1929. The only thing that went up was the peasants' taxes.

One of the big controversies among historians of Fascist Italy is the rate and significance of its overall economic growth. Some historians have correctly pointed out that the growth rate was higher both during the pre-Fascist Liberal era and again after World War II.

Other historians, however, have noted that raw growth statistics for the pre- and post-Fascist eras do not take into account the impact of the Great Depression. Once that is done, the Italian case looks moderately successful for a country in its stage of development. During the Depression, imports fell by 29 percent in Italy while exports fell by one-quarter. The index of manufacturing, with 1938 being 100, stood at 90 in 1929 and at 77 in 1931–32. Unemployment, which was 300,000 in 1929, more than tripled to 1 million in 1933, but was partially alleviated by popular welfare relief for children and war veterans dispensed by the Fascist party. In the meantime, workers saw their real incomes fall by about 10 percent.

These figures, however bad they were, compare rather favorably to other countries during the same period. For example, imports dropped 49 percent in Germany, 51 percent in France, and a whopping 64 percent in the United States. Unemployment increased tenfold in Germany between 1928 and 1932 while real wages fell 20 percent. In Britain, with about the same population as Italy, there were 3 million unemployed by 1932, although its larger nonfarm population would account for much of the difference. Using 1913 as one's base, the Italian growth of industrial production was even more impressive, with the index reaching 153.8 by 1938, as compared to Nazi Germany with 149.9 and France with 109.4. Only the Scandinavian countries, and Britain with 158.3, did better during the same twenty-five-year period.

## THE ECONOMY
## OF NATIONAL SOCIALIST GERMANY

Thinking in economic terms was basically alien to the Old Guard Nazi leaders, including Hitler himself. Political goals were placed ahead of economic ones because, if achieved, they would produce economic benefits anyway. Before the outbreak of World War II, there was not even a central agency to examine and coordinate the material demands of the armed forces. Until 1942, there were no real economic experts in Hitler's inner circle of associates. No fundamental restructuring of Nazi Germany's economy ever took place. None of this is meant to imply, however, that Hitler was disinterested in economic matters.

The early economic program of the Nazis, especially their famous Twenty-five Points announced by Hitler in February 1920, was extremely anticapitalistic. The Twenty-five Points called for the abolition of unearned income, or interest, the confiscation of the profits of munitions makers, and land reform. These ideas, however, although never officially renounced by the party, were quietly ignored so as not to antagonize the middle class or discourage support from big business. Nazi propagandists began to explain that they had nothing against patriotic businessmen; they merely opposed Jewish capitalism. Not so quickly forgotten, however, were Nazi attacks on large, mostly Jewish-owned department stores, mail order firms, and consumer organizations, all of which hurt the proprietors of small, family-owned enterprises who furnished much of the Nazis' electoral support right up to 1933.

Once in power, however, the Nazis quickly changed their economic tune. Even Jewish businessmen, including department store owners, were left largely undisturbed by the Nazis. Hitler was pragmatic enough to recognize that the replacement of competent Jewish businessmen by incompetent Nazi party members would only increase the economic chaos and unemployment that had plagued Germany for more than three years. Consequently, Jewish industrialists sometimes even received government contracts, and as late as 1937 Jewish unemployment still stood at a fairly modest 10 percent, which, though well above the unemployment rate for the rest of the German population, was extremely low when compared to the general American rate of 16 percent. Thereafter, however, Hitler no longer felt that the expertise of Jewish businessmen was essential, so their status, as well as that of all other German Jews, radically worsened. They lost not only their jobs, but also their property, and in many cases their lives.

After 1938, however, the status of non-Jewish factory owners and managers remained largely unchanged. Although they had had relatively little to do with the Nazis gaining power in 1933, they did profit from the new regime as long as they cooperated with its policies. Like Stalin's attitude toward collective farms, Hitler believed that a relatively small number of big industrialists and department store owners would be more efficient, productive, and easier to control than a much larger number of small businessmen. German industrialists, in most cases, were willing to go along with the Nazi regime, in part because they had never been happy with the Weimar Republic, with its strong unions and generous welfare benefits, not to mention its poor economic record. They were pleased with the abolition of free trade unions in May 1933 and the rapid return of prosperity

On the surface, laborers were among the biggest losers in the Third Reich. They lost their right to organize, their freedom of movement, their right to collective bargaining, and to some extent even their vocational choice. These losses were no doubt keenly felt by the half or so of the work force that had been fully employed at the beginning of 1933. To someone who was unemployed or underemployed, however, which included a disproportionately large number of young people, these losses were mostly on paper. Industrial workers were by far the biggest victims of unemployment in the late Weimar Republic. But by the middle of 1934 the unemployment rate of 1932, the worst year of the Depression, had been cut by 60 percent; by 1936 it was back to the level of 1928, and by 1939 there was actually a labor shortage of about 500,000. At the same time, their wages, which by 1932 had fallen to only 65 percent of their 1929 level, grew by 50 percent between 1933 and 1937 although this increase was not nearly as impressive as the rise of the gross national product by 81 percent by 1939.

Hitler, like Martin Luther four centuries earlier, flattered workers by repeatedly talking about the nobility of honest labor, saying that the workers merely had been led astray by their Marxist and Jewish leadership. Through this propaganda, and by being included in large Nazi subsidiary organizations, workers began to lose their isolated proletarian social environment, which disappeared altogether after 1945. Workers also benefited from fixed rents and a relative decline in heating and lighting costs. An eight-hour day was made the ideal and practiced until shortly before the war in most industries. A "Beauty of Labor Office," established in November 1933, helped improve the external appearance of more than 112,000 factories by clearing away rubble and cleaning up unkempt areas. Lawns and parks were created near factories for rest and recreation. Within many factories themselves, the lighting was improved, more space was created between machines, rooms were painted, floors were washed, and rest rooms were installed or upgraded. In 1935, an effort was even made to reduce factory noise.

However, there was also a negative side to the changes affecting labor. In 1935, a labor pass or *Arbeitsbuch* was reintroduced after having been abandoned in the middle of the nineteenth century. This document contained information about training, employment history, and family status among other things. No one could be hired without one. Full employment also eventually became too much of a good thing. By 1938, the average work week had increased to over 46 hours and workers in the aircraft industry were sometimes expected to work 60 hours a week. The lengthening work week began to erode the social harmony that the Nazis had created.

Peasants, like industrial workers, were also lavished with praise by the Nazi regime, and jokes about them were forbidden. They were racially the purest of the Germans and the backbone of the nation. They worked with the German soil and grew products without which the rest of the population could not live. They retained ancient German folk songs, dances, and costumes. They were almost completely unaffected by wicked foreign and Jewish influences. Hardly a parade or public celebration could take place without at least a small group of German peasants, in their colorful native costumes, being present.

Besides the compliments, the government guaranteed higher prices for farm products; it also took measures to reduce indebtedness, taxes, and interest on loans to stimulate production. These policies did have some limited success. By 1938–39, farm production was meeting 80 to 83 percent of Germany's needs as compared to only 68 percent in 1927–28. Meanwhile, however, industrial production was rising by 90 percent. However, farm income as a percentage of national income declined from 8.7 percent in 1933 to 8.3 percent in 1937. And the flight from the countryside was not reversed. By 1939, the allegedly simple pleasures of the rural life were enjoyed by only 18 percent of the population as compared to 20.8 percent in 1933, a decline that was also occurring in Italy as in all industrialized countries. All in all, peasants were affected less by the Nazi regime than any other social or economic group, in sharp contrast to the Soviet Union.

Without question, Hitler's greatest economic achievement, and the thing that did the most to boost his popularity, was his success at wiping out unemployment. Here demography once again was an ally of Hitler. Unemployment declined in part simply because fewer young people entered the job market during the early years of his dictatorship because of the low birthrate during the World War. Critics have often attributed this success to rearmament, but that is at best an exaggeration. Rearmament began on a large scale only in 1936 by which time unemployment had already been nearly eliminated.

Rearmament accounted for only 10 percent of the gross national product between 1933 and 1937 and 15 percent in 1938. The latter figure was half again as high as the comparable figures for Britain and France. Nevertheless, Germany did not begin an all-out militarization of its economy until after the battle of Stalingrad that ended in early 1943. Rather, unemployment had been gutted by an ambitious public works program, not unlike that undertaken by President Roosevelt in the United States but far more successful. Why this was so is not easily answered, but it probably had something to do with the long-term German tradition of government intervention in the country's economy. The regime's elimination of trade unions also made the economy more competitive.

In 1933, *Reichs Marks* (RM)1 billion—equal to over $5 billion to-day—was allocated for public works projects such as highways, canals, public buildings, and bridges. "Pump priming" grants were also issued to employ construction workers in the renovation of old buildings and the creation of new housing. Germany thus undertook deficit spending on an unprecedented scale for a capitalist country. Work creation projects were responsible for 25 percent of the German recovery. Unemployment was eliminated three times faster than in the United States.

Among the public works projects was the world's first system of divided super highways or *autobahns*. They were and still are undoubtedly the most impressive of these public projects, but there are several popular misconceptions about them. Contrary to public opinion, they were not conceived by the Nazis. A prototype had been built in Italy already in 1922 and the Weimar Republic had already approved the legislation and funding that made their construction possible. It was only after Hitler took over power, however, that the actual construction began, so he has undeservedly received all the credit. It is also unlikely that they were built primarily to facilitate military aggression, although it is true that they were less vulnerable to bombing than railroad tracks and in the late stages of the Second World War were sometimes used as substitute landing strips for airplanes. However, their intended purpose was to relieve unemployment, to bolster the construction and the steel industries, and to encourage tourism. Unlike the American interstate highways, whose construction did not even begin for another twenty-five years, the autobahns did not cut through the center of cities and compete with urban public transportation. And every effort was made to make the roads blend in with their natural surroundings. Rest areas were built to allow motorists to admire the German countryside. Ironically, even by 1939 only 2.3 percent of the German population owned a motorized vehicle compared to more than 20 percent in the U.S., thus leaving the magnificent highways almost deserted.

In addition to public works projects, a Four-Year Plan was started in 1936—the purpose of which was to prepare the economy for war. Instead of radically changing the German economy, however, the Plan simply added another layer of bureaucracy to the economy. Now state and party officials, representatives of private industry, the armed forces, the SS, and other Nazi organizations all had a voice in how the economy should be run. There was no proper arrangement for the allocation of raw materials, and industrial investment remained largely unplanned. The Plan dictated what companies should produce, the kind and level of investments they should make, what prices and wages they could set, and how much profit they could make. Although it did not involve as much central planning as the Five-Year Plans of the Soviet Union, the Four-Year Plan also proved to be inefficient.

Equally ill advised were efforts, resembling those of Italy and other industrialized countries, to make Germany self-sufficient. In part this was another preparation for war. But it was also inspired by the traumatic memories of World War I and its immediate aftermath, when hundreds of thousands of Germans starved to death and millions more were malnourished because the British blockade had cut them off from trade with the rest of the world. Consequently, low-grade ore was mined, the production of synthetic rubber was pursued, and even substitutes for coffee and cloth were manufactured. Imports declined from RM 14 billion in 1928 to between RM 4 billion and RM 5 billion from 1933 to 1938. Self-sufficiency was increased but not complete, and the German standard of living suffered as a result.

Like the economy of Fascist Italy, that of Nazi Germany did not match the growth rates of the late German Empire or the post–World War II Federal Republic. The rate of growth for interwar Germany as a whole, including the Weimar Republic, also did not match that of the United States, Italy, or the United Kingdom. Moreover, the real wages of Nazi workers were only slightly ahead of those of the Weimar Republic. If the wages of 1936 are indexed at 100, those of 1928 were 102.2 and those of 1938 were 107.5 with the difference being created by more overtime work being performed, as opposed to real increases in wages. Consumer goods were also only slightly more plentiful than in 1928. The German public was probably unaware that Germany, like most of the rest of the industrialized world, had started to recover from the Depression in the summer of 1932. What the public did know was that the 6 to 8 million unemployed workers of 1932 had almost miraculously disappeared from their streets by 1937.

In generalizing about the economies of the three totalitarian states one simple fact stands out: they were moderately successful as long as they pursued traditional and pragmatic goals. The New Economic Policy, which allowed an independent peasantry and small-scale free enterprise, was quite successful. So too were the economies of Italy and Germany as long as businessmen were relatively free of unrealistic government regulations. Trouble began for both fascist states when they tried to become too economically self-sufficient, a policy the Soviet Union had pursued ever since its founding and especially under Stalin. For Germany, new problems were created by the Four-Year Plan and when war preparations were intensified in the last two prewar years. For the Soviet Union the centrally planned economy of Five-Year Plans, especially collectivized farms (with the exception of the allowance of small private plots), was an absolute catastrophe. For all the totalitarian states, the more pragmatic their programs the more successful they were; the more doctrinaire and fanatical their policies became, the more disastrous. This was a pattern found in more than one aspect of life in the totalitarian states.

# 5 / PROPAGANDA, CULTURE, AND EDUCATION

## THE LIMITATIONS OF PROPAGANDA

Propaganda, culture, and education may at first glance appear to be three unlikely subjects to combine in a single chapter. Propaganda, it is usually assumed, consists of nothing but lies and gross exaggerations, whereas culture and education are reflections of truth, beauty, and enlightenment. In fact, however, the totalitarian parties did not make a big distinction between the three topics. Culture and education were propaganda in more subtle forms. Like propaganda, culture had to be simple enough that everyone could understand it. And like propaganda, the purpose of culture and education was to buttress the state and popularize its policies.

Propaganda is not a modern concept. It has existed since ancient times. Archaeologists and historians believe that Assyrian reliefs, showing the severed heads of enemies, were a form of propaganda intended to terrorize potential enemies. Julius Caesar's literary account of campaigns in Gaul was propaganda to build up his political base in Rome. The Roman Catholic Church was the first to use the term during the Counter-Reformation in 1622. The first secular use of the word came during the Revolution of 1830 in France. Modern democracies do not hesitate to use propaganda; public schools, newspapers, radio, and television all make it easier for them to get their message to the general public. Contrary to popular belief, propaganda does not necessarily consist of lies or even distortions. At its most effective it is selective truth, half-truths, truths out of context, or statements about the future that cannot be proved or disproved. Nothing is more harmful to a propagandist than to be caught in an out-and-out lie. Totalitarian propagandists were also well aware of the universal fact that negative statements unite people whereas positive ones tend to divide them.

Propaganda has acquired a negative reputation since the 1930s because it is closely connected to the Nazis' chief purveyor of propaganda, Josef Goebbels. However, Nazi propaganda was neither as unique nor as effective as is commonly supposed. Propaganda is simply a form of advertising that is part of all organizational activity in a highly literate society. Like commercial advertising, in the long run it cannot be any more potent than the product it represents. Success makes the work of the propagandist easy; failure makes it next to impossible. Propaganda works best only with those people who are already inclined to believe it. It is much better at reinforcing old ideas than changing them. In other words, it must build upon already existing values and mentalities. It does not work when it flatly contradicts the experiences or observations of its intended audience. For example, it did not succeed in convincing the German people that Italy was a powerful ally or that the United States was an evil enemy. It is also certainly not the monopoly of totalitarian states.

Historians have been all too inclined simply to assume that totalitarian propaganda was effective. Newsreels of cheering crowds seem ample proof that a government's message and policy were being enthusiastically received. Looks, however, can be deceiving. It is far easier to see what the people of totalitarian countries were doing than to know what they were thinking. There were, after all, no free elections and no public opinion surveys. Police reports, which have come to light since the fall of Nazi Germany and Fascist Italy, and more recently the German Democratic Republic (East Germany) and the Soviet Union, help fill in some of the missing gaps in our knowledge. But even these reports, though confidential, cannot always be taken at their face value. The informant may well have been telling his supervisor what the latter wanted to hear.

The totalitarian states exercised a far greater control of the mass media and cultural outlets than did the democracies. No form of cultural expression remained uninfluenced by the policies of the totalitarian governments although the degree of control varied from country to country and from time to time. Democratic governments must deal with an often cantankerous press, which is often looking for ways to embarrass the powers that be. The democracies also have very little control over the cinema, theater, and the fine arts in general, at least in peacetime, although wartime controls can be nearly totalitarian.

Another common myth is that people in the totalitarian states were especially gullible. The contrary was more likely the case. They were well aware of the monopolistic control of the mass media. This awareness made them suspicious of anything they were told by their government, even when it was absolutely true. But because people were not allowed to express their views openly, their real gullibility was toward rumors, which were rife.

## SOVIET PROPAGANDA

The Soviet Union was the first country in the world to use propaganda to mobilize an entire nation. The tasks of Soviet propaganda were in some ways easier and in other ways far more difficult than those of the fascist states. Prior to World War II, the fascists' goals of full employment and the establishment of German and Italian grandeur in the eyes of other nations were popular. The Soviet goals of the collectivization of farms and rapid industrialization demanded huge sacrifices. So daunting were these tasks that Stalin mostly resorted to force, especially with regard to collectivization. After the German invasion of Russia in 1941, Nazi atrocities did far more to convince Soviet citizens that the motherland had to be defended than anything Soviet propaganda ever did.

The generally low level of Soviet education, at least during Stalin's lifetime, was both an advantage and a disadvantage for Soviet propagandists. While it may have rendered the masses less sophisticated, it also made it more difficult or even impossible to reach them through the printed word. However, the drive to raise the literacy rate in the Soviet Union was itself closely connected with propaganda. Newly established reading rooms became propaganda centers. Then, with the improvement in Soviet education, especially after Stalin's death in 1953, the Soviet people became better educated, more politically sophisticated, and more difficult to influence. When Stalin first consolidated his dictatorship in 1927, around 25 percent of the members of the Communist party were illiterate, only 7.9 percent had secondary educations, and a scant 0.8 percent had graduated from a university. These statistics are particularly relevant when it is remembered that neither Lenin nor Stalin, nor any of their successors, had to campaign in a general election. Theoretically, they only had to win over the party's general assembly, the Congress of Soviets. In reality, however, they only needed the approval of the party's tiny Politburo, and even there Stalin substituted terror for persuasion.

The geographic isolation of the Soviet Union also greatly reduced the possibility that Soviet citizens would be able to make embarrassing comparisons between themselves and those in the West. From the beginning, the government made it impossible for individuals to travel freely in the West and placed severe restrictions on foreign travelers in the Soviet Union as well. Those foreigners who were allowed to enter the country were carefully searched to make sure that they were not bringing in any "dangerous" literature. Foreign newspapers, except those that were the official organs of Communist parties, were also unavailable for the general public in the Soviet Union right down to the collapse of the regime in 1991. Even though few Russians could afford radios during Stalin's rule, foreign radio broadcasts were jammed by transmitters set up along the Soviet Union's western borders.

On the other hand, Soviet propagandists also faced some formidable challenges not found in Germany or Italy. Prior to collectivization, the illiteracy and geographic dispersion of peasants made them difficult to influence. Collectivization opened up new avenues of political influence. However, it was almost a hopeless task for propagandists to convince Soviet peasants that it was in their interest to join a collective farm; hence the resort to force. Soviet propaganda was also hampered by the low technical quality of its newspapers. To compensate for this problem the regime created a network of oral agitators, which was especially important in reaching the illiterate masses in the countryside.

The close relationship between propaganda and culture in the totalitarian states is seen in the union of the two in a single office in Russia and in Germany. In the Soviet Union the Central Committee Secretariat had a Department for Culture and Propaganda, which dealt with education, the press, party propaganda, and general culture. The Department made sure that all books, magazines, newspapers, films, poems, plays, radio scripts and even scientific papers were approved in advance of distribution by government censors. In order to pursue a career in the arts and culture one had to belong to a certain union. Expressing the wrong ideas could lead to expulsion from the union and the end of one's artistic pursuits.

One of the main functions of propaganda in Russia and the other totalitarian states was to enhance the leadership cult. Photographs of Stalin were published in the daily press showing him smoking his pipe, walking with his comrades across the grounds of the Kremlin, surrounded by small children, or with his arms around his daughter, Svetlana. Like politicians everywhere, the totalitarian dictators believed that the company of children made excellent propaganda. (See figure 18.) Stalin especially loved to be seen receiving little girls with bouquets of flowers as he observed great events from the reviewing stand atop Lenin's mausoleum on Red Square.

Aside from these appearances at parades and various national holidays, Stalin was rarely seen in public, whereas Hitler and Mussolini were omnipresent in peacetime. Prior to the German invasion of Russia in 1941 Stalin had spoken on the radio only once. He was essentially an office dictator. His slow, laborious, uninspired speaking style would have bored listeners to death in the West, but its simplicity seems to have been well received by his hand picked and unsophisticated audiences in Russia. Most Communist party members were not intellectuals or theoreticians. They merely wanted to be told what to do, something Stalin had no problem obliging.

## FASCIST PROPAGANDA

An entirely different set of problems confronted fascist propagandists in both Italy and Germany. Italy still had a partially free press until 1925; Germany's 4,700 newspapers were the largest per capita and probably the most diverse in the world at the beginning of 1933. Therefore, the fascist parties had to compete in the marketplace of ideas in a free society where their claims could be refuted or challenged by an opposition press or an unfriendly government. Even after they consolidated power, the fascist states did not enjoy the advantages of geographic isolation with which Stalin was blessed. Foreigners were free to travel wherever they wished and to talk with whomever they pleased. Foreign newspapers and magazines were also available on newsstands, especially in Germany. Germans and Italians were also allowed to travel abroad. During the Winter and Summer Olympic Games of 1936 the German government made every effort to encourage foreigners to visit the Third Reich.

Although these differences with the Soviet Union were very real, the fascist states were far from being wide-open societies. Hitler and no doubt Mussolini were unconcerned with the presence of foreign newspapers and foreign radio broadcasts because in those days only a few highly educated people, probably no more than 5 percent of the population in Germany, and even fewer in Italy, could understand them. Few foreign newspapers were sold in Italy, and those that were seldom commented on Italian affairs. Traveling abroad for Italians and Germans was easier in theory than in practice because they were limited as to the amount of currency they could take with them. Foreigners traveling in Italy and Germany were likely to find natives reluctant to express their true feelings about their government. It should also be remembered that foreign tourism, especially during the Great Depression, was only a small fraction of what it was to become during the second half of the twentieth century.

Nevertheless, it is true that prior to the outbreak of World War II, Italy and Germany were infinitely less closed to the outside world than was the Soviet Union. The most obvious explanation is that they had much less to hide. By 1936, unemployment had nearly disappeared in Germany at a time when it still stood at nearly 17 percent in the United States. The streets were clean, the population well fed, and the country's pride had been restored. Italy was much slower to emerge from the Great Depression than Germany, and its standard of living was still well below that of the democratic states, but to those foreigners who had not seen the country since 1922, Italy seemed to be progressing nicely. Italy's international prestige in the modern world, prior to its invasion of Ethiopia in 1935, had probably never been higher.

Propaganda was important in Fascist Italy in large measure because Mussolini had begun his career as a journalist and never lost his interest in newspapers, domestic or foreign, and read them daily. He cultivated relationships with foreign correspondents, especially those of *The New York Times* and pro-Fascist Italian-language newspapers in the United States. He also wrote numerous newspaper articles and prepared daily instructions for the press. By 1928, every journalist in Italy had to be a registered Fascist. Mussolini made sure that newspapers did not carry stories on crimes of passion or suicides, epidemics, natural disasters, or even bad weather reports. There is no solid evidence that crime decreased substantially during his dictatorship, but the absence of information about it in the press left the impression that it had indeed abated. Mussolini was surprisingly slow in establishing a department of propaganda. However, in 1934, in imitation of the Nazis' Ministry of Popular Enlightenment and Propaganda created a year earlier, Mussolini set up an undersecretaryship for press and propaganda headed by his son-in-law, Count Galeazzo Ciano.

Certain conditions in Italy made the spread of propaganda more difficult there than in Germany. As late as 1931, 21 percent of the Italian population was completely illiterate, and a much higher percentage was only semiliterate, effectively ruling out written propaganda as a tool with which to influence them. Illiterates were even more vulnerable to the spoken word; but the relative poverty of the country meant that radios became available as a medium of propaganda at a much slower rate than in Germany. Whereas 13.7 million radio sets were owned in houses containing 70 percent of the population in Germany in 1939—the highest percentage in the world—only 1.2 million radio sets existed in Italy in the same year. There were also 6,000 commercial movie theaters in Germany, as compared to just 2,700 in Italy. A partial compensation for the absence of radios in Italy was the erection of loudspeakers in the main squares of small towns to carry radio speeches by Mussolini. In Germany there were 6,000 "loud speaker pillars" in public squares all over the country so that almost no one was outside the range of Hitler's voice.

## NAZI PROPAGANDA

The presence of radios was just one advantage Nazi propagandists had over their counterparts in Italy and the Soviet Union. Virtually 100 percent of the German population was literate. Huge beer halls were commonplace and frequently used for political meetings. Germany's super efficient railroads whisked Nazi speakers from town to town, and Hitler was the first politician in the world to make frequent use of airplanes in his electoral campaigns beginning in 1932, twenty years earlier than in the United States. Another first was Hitler's appearance on closed-circuit television screens before the end of the 1930s.

Nearly all historians regard the Nazis' form of propaganda as the most original and successful aspect of the regime. Although generally true, this assertion needs qualification. Hitler himself acknowledged that he was influenced by the huge marches and massive display of banners utilized by the pre–World War I Austrian Socialists. And he openly admired and imitated the highly emotional and inflammatory propaganda used by Britain and the United States during World War I, which frequently depicted Germans as subhumans in order to induce men to volunteer for the armed services. (See figure 19.) Hitler also borrowed the use of the Roman salute—an outstretched right arm—from Fascist Italy, and probably also the frequent use of uniforms and symbols. As for its success, it would be safe to say that the Depression had far more to do with the Nazis coming to power than their clever propaganda. It also failed to whip up much enthusiasm for war when fighting appeared imminent in 1938 and again in 1939 and could not overcome the blows to public morale from military defeats after the Battle of Stalingrad ended in early1943.

What, then, was original and successful about Nazi propaganda? Most of all it was its sheer quantity. During the Kampfzeit, preceding their takeover of power, the Nazis held more public rallies than all the other political parties of Germany combined. For example, in 1932, when five major elections were held, the Nazis held as many as 3,000 meetings in a single day. It had been customary in Germany for political parties to campaign only during the last few weeks preceding an election. The Nazis did it continuously.

Another novel feature of Nazi propaganda was its systematic and almost scientific organization. Every region in Germany had its own propaganda leader, all of whom were expected to follow the activities of Nazi opponents with great care prior to the elimination of non-Nazi parties in 1933. Quarrels and conflicts within a rival party were to be quickly publicized, and all contradictions between theory and practice, and between promises and fulfillment, were to be exposed in the Nazi press. Party members were to use every opportunity to proselytize, whether it be at work or in a streetcar. They were especially eager and successful at recruiting schoolteachers, who then became part of an army of Nazi public speakers who memorized speeches and rehearsed answers in special speakers' schools.

After arousing the interest of an acquaintance through casual conversation, and then perhaps after having given the person some party pamphlets or newspapers to take home to read, recruiters would invite potential converts to a meeting. Nazi party meetings differed radically from those of other political parties. Hitler graphically expressed his contempt for opposition party meetings when he wrote in *Mein Kampf* that "they always made the same impression on me as in my youth the prescribed spoonful of cod-liver oil. . . . The speakers did everything they could to preserve [a] peaceful mood. They spoke, or rather, as a rule, they read speeches in the style of a witty newspaper article or of a scientific treatise, avoided all strong words, and here and there threw in some feeble professorial joke. . . ."[1] Nazi party meetings, by contrast, were anything but dull. Far from being mere occasions for speechmaking, the acoustics, background music, flags and other symbols, and the timing of entrances and exits were all designed to create the maximum possible emotional appeal. Hitler wanted the meetings to be so colorful and popular that people would actually pay to attend them. For example, at one of the party's annual rallies in Nuremberg, three gliders, in tight formation, landed directly in front of Hitler. Consequently, the NSDAP was the first party in the world and the only party of interwar Germany, or Austria, to charge admission fees to its meetings.

When the public began to tire of politics, especially in late 1932, the Nazis devoted many of their meetings to almost pure entertainment such as films (which in some small towns were still a novelty), plays, acrobatic stunts, lotteries, dances, athletic contests, and even recitals by children. In such ways they could prove their devotion to German culture and also appeal to the broadest possible social spectrum. So successful were the rallies that the price of admission not only paid for the meetings themselves, but also covered some of the Nazis' other propaganda expenses such as newspapers and posters. Hitler also later noted that the annual rallies in Nuremberg were good preparations for war because the 4,000 special trains were a foretaste of the requirements of mass military mobilization.

Nazi propaganda generally followed certain guidelines laid down by Hitler in *Mein Kampf*. First, it had to be simple and repetitive so that even people of modest intellectual prowess could understand and remember it. Second, it had to be emotional. And third, whenever possible the spoken word had to be favored over the written word. In speaking to live audiences Hitler realized that he could adjust his message and delivery in response to his listeners' mood swings. A great deal more emotion could also be conveyed in speaking than in writing.

Hitler himself carefully followed his own guidelines. *Mein Kampf*, written at a time when he was not allowed to speak publicly, was his

1 Adolf Hitler, *Mein Kampf* (Boston, 1943), 480, 481.

only important publication. His speeches were not without faults. They were too long, repetitious, chaotic, and full of contradictions. But these drawbacks were overshadowed by the emotion and compelling conviction that they aroused. He instinctively seemed to know how to tell every audience exactly what it wanted to hear. In this respect Hitler was without peer. Hitler was phenomenal especially because Germany was not a country with a great tradition of oratory.

The task of Nazi propaganda became a good deal easier after the party's takeover in 1933. Within a few weeks there were no more opposition newspapers or public speakers to challenge and contradict Nazi assertions and allegations. The government-owned-and-operated radio station was now a Nazi monopoly and was frequently used by the Führer. But most important, Hitler was now the chancellor and could make policy, not merely talk about it. Like any incumbent politician, his words now had to be taken seriously.

In March 1933, just six weeks after seizing power, Hitler established the Ministry of Popular Enlightenment and Propaganda, headed by Josef Goebbels, who had been in charge of Nazi propaganda during the Kampfzeit. Many commentators have noted that Goebbels was devoid of inner convictions. He merely knew how to display the convictions of others. His cynicism, however, seems to have stopped short of Hitler. Goebbels was one of the few Nazi leaders to commit suicide, along with Hitler, in the waning days of the Third Reich.

Goebbels was actually a more polished speaker than Hitler. However, his intellectual skills proved to be his most important asset. Unlike his master, who thought that the importance of propaganda would decline after the seizure of power, Goebbels believed that it would still be necessary to mobilize support and maintain enthusiasm. Probably his most important achievement was creating a semireligious myth of an infallible German Messiah and thereby forging an extraordinary bond of loyalty between the masses and their Führer.

Goebbels controlled the news by holding daily press conferences at the Propaganda Ministry where editors were told what to write, although they were given some leeway in how they wrote, so as to avoid obvious conformity and monotony. Thus, German (and also Italian) newspapers were manipulated, but unlike those of the Soviet Union they were not nationalized. Goebbels's ministry also demonstrated the close connection between propaganda and culture; after September 1933 it included a Reich Chamber of Culture, which was subdivided into chambers not only for the press, but also for broadcasting, literature, theater, music, film, and the fine arts. In his control of German culture, Goebbels was guided by his personal conviction that propaganda was most effective when insidious, that is, when its message was concealed in popular entertainment. He knew that once propaganda was recognized as such it lost its effectiveness. When he occasionally departed from this ideal and used "hard sell" techniques, the attempt usually failed miserably. The entertainment content of the Nazi's propaganda after their takeover of power can be seen in elaborate ceremonies honoring Nazi martyrs, marching songs, which replaced hymns, and festivals commemorating great Nazi events, which replaced religious holidays.

## TOTALITARIAN CULTURE

Authoritarian states have always censored literature and the arts. What was unique about the totalitarian states was their attempt to create a new culture, a kind of cultural autarky that would match their attempted economic self-sufficiency. Their success should not be exaggerated, especially in the fascist states, which lasted only a generation or less. For them especially, controlling the already existing culture was probably just as important as creating a new one. One should also not exaggerate the uniformity of culture in any one totalitarian state or generalize between all three. Nowhere were controls over culture imposed overnight, let alone did a new culture suddenly emerge full blown.

Nevertheless, a few generalizations can safely be made. All the dictators rejected the idea of art for art's sake. For them, culture was an important handmaiden to the overall success of their regimes. All of them, but especially Stalin and Hitler, favored hugeness, especially in architecture, as a means of impressing the masses. The same two dictators and Lenin, and to a lesser extent Mussolini, were suspicious of anything modern, avant garde or abstract. Hitler described modern art as the "mental excrement of diseased brains."[2] By 1938 almost 16,000 works of art, by foreign as well as German artists, deemed offensive by the Nazis had been removed from German galleries and either sold abroad or burned. The dictators liked art that was happy,

2 Quoted in Henry Ashby Turner, Jr., ed., *Hitler: Memoirs of a Confidant* (New Haven, 1985), 309.

optimistic, and extroverted, not pessimistic, unpleasant, ambiguous, or philosophical. Authors were supposed to use plain words and uncomplicated writing styles. The dictators wanted culture to be inspired by heroic episodes in their country's past. In the Soviet Union, the new style was called "socialist realism." No similar term was ever coined in the fascist states—Hitler sometimes talked about the necessity of art being "idealistic"—but the fascists could easily have called their style "bourgeois realism" because it was both middle class and representational. However, artistic realism in Germany and the Soviet Union by no means meant photographic accuracy of real people or places. Rather it was a romanticized and idealized depiction of what society should become in the utopian future. Paradoxically, totalitarian art was, therefore, in a sense symbolic.

To root out artistic heresy, artists and literary figures of all kinds in Germany and the Soviet Union were to belong to state-controlled unions. Anyone not belonging to such an organization could not continue to practice his craft. But those who did conform were often handsomely rewarded. In Italy, on the other hand, artists merely had to pledge their loyalty to the state, but not to any aesthetic dogma. Nor did they have to belong to professional unions.

The fascist states shared some similarities with each other that they did not share with the Soviet Union. Mussolini and Hitler were both fascinated by the brutal strength of Roman architecture. Neither of them promoted paintings or statues of industrial workers, a favorite theme in Soviet art. Soviet artists were not interested in painting pictures of peasants in folk costumes or even pictures with family settings. On the other hand, many pictures of Hitler Youth and Komsomol (Soviet) youth groups could be found in both Nazi Germany and the Soviet Union. All three dictatorships also favored pretentiousness, pomposity, and neoclassicism. Stalin tore down national monuments and whole neighborhoods to make way for his giant buildings, and Hitler was prepared to destroy the center of Berlin in order to build monstrous new government structures.

Historians have often unjustifiably credited Lenin with being the most culturally tolerant of the totalitarian dictators. Publicly he declared himself incompetent to judge art. As recent research has revealed, however, behind the scenes he did not hesitate to lay down the law in artistic matters. He hated avant-garde art, closed the Bolshoi Theater for ballet, and rarely attended plays, or if he did, often left after the first act. The golden age of Soviet film, during the second half of the 1920s, occurred only after his death in 1924.

The comparative freedom of the late 1920s was to change drastically under Stalin. In all aspects of culture there was a return to patriotic themes, which reflected Stalin's slogan of "Socialism in one Country." It was also unthinkable that there be freedom of choice in culture, but not in whether one wanted to join a collective farm or work in a factory. Soviet society could not be partially free and partially repressive. Stalin was particularly intolerant of writers. During his dictatorship a thousand of them were executed and another thousand survived in captivity. Much more to his taste was the work of Maxim Gorky, who was put in charge of all Soviet culture. In speeches, letters, and articles Gorky debunked what he called "legends" concerning forced labor and terror, collectivization, and famine in the Soviet Union.

Of the three totalitarian dictatorships, Fascist Italy made by far the least impact on the continuity of its national culture. American mass culture, in fact, was more influential in Italy during the Fascist era than the Fascists themselves. Mussolini's government was more authoritarian than totalitarian in allowing all sorts of heterodox ideas as long as they did not directly challenge the regime. Consequently, few creative writers or artists felt compelled to emigrate or were forcibly deported. The conductor Arturo Toscanini was a rare exception. On the other hand, a fairly large number of important intellectuals, such as the well-known historian Gaetano Salvemini, were driven out of the country or imprisoned for their opposition. However, most intellectuals merely censored themselves to avoid offending the authorities. Those that did offend could find themselves isolated, but at least alive and healthy. Roman Catholic culture remained untouched in part, no doubt, because the clergy frequently praised Fascist anti-Communism.

There was no one Fascist style, but as in the other totalitarian states, culture was supposed to be straightforward and useful. There were no book burnings and only a modest purge of existing literature. But the scores of literary competitions for poetry, history, and essays on themes set by the Fascist party obviously had a political purpose. Political articles in Fascist newspapers were thoroughly censored, but cultural and artistic criticisms were lively and honest. As in Germany, newspapers were allowed to retain their own style and character, so as not to alienate their readers. Only after 1937 was Mussolini more interested in positive indoctrination than mere negative censorship. In that year a "Cremona Prize" was established for the "best Fascist art," and beginning in 1938 Italian art began to become more realistic. The state-owned radio was thoroughly Fascistized, but this was of relatively little significance in a country that had so few receivers.

Film was a relatively new art form that all of the totalitarian states attempted to exploit for propagandistic reasons. The fascist states, however, discovered that hard-core propaganda films were not well received by the general public. Consequently, only a half dozen or so were ever made in Germany, and only three or four were made in Italy, even though Mussolini actively supported the film industry. Films that made a profit were more likely to win prizes than those that contained much propaganda. Fascist themes, however, were sometimes introduced in a subtle way. Some films depicted heroines whose main role was to enhance the role of the male and the family. Other films were historical dramas that glorified militarism. The vast majority of them, especially in the 1930s, were escapist and sentimental, as were those made in Germany (and the United States at the time). Newsreels were a more promising means of indoctrination than feature films because propaganda could easily be disguised as news. In 1926, Italian theaters were required by law to show a newsreel with each feature film.

Lenin immediately recognized the importance of the cinema, calling it the art form of the twentieth century. It was a particularly useful propaganda medium in a country where 60 percent of the population was illiterate. It was during the NEP that the movies of Sergei Eisenstein drew international acclaim for their novel techniques and many foreign films were imported. To eradicate nationalism, which was associated with the tsars, historical films emphasized the class struggle. During the New Economic Policy, however, escapist films from the United States were more popular than the innovative Soviet-based work of Eisenstein.

Stalin, it almost goes without saying, made sure that Soviet movies glorified the Bolshevik Revolution and the five-year plans and showed how happy all the nationalities of the Soviet Union were with the new regime. He was especially interested in film and was well aware of the medium's value as propaganda. Foreign films were no longer imported although this did not stop Stalin (like Hitler) from enjoying westerns and detective stories. The second half of the 1930s saw the emergence of musical comedies, perhaps because films that attempted to persuade Soviet citizens to work harder failed in their mission. Stalin micromanaged the production of movies even to the point of objecting to experimental camera work. He made sure that he previewed all Soviet films before they were released to the public.

The Nazis' impact on German culture was far swifter and more profound than the Fascists' impact on Italian culture. The large number of radios, newspapers, and cinemas in Germany also gave its totalitarian regime more media outlets than its counterpart in Communist Russia. On the other hand, Nazi propagandists were not attempting to change the lives of German citizens as much as their Soviet counterparts.

Literature was the first branch of the arts affected by the Nazis. As early as April 1933, the Nazis had compiled a long blacklist of "leftist," democratic, and Jewish authors which included several famous authors of the nineteenth century. Two thousand five hundred writers, including Nobel prize winners and writers of worldwide best sellers, left the country voluntarily or under duress, and were replaced by people without international reputations. To the average German reader, however, this mass emigration and censorship may not have seemed as serious as it does today. Of the twelve best-selling authors, seven were actually supported by the Nazis, three were tolerated, and just two were banned. Many middle-class Germans also applauded the government's quickly eradicating both written and pictorial pornography, as well as its campaigning against prostitution. The decrease in new, quality reading matter also appeared to be compensated by the increasing popularity and availability of literary classics, a phenomenon that also occurred in the Soviet Union.

The Nazis quickly purged all public libraries of books by Jewish and left-wing authors. This campaign reached a climax with book burning orgies in numerous university towns around the country in May 1933. These events so outraged world public opinion, however, that Goebbels never allowed a repetition. Somewhat surprisingly, there was no precensorship of books; publishers generally knew what they could and could not publish. If they guessed wrong, they could have an entire edition confiscated by the Gestapo.

The theater in Nazi Germany was not as negatively affected by the regime as literature, but the brilliance of the Weimar era disappeared overnight. The works of almost all the famous playwrights and directors of the Weimar period, many of whom were Jews, were banned by the Nazis. However, the revival of prosperity and government subsidies to municipal theaters helped double the size of theater-going audiences by 1942. Comedies were the most popular plays, but the regime subsidized productions of the work of classical playwrights like Goethe and Schiller to compensate for the lack of new dramas.

Basically the same trend took place in art, music, and film. Serious, innovative, and intellectually challenging new works were stifled, although the classics of music and literature were supported in all three totalitarian states. Actually, prior to coming to power in 1933 the Nazis had only the vaguest idea of what their policy toward music should be. This ambiguity, for the most part, continued once they were in power, and the Nazis never did produce a new style. They knew they were opposed to jazz, which they associated with American blacks. (The Soviet regime considered jazz to be "cultural sabotage.") However, jazz was already so popular in Germany that they decided that "German" jazz was acceptable. They were also opposed to atonal music, but could not agree on what music was atonal. The only certainty was that Jewish musicians could only perform before Jewish audiences and Jewish compositions could not be performed in public. Fortunately for the international reputation of the regime, most famous German musicians did not emigrate, and the performance level of German orchestras and opera houses remained high. The Wagnerian music festival at Bayreuth (Bavaria) also benefited from Hitler's subsidies and attendance.

The cinema industry, which was the second largest in the world after Hollywood, became increasingly popular during the Third Reich. Attendance grew from 250 million in 1933 to 1 billion in 1942. Contrary to conventional wisdom, German feature films consisted mostly of light, sentimental, and popular works. As such they were far closer in character to American movies of the same period than to those produced in the Soviet Union. For example, of 1,097 feature films produced during the Third Reich, the vast majority were love stories, comedies, musicals, detective stories, and mountaineering films, the latter being a specialty of the Third Reich. Only one in twenty was overtly political, and even that ratio declined after the Battle of Stalingrad. Surprisingly, only a handful of hard-core anti-Semitic films were produced. The most famous of these, *Jüd Süss*, which was the story of a blonde Nordic girl who was raped by a Jewish brute, was poorly received in Germany, except for ardent party members, but broke all box-office records when it was shown in occupied France in 1941.

As in Italy, newsreels and documentaries were considered by the regime to be an important outlet for propaganda, but they remained popular only as long as they were able to show Nazi domestic successes and military victories. Needless to say, the newsreels did not show book burnings, pogroms, concentration camps, sterilization, or euthanasia. Beginning in 1938, all of Germany's cinemas were required to show the latest newsreels, which during the war increased to 30 minutes in length.

In architecture, the antimodern bias of the Nazis was less apparent than in other cultural fields. They tore down no modern buildings and there was no uniformly Nazi style. Radical architects were not terrorized, but they were also not given commissions. New buildings were constructed in a variety of styles reflecting the preferences of local Nazi leaders. Hitler insisted only that Nazi architecture be heroic, meaning monumental in scale. Monumental is hardly an adequate word to describe the gargantuan buildings Hitler had his pet architect, Albert Speer, design for the center of Berlin and elsewhere. Speer's "People's Hall," for example, would have held 200,000 people, far more than any other building in the world. Its dome would have been seven times larger than St. Peter's in Rome. Fortunately, most of these proposed buildings were never built.

The fascist regimes were not only interested in controlling culture but also in making it readily available to the masses. The Nazis increased the number of state-run libraries from 6,000 in 1933 to 25,000 at the height of the war. They also provided soldiers with 45,000 front-line libraries, which held 43 million books donated by civilians. More novel were the leisure-time organizations created by both fascist regimes, which were arguably their most popular institutions.

The *Opera Nazionale Dopolavoro* (OND or "After Work") was Fascist Italy's largest and most active recreational organization for adults, its membership rising from under 300,000 in 1926 to 5 million in 1940. It was about evenly divided between people who considered themselves lower-middle-class and those who were farmers or blue-collar workers. It was responsible for operating and maintaining over 11,000 sporting grounds, over 6,400 libraries, nearly 800 movie houses, more than 1,200 theaters, and well over 2,000 orchestras. By the late 1930s every town and village throughout the country had a Dopolavoro clubhouse replete with a small library and a radio, and often athletic equipment, auditoriums for films and plays, and sometimes even a small travel agency. All the activities were provided at reduced rates including 50 percent discounts for train fares for travel within Italy. Membership was voluntary and the clubs' activities were relatively nonpolitical—which may well have been the cause of the organization's popularity. However, because of the poor quality of its plays and concerts, the Dopolavoro was looked down upon by the middle class, even though these performances were probably the most successful part of the OND. For children there were over 5,800 campsites with an annual enrollment of nearly 1 million.

Much more bourgeois was Germany's *Kraft durch Freude* (KdF) or "Strength through Joy organization." It too was enormously popular, growing from 9 million participants in 1934 to 55 million five years later, no doubt in part because it provided a much greater variety of activities than Dopolavoro. As its name implied, the Strength through Joy program was supposed to increase productivity by refreshing workers, an interesting idea although there is no evidence that it worked in the way intended. It provided various fringe benefits for its members including subsidized theater performances, concerts—some of them staged in factories—art exhibitions, sport and hiking groups, social and folk dancing, and films and adult education courses. It also owned its own enterprises including a Volkswagen factory and a dozen of its own snow-white sea-going ships, which took members on vacation cruises from Spain's Madeira islands, Italy, and Istanbul in the south to the Norwegian fjords and Finland in the north. It was no coincidence that the Nazis regarded all of these destinations as actual or possible allies of Germany. Having only one class instead of the customary three classes of cabins, KdF ships were designed to help build the classless *Volksgemeinschaft* although in reality only wealthier Germans could afford the cruises. Although it undoubtedly produced some goodwill for the regime, like its Italian counterpart, the main reason for its popularity was because it was relatively free of political pressure.

Nothing exactly comparable to Kraft durch Freude or Dopolavoro existed in the Soviet Union. However, youth organizations (discussed below) organized camping trips and took over confiscated palaces and mansions of the nobility and upper bourgeoisie and used them for various activities including the showing of movies. As for adults, labor unions subsidized tickets for theater, opera, and ballet performances; provided vacation rest homes; and arranged vacations, for example, to the Black Sea. They also provided literacy classes, elementary and secondary education classes at factories, and on-site child care centers. Consequently, by one way or another, the Communist party directly controlled all athletic and social activities in the Soviet Union.

## SOVIET EDUCATION

Education was merely another branch of propaganda, and a very effective one at that, in the totalitarian states. All states try to instill a love of one's country and its institutions in their people, and democracies are no exception. It is doubtful whether any state could function without the glue provided by patriotism. Superpatriotic organizations in democratic states have even tried to make certain courses instruments of propagandistic indoctrination. The difference between totalitarian states and democracies in their educational policies is therefore at least partly one of degree. In the former, teachers and students were constantly under government pressure. Teachers were forced to join party organizations, and there was no such thing as tenure. As in other aspects of totalitarian culture, the schools were not immediately transformed. Not all teachers could be replaced by party members overnight, and new and politically correct textbooks required years to write and publish.

In all three states there was a strong emphasis on political indoctrination. Nazi Germany also stressed practical subjects and physical education as a preparation for war. Teachers and university professors in all three states were brought under state control through professional organizations. Untrustworthy teachers were dismissed. In all three states universities lost their autonomy and were subjected to rigid bureaucratic control. Freedom of research was also impeded in all three states though not always in the same way. The dictatorships were especially interested in controlling political subjects like history and political science and less interested in influencing the natural sciences like mathematics, physics, and chemistry; even here, however, there were exceptions. Both Stalin and Hitler imposed their views on biology.

During the 1920s the Soviet Union was an exception to some of the above generalizations. In fact, the same spirit of revolt and experimentation, which existed in the culture of the NEP, was found in the country's educational system. The authority of teachers—who had been trained in the tsarist period—was minimized; homework and examinations were abolished. Traditional subjects were neglected. Soviet educators consciously borrowed techniques from abroad. Pupils were largely expected to acquire an education while participating in society.

All this changed with the introduction of Stalinism in the early 1930s. Schools were now required to participate in the conversion of a technologically and culturally backward society into a modern one. Academic ranks were restored in 1932 and salaries for teachers raised. Strict classroom discipline and respect for teachers was restored, as was mass recitation. School children wore uniforms: jumpers for girls and military-style outfits for boys, in both cases to make them feel more like members of a group than like individuals. Textbooks were introduced and a decree of February 1933 stipulated that they all had to be approved by the Commissariat of Education. Traditional subjects like history and literature reappeared. Pupils were expected to master foreign languages, mathematics, and science. More and more the schools began to resemble their tsarist predecessors. The educational system was intended to train young people for slots in the economic, social, political and cultural life of the state.

Under Stalin, real progress was made in eliminating illiteracy in the Soviet Union, although no more so than in the Balkan states during the same period. In order to make the country more modern, that is to say, more industrial and technological, the educational system had to be greatly expanded. During the 1930s, seven years of schooling were required of all children in the Russian Republic and in the cities of the other republics of the USSR. Starting in 1935–36, even children of the former bourgeoisie had free access to education including universities. School attendance increased from 7.8 million in 1914 to 32 million in 1939. Adult illiterates had their workdays reduced by two hours with no loss of pay if they attended school. As a consequence, illiteracy was reduced from 50 percent in 1927 to 19 percent on the eve of World War II. Education was free at all levels. The most advanced students even received living expenses, but in exchange had to serve five years (later reduced to three) in areas assigned by the government. By 1940, there were seven times as many specialists with higher educations in the Soviet Union than there had been in 1913. (See figure 20.) Women especially benefited from their increased access to higher education. According to the census of 1939 they held 44 percent of the posts at universities in the fields of education, science, and art. These achievements, however, were offset by low pay and an insufficiency of child-care services.

However much Stalin may have thought he was merely training specialists for slots in the Soviet economy, he was unknowingly laying the foundations for his regime's destruction. At the risk of overgeneralizing, it would be fair to say that uneducated people are usually much more in awe of authority than educated people; uneducated people are much easier to command than those with advanced degrees. Even persons trained in narrow specialties are more likely to ask questions and less likely to be satisfied with simplistic answers. Essentially this was the evolution that occurred in the Soviet Union between the 1930s and the 1980s. Stalin did his best to retard the process, however, by serving as a supreme arbiter on all matters involving the arts and sciences; suppressing the plurality of opinions which is the heart and soul of scientific progress. Because of this, the Soviet Union fell further and further behind the West scientifically, especially in nonmilitary fields.

## EDUCATION IN THE FASCIST STATES

In some ways education in the fascist states resembled that of the Soviet Union in the 1930s. Italy, as mentioned, also had an illiteracy problem, albeit less serious than the Soviet Union's. New schools were built in Italy and old ones improved; the minimum school leaving age was raised from twelve to fourteen and attendance was far more strictly enforced than earlier. As a result, state expenditures on schools increased by 50 percent. State approved textbooks were introduced in 1929. Children were taught that they owed the same loyalty to Fascism as they did to God. Also in 1929, secondary-school teachers were forced to take a loyalty oath. The same demand was made of university professors in 1933, a demand supported by Pope Pius XI. Of approximately 1,250 professors, only eleven refused to comply. After 1933, teachers at all levels had to be members of the Fascist party.

In general, however, Italian schools and universities were far less affected by totalitarianism than the educational systems of the Soviet Union or Nazi Germany. It is true that Mussolini's first minister of education, the philosopher Giovanni Gentile, who served between 1922 and 1924, said that the educational system should inculcate Italian young people with the ideology of the Fascist state including obedience and respect for authority. However (in contrast to his counterparts in Nazi Germany and the Soviet Union) he catered to the traditional preferences of the bourgeoisie by putting less emphasis on the sciences and even more on Italian literature and history, as well as Latin, than there had been in the pre-Fascist era.

Indoctrination in Fascist principles became intense only after 1929 and textbooks did not become a state monopoly until 1936. Only in the late 1930s, thanks to the reforms of Giuseppe Bottai, would physical fitness and manual work be emphasized in an effort to unite the school experience with "real world" experiences. Even though the basic subject matter for many years remained much the same, the treatment did not. History textbooks showed the divine civilizing mission of Italy throughout history. Ancient history was virtually synonymous with ancient Roman history. The rebirth of Italian nationalism in the mid-nineteenth century, known as the *Risorgimento*, became a mere prelude to Fascist Italy. Nevertheless, the attempt to indoctrinate chauvinism, militarism, and imperialism frequently remained superficial at best. Italian homes remained more important than schools as places where morals and values were taught. Special leadership schools for promising young men between the ages of twenty-three and twenty-eight were established in 1940, but their inauguration coincided with Italy's entrance into World War II, which drew away some of the best candidates.

The one Fascist educational policy that made a big and negative difference was the introduction of anti-Semitism in 1938. About two hundred professors and teachers lost their jobs as a consequence, a loss that at the university level was significant because about 10 percent of all professors were of Jewish origin. Not only did this new policy harm the universities, but it also proved to be extremely unpopular with the general public.

The Nazis' impact on the educational system of Germany was far more immediate, profound, and negative. The curriculum was made more practical, reflecting Hitler's anti-intellectualism. History at every level was thoroughly Nazified; Jews were blamed for every disaster in German history. German geography and German culture were stressed, as were such specifically Nazi subjects as racial biology and population policy. A great deal of time was devoted to physical education as a means of building character and discipline. Character building was regarded as more important than book learning because it created a willingness for service and obedience to the Volk and the Führer. Physical strength was thought to build confidence and a sense of superiority, as well as a means of improving the health and size of the German population. The reshaping of the curriculum, however, varied considerably from place to place, depending on individual teachers and principals. For example, until March 1938, the censorship of textbooks was haphazard. But Nazification was aided by the fact that many teachers already were members of the party before Hitler's rise to power.

German universities were much more profoundly affected by anti-Semitism than their Italian counterparts. There were around 550,000 Jews in Germany in 1933, as compared with just 50,000 thoroughly assimilated Jews in Italy, a country with almost no anti-Semitic tradition. Eighteen percent of the faculty was dismissed from German universities. Of these, a third were Jews dismissed on strictly racial grounds. But it would be safe to assume that there were many Jews among the 56 percent who were dismissed for political reasons. Whereas eleven Italian professors lost their jobs when they refused to take the loyalty oath, one hundred times that number lost their academic jobs in Germany. Those professors who were retained were required to belong to the National Socialist Association of University Lecturers. Academic work in Germany was also disrupted by the constant presence of informers among both the student body and the faculty.

The Nazi regime also reduced, at least temporarily, the number of university students, especially young women, partly as a means of reducing unemployment among professionally trained people and partly as a consequence of Nazi antifeminism. Enrollment at German universities shrank from nearly 128,000 in 1933 to 51,000 in 1938, including just 6,300 females although some of this decline was due to the very low birthrate during the World War. Fifteen times as many students, per capita, attended American universities at this time. Even in secondary schools the number of girls declined from 437,000 in 1926 to 205,000 in 1937. After 1938, however, the shortage of specialists needed for war production and the conscription of young men broke down the Nazi resistance to higher education for women, and the number of German students actually rose to 82,500 in 1944, of whom nearly half were women.

Academic disciplines were affected differently by the Nazis. The teaching of the social sciences and economics were seriously influenced because of their political implications. Biology was thoroughly Nazified with racial, and racist, theories. The quality of courses in psychology and physics was badly damaged simply because so many brilliant Jewish professors had worked in these areas. On the other hand, medical science does not appear to have been seriously harmed; more medical journals were published in Germany between 1933 and 1937 than in any other country. Moreover, they contained few or no references to larger political events. The practice of medicine, however, as opposed to medical research, is another story altogether, as will be seen in the next chapter.

## YOUTH GROUPS

The totalitarian states were not content to leave the political indoctrination of young people to their educational systems alone. To some extent they regarded the older generation, which had grown to maturity and had acquired their values during the old regime, as beyond redemption. Those in power saw themselves as movers of the young and daring against the old and fossilized. The youngest generation, moreover, was malleable; their values were still very much in flux. If by indoctrinating them in the party's ideology, dressing them in uniforms, and engaging them in enjoyable activities, they could be converted to the cause, the young would likely pass their convictions on to the next generation and perpetuate the regime. All three totalitarian parties had exceptionally young memberships, at least in their early years.

In Russia, a Communist League of Youth (*Komsomol*), for fifteen to twenty-three year olds, was established in Petrograd as early as 1917. It sponsored and oversaw many sporting, cultural, and social activities. Stalin exploited the idealism and romanticism of the early movement by having the Komsomol play a vital role in the First Five-Year Plan, and especially in the collectivization campaign. By 1939, it had 9 million members in its three subdivisions. The youngest children belonged to the Little Octobrists and sang patriotic songs and went on excursions to monasteries, where they were told about the depravity of religion. At the age of nine they graduated into the Young Pioneers, who played war games and helped illiterates of all ages learn to read. They also engaged in sports and went on camping trips where campfire talks included stories about Lenin's life and anecdotes about the history of the revolutionary movement. The oldest Komsomol members helped organize demonstrations to promote Stalin's policies. The best of the Komsomol's graduates were invited to join the Communist party: during Stalin's time it was not good for one's health to refuse the invitation. The entire youth organization was modeled on the party's, with the same regional and district network.

The Italian effort to organize youth was handicapped by the lack of youth groups in the Liberal era. The Fascist equivalent of the Komsomol was the *Opera Nazionale Balilla* (ONB), which included, in theory at least, children of all classes and both sexes between the ages of six and eighteen. In practice, however, relatively few children from peasant or working class families belonged to the ONB. Founded in 1926, but with antecedents dating back to 1922, it avoided overt political indoctrination. More important was simply submerging oneself in a mass organization that built character, meaning obedience to authority. Most of the ONB's members enjoyed getting together in their uniforms, shouting slogans, and sharing a prescribed patriotic ritual. Children who were kept out of the organization by anti-Fascist parents often felt deprived and in fact were subjected to discrimination in school and when it came time to start their careers.

One area in which the ONB enjoyed considerable success was in making young Italians more sports minded. Calisthenics and mass gymnastic exercises of identically dressed young people singing Fascist songs were intended to demonstrate the unity, order, and force that Fascism had created. Ostensibly, the payoff of this new emphasis was Italy's strong showing in the Olympic Games of 1932 and 1936 when Italian athletes finished second and fourth in the overall results. Nationalistic pride soared.

Probably no totalitarian movement was more successful at capturing the fanatical support of young people from the very beginning than the Nazis. (See figure 12.) It was young people who distributed Nazi newspapers and leaflets free of charge when other political parties had to pay for these services. By July 1931, eighteen months before Hitler came to power, the League of German Students, an association of university students in Germany and Austria, already had a Nazi majority and leadership.

Unlike the Fascists, the Nazis could build on a youth movement that dated back to about 1810. From the beginning it was nationalistic, and after 1890 it also became anti-Semitic. At that time a group called the *Wandervögel* (literally, "wandering birds") rebelled against the Industrial Revolution by romanticizing the beauty of nature as opposed to the ugliness of big cities where Jews were concentrated. Although the *Hitler Jugend* ("Hitler Youth" or HJ) was not founded until 1926, Nazi youth groups had existed since 1922. Young people between the ages of ten and eighteen were eligible to join the HJ. Children under fourteen were assigned to the *Jungvolk* if they were boys and the *Jungmädel* if they were girls. Teenage girls belonged to the *Bund Deutscher Mädel* (BDM or "League of German Girls").

The Nazis were ingenious at exploiting the enthusiasm and sense of adventure of young people. The young were provided with duties, free from parental supervision, which were sheer pleasures and which gave them a sense of importance. The HJ, unlike the ONB in Italy, was quite successful in breaking down social and intellectual distinctions between classes. It was also democratic in that it gave every child, regardless of family background, an opportunity for advancement within the organization. Between 1933 and 1936, membership in the various youth groups grew from 1 million to 5 million as the Nazis absorbed non-Nazi youth groups which by 1936 were eliminated altogether. By early 1939, membership in the Nazi youth groups had reached 8.7 million and became fully compulsory for every healthy boy (but not girl) over the age of nine; 82 percent of all boys belonged to the HJ or to one of its affiliate organizations.

The HJ would now be called very sexist. Boys were to develop "manliness" through exercise, competitive sports, and premilitary training; girls, in their separate organizations, were to learn how to become good wives and mothers. They were discouraged from using makeup because it conflicted with the Nazis' concept of natural Aryan beauty. Teachers and intellectuals, toward whom the HJ displayed an undisguised hostility, as well as parents, were less enthusiastic about the program than young people. The former resented their diminished authority and the classroom time lost through HJ activities, such as celebrating Hitler's birthday and taking part in the charitable Winter

Aid campaign and the Harvest Festival, all of which came at the expense of time spent in the classroom.

In two areas the HJ was undoubtedly successful: athletics and premilitary training. No doubt as a result of the HJ's stress on physical fitness, Germany did exceedingly well in the 1936 Olympic Games held in Berlin and Garmisch-Partenkirchen, winning a total of eighty-nine medals, as compared to only fifty-six for the second-place U.S. delegation. The Games, which were the first to be broadcast live internationally over the radio, raised the image of Nazi Germany to unprecedented levels. The physical fitness program promoted by the HJ consumed four hours during the week and three entire weekends a month. Together with war games, which included the use of lethal weapons, and map reading, the Hitler Youth helped make the German army the best trained in the world when World War II began. The Hitler Youth also served as an indispensable recruiting ground for the SS.

Of the three totalitarian youth groups, the HJ appears to have been by far the most successful in achieving the goals set for it by the party. No other demographic group remained as loyal to Hitler to the bitter end as young people. The flag raisings, parades, hikes, camping excursions, and war games all seem to have made an indelible impression on young Germans, especially on the youngest among them. Whereas 80 percent of the general population continued to support Hitler before Stalingrad, 95 percent of the youth did so *after* Stalingrad. This is not to suggest, however, that there was no opposition to the Nazis among the young. German youth originally had been attracted to the Nazi party because it was a protest movement. By the middle 1930s the HJ had become part of the new establishment, and its mammoth structure and regimentation were resented by a minority of young people. In protest, some from working-class families joined the "Edelweiss Pirates" and went hiking, cycling, or hitchhiking on their own in defiance of wartime travel bans. Upper middle-class young people joined the antipolitical "Swing Youth," whose members outraged adults by listening to "decadent" jazz and dancing the jitterbug. During World War II some of the most courageous opposition to the Nazis was provided by a group of university students in Munich called the "White Rose," whose members paid for their idealism with their lives.

The relative loyalty of young Germans to Hitler may simply have resulted from the Third Reich lasting only twelve years, not giving more of them enough time to become disillusioned. In Italy, young people began to realize after 1936—fourteen years after Mussolini had come to power—that the regime had not lived up to its own promises. They were especially opposed to the military alliance with Germany. The Fascists were simply unable to create a new ideological consciousness among the young. In Russia, the shocking revelation made in 1956 by General Secretary Nikita Khrushchev about the crimes of Stalin contributed to an already growing disillusionment among the younger generation, which grew increasingly cynical about the promises of imminent prosperity made by the regime's (now) elderly leaders. They were also bored by the routine of the Komsomol. By the 1980s, the younger generation was almost completely lost to the regime, in stark contrast to the 1920s and 1930s.

The totalitarian states all achieved some successes in the areas of propaganda, culture, and education. Their propaganda machines certainly succeeded in creating cults of personality for the dictators whose popularity remained far higher than that of their parties. The regimes also managed to spread culture and education to the masses, who often had been neglected by the old pretotalitarian governments. Under the totalitarian dictators, illiteracy was virtually eliminated in Russia and Italy. Young people, at least for a time, were thoroughly indoctrinated by the new dogmas in youth groups and became more athletically inclined. However, the most popular forms of entertainment of the totalitarian parties were precisely those films and plays with little or no political content. The most popular organizations like Dopolavoro and Kraft durch Freude were voluntary and almost completely nonpolitical.

As in so many other aspects of totalitarianism, the failures outnumbered the successes even if the failures were not always immediately apparent. In the long run, propaganda was only as successful as the achievements it hoped to advertise. It could not convince Italians that the regime was worth defending in World War II; it could not convince Germans that Germany was winning a war it was actually losing; and it could not convince Soviet citizens that they were prosperous. Young people were easier to fool, but given time even they began to realize that they had been betrayed. In the name of culture and education, the totalitarian states, especially Russia and Germany, harassed, deported or killed some of their most creative people—much to the benefit of other countries, especially the United States. Although educational levels were raised in Russia and Italy, educated people were the most likely to question the dogmas of the regimes that had given them their training.

# 6 / FAMILY VALUES
# AND HEALTH

## THE CONSERVATIVE TREND IN VALUES

The attitude toward women and the family, and even health, in totalitarian society, like economics and a good many other subjects, was initially very different in the fascist states from that in the Soviet Union. The Communists believed the Bolshevik Revolution and the Soviet Union represented a sharp break with the bourgeois past with its glorification of private property and the subordination of women. This ideology led to the conclusion that when private property was abolished, men and women would own everything in common and all people would therefore be free and equal. Women would be emancipated from the very restricted role they had played, not only within the family but also within society as a whole.

Fascist ideology, at least in its more mature stages, purported to defend traditional values, including the role of women, religion, and the family against the (modern) challenges of Communism and liberalism. Western civilization, they claimed, had been undermined by the Industrial Revolution, which had given birth to Marxism and atheism and threatened to destroy the family by luring women out of the household and into traditionally "male" jobs in factories and offices. They also believed, at least in Germany, that the Industrial Revolution had undermined health by polluting the air and water and that modern medicine, as practiced by Jews, with its emphasis on drugs, was ineffective in restoring the health of the nation's people.

Prior to the Russian Revolution, and during the New Economic Policy, the Communists deprecated the family and associated it with private property and the bourgeoisie. The early Bolsheviks had often led a bohemian existence and had sometimes not bothered to marry their live-in partners. They expected the family to "wither away" right along with the state. Once in power they saw to it that divorce was made easy and incest, bigamy, adultery, and homosexuality were all de-criminalized. After seizing power they did not at first perceive the importance of stable personal relations within a bureaucratic structure. Women were fully emancipated during the NEP. They were allowed to enter all professions. Divorce, birth control, and abortion were all easily obtained.

Stalin, however, could not tolerate a libertine attitude toward such a basic institution as the family. Just as he could not allow freedom in cultural affairs to exist at the same time he was applying dictatorial controls over the economy, so too did he feel that conservative family values had to be restored if he hoped to bring about a disciplined Soviet society. Oddly enough, then, the "left-wing" ideology of Communism began to resemble more and more the ultraconservative values of the fascists during the 1930s.

The conservative thrust of totalitarian family values was not as unusual in the 1920s and 1930s as one might suppose. Even in non-Communist Europe and North America the tidal wave of feminism, which had reached its peak shortly after the end of World War I, had already begun to ebb well before the end of the Roaring Twenties. The war broke down the resistance of both men and women to female suffrage throughout most countries in Western, Central, and Northern Europe as well as in North America. For politicians who had previously opposed woman suffrage, it became a convenient fiction to say that female suffrage was a war measure and a reward for patriotic service. Consequently, women won the vote in Britain in 1918, in Germany it was written into the Weimar constitution in 1919, and in the United States the Nineteenth Amendment was approved in 1920. In Italy and France, however, women did not get the right to vote.

Far from energizing the women's rights movement, the winning of the franchise dealt it a major setback. Members of the movement—which by no means had included all women to begin with—could agree on little except the franchise. With it now safely won, there were no more truly unifying goals. Men who had grudgingly agreed to let women vote, dug in their heels when it came to other issues such as jobs and wages. After World War I, returning veterans wanted their old jobs back, and politicians, especially in totalitarian parties, were eager to curry their favor. By 1921, there were actually fewer women working outside the home in Great Britain—and most other former belligerent countries—than a decade earlier. The demand for equal pay for equal work failed everywhere. Even the enrollment of women in universities declined. In the United States, a higher percentage of women attended colleges and universities in the 1920s than in the 1950s. The coming of the Great Depression only accelerated this literally reactionary trend on both sides of the Atlantic as more and more men in all the industrialized countries demanded that women give up their jobs to unemployed men, especially if they had husbands who were employed.

## SOVIET WOMEN: THE MIXED BLESSINGS OF EMANCIPATION

The early Bolsheviks committed themselves to a thorough program of women's emancipation and had a number of female party members ready to enact their program when they came to power in 1917. Religious marriages were no longer necessary. The first Soviet constitution of 1918 gave women full political equality and legalized divorce. Either spouse could demand a divorce and no grounds were necessary for its approval. Legislation provided for maternity pay and child-care facilities as advocated by Marx and Engels. The status of illegitimacy was eliminated. The principle of equal pay for equal work was also established in law. In 1920, the Soviet Union became the first country in the world where abortions were not only legal, but also free. The *Zhenotdel*, or Woman's Department of the Soviet government, made great contributions to women's causes, especially in the areas of health issues and literacy, before it was suppressed by Stalin in 1930. Soviet women were especially prominent in the arts, where their radically abstract paintings and posters broke dramatically with artistic conventions. Meanwhile, the Soviet government was expanding educational opportunities for women as well as job-training programs. The tsarist government had finally opened higher education to women during the First World War. However, it was the Bolsheviks who freed education from gender, class, ethnic, and linguistic restrictions. The Soviets even went so far as to mandate that 30 percent of the students at institutions of higher education had to be women, a rule that was far more egalitarian than anything existing in other European countries at the time.

However, it was easier to enact laws than to have them realized in practice. The force of tradition among both men and women often made the laws a dead letter, especially on the matter of equal pay for equal work. Moreover, Lenin and other early Bolsheviks never fully trusted women, especially members of the peasantry and working class who were assumed to be religious and hostile to trade unions and political parties. They feared that the new laws could facilitate personal irresponsibility and marital instability. Most Bolsheviks wanted men to lead and women to stay at home or devote themselves to some traditional "women's work." A survey in the Vyborg area near Leningrad in 1926 had revealed that only 7 percent of the divorces in one Russian town in that year were by mutual consent and that 70 percent were initiated by men. Either partner, at that time, without even informing the other, could obtain a divorce by merely sending a postcard to the proper ministry.

Not all of the changes in marriage laws were necessarily enthusiastically received by women or even worked the way the government had anticipated. Women were reluctant to give up church weddings. Many women (and some men) were opposed to liberalized divorce because it did not require either fathers or the state to provide child support. Peasant women resented being excluded from maternity benefits. Where maternity benefits did exist, employers during the NEP often fired women and replaced them with men so they could avoid assisting pregnant women and nursing mothers.

Free and easily obtainable abortions led to even more serious consequences. By the 1930s there were twice as many abortions as live births. Abortions, in fact, were the most common means of birth control. So far did the birth rate drop that abortions were outlawed in 1936 in order to increase the birth rate. Exceptions were made only for women suffering from a physical or mental disease. Physicians performing illegal abortions were subject to one to three years in prison. However, the prohibition, which was opposed by women, only led to a large number of illegal and dangerous abortions.

After Stalin's emergence in 1928 as the dictator of the Communist party, women almost vanished from the higher levels of the state and party bureaucracy, but they did not stay at home. Stalin's ascendancy marked both the end of the relative freedom of the New Economic Policy and progress in women's rights. Stalin silenced the discussion about women's rights by simply declaring that the problem had been solved. Not only Stalin, but most other Communist leaders as well, were hostile to the very idea of women's organizations. They often implied, especially in Muslim areas, that Zhenotdel workers were either immoral or incompetent. Only a minority was ever served by women's organizations and even fewer women joined the party.

During Stalin's dictatorship and until the *glasnost* (openness) policy of the last Soviet leader, Mikhail Gorbachev, the official Soviet view was that Stalin was the champion of the family. To promote marriage, the right to discuss lesbianism and homosexuality was revoked in 1933. Male homosexuality became a crime punishable by five to eight years' imprisonment, a law that remained in force in the 1980s. Another law of 1936 attempted to discourage divorce—which had reached 37 percent in Moscow in 1934—by making it so expensive that it became virtually impossible. Second or subsequent divorces were three and six times as expensive as a first one. The Russian traditional cult of motherhood was reinforced, and divorce further discouraged in 1936 when child-support payments from divorced fathers were increased. The latter had to pay one-fourth of their wages to support one child and one-half of their wages to support three or more children. Women having five or more children were actually rewarded with prizes and medals. In 1944, cash bonuses were given to women having two or more children, with the amount increasing with each new baby; ten children earned one the title of "Heroine Mother."

Neither the emancipation laws, nor those that attempted to reinforce the nuclear family, benefited women or even worked as intended. The number of job-holding women rose from 3 million in 1928 to over 13 million in 1940. By 1945, they constituted 56 percent of the work force, probably the highest percentage in the world. But as in other countries, both fascist and democratic, nearly all women held jobs that were either menial or low paying or both. By the end of the 1930s, women constituted 57 percent of all farm workers, but held just 3 percent of the managerial positions on the collectivized farms. Very few leading positions in the party were filled by women. They did become the majority of the country's teachers and physicians, but these positions were very poorly paid. Moreover, their greater presence in the workplace did nothing to reduce their responsibilities at home, where Russian husbands remained notoriously stubborn about not sharing household chores. The laws against divorce and legalized abortions simply meant that couples informally separated and women were forced to have illegal abortions. Consequently, the birth rate remained relatively low. Finally, Stalin's effort to strengthen the family was undermined by his extremely suspicious character. Children's newspapers urged their readers to spy on their parents and to report any questionable activities to the authorities.

At best, one can say that the Bolshevik Revolution was a mixed blessing for Russian women. They were able to enter professions previously closed to them. Like their male counterparts, their educational opportunities improved. They were honored as mothers and, if divorced, they were assured of child-care payments. However, by the end of the interwar period they found themselves overworked and underpaid. Their new political "rights," such as the right to vote, were meaningless because the elections themselves were meaningless.

## FASCIST ITALY:
### THE FAILURE OF ANTIFEMINISM

The same picture of mixed blessings can be painted for the women of Fascist Italy. Italy was by no means in the forefront of the women's rights movement prior to World War I. A high rate of illiteracy, low civic participation, the prevalence of small towns and villages where traditional paternalistic values remained strong, and slow economic growth all worked to retard the feminist movement. Traditional patriarchal values were strongest in southern Italy, especially Sicily, where it was taboo for women even to appear in public.

Although the Fascist program of 1919–20 called for female suffrage and social equality, Mussolini soon reversed his position on women's rights as indeed he did about almost everything. This about-face is not surprising, because Mussolini regarded women as being intellectually, physically, and morally inferior to men. Faithful wives would, in any case, vote in the same way as their husbands. It soon became apparent to the Duce that to win over veterans he would have to promise them job preferences at the expense of women. Women had entered the job market when men had gone off to fight between the beginning of the war with the Ottoman Empire in 1911 and the end of World War I in 1918. Women did not merely lose jobs after the Fascist takeover; a law enacted in 1927 decreed that women's salaries could be only half that of their male counterparts.

Mussolini's imperialistic goals also required a large population and an increased birth rate. This policy inevitably alienated feminists, but it attracted ardent Roman Catholics. Ultimately, the conservative Fascist and Catholic views toward the role of women reinforced each other, although friction was caused by competition between Catholic women's organizations and expanding Fascist counterparts.

As Mussolini's ideology became increasingly conservative he blamed liberal agnosticism for numerous family problems from a declining birth rate, to illegitimacy, infant mortality, and juvenile delinquency. The Fascists also had harsh words for the Soviet Union, which had presumably collectivized the family out of existence, and the United States, where commercialism had led to a high divorce rate and racial mixing. These problems could all be avoided or corrected, Mussolini argued, by appropriate state action.

Mussolini's efforts to please his conservative, middle-class supporters with antifeminist programs were not fixed when he came to power in 1922. Not until 1925 did he enact any legislation involving women. When he did, not all of his policies were part of a patriarchal reaction. To turn Italy into a modern, industrialized state with a powerful army capable of conquering new colonies for the country's hoped for rapidly expanding population required promoting some of the very changes the regime sought to curb. This ambiguity toward feminism could be found in youth groups. They sought to encourage traditional domesticity, but also involved girls in party activities outside the home, which undermined parental authority. The reform of the school system in 1923 was blatantly antifeminist yet allowed a substantial number of women to pursue their education beyond primary school. Female enrollments at Italian universities increased from 6 percent of the student body in 1913–14 to 20 percent in 1938. However, fees charged to female students were double those paid by males.

Until the late 1930s, the regime tolerated non-Fascist bourgeois organizations for both men and women, as long as they did not compete with the party for middle-class loyalties, although the same tolerance was not shown toward working-class organizations. However, the pace of recruiting for Fascist women's groups increased during the 1930s so that by 1940 they had nearly 3.2 million members or about 25 percent of all women over the age of twenty. Fascist organizations for girls were clearly differentiated from those for boys in emphasizing traditional female roles such as first aid, child care, and charity, in addition to rhythmic exercise. Highly regulated gymnastics were practiced to strengthen and beautify the body and as an exercise in obeying rules. On the other hand, sports for women were avoided after 1930 because of Vatican protests and the fear that women might regard them as a step toward emancipation. Mussolini also feared that rugged "masculine sports" like skiing and horseback riding might cause infertility in women.

The reaction against the emancipation of women could also be found in marital laws and women's fashions. Severe punishments for adultery were enacted, which were even harsher for women than for men. The authority of the husband was increased. Divorce was strictly forbidden and penalties for abortion were increased from two to five years imprisonment for anyone either having or abetting one. Prudish rules about the shape of bathing suits and the length of skirts were prescribed. Fascist leaders made derogatory remarks about high heels and the use of cosmetics. Erotic literature was outlawed. No pictures of women in short skirts or skimpy bathing suits were permitted in Fascist newspapers. Nightlife was also rigorously restricted, much to the pleasure of the pope.

The coming of the Great Depression to Italy simply accelerated the trend away from women's rights already apparent in the early years of the Fascist regime. One of the most important reactionary movements was in the limitation of the right of women to work outside the home, a trend also found in democratic countries. Limiting female employment would accomplish two purposes: it would open jobs for unemployed males, and it would eliminate a major distraction to reproduction, thus increasing the birth rate. In addition, staying home would make it more difficult for women to "waste" money on cosmetics and sweets. Even during the 1920s, women had been restricted from teaching in some predominantly male secondary schools and certain subjects like philosophy in any school. After the start of the Depression, at a time when one-quarter of the national work force was female, preferences were given to men for civil service jobs. In 1933, new regulations limited the rights of women even to compete in state civil-service examinations. A law of 1938 limited females to no more than 10 percent of the work force in both private and state employment. A year later exceptions were made for certain "female" jobs like telephone operators and typists. In all fields women were the last to be hired and the first to be fired.

Fascist discriminatory legislation had only very limited success. It did manage to prevent the number of women in the so-called free professions like teaching, jurisprudence, medicine, and journalism, from ever exceeding 108,000, or 10 percent of all professionals. On the other hand, it utterly failed in forcing even married women out of the work force, let alone unmarried women. In 1931, 12 percent of married women held jobs; by 1936, the percentage had risen to 20.7, almost certainly because employers wanted to retain cheap labor. Fascist employment policies were less drastic than those of Nazi Germany, where women were sometimes dismissed from state jobs. However, the difference is less obvious than it appears because Italian women were far less likely to have held highly qualified positions in the first place.

By far the biggest concern of Fascists regarding women was raising the birth rate. This interest also preceded the Depression, but was deepened by it. Fascist hysteria about demography also reflected, in highly exaggerated form, common concerns throughout Europe and North America in the late 1920s and 1930s, when the birth rate in many countries fell below replacement levels. Since the mid-nineteenth century, and to only a lesser extent in the 2000s, population has frequently been equated with national power and prestige as well as with a healthy economy. Moral values have even been attached to population. A country with a rapidly growing population has been considered young, virile, and vigorous. A country with a stable or declining population has been regarded as old, decadent, and decrepit.

Mussolini was determined that Italy would not fall into the latter category. His goal was to raise the country's population from around 40 million in 1927 to 60 million by the middle of the century. A large number of laws were enacted to fulfill this policy. A punitive tax was enacted on bachelors in 1926. In the same year the sale and display of contraceptives along with their possession, manufacture, or importation were outlawed along with contraceptive literature. After 1928, taxes for families with six or more children were phased out. At the same time marriage loans and baby bonuses were inaugurated. The legal marrying age for girls was lowered in 1929 from fifteen to fourteen and for boys from eighteen to sixteen. Homosexual acts were outlawed in 1931 and abortion remained a criminal act. In 1937, marriage and children became preferential factors in government jobs. Special prizes were given to women with twelve or more children. When introducing themselves to Mussolini, women were expected to tell him how many children they had.

Ironically, all the laws against contraception and abortion and favoring population growth had no effect on reversing Italy's declining birth rate. Nothing could overcome the effects of poverty and women's desire for more freedom. There had been 1,176,000 births in 1922 or 30.7 per 1,000 women. These figures shrank almost every year until they reached an absolute low in 1936 of 963,000 births, or 22.4 per 1,000, before both figures rose slightly the following year.

Mussolini's population policy did produce some long overdue legislation favorable to mothers, children, and health. After 1934, women were given two months of paid leave—one month before childbirth and another month afterward—and their jobs were guaranteed from the sixth month of pregnancy to six weeks after the birth of the child. The same law also provided lump sum payments for the birth of each child. Working mothers were guaranteed time off for breast feeding. Factories employing more than fifty workers were required to have feeding rooms for new mothers. Free, month-long summer camps were established for children belonging to Fascist youth groups; doctors decided whether they would benefit more from a holiday in the mountains or at the seaside. Social diseases such as tuberculosis were vigorously attacked; free meals were distributed to the poor.

All in all, women's programs in Fascist Italy were failures within the context of what the Fascists were trying to accomplish. Two decades of trying to reverse rising female employment and declining birth rates resulted in total bankruptcies. The most that can be said for Fascist policies is that they improved the health of mothers and children.

## WOMEN IN NAZI GERMANY: KINDER, KIRCHE, UND KÜCHE?

The Nazi attitude toward women was in many respects the mirror image of that found in Fascist Italy. There was the same rejection of female emancipation, the same desire to get women out of the workplace, and the same effort to increase the birth rate, policies summarized in the slogan *"Kinder, Kirche, und Küche"*: Children, Church, and Kitchen. The differences were mostly matters of degrees. Far more women were working in Germany when Hitler came to power than in Italy in 1922, and the birth rate in Germany had fallen even further. German women had also gained the vote in 1919, whereas Italian women had not, although winning the franchise in Germany was in part more the product of defeat in war, not of a long suffrage campaign. However, the idea of rewarding women for their wartime contributions had also been current in Germany just as it had been in the West. On the other hand, soon after the war most Germans thought that a woman's place was in the home. Female deputies in the Reichstag were taken seriously only when discussing "women's" issues. Male members of the German Parliament, with the exception of the Communists, rejected the notion of equal pay for equal work. Newspapers ridiculed women who had boyish-looking hairdos.

Nazi policies toward women did not appear as reactionary at the time as they do to us today. Their attitude toward increasing the population did not differ significantly from that of Italy or even France. The Nazis were also less prudish when it came to sexual matters than the Fascists, probably because the influence of the Catholic Church was much weaker in Germany. Realistic paintings of nudes in sensuous postures were common in Germany. The cults of the body, sport, and of sex, which had started in the 1920s, continued unabated in the 1930s and early 1940s. Nazi Germany was one of the first countries to encourage girls to engage in athletics. Physically fit women would then be more likely to produce healthy babies. Finally, the Nazis strove for a classless society or *Volksgemeinschaft*, whereas the official Fascist goal was a stratified corporate society, which meant very different roles for upper- and lower-class women.

The Nazis no more had a fixed policy toward women when they came to power in 1933 than the Fascists did in 1922. In fact, they had not thought much at all about women, although what they did think was conservative, reflecting Hitler's bourgeois background. Since the Nazis, in theory at least, rejected liberalism, Marxism, urbanization, and modernization, it was natural that they would also reject feminism, which was closely associated with these movements. Equality between the sexes seemed to undermine the traditional authority of the father and therefore of authority in general. Although there had been a few women in high positions in the early Nazi party, they were explicitly barred from top posts in January 1921. Few women, in fact, ever gained prominence in the Third Reich, and in 1935 only 2.5 percent of the 2.5 million members of the NSDAP were women.

Although Hitler considered women every bit as inferior as did Mussolini, the official Nazi policy, as it eventually evolved, claimed only that they were different. Following arguments commonly advanced by conservatives in the late nineteenth century, the Nazis alleged that they were merely drawing natural distinctions between men and women.

Politics was inherently dirty and it was therefore better that women remain aloof from its corrupting influence. However, women were fully entitled to have (and run) organizations of their own, and they were to be honored for their roles as wives and mothers.

During the Kampfzeit, Nazi women's organizations tended to be of the ladies-aid type. They were supposed to help out poor Nazi families, care for wounded SA men, sew torn brown shirts, and cook meals for Nazi rallies. After the takeover of power, a special Women's Bureau was created and headed by Gertrud Scholtz-Klink. The Bureau was involved in areas traditionally regarded as women's concerns, but also in many that were regarded as private, such a childbearing and child care, consumer purchasing, menu planning, ethical values, social life, religious faith, eugenics, ideological indoctrination, and anti-Semitism. By 1939, 8 million women belonged to Nazi associations under the general supervision of Scholtz-Klink, and another 3 million girls belonged to the Hitler Youth.

The Nazis' major goal after 1933 was to increase male employment by decreasing the number of female jobholders. The more men who worked meant the more men who could afford to marry. The fewer women in the workplace the more there would be at home having babies for the fatherland. In early 1933, there were 11.5 million German women who were still employed, or about 36 percent of the total labor force. About twice as many women worked in Germany as in the United States, even though Germany had only half the population. Whereas male unemployment stood at 29 percent, female joblessness was a relatively low 11 percent. The main reason for the difference was that heavy industry and construction—both of which employed mostly men—were hardest hit by the Depression. A secondary reason may have been the low wages earned by German women. Like women in other industrialized countries, they were paid far less than men for the same work: only 66 percent of men's wages for skilled work and 70 percent for unskilled labor.

The effort to get women out of the work force succeeded only partially and temporarily. The Nazis let stand a law passed in May 1932 permitting the dismissal of economically secure female civil servants. All women school administrators lost their jobs within months of the Nazi takeover, and the number of female teachers at girls schools declined by 15 percent between 1933 and 1935. After 1934, however, women were gradually allowed to return to university teaching positions. The percentage of university coeds was supposed to drop from 20 to 10, which it did in fact do in the late 1930s. Thereafter, however, it rose again as the Nazis realized that there were not enough men to fill professional jobs. After June 1935, women could no longer be appointed judges or public prosecutors, but this law did not affect those women who already held such positions. Women were also declared ineligible for jury duty on the grounds that they could not think logically or objectively since they were driven only by emotions.

As for overall female employment, the Nazis succeeded only in temporarily reducing the percentage of women in the work force, which dropped to 31 in 1936 before it rose again to 36 in 1938, the highest percentage in the world. In absolute numbers there was actually a steady increase from 11.5 million female workers in 1933 to 12.8 million in early 1939 (within the German territory of 1937). The need for workers, brought on by industrialization and rearmament, in the long run outweighed the government's desire to get women out of the work force.

The primary means of inducing women to leave their jobs was to offer people marriage loans. Enacted in June 1933, the Nazis provided married couples with tax-free loans of up to RM 1,000—roughly equal to $5,000 in the currency of the 2000s—in vouchers to be used for household goods. Repayment was to be at the rate of 1 percent per month, but 25 percent of the loan was to be canceled with the birth of each child. Money for the loans came from a tax on childless single people. To obtain a loan, however, the wife had to give up her outside work (although this requirement was eliminated in 1937). The loans enjoyed some success because the number of marriages in Germany increased from 517,000 in 1932 to 774,000 in 1934. However, this fact did not prevent the percentage of married women working outside the home to rise from 28.2 in 1933 to 41.3 in 1939. Income tax deductions for dependent children and subsidies for poor families were also enacted in 1934 and 1935.

The birth rate climbed from 14.7 per 1,000 in 1933 to 18.4 per 1,000 just a year later, although at no time did women have the average of four children which the Nazis regarded as ideal. As in Italy and Russia, as well as France, prolific German mothers were decorated with medals. August 12, the birthday of Hitler's mother, was the day on which the Honor Cross of German Motherhood was awarded, starting in 1939. Like war heroes, mothers were said to have risked their health for the fatherland. As though they were Olympic champions they received a bronze medal for having four children, a silver one for six, and a gold medal for eight or more. Other positive steps to increase the birth rate included liberalizing divorce in the hope that people would remarry and have more children. Unmarried mothers were also treated more humanely than was the case in most parts of Europe during the 1930s.

The Nazis did not rely entirely on positive inducements to raise the birth rate. Immediately after seizing power they outlawed the sale and advertisement of contraceptives as well as voluntary sterilization. Homosexuality was also forbidden and severely punished. Abortion, already penalized in the Weimar Republic, was regarded as a crime against the German people. People who performed abortions, except for purposes of "racial hygiene"—in practice, on women who were mentally retarded, "asocial," or Jewish—were at first subject to up to two years imprisonment; physicians performing abortions could receive ten years imprisonment after 1937; during the war the death penalty was meted out in some cases. Nevertheless, as was the case in the Soviet Union, the criminalizing of abortion merely drove the practice underground. An estimated 500,000 illegal abortions were performed in 1936, and the figure may have reached 1 million by 1939.

Although many Germans did their part to see to it that the birth rate did increase under the Third Reich, with the notable exception of the Nazi party's most prominent leaders, it is by no means certain that Nazi procreation policies had anything to do with it. Couples receiving marriage loans had an average of only one child. In reality, the loans did not begin to cover the costs of a larger family. The overall increase, that actually began in the late Weimar Republic, may have simply resulted from greater prosperity and a new cohort of young men whose numbers had not been decimated by World War I. (It is noteworthy that Russia's current [2008] modest baby "boomlet" is not the result of the government's pro-natalist policies but because of rising prosperity.) As for the welfare of the family as a whole, it almost certainly was weakened rather than strengthened by the Nazi experience. The staggering popularity of organizations and meetings, especially for men and boys, but also for women, could only disrupt family life, undermine the authority of the parents, and harm the education of children.

Although the Nazis enjoyed a modest success in raising the birth rate, their drive to establish an Aryan ideal of feminine beauty was almost a total failure. The perfect German woman was supposed to do without cosmetics, a decadent import from the West, dress simply, refrain from wearing corsets and trousers, and be athletic. She was to have radiant blonde hair tied in a bun, or else braided. This ideal never came close to being realized, least of all by German movie stars. Even Hitler's mistress, Eva Braun, continued to wear lipstick. In Italy, as well, there was no decline in the number of the society ladies so hated by Mussolini.

Once more, totalitarian goals had been largely thwarted. German women were no more likely to be at home in 1939 than they had been a decade earlier. Unlike in Fascist Italy, the birth rate was up, but not simply due to Nazi policies.

## HEALTH AND EUGENICS IN NAZI GERMANY

Pronatalist legislation in the totalitarian states was just one aspect of health care, albeit a very important one. Health care was free in the Soviet Union and far more available than it had been in tsarist Russia, especially in rural areas. The Fascist regime enacted sickness insurance in most labor contracts after 1928. However, social security benefits were more modest than those found at the time in the Soviet Union and in the Scandinavian states. It was rather in Nazi Germany that the most dramatic changes in health care occurred. Some of them were sensible and even far ahead of their time. Others were utterly criminal.

When the Nazis came to power, Germany led the world in the physical and life sciences as well as the social sciences. Even though by 1935, 20 percent of German scientists, most of whom were Jewish, had lost their jobs, the Nazis profited from their scientific inheritance. In Hitler's first four years in power the German government had helped raise the standards of health to such an extent that even foreigners were impressed. Infant mortality was greatly reduced. Diseases were caught in their early stages because physical examinations were required for couples prior to marriage or obtaining a marriage loan. Tuberculosis and other diseases were also noticeably diminished.

The Nazis were concerned about the long-term effects of environmental pollutants including asbestos—more than two decades before American scientists. They also established policies to lessen the toxic effects of alcohol and especially tobacco. A German scientist had already established a statistical link between second-hand smoke and lung cancer in 1928. In the early 1940s German scientists—again long before their American counterparts—maintained that smoking was addictive. The Nazi regime launched the world's first aggressive antismoking campaign. Tobacco advertisements could not use female-centered images, athletes, or sports fans. They also could not ridicule nonsmokers. Some nonsmoking restaurants were also established. Hitler, who had smoked up to 25 cigarettes a day during his Vienna sojourn, was depicted as the country's number one nonsmoker.

German scientists also realized the importance of eating less meat, especially fatty kinds, and eating more fresh vegetables and fruits, as well as more cereals. Hitler himself, with only occasional exceptions, had been a vegetarian since 1924 and referred to meat eaters as "corpse eaters." The Reich Physician Führer, Gerhard Wagner, attacked the recent popularity of highly refined white bread at the expense of whole-grain bread. The latter was supposed to be the "final solution of the bread question." German medical journals warned against the possible side effects of artificial preservatives and colorings in food and drinks. Other health hazards that the Nazis abolished or at least tried to control included lead-lined toothpaste tubes (again, fifty years before similar measures were taken in the U.S.). They also outlawed narcotics such as cocaine and heroine and ads for alcoholic beverages directed at children. Drug companies could not make exaggerated claims about the potency of their products, and Coca-Cola was declared unfit for young people.

In part because of these enlightened views, medical people were among the earliest adherents of Nazism. Eventually, 45 percent of them became party members, a higher percentage than any other professional group. The primary impetus for German doctors to join, however, was the party's anti-Semitism, not its medical policies. In 1933, half of Germany's physicians were Jewish. If they were excluded, the overcrowding and financial stress in the profession would be eliminated for those "Aryans" who remained.

Another reason that many German physicians were pro-Nazi was the party's policy on eugenics, that is, improving the human race through breeding. Eugenics was far from being either a Nazi or even a German phenomenon. It was also popular in Canada, Switzerland, and Scandinavia. Fascist Italy had a strong and highly vocal eugenics movement, but it ran into the brick wall of Vatican opposition. From its inception in the late nineteenth century it had been associated with progressive politics. Eugenicists in the early 1920s were more concerned about the declining birth rate and the increase in mental illness than they were about eliminating Jews.

The United States was probably the world leader in the field of eugenics during the 1920s. Twenty-eight states had passed sterilization laws by 1933. Eugenicists held prestigious positions as professors and as members of major research institutions. American immigration laws, which eugenicists helped to shape in the middle of the decade, were based on the idea that certain "races" in Northern and Western Europe were superior to Eastern and Southern European and non-European races. By 1928, over 75 percent of American colleges and universities offered courses that included eugenics. The United States was also the first country in the world to permit sterilizations to "purify" the race; by 1939, some 30,000 such operations had been performed in twenty-nine states. Early Nazi eugenics laws were based on American models.

American eugenicists admired Germany for having nationwide laws concerning sterilization instead of the hodgepodge of legislation that existed in the forty-eight American states. In fact, American eugenicists were the strongest supporters in the world of Nazi eugenics outside of Germany itself. Among the general public in the U.S., 66 percent favored compulsory sterilization of habitual criminals, a practice that had existed in America since before the First World War. Sterilization for other purposes also increased in the U.S. during 1930s with 30,000 having been sterilized by the end of the decade. However, Americans, including eugenicists, were critical of the Nazis' anti-Semitic legislation. The Nazis responded by pointing out (at least prior to 1938) that German Jews were better treated than were American blacks and were not lynched. However, the extreme persecution of Jews in Nazi Germany that began in the late 1930s alienated the American public in general, as well as American eugenicists, from the Third Reich. After the war American eugenicists pretended that they had had only a very distant and critical relationship with their Nazi counterparts which included vague categories such as "extreme feeblemindedness."

In Germany, a law of July 1933 listed a host of supposedly hereditary mental diseases, along with chronic alcoholism, that required people so classified to be sterilized. By 1945, as many as 375,000 men and women had undergone the procedure But the Nazis did not stop at mere sterilization, most of which had taken place before the outbreak of the war in 1939. Eugenics evolved into euthanasia, that is, the actual killing of "racial inferiors" and "life unworthy of living." Starting in October 1939, about 72,000 people were euthanized in semisecrecy before Hitler called a temporary halt to the program in August 1941. The interruption has usually been credited to a sermon by Bishop Galen of Munster that induced other Catholic and Protestant clergymen to denounce euthanasia publicly. This sermon was given on August 3, three weeks before Hitler issued his decree. His decision, however, may have rested on the simple fact that an earlier target of 70,000 killings had already been attained. The victims included Jews, Gypsies, homosexuals, Communists, the mentally infirm, people suffering from tuberculosis, and a large group of individuals loosely referred to as "antisocials," which included drug addicts, alcoholics, prostitutes, homeless people, and others—who were often killed in portable gas vans. When the program was later resumed in Poland another 130,000 victims died.

Although some parents of mentally or physically disabled children were, sadly, actually eager to get rid of them, Hitler kept his program as secret as possible because he was unsure of public reaction as a whole. The euthanasia program turned out to be a mere prelude and preparation for the Holocaust because the same killers and to some extent the same methods of killing were used for both actions. The Holocaust, however, was conducted with even greater secrecy.

## RELIGION: THE BASIC INCOMPATIBILITY

Religion is another area of "family values" in which the totalitarian states differed radically from each other in theory but followed somewhat similar practices. In the Soviet Union the attitude toward all forms of religion was usually one of overt hostility, although this policy was temporarily reversed during World War II. The fascist regimes pretended to be the defenders of Western civilization against atheistic Communism, but their practices were only marginally friendlier to religion, especially in Nazi Germany. Unfortunately, high-ranking church officials in the fascist states for a long time failed to recognize the basic incompatibility between the claims of totalitarianism and those of Christianity.

Although Karl Marx changed his views on a number of things, he consistently preached that "religion was the opium of the people."

It kept the masses in a kind of drugged stupor so that they would tolerate the evils of this world—to the enormous benefit of the bourgeoisie, which exploited them—in hopes of a great reward in the next world. Marx and his followers especially resented the close links between church and state that existed in many countries, including tsarist Russia.

From the moment they seized power in November 1917, the Communists' policy toward the Russian Orthodox Church and all other religious institutions, was one of unremitting antipathy. Communist doctrine and the Soviet constitution proclaimed that once church and state had been separated, religious beliefs would be left to individual choice. Yet Communism also maintained that religious beliefs were socially destructive superstitions that had to be fought.

In practice, not just beliefs, but also the clergy, religious organizations, and religious buildings were regarded with hostility. One of the first acts of the Bolshevik government was to place the Patriarch of the Russian Orthodox Church under house arrest when he became openly critical of the new regime. The passive resistance of the Russian Orthodox Church against the antireligious policies of the state resulted in the confiscation of its property and long prison sentences and the execution of 8,100 Orthodox priests, monks, and nuns in 1922 alone. During the Great Purges of the 1930s three out of four priests and church leaders, 18,000 in all, were killed. Hundreds of churches were destroyed in the 1920s and 1930s, including priceless cultural monuments, for their building materials. The country's largest house of worship, the Church of Christ the Redeemer in Moscow, was leveled in 1932 in order to make room for the world's tallest building but ended up being replaced by a swimming pool. Thousands of other churches were closed or turned into warehouses. By the end of 1930, 80 percent of village churches had been closed. The printing of religious books, magazines, and newspapers was forbidden. The only religious teaching permitted had to be conducted in private and was only tolerated at all for people over the age of eighteen. Parents were not even allowed to tell their children about God in the privacy of their own homes. Antireligious propaganda was carried out in schools by the Komsomol and by a special party auxiliary called the League of the Militant Atheists, which was founded in 1925. Antireligious museums were opened in Moscow in 1926 to reveal religious hoaxes.

Even though Stalin relaxed the antireligious campaign in 1934 and then called it off altogether for the duration of World War II, tremendous damage to Russia's international reputation had already been caused. Almost certainly nothing else the Communists did, not even the atrocities associated with collectivization and the purges of the late 1930s, caused so much revulsion in the West as the Communists' militant atheism. Even domestically, its efficacy can be doubted. Probably two-thirds of the rural population remained believers, including children who were raised by their religious grandmothers while their parents were away from home working.

By contrast, for many years church-state relations actually aided the international reputation of Fascist Italy. Mussolini's policies regarding the role of women, birth control and abortion, and pornography were all heartily endorsed by the Vatican. The Holy See also applauded the regime's aggressive anti-Communist ideology and its stress on hierarchy and discipline over chaos and anarchy. Both church and state believed that human beings needed to be corrected, guided, and restrained and were suspicious of individualism. Both taught the importance of submitting to authority and an infallible leader. The church was pleased when crucifixes were returned to classrooms and other public buildings in November 1922. The following year the regime recognized some religious feasts as state holidays. When there were disputes they were rarely in the open, except those over Catholic youth groups in 1931.

Almost certainly the most popular thing that Mussolini ever did was to resolve the dispute between the Italian state and the Papacy that had existed since the confiscation of Papal territories by the state in 1870 during the unification of Italy. In protest to the loss of his territories, and later to anticlerical legislation, the pope became a voluntary prisoner inside the Vatican City, a tiny enclave in the middle of Rome, and forbade practicing Catholics to participate in Italian politics. A kind of cold war was thus created which lasted for nearly six decades. Actually, church-state relations had begun to improve even before Mussolini became the Italian prime minister in 1922. But Mussolini succeeded in healing the rift with the Papacy primarily because, unlike his predecessors, he did not have to deal with an opposition after 1926.

The Lateran Accords of February 1929 made Roman Catholicism the only state religion and granted the pope sovereign rights in the Vatican. It also gave the Vatican $92 million in cash and bonds (equal to well over $1 billion in the currency of the early 2000s). Mussolini also agreed to enforce the Church's canon law in the state, including the ban on divorce and to make religious education compulsory. Catholic youth groups were permitted to exist as were parochial schools. In exchange, the Duce received the goodwill of Pope Pius XI and the country's practicing (as opposed to nominal) Roman Catholics, who made up about 24 percent of Italy's population.

Despite the existence of what seemed like a mutual admiration society, church-state differences soon emerged. For example, in 1931 Mussolini attempted to ban a youth organization called Catholic Action for being too political and a rival of Fascist youth groups. Following a bitter response by the pope, Catholic Action was reinstated after agreeing to forswear political activities. Mussolini's generally friendly attitude toward the church was strictly a matter of political pragmatism. He had long been a militant anticlerical during his years as a prominent Socialist and his inner beliefs toward religion never changed. He did not go to church or observe the Church's holy days and paid only one visit to the pope. An open clash reemerged in 1938 with the regime's adoption of anti-Semitic policies (to be discussed in the next chapter). Ultimately, there was a kind of standoff between church and state. The regime could not stamp out Roman Catholic values and in most cases did not even want to. The church, on the other hand, could not seriously restrict Mussolini's power. Its resistance was limited to pastoral letters or encyclicals to the faithful. When it came to the even more crucial issue of Italy entering World War II in 1940, it was helpless to prevent it.

Nazi Germany occupied a middle ground between Communist Russia and Fascist Italy on the question of church-state relations. Ideologically, it was very close to Italy in posing as a defender of Christianity and Western civilization against Communist atheism. No churches were dynamited into oblivion. On the other hand, its relations with church officials were rarely as close as the Fascists' were in Italy, and the regime's policies brought it into harsh conflict with ecclesiastical authorities far more frequently.

The Nazis and the Fascists greatly benefited from the general swing away from liberal values toward conservatism that swept through the entire Western world in the interwar years. The results of this conservative reaction with regard to women's rights have already been observed. By 1918, war, defeat, and revolution had left the Lutheran and Reformed Calvinist churches of Germany in disarray and brought into the open long-standing theological and ideological rifts. Liberal theology—so strong in prewar Germany—was discredited and replaced by a new wave of fundamentalism closely associated with nationalism. The Christian nationalists demanded a revival of German power and spirituality. Not surprisingly, therefore, the vast majority of Protestant clergy remained hostile to Weimar democracy. The Nazis appealed to these people by calling their party a "movement of renewal." Nazi propagandists frequently talked idealistically about self-sacrifice and overcoming selfish materialism.

The Roman Catholic clergy of Germany were for a long time more skeptical of the Nazis than were Protestant theologians. Catholicism had been the religion of only about one-third of the German people since the country was unified in 1871. Sporadic discrimination by Chancellor Otto von Bismarck made Catholics more suspicious of the state than were the dominant Protestants. Catholic clerics went so far as to denounce extreme German nationalism and racial anti-Semitism and, in 1932, said that Roman Catholics could not remain in good standing with the church and at the same time be members of the party. Their opposition, however, was weakened by their toleration of cultural anti-Semitism as well as by their own authoritarianism. As in Italy, Catholic clergy and laymen applauded Nazi attacks on abortion, birth control, pornography, venereal disease and Bolshevism. Nevertheless, the Nazis were less successful at attracting Catholic votes than they were the ballots of Protestants.

Privately, Hitler and other leading Nazis viewed Christianity as a weak and obsolete religion. Hitler told his intimates during his "table talks" that Jesus was an Aryan, and St. Paul had mobilized the criminal underworld into a kind of proto-Bolshevism. But Hitler, at least, was wise enough to keep his religious opinions largely to himself and sometimes even restrained his more radically anti-Christian subordinates. Almost as soon as he came to power he moved to conciliate Catholics who, after 1930 had been much less inclined to vote for the Nazis (only half as many did so in July 1932) by promising the Center party to uphold the rights of the church, including denominational education, in exchange for the Center Party's vote for the Enabling Act of March 1933. It was this Act, which had the support of the Vatican, that put the Reichstag's official stamp of approval on the Nazi dictatorship. At the end of that month, a conference of Catholic bishops responded by withdrawing their objections to Catholics belonging to the NSDAP. Bavarian bishops in May issued a pastoral letter supporting the government's program of "spiritual, moral and economic rejuvenation."[1] The biggest coup for Hitler was the Concordat or treaty with the Papacy in July, which granted independence to Catholic religious and social organizations in exchange for the Vatican recognizing the regime and renouncing clerical interference in "politics."

Despite this promising beginning, conflicts were not slow in developing between the Nazi regime and both the Protestant and Catholic clergies. Of 17,000 Protestant pastors, about 3,000 nationalists had formed their own group of "German Christians" within the NSDAP as early as 1932. They accepted so-called positive Christianity, which meant a "racially pure" church, and the renunciation of the Old Testament and pacifism. Some, like Hitler, even tried to make Jesus into an Aryan. Like the Nazis, they favored the leadership principle and temporarily took over all Protestant offices in July 1933, after the holding of fraudulent elections.

These moves alarmed about 4,000 of the more liberal Protestant clergy, who established an "Emergency League" in late 1933. The League set up a "Confessing Church," which, in the "Barmen Confessions" of May 1934, supported traditional Christian beliefs and denied the right of the Nazi party to impose its policies on all aspects of life. Otherwise, however, the Confessing Church did not even seek to undermine the Nazi state, let alone overthrow it. Nevertheless, Nazi authorities were not pleased by the Barmen declaration and arrested numerous bishops. Adverse reaction both at home and abroad, however, caused Hitler to back down. The German Christian movement was dissolved. However, denominational schools and youth groups, both Protestant and Catholic, were harassed and eventually banned, and by 1937 over 700 Protestant clergy were in concentration camps, where about fifty of them died, a fate suffered by even more Catholic clerics. The Vatican responded in March 1937 with an encyclical entitled *Mit brennender Sorge* (with burning sorrow) in which it denounced Nazi breaches of the concordat and the worship of the false gods of race and state. This did not prevent the Nazis from closing all denominational schools by 1939.

Clashes continued to occur between the regime and especially the Catholic Church over euthanasia and crucifixes being removed from Bavarian schools. These confrontations once again ended with Hitler

1 Quoted in Ian Kershaw, *Popular Opinion and Political Dissent in the Third Reich: Bavaria, 1933–1945* (Oxford, 1983), 191.

backing down, at least temporarily, and gaining credit for his "moderation." However much Hitler sympathized with Nazi radicals on religious issues he wanted to postpone major confrontations with the churches until after the war. In the meantime, as in the case of Italy, the state was the big winner in the church-state struggle. With the notable and courageous exception of Jehovah's Witnesses, 2,000 of whom out of 10,000 wound up in concentration camps, the Christian churches did not question fundamental Nazi institutions or practices and supported rather than opposed German involvement in World War II, especially the invasion of Russia, which was explicitly endorsed by the Catholic bishops as a holy war. Protestant and Catholic clergy also did next to nothing to save Jews from the Holocaust, let alone take any steps to prevent it. As in the other two totalitarian states, the church was little more than a nuisance with which compromises occasionally had to be made. On the other hand, none of the three states ever came close to stamping out religion. Although in general, religious beliefs and institutions declined in the totalitarian states, especially in the Soviet Union and among young people in the fascist states, direct attacks on the church in many cases only strengthened the allegiances of the faithful.

The family values of the totalitarian states were a mixture of enlightenment and brutality. All of the states took positive steps toward helping mothers and children. Although their attitude toward birth control, abortion, and demography seems extreme to us today, they were not particularly unusual in their day, when the threat of declining populations following the bloodbath bath of World War I was a widespread concern. There is little or no evidence that the women's policies of the totalitarian states, especially in the fascist countries, were unpopular even with women themselves, and considerable evidence exists that they were well received by them as a group. Health care also improved in the three dictatorships. But when the Nazis turned to their most radical health care policy of euthanasia, they so feared hostile public reaction that they kept it secret.

The religious policies of the totalitarian states were far less uniform and also far less popular. The Soviet government needlessly alienated millions of its own citizens and outraged public opinion around the world with its religious policies. Mussolini was by far the most cautious of the dictators toward religion and was rewarded with the warm support of the Catholic Church throughout most of his dictatorship, until he turned to anti-Semitism and world war. Hitler's religious policy was more negative and aggressive than Mussolini's, but he knew how to restrain his more radical followers, and he also knew when to back down.

In family values and health care, as in so many other aspects of totalitarian society, moderate and relatively traditional policies were popular and worked reasonably well or at least did not have catastrophic consequences. Radical policies, on the other hand, resulted in popular hostility and ultimate failure.

# 7 / TOTALITARIAN TERROR

If the treatment of women was an area in which the totalitarian states differed relatively little from the democracies, the use of terror was what most differentiated the two systems. The constant rejection of the status quo for the sake of utopian changes in the lives of ordinary people was bound to create resistance, which could only be overcome with terror, or at least the threat of terror. The more grandiose the changes, the more terror was required. Each dictatorship created its own morality which justified the use of terror against anyone who opposed the new utopia. Not surprisingly, therefore, Stalin, who demanded a top-to-bottom change of Soviet society exercised the most terror, whereas Mussolini, with his much more modest program, relied on terror by far the least of the three dictators.

Contrary to expectations, terror increased with time in all three dictatorships. Opponents of the Fascists and Nazis, who were horrified by the use of terror by which both parties gained power, consoled themselves with the belief that once in power the responsibilities of governing would force the dictators to become more moderate and responsible. Although there were periods of consolidation and retrenchment—the New Economic Policy in Russia, the years 1926 to 1935 in Italy, and from the middle of 1934 to the end of 1937 in Germany—in the long run all three of the totalitarian states became more radical and terroristic. The only exception was the Soviet Union after Stalin's death in 1953.

It is easy, especially when reading a brief book such as this one, to imagine that terror in the totalitarian states was constant, that all citizens lay awake at night trembling with fear that a knock on the door from the secret police could come at any moment. Such fears did exist with some people some of the time, but they were by no means uniform or universal. People who were not interested in politics, who did not belong to some pariah group like the kulaks in the Soviet Union or the Jews in Nazi Germany, usually learned what not to do and what not to say. Even for them, however, security was by no means certain, especially not in Russia during the late 1930s, or in Germany toward the end of World War II.

A "purge" was a refinement of totalitarian terror. By definition it was limited to party members. It was a luxury that only a stable regime with a multitude of reliable supporters could afford. It was also a means of invigorating a movement with new blood and restoring revolutionary fervor. Purges were a regular feature only in the Soviet Union, but this fact may have simply been a product of the Communist regime's longevity. It is difficult to imagine a purge not taking place in Italy and Germany after the deaths of Mussolini and Hitler if the Fascist and Nazi regimes had continued to exist after their founders' demise.

## THE GREAT PURGES IN THE SOVIET UNION

Terror was so pervasive and lasted so long in the Soviet Union that it is not easy to isolate it from Soviet history in general, especially during the long dictatorship of Joseph Stalin. Terror began the moment the Bolsheviks seized power by force. It intensified with an abortive attempt to assassinate Lenin in 1918 and much more so during the Civil War. It receded, but did not disappear, during Lenin's NEP. Certainly, the collectivization of Russian farms was nothing if not a gigantic act of terror in which millions of Russian peasants were killed or imprisoned and nearly all the rest were traumatized. All of these early waves of terror, however, were connected to some clearly recognized political or economic goal: the seizure and consolidation of power and the economic transformation of the countryside. The terror was directed against people who opposed the government's goals. What is remarkable about the Great Purges in the 1930s is that they were aimed at loyal party members who at most had only verbally objected to Stalin's plans or criticized Stalin privately in small groups. They posed no immediate threat to the great dictator. For Stalin, who had the phones of dozens of Communist leaders tapped, criticism was tantamount to personal betrayal and treason. In time, the purges developed a dynamic of their own and enveloped people who had never even been oppositionists.

The Great Purges of 1934 to 1938 have provoked more controversies among historians than perhaps any other aspect of Soviet history. Was there a conspiracy to overthrow Stalin? On what basis did Stalin choose his victims? Why were there confessions to absurd allegations like plotting to restore capitalism or conspiring with Nazi Germany? How many people were killed? What impact did the purges have on Russia's image in the West? How did the purges affect Russia's performance in World War II? Only educated guesses have been offered as answers for these and other questions; definitive explanations await the further opening of Soviet archives.

Most historians believe that we must look for answers to these questions in Stalin's highly suspicious and even paranoid character. He made sharp divisions between his trustworthy friends and vicious enemies. Moreover, anyone who appeared to contradict Stalin's idealized image of himself became his enemy. Even to have associated with a former enemy of Stalin's, especially Leon Trotsky, was enough to brand a person Stalin's enemy. Many Communist leaders had opposed the drastic nature of collectivization and made dire predictions about the possible consequences, which turned out to be all too true. Many of these critics had been members of the Bolshevik party long before the revolution and enjoyed great popularity in the general public. They were also aware of Stalin's modest role in the Revolution, which clearly exposed his effort to rewrite history with himself being Lenin's right-hand man. Even if Stalin did not believe that a conspiracy to unseat him was afoot, he might well have believed that the establishment of an alternative government at some future date was possible.

In other words, the purges may have been a preemptive strike against anyone with a power base or any traces of independent thought. Stalin must have also realized that the Communist regime itself smelled of illegitimacy. It had come to power through force and had never won a free election. It did not enjoy the sanctity of the tsarist regime that had ruled for centuries by divine right. Stalin's support was strong only among his own appointees.

The Great Purges were instigated by the assassination of Sergei Kirov, the popular leader of the Communist party in Leningrad, in December 1934. Kirov had committed the unforgivable sin of getting more applause and more votes at a party congress in 1934 than Stalin. Although the circumstances of the assassination are still uncertain, most historians think that Stalin ordered the murder himself. According to this theory, he wanted to destroy a potential rival for the party's leadership and someone with whom he had had serious policy differences. No other assassination could have stirred up as much outrage and alarm as Kirov's. Another hypothesis is that Stalin may have been inspired by the Reichstag fire in Berlin the previous year, which Hitler had used as a pretext for eliminating the Communist party of Germany.

Immediately after Kirov's assassination, the secret police, now known by its acronym NKVD, began rounding up Old Bolsheviks, those party members who had joined the party before 1917, well before Stalin had reached his ascendancy. Although the Old Bolsheviks were the best-known Communists to be arrested, and their trials drew by far the most attention, they were by no means alone. Actually, the brunt of the purges fell on Communists who had joined the party during the Civil War and who had risen to some of the top ranks during the 1930s. They had always been loyal Stalinists, but they knew about Lenin's Political Testament and some of them were also aware of Stalin's responsibility for the collectivization disaster. Those people holding high party offices, along with their associates, were five times more likely to be arrested than rank-and-file members.

These highest-ranking party members were given show trials between 1936 and 1938. None of the accused was provided a lawyer. By 1937, there were so many defendants that to expedite matters NKVD officials conveniently wrote out confessions in advance to literally incredible crimes such as plotting to restore capitalism, attempting to wreck the socialist system, or wanting to cede Soviet territory to Germany or Japan. Rarely were the party members convicted on the basis of any evidence other than their own confessions. The mystery is, why did they confess, why were their confessions apparently believed by so many Soviet citizens, and why was there not a revolt in the party against these miscarriages of justice?

Historians have again been forced to resort largely to speculation to answer these questions. The accused were in no position to object in principle to fake trials. They had not protested against such trials in the past when the victims had been non-Communists and when the accusations against them were based on false evidence. Nor had they ever rejected the idea that the party's leaders had the right to determine who were class enemies. They had also subscribed to the idea that the party as a whole was always right and that to disagree with the party line was to commit the unpardonable act of "factionalism." Now that these principles were turned against them they had no recourse. Some historians have suggested that in confessing they were doing a final service to the party. It seems just as likely, however, that they were hoping that confessions would spare their lives or at least the lives of their family members. Threats against relatives were unprecedented in Russian history. Even revolutionaries had not feared for their families in tsarist times.

It is known that recalcitrants were physically tortured and kept awake up to ninety hours at a time; threats were also made against their loved ones. Those arrested were kept utterly isolated. Not even family members were allowed to visit them. They were interrogated night and day while being kicked and insulted and forced to rehearse their confessions. There were no opportunities to make heroic scaffold speeches. None of the major defendants was spared, and only 1 percent of all defendants in political trials was acquitted. For Stalin, who secretly watched the major trials, the confessions were the ultimate way of humiliating his rivals and a means of giving the procedures an appearance of legality.

The show trials of party bigwigs represented only the tip of the iceberg during the purges. Stalin found the purges of both major and minor party officials and nonparty members a useful way of explaining to himself and to others the failures of collectivization and industrialization. Those atrocities could now be blamed on "wreckers" who had deliberately sabotaged the heroic efforts of Soviet workers and peasants to modernize their country. Stalin had a limitless number of accomplices in this process, from the Politburo, to the secret police, to writers and numerous anonymous informers. The members of the secret police, over which there were no external controls other than Stalin, were handsomely rewarded for their efforts, having their pay quadrupled until they became the highest paid government agents. Their handsome salaries and other privileges only made them more eager to justify their existence by finding still more "traitors." If they could not, their turn might come next, something that even the Gestapo and SS did not fear in Nazi Germany.

The mechanics of the purge, like those of collectivization, soon acquired a momentum of their own and developed into what is known as the "Great Terror," which involved perhaps eight or nine times as many nonparty members as Communists. The more people Stalin killed, the more family members and friends of the dead he had to fear. Denunciations, which the government had encouraged during collectivization, once again became popular. An anonymous letter to the authorities was sufficient for a student to get rid of an unpopular professor or for a secretary to destroy her boss. Anyone could be accused of anything. The circumstances were ideal for settling old scores and at the same time proving one's loyalty to the party. Every meeting of writers and all literary journals were filled with malicious accusations. In the end, the majority of members in the Union of Writers was either shot or sent to labor camps. Lists of enemies were also drawn up in mass meetings on collective farms and in factories for the ostensible reason of discovering "wreckers" who had disrupted production. Anyone could be included on the list on the basis of hearsay evidence, but most of the accused were people who drew relatively high salaries.

The Terror climaxed with the decimation of the armed forces in 1937–38. In early 1938, Hitler went to a great deal of trouble to dismiss (but not kill or imprison) two of his top military leaders. Stalin, who like Hitler had a long-standing distrust of the military, by contrast, had his top military and naval officers shot by the hundreds with or without a trial. The executions included 3 of the country's 5 marshals, 3 out of 4 full generals, all 12 lieutenant generals, 60 of 67 corps commanders, and 130 out of 199 divisional commanders. The navy lost all 8 of its admirals. Altogether, the army lost 35,000 men, or half of its officer corps, although 30 percent of those arrested were later reinstated. Nevertheless, by the time that the last purged officer was shot two weeks before the German invasion in June 1941, one-third of the Soviet officer corps had been killed. No officer corps in modern times, including the Soviet Union's during World War II, ever suffered such staggering casualties as the Soviet officers sustained in peacetime. Stalin at least carried out the military purges in stages, to allow time for new officers to be trained, and to avoid the complete destruction of the country's striking power. However, this training was far from complete so the effectiveness of the army was undoubtedly severely damaged, particularly during the war with Finland in the winter of 1939–40.

Numbers alone do not tell the whole story about the effects of the military purge. Officers with the most experience in mechanized warfare and who had developed the habit of thinking independently during the Civil War (as well as those who had been close to Trotsky) were the most likely to be purged. For example, General Mikhail Tukhachevsky, who had served the Communists heroically during the

Civil War, and who had created the largest tank force in the world, was one of Stalin's prime targets. He was convicted of conspiring with the Germans on the basis of documents forged by the Nazis and conveyed to Stalin by German Communists.

Estimates of all the people killed during the purges vary considerably. Those authors who have given high estimates have been accused by other scholars of being unreconstructed cold warriors. Those who have made low estimates have opened themselves up to the charge of being pro-Soviet. The latest estimate is that around 3,850,000 people were arrested although some estimates range as high as 7 million. Whatever the number, they were tried secretly after which somewhere between 400,000 and 1 million were executed, with the remainder sent to labor camps. Estimates of those who died of overwork and malnutrition in the Arctic camps vary even more wildly, from a conservative 3 million to a not impossible 12 million. By 1939, 850,000 members of the Communist party had been purged of whom 780,000 had been shot, about one-third of the membership in 1937. Of the 1,966 delegates to the Seventeenth Party Congress in 1934, 1,108 were subsequently purged, arrested, or killed. Seventy of the 139 members of the Central Committee elected by that Congress were executed. Without any question, Stalin killed more Communists than did the fascist dictators. So many people died of unnatural causes during the 1930s, including the state-induced famine of 1931–32, that Stalin had the chief census takers shot as "enemies of the people" and a falsified census was published.

By the end of the purges, somewhere between 3 million and 8 million prisoners languished in something like 125 slave labor camps or gulags where 90 percent of them died between 1936 and 1938. The *gulags* had existed since the time of Lenin, but it was only in Stalin's day that their number reached truly mammoth proportions. Following the purges, the number of inmates never declined and may have reached 15 million by the end of World War II. The total land area of these camps, together with the surrounding land worked by the prisoners, was larger than that of any European country west of Russia.

Perhaps the most amazing thing about the purges and the Terror is that they did not generate a single assassination attempt against Stalin. (By contrast, there were at least forty-two plots to kill Hitler.) Popular reaction to the purges and Terror appears to have been mostly positive. To the still poorly educated Russian in the street who was prone to believe in conspiracies, there did indeed seem to be plenty of evidence that the economy had been "wrecked." Soviet citizens did not want to believe that their government's miscalculations and incompetence had caused the economic chaos. To most people, the trials and arrests seemed to provide logical answers. If someone knew of an innocent relative being arrested, they merely assumed that this was an isolated mistake about which Stalin had no knowledge. Many people, particularly recently collectivized peasants, must have taken a grim satisfaction in seeing some of the people who had caused them so much misery suffering a well-deserved retribution.

Stalin's exact role in the purges has been another of the many historical debates about the phenomenon. Few if any historians doubt that the purges could have taken place without his instigation and support. His office in the Kremlin was the command post of the Terror. However, Stalin himself kept a low profile throughout the whole ordeal, giving no public speeches for two years and granting interviews for publication only twice after March in 1937 and once in all of 1938. Other people such as the trial prosecutor, Andrei Vyshinsky, and the head of the NKVD, Nikolai Yezhov, were much more prominent in the whole affair. It was Yezhov who turned over to Stalin long lists of alleged "wreckers," with proposed sentences, for the dictator's signature. Stalin approved 383 such lists of the names of 44,000 party, government, military, Komsomol, and economic officials as well as leading individuals in the nation's cultural life.

Out of all of the names presented to him, Stalin probably personally considered only the cases of the members of the Central Committee, the High Command of the army, and the provincial secretaries of the party, both past and present. He took the trouble to call the victims just before their arrest to assure them that they had nothing to fear. After meeting with the Central Committee in February and March 1937, Stalin no longer regarded it as necessary for him to consult that body before having people arrested, including members of the Central Committee itself. He was concerned with every detail of the purge trials and saw to it that the "conspirators" in the show trials were assured that their lives would be spared if only they confessed. Later he relished the reports of their executions.

Some historians, while not contesting Stalin's central role in the Terror, have argued that he had no carefully laid out plan. He was at times indecisive and made several false starts and retreats. It is also apparent that once begun, the Terror, like collectivization, developed a momentum of its own marked by personal hatreds, confusion, and a lack of coordination. Such chaos finally gave Stalin the excuse to authorize a decree blaming local authorities for excessive vigilance, just as he had blamed local party officials in early 1930 for being "dizzy with success" in the middle of collectivization.

The Terror of the late 1930s had consequences that went far beyond those people who were killed or imprisoned. The Soviet Union suffered another huge loss of prestige abroad. If the incredible charges made against high party, government, and military officials were actually true, then the country was filled with traitors and ripe for counterrevolution. If they were false, what was one to think of a government that had manufactured spurious charges against its highest government and military officials and published them abroad? How much did one have to fear—or hope for—from a military that had just been decimated by its own leader?

Domestically the results were equally serious. The largest factories lost most of their highly qualified engineers. The Kharkov Physics Laboratory, one of Europe's best, was ruined by the arrest of most of its senior staff. The most serious consequences, however, were intangible. Senior and competent civilian and military officials were replaced by people who were much younger and less qualified. The replacements were often careerists who were unwilling to take risks. Managerial authority was badly undermined. Workers were encouraged to criticize their supervisors, but managers were not eager to discipline workers for fear of subsequently being denounced by them.

For Stalin personally, the purges and Terror were a complete success. His cult of personality was more firmly entrenched than ever. He was now surrounded not by colleagues, but by accomplices who were implicated in his crimes. The Communist party was eliminated as a ruling class. Only local bosses had any real authority, which existed solely at the pleasure of the great dictator. The party was now less important than the police and even the state. Its deliberative bodies like the Central Committee and Politburo rarely even met. Stalin had removed all possible alternate sources of power or even criticism. When he was faced by the ultimate test of the Nazi invasion in 1941, he had no need to fear a domestic revolt or the rise of a Soviet Napoleon. On the other hand, there was no one left to protect him from his own stupidity.

## TERROR AND PERSECUTION
## IN THE FASCIST STATES

Nothing comparable to the Great Purges and the Terror existed in the two fascist states, at least before World War II. In general, the fascist dictators, unlike Stalin, were interested only in actual, not potential opposition. It is revealing that the NKVD had 366,000 employees in 1941 in a country of 183 million. By comparison 20,000 people (including clerks and typists) worked fulltime for the German secret police, the *Gestapo*, in 1939, out of a population of 68 million. Hitler and Mussolini were far more popular than Stalin, and therefore much less dependent on terror to prop up their regimes. The only major peacetime purge in either country was the Röhm Purge of June 1934 in Germany. Although it was not restricted purely to the top leadership of the SA—Nazis used the opportunity to even "old scores" with former anti-Nazis—the best guess is that about eighty-five people were killed in a single night (not the 1,100 estimated by some foreigners at the time). The outrage that one might assume would have arisen from the purge was tempered by the knowledge that many of those killed were notorious murderers and sadists. Compared to Stalin, therefore, Hitler was a rank amateur when it came to purging. Mussolini, also, had the power to purge and his party secretaries resorted to it thousands of times, but usually with nonlethal consequences. The expulsions from the Fascist party demonstrated that members had to be careful with their speech and actions or they would lose their privileged status.

Nevertheless, terror and persecution certainly did exist in Italy and Germany prior to World War II, even if the result was not as overt and bloody as it was in Stalinist Russia. In both fascist states the use of terror was most common during the rise to power of the regime and the following period of consolidation before flaring up again in the year or so preceding World War II. Contributing enormously to the terror were denunciations by private citizens in all three of the totalitarian states. In Germany, the Gestapo was flooded by denunciations from angry people of all classes who had grudges against their neighbors and relatives; only 10 percent of the denunciations came from other Nazi organizations. Faced with an embarrassment of riches, the Gestapo was forced to choose which allegations to pursue and which to ignore. Even Hitler was concerned about this deluge, but neither he nor the Gestapo could stop it. In most cases no real proof of antistate activity could be found. Grumbling about various aspects of Nazi policies, although common, did not necessarily represent opposition to the regime as a whole. In Italy the Blackshirts, or *Squadristi*, made a habit of beating up their opponents and torturing their leaders by pouring castor oil down their throats. The last rampage of the Blackshirts occurred in Florence in October 1925, sixteen months after the murder of Matteotti. They killed several Fascist opponents and injured many others, even as foreign tourists watched in horror.

In 1926, a secret police was created in Italy to augment propaganda as a means of consolidating the regime. The Fascist judicial system sometimes recommended torture, but rarely the death penalty for political offenders. A Special Tribunal handed down prison sentences totaling over 28,000 years to more than 5,000 of the accused, but 80 percent of the defendants were acquitted or let off with a reprimand or a warning. For others, loopholes and corruption allowed them to escape punishment altogether. As many as 5,000 people at any one time and 17,000 altogether, were less fortunate and became political prisoners on small penal islands or under "controlled residence," often in some diseased-infested village in the southern part of the country. Another 160,000 were kept under some kind of surveillance. However, only twenty-nine Italians were executed for political crimes, including spying, between 1926 and 1943, in large part because there simply was not much opposition to the regime, at least prior to the late 1930s. Many hundreds of other anti-Fascists were tried by the regular courts. In these cases there were somewhat better opportunities for acquittal because many judges were not Fascists. Most of the opponents of Fascism were intellectuals, especially those living abroad.

A major reason for the lack of opposition and persecution, however, was the prevalence of fear that had been instilled by the Fascists between 1919 and 1925. Consciously or unconsciously, Mussolini followed the advice of Nicolo Machiavelli in believing that it was impossible to rule without first being feared. The early examples of terror were enough to keep nearly all Italians in line in later years. Ordinary Italians feared the authorities, anyone they did not know, and even their friends and family who might get them in trouble.

## THE PERSECUTION OF JEWS

After 1945 it became apparent that Hitler had come a long way in matching Stalin's achievements as a mass murderer. In addition to 5 to 6 million Jews, he was responsible for the deaths of hundreds of thousands of disabled Germans and millions of Sinti and Roma (better known as Gypsies). In other countries occupied by the Nazis during World War II still more millions of people were killed, probably 11 million noncombatant deaths in all. In light of Hitler's ruthlessness in launching a new war in 1939, and brutally exterminating millions of innocent people, it is surprising that, in contrast to Stalin, he was relatively cautious about the use of terror in peacetime, especially before 1938.

There has been a considerable controversy about the role of anti-Semitism in the Nazi rise to power. The older view held anti-Semitism to be crucial to the Nazis' success. More recently, however, historians have tended to downplay its centrality. A major reason for the new interpretation is the realization that Nazi anti-Semitism was far from unique in the Weimar Republic. Nearly all the other political parties except for the Social Democrats exploited the widespread prejudice for their own political gains. Moreover, even Nazi anti-Semitism was stronger in the early 1920s than it was in the early 1930s, when the Nazis finally achieved power. The biographies of numerous leading Nazis have also revealed that surprisingly few of them were anti-Semites before 1925. Among those who were not anti-Semitic were Josef Goebbels, the SS leader, Heinrich Himmler, Albert Speer, Baldur von Schirach, and one of the key players in the Holocaust, Adolf Eichmann. A survey of rank-and-file Nazis carried out during the 1930s showed that only 12.9 percent of them had joined the party because they were strongly anti-Semitic, and 48 percent of the early Nazis were not anti-Semitic at all.

Another misconception about the Nazis that has recently been rectified by historians is that anti-Semitism was strongest among the lower middle class, people like small businessmen, clerks, and civil servants, including elementary school teachers. Anti-Semitism did indeed exist among these groups, and their sheer size made them an important element among Nazi voters. However, anti-Semitism was much stronger within the more respectable upper middle class, especially professional people like physicians, lawyers, journalists, young university instructors, and university students, who were hoping to become professionals. These were the people most likely to be in direct economic competition with the Jews, who were very prominent among German professionals. For example, 22 percent of German lawyers were Jewish in 1930. Nevertheless, with the possible exception of the students, what these anti-Semitic groups wanted was at most the deportation of German Jews; nearly all of them would have been horrified at the prospect of the Jews being murdered en masse as Josef Goebbels hinted at in his diary. Their preferred solution to what was commonly called the "Jewish question" was a *numerus clausus,* or cap on Jewish representation in various economic fields based on their proportion of Germany's total population, meaning no more than 1 percent.

For the first five years of the Nazi regime Hitler seemed to be moving toward this seemingly "moderate" solution. He had personally toned down the crudeness of his anti-Semitism in his speeches after 1928 to appeal to the respectable middle class. In October 1930, he publicly announced that he had nothing against "decent" Jews and rejected violent anti-Semitism. When he came to power in January 1933, there is no evidence that he had decided what he would do about the Jews beyond legal discrimination as outlined in *Mein Kampf.* As for the German Jews themselves, the majority thought that Nazi anti-Semitism was pure demagoguery and need not be taken seriously; nothing bad would happen to them. The pessimists feared that they would lose their civil liberties and perhaps some of their jobs, but nothing more.

Prior to 1938, political persecution was by no means focused exclusively on Jews. Of the nearly 100,000 Germans who had been thrown into makeshift or permanent concentration camps at one time or another during 1933, none was there specifically because he was Jewish. Anti-Nazis, especially Communists and Social Democrats were the most likely candidates for imprisonment, and Jews were incarcerated only if they belonged to an anti-Nazi political party. Most of the early concentration camp prisoners were released within a few weeks. After 1933, the peacetime camp population declined to a low of 5,000 in 1936. Following the annexation of Austria and parts of Czechoslovakia in 1938 and 1939, the number ballooned to at least 21,400 although these figures do not reveal the total number of people who passed through the concentration camp system before the war. In the middle 1930s, the majority of inmates were habitual criminals, prostitutes, homosexuals (who were treated as the lowest category and who were there to be "cured" of their orientation), pimps, drunkards, beggars, the "work shy," and Jehovah's Witnesses (because of their refusal to serve in the armed forces).

One of the biggest misconceptions about Nazi concentration camps that were established in Germany before the war is that they were secret. It is true that released prisoners were forbidden to discuss their imprisonment on pain of being reincarcerated. The existence of the camps themselves, however, was anything but secret. Heinrich Himmler actually held a press conference to announce the establishment of the first "permanent" concentration camp at Dachau two days before it was open for business. (See figure 21.) In early 1938, he invited journalists to visit the Sachsenhausen concentration camp near Berlin. Because the camps were intended in part to intimidate Nazi opponents it would have made no sense to keep them a secret. On the other hand, the Nazis attempted to keep the existence of extermination camps that were erected outside Germany during the Second World War totally secret, fearing both domestic and international repercussions in case their existence were exposed. (See figure 22.) Although the prewar camps were clearly designed to strike fear in the minds of actual or potential opponents of the regime one should not assume that most Germans opposed them. On the contrary, most Germans welcomed them as a way of cleaning up "lawlessness." The Nazis also presented them as educational work camps where asocials would be rehabilitated. (See figure 23.)

Although the persecution of German Jews began soon after the Nazi takeover it was not terribly intense at least by later standards. Some Austrian Catholic anti-Semites even complained in 1933 that Nazi anti-Semitism was a fraud! A party-directed boycott of Jewish businesses, doctors, and lawyers in April 1933 failed miserably after just one day when few Germans supported it despite the presence of intimidating SA men standing in front of Jewish-owned stores. The only concrete result of the boycott was the arousal of international indignation. People with just one Jewish grandparent were excluded from the civil service, including teachers in public schools, later in the same month. A quota was placed on Jewish university students, but Jewish pupils could still attend public schools although they had to sit on segregated benches.

The impact of the civil service law was lessened at the insistence of President Hindenburg and Hitler's German Nationalist partners.

Jews who had been practicing their professions before the outbreak of World War I, war veterans, and children of Jews who had been killed in the war, were excluded. These exceptions turned out to be much more numerous than Hitler had imagined. For example, half the country's 717 judges and 70 percent of its lawyers were not covered by the new law. Jewish businessmen, who were far more numerous than Jewish civil servants or professional people, were only moderately affected by anti-Semitic actions until 1937, especially in comparison with what they were to confront later. Nevertheless, 53,000 Jews were frightened into leaving Germany in 1933. However, the anti-Semitism of host countries, including the United States, and homesickness for Germany, caused 16,000 of these refugees to return to Germany.

The second phase of Jewish persecution began with the enactment of the Nuremberg Laws in September 1935. The laws have often been seen as the real beginning of the Holocaust because they deprived Jews of their German citizenship and subjected them to a number of discriminatory regulations. Jews themselves, however, did not universally hold this negative view at the time. After the chaotic treatment of Jews during the first two years of Nazi rule, the laws seemed to ensure German Jews a secure if second-class position in German society, an attitude shared by most Germans except for the more radical Nazis who thought they did not go nearly far enough. Jews lost their right to vote in German elections (but not in their own communal elections), but general elections were now meaningless anyway. Marriage and sexual relations (subsequently very loosely defined) were forbidden between Jews and gentiles, but this proscription did not prevent liaisons from taking place despite numerous denunciations by "Aryans." Ultraconservative Jews (in both Germany and Austria) actually welcomed the laws because they would create Jewish cultural autonomy. They would also disabuse Jews of the notion that they would ever be accepted into German society and would encourage them to return to the traditional faith. The Zionist leadership in Palestine also showed little if any concern about the legislation and would help German Jews emigrate only if they came to Palestine.

In answering the vexing question of who was a Jew, Hitler chose the most restrictive definition of the four proposed to him. To be classified as a full Jew one had to have three Jewish grandparents or two if one actively practiced Judaism. There were also around 200,000 first- and second-class *Mischlinge*, who had only one or two Jewish grandparents, but they were merely ineligible for certain jobs. The German public evidently viewed these laws as reasonable and necessary. Academic journals at the time pointed out that American (black-white) antimiscegenation laws defining Negroes were far more encompassing than the Nuremberg Laws. German and Austrian Jewish newspapers generally welcomed the laws as a return to order.

Severe persecution of Jews began only in 1938, when Hitler felt Germany's armed forces were strong enough that he no longer had to fear international reactions. Until then Jews who felt they had been abused could still appeal to the police with a reasonable expectation that their complaints would be taken seriously. However, already in 1937, individual local Nazi bosses, called *Gau* leaders, began attacking Jewish business owners and forcing them to sell, or "Aryanize," their property at artificially low prices. The major turning point, however, came with the annexation of Austria in March 1938. The takeover of Austria not only added over 200,000 Jews to the Third Reich's population—more than compensating for the 129,000 Jews who had emigrated prior to 1938—it also added a large number of rabid anti-Semites. Austrian anti-Semitism had long been much more virulent than the German variation. The difference was caused by the continuing strength of Catholic religious and cultural anti-Judaism, the rapid increase of Vienna's Jewish population after the middle of the nineteenth century, and the impoverishment of the country as a result of the breakup of the Austro-Hungarian monarchy. Attacks by Austrian anti-Semites against Jews, following the *Anschluss*, or union of the two countries, were so violent and the pace of Aryanization so rapid, that German Nazis came to Vienna to study the Austrians' techniques. The overall impact of the Anschluss, therefore, was to speed up the persecution of German Jews.

This persecution persisted through the spring, summer, and fall of 1938. In June, 1,500 Jews were sent to concentration camps, this time simply for being Jews. Sporadic acts of violence were perpetrated against Jews during the summer. Hitler ordered Goebbels to stop these activities. However, since no general ban was placed on them party activists interpreted this silence to be a green light. Between July and September the German government issued decrees restricting the employment of Jewish doctors and lawyers. Jewish men were forced to add "Israel" to their names, and Jewish women had to attach "Sarah" to theirs. Even before the catastrophe of November 1938,

Jewish capital assets had been reduced by almost 60 percent, from RM 12 billion in 1933 to only RM 5.1 billion in 1938, even though the Jewish population had declined by only one-third.

The prewar climax to the persecution of German Jews came in November. On the 7th of that month a seventeen-year-old Jew of Polish extraction named Herschel Grünszpan shot a German diplomat in the German embassy in Paris. Two days later the diplomat died, unleashing a ghastly night of looting, burning, and murder commonly known as *Kristallnacht* or "crystal night," a euphemism (which referred to the shattered glass of the windows of Jewish-owned shops) invented by the atrocity's chief promoter, Josef Goebbels. Disguised to look like a spontaneous outburst of righteous indignation, Kristallnacht was actually a well-orchestrated pogrom carried out variously by party leaders and by members of the SA, SS, and the Hitler Youth although all three groups had been ordered not to wear their uniforms. The SA men were the worst, dragging numerous Jews from their beds and beating them, sometimes literally to death. When the smoke cleared, 11,200 synagogues and temples throughout Germany (including Austria) had been burned (see figure 24), 7,500 Jewish-owned businesses lay in ruins, officially ninety-one Jews had been murdered (but the actual figure was probably in the hundreds), at least 300 committed suicide, and between 26,000 and 35,000 Jews had been arrested and sent to concentration camps where most were released a few weeks later but not before several hundred other Jews died of abuse, trauma, and exposure.

Like the boycott of April 1933, Kristallnacht was anything but a public relations coup. Throughout Germany, foreign diplomats reported local crowds being aghast and ashamed of their government and their fellow Germans. They were indignant about the destruction of property at a time when they were supposed to be frugal. However, revelations from private diaries have more recently shown that many Germans were also disturbed by the immorality of the action. The pretense of spontaneity was universally rejected as ludicrous. Only the most hard-core Nazis approved of the pogrom. Even many Nazis thought it was a cultural disgrace and a blow to Germany's international image. Indeed, in the United States, previously neutral Americans, including German-Americans, now became staunchly anti-Nazi. Some leading Nazis such as Hermann Goering were furious with Goebbels because of the wanton destruction of property. However,

Goering then simply forced the Jews to pay for the damage by fining them RM 1 billion, equal to about $2.5 billion today. Kristallnacht was the first and last action of its kind in Nazi Germany. Further anti-Jewish measures were systematic, "legal" (by Nazi standards), and often secret.

The November Pogrom was essentially designed to accelerate Jewish emigration from Germany. Indeed, Jews who promised to leave Germany quickly were released from concentration camps within a few weeks. Kristallnacht occurred near the beginning of a new wave of anti-Semitic legislation. Jewish children were expelled from public schools on November 15 and forced to attend all-Jewish schools. All Jewish physicians who still had gentile patients were allowed to practice only on Jews after the end of September 1938. On November 12, a new law forbade Jews from undertaking any form of independent business activity. Management-level workers were to be dismissed from their jobs without any severance pay or pension rights. Other laws during the next three years prevented Jews from using parks; attending cultural events like films, exhibitions, and concerts; owning an automobile; publishing; or even using public telephones. The laws served their intended purpose. Deprived of any way to earn a living, Jews hastened to emigrate. Whereas only 23,000 Jews left Germany in 1937, over 35,000 did so in 1938, and another 63,000 fled recently annexed Austria. In 1939, a combined total of 128,000 Jews left the Greater German Reich. These people were the lucky ones. Those who remained, mostly old people and women, were soon to be swept away by the Holocaust.

Historians have disagreed about Hitler's role in the above events. His habit of not putting his orders in writing has only added to the mystery. This much can be said with certainty: Hitler, like Stalin, wanted to avoid direct responsibility for anything that might be perceived at home or abroad as disreputable. During the anti-Semitic outbursts in 1933–34 he did not make a single speech in which the Jewish question was even mentioned. A firm believer in the idea of a powerful international Jewish conspiracy, he refused to countenance any anti-Semitic measures while Germany was still militarily weak, for he was fearful of provoking an international response from mythical Jewish wire pullers in the United States, Britain, and France.

By the fall of 1937, however, Hitler was beginning to lose his inhibitions. At the annual Nazi party rally in Nuremberg in September, he made a frenzied attack on "Jewish Bolshevism." It can hardly be a coincidence that this was about the time when physical assaults on German Jews and the "Aryanization" of Jewish property began to accelerate. But just prior to Kristallnacht, he made no speeches and issued no written orders; following the pogrom he also maintained his public silence so that he could once again remain aloof from responsibility. Moreover, the pretense of the spontaneity of the violence could be maintained. Nevertheless, at the very least, Hitler was morally responsible for the anti-Jewish campaign. Subordinate Nazis were well aware of Hitler's opinions concerning Jews and sought to implement them. When Hitler thought they had gone too far he could and did intervene, but for tactical, not ethical reasons.

Meanwhile, the anti-Semitic orgy in Germany found an echo in Italy, where there were at most only 50,000 Jews, most of them well integrated. Mussolini's motivations for introducing a policy of anti-Semitism over the objections of government officials have been hotly disputed by historians. On numerous occasions he expressed his skepticism about "racial science." He had a Jewish mistress, Margherita Sarfatti, at times condemned Nazi anti-Semitism, and even gave German Jews temporary haven. He told a foreign journalist in 1932 that "Italians of Jewish birth have shown themselves good citizens, and they fought bravely in the war."[1] However, some historians believe that he may have discovered the political usefulness of anti-Semitism during his well-publicized four-day state visit to Germany in 1937. Others think that he gave in to Nazi pressures or was at least trying to please Hitler and strengthen ties between Italy and Germany although there is no evidence of overt pressure coming from Germany. Still others, however, believe that Mussolini had long been a racist as well as an anti-Semite. In 1930–31, under his leadership, the Italian army deported 100,000 Libyans to a concentration camp where they were left to starve. In 1935, Mussolini saw a Jewish conspiracy in the international opposition to his war in Ethiopia in 1935–36. The inference of that conquest, as well as Italy's possession of several other African colonies, made racism a logical way to prevent fraternization between natives and colonial administrators. Antimiscegenation laws had been enforced in Italian East Africa since 1933 and were introduced to Ethiopia in 1937.

1 Emil Ludwig, *Talks with Mussolini* (Boston, 1933), 70.

In any event, the campaign against Italy's Jews began in July 1938, with the publication of a "Manifesto of Fascist Racism." In September, the citizenship of foreign-born Jews, who had become citizens only after January 1919, was revoked. At about the same time, Jewish students and teachers were banned from public schools and were required instead to attend Jewish schools. In October, the Fascist Grand Council prohibited Jewish membership in the party. Jews were also expelled from all civil and military service positions as well as from professional, journalism, law, and cultural, and academic associations. Ninety-eight university professors, or nearly one in ten, lost their jobs as a consequence. Now Jews were not allowed to own land or run businesses having more than 100 employees or to hire non-Jewish servants. A campaign to purge the country of modern, "Jewish" culture, especially avant garde literature and textbooks by Jewish authors, also took place in 1938. Finally, mixed marriages were forbidden and Jews were forced to change their names to something more "Jewish." As in the case of some of the early anti-Semitic laws in Germany, exceptions were made for war veterans and their families and children of mixed marriages who did not practice Judaism. In November, still more legislation was aimed at deporting foreign-born Jews, and indeed, 6,000 Jews did subsequently leave the country.

Aside from the murder of Matteotti, The Defense of the Race Laws was the most unpopular action taken by the Fascist regime prior to its entering World War II, although they engendered little open opposition from Gentiles. Only some of the Fascist leadership and the Fascist University Groups, both of which had pushed for the laws, strongly supported them. Among the general public they won approval only in Trieste, perhaps because of the strong tradition of anti-Semitism it had inherited from the Austrian Empire, and perhaps because the city had a relatively large Jewish population. Otherwise, however, there was a great deal of public disgust over the legislation, especially since it coincided so closely with anti-Jewish atrocities in Germany. Even the royal court and some members of Mussolini's family objected to it, but to no avail. Rightly or wrongly, it was widely believed that the regime had meekly submitted to Nazi pressure. Academic and business elites, unlike those in Germany, were particularly outraged by the laws. Another long-time supporter of the Fascists, the Vatican, regarded the legislation as a clear violation of the Concordat of 1929 because it forbade the marriage of Christians to baptized Jews.

This summary of terror and persecution obviously shows that prior to World War II, at least (but not thereafter), Stalin was in a class by himself. Whereas his fatalities could already be counted in the millions, those who died in Nazi persecutions totaled at most a few hundred. Mussolini's prewar victims amounted to only a couple of dozen. Similar comparisons could be made between the imprisonment of political prisoners in the three totalitarian states. However brutal the Nazi camps were in this period, most inmates survived the ordeal, as did political prisoners in Italy.

The persecutions in all three totalitarian states were profoundly self-destructive. Stalin's persecutions were on such a massive scale that the very efficiency of the Soviet economy and military were badly undermined. He was especially eager to get rid of the most senior members of the Communist party, the Old Bolsheviks. Hitler and Mussolini went to the opposite extreme as far as party members were concerned. They tolerated any amount of corruption and inefficiency, especially if committed by old cronies; only disloyalty could lead to serious consequences for a party official. As a result, however, their systems became much less efficient and their political parties steadily declined in public esteem. The Russian and German general publics approved of the purging of party officials, but many Germans and Italians objected to harsh measures taken against their Jewish fellow citizens. The persecution of Jews in Germany and Italy probably did more to damage the international reputations of the Nazi and Fascist regimes than the Terror did for the Soviet Union's image abroad, although lack of information about Russia at the time probably accounts for much of the difference. The forced emigration of leading Jewish intellectuals and scientists also had serious consequences for the two fascist countries culturally, economically, and even militarily. For Mussolini, Fascist racial laws were also a real turning point in the legitimacy of his regime domestically. All three of the dictators succeeded in remaining remarkably aloof from any negative public reactions to the use of terror with the exception of the murder of Matteotti in the early years of Mussolini's rule. However, the dictators' continuing personal popularity at home did nothing to save the reputations of their regimes abroad.

Fig. 1. The antiques of history. Portraits of Lenin, Stalin, and Marx for sale in an antique store in Hong Kong. Part of a poster showing the first ruler of Communist China, Mao Tse-tung, is on the far left. *Photograph by the author in 2008.*

Fig. 2. Lenin haranguing a crowd in Petrograd during the Bolshevik Revolution. This copy of a famous scene is located in the Museum of the Revolution in Hanoi, the capital of Communist Vietnam. *Photograph by the author in 2008.*

Fig. 3. The Winter Palace in St. Petersburg. Palace of the last tsar of Russia, Nicholas II. Later it was the headquarters of the Russian Provisional government that was overthrown by the Bolsheviks in November 1917. *Photograph by the author in 1996.*

Fig. 4. Poster showing Soviet border guards. The poster says: "Glory to the border patrol soldiers. The keen guardians of the Soviet borders." At a time (1946) when there was absolutely no danger of an invasion of the Soviet Union the poster illustrates a siege mentality that existed throughout Soviet history almost to the end of its existence. *Courtesy of Hollingsworth Fine Arts.*

1921 ДА ЗДРАВСТВУЮТ НАШИ СЛАВНЫЕ ПОГРАНИЧНИКИ, ЗОРКИЕ ЧАСОВЫЕ СОВЕТСКИХ ГРАНИЦ! 1946

Fig. 5 Monument in Bolzano (Bozen in German) Italy. It was erected in the Fascist era to celebrate the Italian victory over Austria-Hungary and the annexation of the South Tyrol. Note that the columns are fasces, the Fascist symbol of power in unity. *Photograph by the author in 1972.*

Fig. 6. Stalin, the "democrat," voting in one of the Soviet Union's uncontested elections. Note that the picture is taken from a distance in order to avoid showing his pockmarked face. *Picture courtesy of the Austrian Picture Archive of the Austrian National Library.*

Fig. 7 Stalin the "congenial colleague" with his foreign minister, Vyacheslav Molotov, seated behind the desk and lamp. *Picture courtesy of the Austrian Picture Archive of the Austrian National Library.*

Fig. 8. A huge wall painting of Lenin in central Moscow. The sign says: "Long live the name and achievements of the great Lenin throughout the centuries." Note the near absence of cars on this major thoroughfare near the Kremlin. *Photograph by the author in 1980.*

Fig. 9. Mussolini, the "respectable" new prime minister of Italy, in formal attire and top hat with King Victor Emmanuel III at a public ceremony in May 1923. The relatively short Mussolini (second from the right) loved to be seen towering over the diminutive king (dressed in a military uniform). *Picture courtesy of the Austrian Picture Archive of the Austrian National Library.*

Fig. 10. Mussolini's chancellery, the Palazzo Venezia in Rome. Mussolini spoke to huge crowds from the balcony in the center of this fifteenth-century palace and it was from this balcony that he declared war against the Allies in June 1940. It now houses an art museum. *Photograph by the author in 2004.*

Fig. 11. Front page of the *Völkischer Beobachter*, the leading official newspaper of the Nazi party. Dated April 20, 1940, Hitler's fifty-first birthday, the semireligious tribute says that the German people are aware of the Führer's sacrifices for Germany. The last stanza says in part: "Therefore our love is so great, because you are the beginning and the end. We believe in you unconditionally."

Fig. 12. Hitler as the hero of German youth. Here he greets a massed assembly of Hitler Youth with his famous salute. Holding out his right arm for long periods of time was his only outstanding physical achievement. *Picture courtesy of the Austrian Picture Archive of the Austrian National Library.*

Fig. 13. The Nazi ladies' men. Hitler and his propaganda minister, Josef Goebbels, loved to be surrounded by adoring, attractive young women. *Picture courtesy of the Austrian Picture Archive of the Austrian National Library.*

Fig. 14. Soviet poster ridiculing slow workers. The caption reads: "Don't rush, Nikolai! You make your comrades look bad!" *Courtesy of Hollingsworth Fine Arts.*

Fig. 15. Soviet poster calling for more quality in consumer goods. The title reads: "Quality is our motto." *Courtesy of Hollingsworth Fine Arts.*

Fig. 16. Tile plaques in Moscow. These tiles on the outside of a Stalinist era customs house show the regime's goals to build modern weapons, industries, and transportation. *Photograph by the author in 1996.*

Fig. 17. The Boulevard of the Imperial Roman Forums in Rome. This avenue, which crosses over and between the ancient Roman forums terminating at the Coliseum in the background, was built during the Mussolini regime and was used for Fascist parades. *Photograph by the author in 1972.*

Fig. 18. Hitler "the humble man of the people" takes time from his busy schedule to have his photograph taken with a little girl. Such an image was designed to prove that Hitler was anything but proud and aloof. It was taken in Vienna shortly after the German annexation of Austria in 1938. *Picture courtesy of the Austrian National Library.*

Fig. 19. First World War American recruiting poster. It depicts a German soldier as a subhuman who had just ravished Europe and is about to step onto U.S. shores. Hitler professed admiration in *Mein Kampf* for such propaganda and used it as a model for Nazi propaganda.

Fig. 20. Soviet poster (1946) which says: "Our country must become the most educated and cultured in the world." *Courtesy of Hollingsworth Fine Arts.*

Fig. 21. Dachau concentration camp near Munich, the first "permanent" concentration camp in Nazi Germany. Note the elaborate means of confining the prisoners. *Photograph by the author in 1969.*

Fig. 22. The entrance to the Auschwitz concentration camp, now in southwestern Poland. The sign over the entrance says "Work will make you free." All Nazi camps used this slogan which predated the Nazi era. *Photograph by the author in 1996.*

Fig. 23. Identification insignia for Nazi concentration camp prisoners at the Mauthausen camp near Linz, Austria. The horizontal bar shows the five major categories of prisoners: political, professional criminals, emigrants, Jehovah's Witnesses, homosexuals, and asocials. Subcategories in the vertical bar are backsliders, prisoners of punishment companies, Jews, and special categories. The prisoners wore these identification patches so guards could instantly identify them. *Photograph by the author in 1988.*

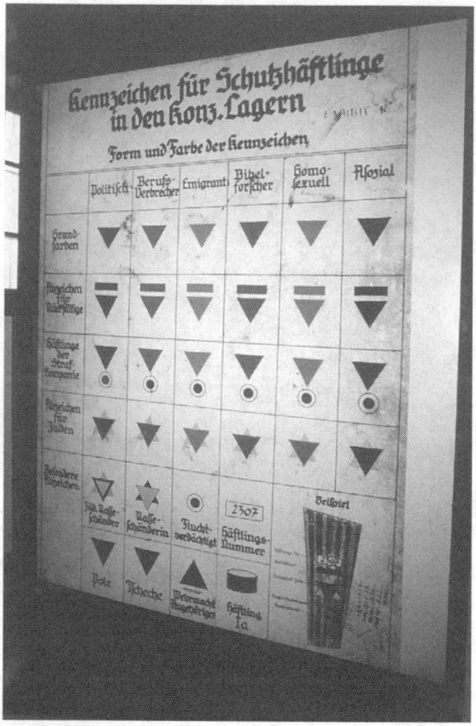

Fig. 24. Ruins of the New Synagogue in central Berlin. It was one of the hundreds of Jewish synagogues and temples that were set on fire by the Nazis during Kristallnacht in November 1938. It was also the only one that was saved from destruction by a German firefighter. Ironically it was gutted by Allied bombers during the Second World War. Since the reunification of Germany it has been partially restored and serves both as a museum and as a functioning synagogue. *Photograph by the author in 1969.*

Fig. 25. The fascist partners. Mussolini and Hitler on parade during the Duce's official state visit to Germany in 1937. The visit impressed Mussolini and helped cement friendly relations between the two fascist countries which had been greatly improved during the Ethiopian war. *Picture Archive of the Austrian National Library.*

Fig. 26. Front page of the *Völkischer Beobachter*, the leading official newspaper of the Nazi party. Dated September 19, 1938, its headlines read: "Mussolini: Plebiscite! Prague threatens Europe with war." Smaller headlines say: "The Duce in Trieste: 'Italy's place in case of a conflict has already been decided.'" "The government newspaper in Prague: We are strong enough to drag all of Europe into war." The cartoon depicts Czechoslovak soldiers executing defenseless Sudeten Germans. A spirit rises from the corpses holding a Nazi flag.

Fig. 27. Painting of the Allied evacuation of Dunkirk in May 1940 in the British War Museum, London.

Fig. 28. Illustration of the arrival of Soviet Prisoners of War in the Buchenwald Concentration Camp. When this picture was taken the camp was located in Communist East Germany (the German Democratic Republic). This glass illustration was a reasonably accurate representation, but it was also designed to evoke sympathy for the big Communist brother of East Germany, the Soviet Union. The Soviet prisoners of war arrived exhausted and emaciated after having marched hundreds of kilometers and usually survived only a few weeks after reaching the camp. There were twenty main concentration camps in Germany by 1944 and 165 subcamps which held millions of "racial inferiors" and POWs. *Photograph by the author in 1969.*

Fig. 29. A World War II monument in Yaroslav, Russia. The slab on the left says: "Honors to the heroes of the war." The slab on the right reads: "Honors to the workers." Monuments such as these along with many motion pictures kept the memory of the war alive and helped buttress the legitimacy of the regime. *Photograph by the author in 1996.*

Fig. 30. The "Wall" dividing East and West Berlin. Note that there were actually three walls. In the center there were 300 hundred guard towers with machine guns, land mines, and lamps. Five thousand East Germans managed to escape, but hundreds died trying to cross this 100-yard no-man's land to reach West Berlin in the background. *Photograph by the author in 1969.*

Fig. 31. The face of the new Russia. A McDonald's restaurant in Moscow. *Photograph by the author in 1996.*

Fig. 32. Campaign poster in Moscow following the fall of Communism. Note the emphasis on a poor old woman and the church in the background, subjects that would have been inconceivable in the Soviet period. *Photograph by the author in 1996.*

# 8 / THE ERA OF TRADITIONAL DIPLOMACY AND WAR, 1933–1941

The same mixture of traditional and totalitarian tactics and goals found in the domestic policies of the totalitarian states can be found in their diplomatic and even their military policies during the 1930s and the early stages of World War II. None of the dictators, moreover, was particularly secretive about his goals, All three of them had delineated at least the outlines of their foreign policy ambitions—for anyone who chose to take them literally, which only a few shrewd diplomats did—in numerous prewar speeches and publications. Mussolini wanted a new Roman empire in and near the Mediterranean—which he would populate with a rapidly growing population—and constantly glorified war. Hitler laid down the outlines of his foreign policy in *Mein Kampf,* in which he stated his desire to make Germany a world power through the conquest of at least large parts of the Soviet Union. To ensure success he would form an alliance with Italy and avoid a conflict with Britain. Stalin wanted to extend Russian influence deep into Europe and if possible have a ring of satellite states that would obey his every command. He also favored the expansion of the Communist ideology and Communist movements abroad provided the ideology remained orthodox (in his view) and the movements remained dutifully subordinate to his commands.

Nevertheless, the actual tactics pursued by the totalitarian dictators for a long time remained relatively traditional and restrained, thus fooling many people, both at home and abroad, into thinking that the dictators had only limited and fairly reasonable ambitions. The restraint turned out to be temporary and resulted not from the modification of long-range objectives, but from the realization by the dictators themselves that their countries were simply too weak either industrially or militarily or both to make aggressive actions a realistic possibility during most of the 1930s. Ironically, as long as they followed policies of self-restraint they enjoyed substantial and sometimes even spectacular success. As soon as they felt strong enough to pursue their doctrinaire totalitarian goals, they were headed for disaster. This outcome was apparent almost immediately in the case of Italy. It took a few years to unfold in Germany, and over four decades to do so in the Soviet Union.

## HITLER'S FOREIGN POLICY STRATEGY

The catastrophic end to the Third Reich should not blind us to the fact that Hitler was at least superficially successful as a diplomat throughout most of the 1930s. Like any good diplomat, he knew how to make a virtue out of a necessity. When he came to power in 1933, Germany still had little more than the 100,000-man army it had been allowed to maintain by the Treaty of Versailles. It had no air force at all and next to no navy. Its western territories near and west of the Rhine were permanently demilitarized: Germany was not allowed to station any troops in these territories nor build any fortifications, thus leaving the country exposed to an invasion by France. Even Poland and Czechoslovakia had stronger military establishments than Germany for the first several years of Hitler's rule. Under these circumstances, Hitler had no reasonable choice but to proclaim his love of peace. By so doing he weakened efforts by foreign statesmen to unite against him.

Historians were slow to begin debating Hitler's foreign and military goals. Until 1960, it was widely assumed that the Nuremberg Trials and Hitler's own statements in *Mein Kampf* had settled the issue once and for all: Hitler had laid everything out in his book in the middle 1920s and then simply followed his own preconceived policy. This view was challenged in 1961 by the British historian A. J. P. Taylor. Taylor argued that Hitler had no such blueprint and simply took advantage of opportunities as they came along. This benign view of the Führer at first evoked a furious response from nearly all professional historians. In time, however, historians have conceded that there was indeed much opportunism in Hitler's tactics and that *Mein Kampf* was far more an outline of Hitler's future foreign policy than it was a detailed blueprint.

Almost no historians, however, have agreed with Taylor that Hitler had no long-range plans that would inevitably lead to war and that the outbreak of war in 1939 was nothing more than an unfortunate accident. Most historians still believe that Hitler had no intention of pursuing a peaceful policy any longer than he absolutely had to. As he himself acknowledged in *Mein Kampf:* "We must clearly recognize the fact that the recovery of lost territories is not won through solemn appeals to the Lord or through pious hopes in a League of Nations, but only by *force of arms.*"[1]

Historians do still hotly debate Hitler's *ultimate* objectives. No one believes that he merely wanted to restore Germany's boundaries of 1914. Hitler himself showed contempt for such an idea, arguing that those boundaries had already become inadequate to feed Germany's prewar population. Hitler thought that the mere annexation of nearby German-speaking territories would not solve Germany's economic problems, even though he pretended otherwise in the late 1930s. The real debate occurs on what Hitler wanted to do *after* he had annexed the territories of ethnic Germans. It is generally agreed that he also sought Ukraine because of its fertile soil and fairly moderate climate. But what was to become of Poland, which stood between Germany and Ukraine? Was it to be conquered and annexed or turned into a satellite? Hitler remained silent on the issue in *Mein Kampf*. And would even the annexation of Ukraine have satisfied Hitler? After he conquered it in 1941–42, he began dreaming of still broader conquests, African colonies, and an eventual showdown with the United States, perhaps in his lifetime, perhaps not until the next generation.

It is probably safe to say that Hitler would have continued Germany's expansionist policy for as long as he could. His model was the nineteenth-century United States, with the Slavs of the Soviet Union playing the role of the American Indians. The Soviet people would be brutally conquered. The racially valuable survivors would be Germanized and the remainder would either be killed or put on Indian-style reservations where they would be closely guarded by SS men carrying a metaphorical rifle in one hand and spade (for farming) in the other.

Leaving aside the unimaginable savagery of such a negative utopia, Hitler's dream shows that, as in so many other aspects of life, he had not adjusted to the realities of the twentieth century. Like members of the pre–World War I generation, he defined power in terms of natural resources and agriculturally usable land; he had no confidence in

1 Adolf Hitler, *Mein Kampf* (Boston, 1943), 627.

Germany's ability to raise its agricultural productivity. If those criteria were valid, however, China, India, and Russia should have been the strongest countries in the world. Hitler also ignored the fact that since the Industrial Revolution a nation's prosperity and power depended primarily on the state of its technology. Therefore, the very premises of Hitler's diplomatic and foreign policies were invalid.

Hitler did not simply bide his time between 1933 and the beginning of his more aggressive moves in 1938 any more than he wasted the late 1920s when the Nazi party was too weak to seize power. He immediately began to rearm Germany, although not as rapidly as was once commonly supposed. He also carried out a steady verbal assault on the Soviet Union. Both policies enjoyed widespread support at home and the second also elicited considerable support from abroad, particularly with conservatives in Britain and the United States. Rearmament helped solve Germany's unemployment problem; big industry and the armed forces were especially enthusiastic.

The timing of Hitler's accession to power was as fortuitous diplomatically as it was economically. As mentioned, he had come to power about six months after Germany began to recover from the Depression, but it was he who received all the credit. Much the same was true in diplomacy. Germany's foreign minister from 1923 to 1929, Gustav Stresemann had already won a number of important concessions for Germany. Reparation payments were sharply scaled back in 1924 and again in 1929. The Locarno Pact of 1925 prohibited a unilateral French invasion of Germany and allowed the Reich to join the League of Nations the next year. The Young Plan, signed just before Stresemann's death in October 1929, arranged for the withdrawal of French and Belgian troops from the Rhineland the following year, five years ahead of the schedule established by the Treaty of Versailles. In 1932, U.S. President Herbert Hoover proclaimed a moratorium on German reparations and Allied war debts. These were all substantial gains for Germany. They were also within the context of international law and usually resulted from negotiations, never from German threats or unilateral faits accomplis. Stresemann had gone far in reestablishing Germany's good name and in creating a kind of treasury of good will. It was Hitler, however, not the democratic Weimar Republic, who made withdrawals from this account.

Hitler also benefited from the historical debate that raged over the Treaty of Versailles in the decade and a half following its signing.

Many historians in Britain and the United States, though not France, had concluded that Germany had been treated too harshly in the treaty. Hitler himself, in countless speeches, pointed out how the World War I victors had violated their own principle of self-determination. Whereas that right had been granted to Poles, Czechs, Rumanians, Lithuanians, and several other European nationalities, it had been denied to the Germans. Germany wanted nothing more than to claim the same right for the roughly 12 million German-speaking people who lived just beyond its new borders. This was a powerful argument for which there were no easy rebuttals based strictly on moral grounds.

The whole Paris Peace Settlement, of which the Treaty of Versailles with Germany was just one part, had been an uneasy compromise between idealism and power politics. A number of new nation-states had been established between Germany and Russia, and between Finland and Yugoslavia. However, the Allies, especially France, had enabled potential friends of the West, such as Poland, Czechoslovakia, Rumania, and Yugoslavia, to gain disputed territories at the expense of Germany and its World War I partners: Austria, Hungary, and Bulgaria. On the other hand, Germany had been left united, was only partially and temporarily occupied by Allied soldiers, and, with 62 million people, was still the second-most populous European country after the Soviet Union. Its industries emerged from the war unscathed, making it the strongest industrial power in Europe.

Not only did Germany remain a potentially powerful country, but it also faced neighbors unable to agree on a common policy toward the Reich. France, Poland, and Czechoslovakia, all beneficiaries of the peace settlement, did not want to make any concessions to Germany. Britain, not being an immediate neighbor, having annexed no German territory, and still feeling relatively safe behind the English Channel—especially now that the German navy was at the bottom of the North Sea—was much more conciliatory. Hitler was masterful at playing these four states off against each other.

As already observed, Hitler was scornful in *Mein Kampf* about restoring Germany's boundaries of 1914. Nevertheless, for many years he posed as a traditional nationalist who merely wanted to revise the Treaty of Versailles. Once Germany's demands for sovereignty and self-determination had been met, Germany would become a bastion of peace and stability and a bulwark against the spread of Communism. Privately, however, he told his senior military officers as early as

February 3, 1933, that Germany's foreign policy had to be aimed at conquering Lebensraum in the east, the population of which would then have to be "ruthlessly Germanized."

## HITLER AS "PEACE LOVER," 1933–1935

Hitler's most brilliant diplomatic moves were probably those that came early in his chancellorship rather than those of the late 1930s as is usually asserted. In May 1933, Germany extended the Treaty of Berlin, a treaty of friendship and neutrality with Russia, which had first been signed by the Weimar Republic in 1926. Two months later, the Concordat with the Papacy, mentioned in Chapter 6, was signed. Still more astonishing was a nonaggression pact with Poland signed in January 1934. The latter, which was in response to a Polish initiative, was a particularly daring stroke because it appeared to contradict the opinion of anti-German nationalists in Poland and France who claimed that Hitler had aggressive intentions and would tear up Versailles and reannex lost German lands in the east at the first opportunity. The pact was all the more surprising and impressive because Hitler had to overcome a great deal of domestic opposition to conclude any deal with Poland, which had acquired far more German territory than any of the other neighbors of the Third Reich. In reality, Hitler got something for nothing. Germany was too weak to attack Poland in 1934 under any circumstances. More important, the pact contradicted the spirit if not the letter of a Franco-Polish alliance that had been concluded in 1921. It also seemed to prove to the world that Hitler was a man of peace, just as his propaganda claimed.

Meanwhile, Germany had withdrawn in October 1933 from a disarmament conference that had begun in Geneva, Switzerland, the preceding year, fearing that the proposed supervision of disarmament would reveal its secret rearmament program. Simultaneously it withdrew from the League of Nations, an organization that Germans had long viewed, with some justification, as a tool of its former enemies. The withdrawal from the conference was actually due more to the German Defense and Foreign Ministries than it was to Hitler, who tended to be more cautious. But the Führer turned what could have been a public relations disaster into a triumph by pointing out that the Treaty of Versailles had stipulated that the disarmament of Germany was to be the beginning of a general disarmament, something which had never formally taken place. (In reality, however, the British and French had drastically cut their armed forces in the late twenties and early thirties.) All he asked for, Hitler claimed, was to be treated equitably. As for the League, it had repeatedly ignored Germany's complaints about the treatment of ethnic Germans in Poland.

Hitler grew bolder in March 1935, when on the 9th he suddenly announced the existence of a German air force, which Britain and France had already suspected and did not protest. He furthermore claimed that it was already as large as the British Royal Air Force (RAF), a total falsehood. A week later, he used a French decision to double the length of its terms of military service—to compensate for France's very low birth rate—as a pretext to announce universal conscription and his intention to build a 550,000-man army. The British, French, and Italian governments all solemnly protested these moves when they met in the Italian resort city of Stresa in April, but they took no concrete countermeasures. The French did conclude an alliance with Russia on May 2, but it was hardly worth the paper it was written on because it was not followed by any conversations between the two military establishments. Moreover, the two countries could aid each other only after taking their complaint to the League of Nations. Hitler used the alliance to claim that the French had "sold out to the Bolsheviks."

To restore his reputation as a man of peace, Hitler agreed to an Anglo-German Naval Agreement in June 1935. The Agreement theoretically limited the size of the German navy to 35 percent of the combined navies of the British Commonwealth. However, if threatened by the Soviet Union, Germany could have 100 percent as many submarines as the British. Once again, Hitler had made a virtue of necessity. As Winston Churchill, the future British prime minister later pointed out, the treaty actually did not limit Germany in any way. Even if it had built ships day and night, it would not have reached the 35 percent limit until 1942, at which time it could have torn up the Agreement. In the short run, the most important consequence was that Anglo-French relations were soured because the French had not been consulted. Hitler looked reasonable and peace loving and the British looked selfish. The Agreement also encouraged Hitler to think that he could count on the acquiescence of Britain for his ultimate goal of attacking the Soviet Union.

## FROM ETHIOPIA TO SPAIN:
## FASCIST ITALY AT WAR

It is easy to forget, in light of what happened later, that in 1935 Hitler's diplomacy seemed almost pacifistic compared to that of his fascist counterpart, Benito Mussolini. Just four months after Hitler had agreed to limit the size of the German navy, the Italian army invaded Ethiopia, a member of the League of Nations.

With some minor deviations, Mussolini's early foreign policy had actually been quite cautious. An exception was his coercing Yugoslavia to surrender to Italy the Adriatic port city of Fiume (Rijeka). Unlike Hitler, he had come to power before he had been able to enunciate his foreign policy goals. Consequently, for several years he depended heavily on the advice of his professional diplomats. Moreover, in the past, Italy's foreign policy had enjoyed its greatest success when there had been a European balance of power. No such balance existed in the first decade of Mussolini's rule. Great Britain, on whom Italy depended for much of its coal, controlled the Mediterranean Sea with its navy, and France's army and allies made it dominant on the Continent. Hitler's ascendance to power offered Mussolini an opportunity to exploit a new balance of power, but also entailed the risk that Italy could be confronted with a dangerous new neighbor should Hitler succeed in annexing German-speaking Austria.

Motivations are always difficult for historians to decipher, and the Ethiopian War is no exception. It appears, however, that the Fascist revolution was growing stale by the mid-1930s. There was little else that Mussolini could do domestically without alienating one of the major conservative groups supporting him. Italy was also significantly slower to recover from the Great Depression than either Germany or Britain. A war against Ethiopia would solve several problems at once. It would divert attention from the economy, avenge Italian defeats at the hands of the Ethiopians in 1889 and 1896, and bring glory to Italy (and especially to Mussolini). All this would be accomplished by establishing an empire in Africa, and theoretically provide an outlet for Italy's excess population, which, because of immigration restrictions, was no longer able to emigrate to the United States in large numbers.

Historians are divided as to whether to describe the Ethiopian War as a milestone on Italy's road to becoming a full-fledged totalitarian state or whether it was merely an old-fashioned colonial war, not unlike those fought by other European powers in the late nineteenth century. A good argument can be made for either case. Mussolini made no attempt to disguise his desire to gain a colony and ridiculed as hypocritical the opposition of the British and French, peoples that had acquired so many colonies themselves by force.

Yet there were elements to this war that were different from the colonial wars. Mussolini did not bother to consult with anyone except the king before starting the war. He exploited every propaganda outlet to make the war popular with the Italian people—and succeeded. (Italian-Americans were equally enthusiastic. Tens of thousands of them attended rallies in support of the war and Italian-American women contributed their gold wedding rings to the cause. Support for Fascist Italy in the Italian-American press, unlike the German-American press, remained strong almost until Pearl Harbor.) The Catholic Church shared in the prowar enthusiasm by blessing departing troops. Cardinal Shuster drew a favorable comparison between the war and the Crusades. The pope celebrated the occupation of the Ethiopian capital, Addis Ababa, as the "triumph of a great and good people."[2] Mussolini boasted how Italy had overcome sanctions imposed by the fifty-member League of Nations that had outraged the Italian public. The brutal treatment of the Ethiopians both during and after the conquest foreshadowed, on a very small scale, the Nazi treatment of the Soviet people during the Russian campaign. Ethiopia's first generation of schoolteachers was slaughtered in order to prevent the emergence of an educated native elite. Other prominent citizens were shot after surrendering and being promised a pardon. Poison gas was used against both soldiers and civilians as well as hospitals marked with the Red Cross.

For Mussolini personally, the war was both the high point in his career and the beginning of his downfall. Historians who argue that Mussolini built a consensus for Fascism—a controversial issue especially in Italy—find the popularity of this war to be convincing evidence. The war undoubtedly brought his popularity at home to new heights. He had, for a time, become the leading personality of world politics. However, it also gave him a grotesquely overblown sense of grandeur. If he could withstand the efforts of Britain, France, and the remainder of the League of Nations to block his conquest, there

2 Quoted in Tracy Koon, *Believe, Obey, Fight: Political Socialization of Youth in Fascist Italy, 1922–1943* (Chapel Hill, NC, 1985), 138.

seemed to be no limit to the triumphs that lay before him. When his generals tried to prevent him from intervening in World War II, he took great pleasure in reminding them of their earlier unfounded timidity over the Ethiopian campaign.

However, the war in Ethiopia, which took longer than expected, far from being a boost to the Italian economy, cost a year's revenue. It drained Italy's meager military and industrial resources. The official end of the war in May 1936 was followed by guerrilla warfare until Italy lost the colony in 1941. Italian military strength, compared to that of the other great powers, peaked in 1935. Thereafter it declined both relatively and absolutely.

Moreover, Italy's recently enhanced influence depended on a balance of power between Germany on the one hand, and Britain and France on the other. The Ethiopian War had alienated the West, albeit not necessarily indefinitely, and caused increasing Italian dependence on Germany, which had not joined the League in imposing sanctions. Hence, it was the real beginning of the German-Italian "Axis," which prevented Italy from continuing its balancing act.

In the middle of the Ethiopian War, and with the West still angry over Mussolini's naked aggression, Hitler decided to move German troops into the demilitarized Rhineland. Even though there were many indications of an impending action, the French had no plans for a military response. They grossly overestimated German strength and feared that a counterattack would spark a major war in which France would be isolated. The cautious and nervous Hitler initially sent only 30,000 troops into the Rhineland, of which just 3,000 soldiers ventured west of the Rhine, not the 295,000 estimated by French intelligence.

The consequences of the remilitarization have been fiercely debated by historians. Some have noted that it changed nothing since the French had long since abandoned the idea of invading the territory to counter any German offensive move. This is true but far too simplistic in the opinion of other scholars. French inaction, though planned, was nevertheless demoralizing to the French people themselves. France's eastern allies also began to have serious doubts about their partner to the West. Most ominous of all, Belgium, disgusted by France's passivity even when German troops approached its border, dropped out of the French alliance system and declared its neutrality. Hitler had also taken the first step in ensuring the security of Germany's western frontier, which was a prerequisite for an invasion of Russia.

For Hitler personally, the remilitarization of the Rhineland had consequences not unlike those of the Ethiopian War for Mussolini. For the first, but not the last time in his diplomatic career, he had taken an enormous gamble and won. Instead of using diplomacy—which had an excellent chance of success—and enhancing his stature as a statesman, he had used force, and did so against the advice of his senior military officials. Although he did not yet have the contempt for his advisors he would eventually develop, he loved to refer back to this episode in later years as a classic example of his superior judgment. He now made the first big withdrawal from the goodwill account established by Gustav Stresemann. The Western Powers acquiesced in his actions thus granting Hitler a huge diplomatic victory they had denied the democratic Weimar Republic. Hitler's victory was not cost free, however. The West resented the German dictator's unilateral action and began to rearm. British armament expenditures in 1936 were two-thirds higher than those of 1934 although still only one-half the size of Germany's.

Only four months after the Rhineland crisis, the world's attention was drawn away from Germany once again, this time to Spain. In July, General Francisco Franco took over the leadership of a conservative-monarchist rebellion against the left-of-center, republican government of Spain. Mussolini eagerly intervened on Franco's side in the ensuing civil war even though Italian troops were still heavily engaged in Ethiopia. Mussolini's motivations for this intervention, which eventually resulted in his committing some 72,000 troops and 5,000 officers, are, again, not easy to fathom but were probably influenced by the following considerations. He may have been overreacting to the recent successes of leftist governments in France and Spain, and he was probably concerned about Soviet aid to the Spanish Republic. His Germanophile foreign minister and son-in-law, Count Galeazzo Ciano, helped convince him that Franco would win easily and that support for Franco would cement a close relationship between Italy and Germany, which also supported Franco. Indeed, it was during the civil war that the "Axis" alliance was cemented. Finally, although Mussolini was not trying to turn Spain into a fascist state, he probably thought that a nationalist, right-wing government in the western Mediterranean would one day help Italy expand its interests at the expense of the liberal democracies. If so, however, he received no such promises in exchange for his very considerable assistance to Franco's cause.

In the end, the Spanish Civil War simply intensified the unfavorable trends already begun in Ethiopia. By the time the war ended in March 1939, Italy had lost 4,000 men, over 700 airplanes, and 9 million rounds of ammunition, which it was unable to replace. It was now more heavily committed to Germany, which had also intervened in Spain, but on a much smaller scale. Only a partnership with Germany offered Italy the prospect of realizing its imperialistic goals. (See figure 25.) The Western Powers, who opposed those very ambitions, were more alienated than ever and largely lost interest in trying to woo Italy back into their camp. Finally, in one major way the Spanish intervention differed from Ethiopia: it was not popular with the Italian people. If, in fact, Mussolini had previously established a consensus, it now began to crumble. Hitler, in the meantime, gained combat experience for the 16,000 pilots and technicians he had sent to Spain, and he quietly continued Germany's rearmament while the world's attention remained riveted on the Iberian peninsula.

## *AUSTRIA AND CZECHOSLOVAKIA: HITLER'S FIRST CONQUESTS*

Although the Spanish Civil War was at its height in 1937, the year was otherwise uneventful diplomatically. Hitler attempted no new faits accomplis and even the persecution of German Jews had not yet entered its most violent phase. Apart from Spain, the only ominous event occurred secretly, and its significance is still disputed by historians. This incident was the "Hossbach Conference," a meeting between Hitler and his senior diplomatic and military advisors, which has been named for the officer who took notes. During the meeting, Hitler, citing Germany's alleged need for Lebensraum, outlined several opportunities for German expansion. At the Nuremberg Trials in 1946 the conference was described by Allied prosecutors as a "blueprint for war." This assessment is at best an exaggeration, since events did not follow the outline Hitler suggested at the meeting. In it he did, however, specifically mention Austria and Czechoslovakia as two early targets for expansion. He also ridded himself the following February of his conservative foreign minister, Konstantin von Neurath, and

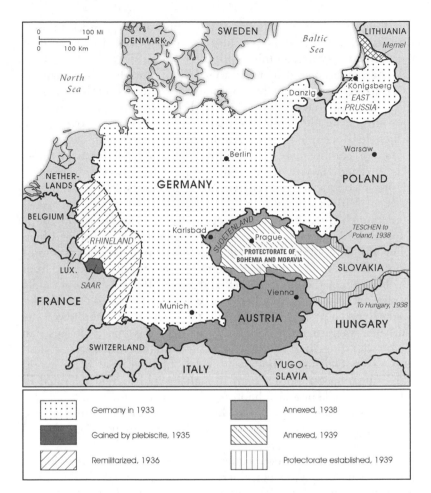

## The Expansion of German Territory and Power, 1935–1939

This map illustrates the enormous success of Hitler's foreign policy between the return of the Saar territory to Germany in 1935 and the recovery of the Memel region from Lithuania in March 1939. Without the loss of a single soldier Hitler regained full sovereignty over the previously demilitarized Rhineland and added more than 11 million people to Nazi Germany's population, along with many valuable natural resources such as coal in northern Bohemia and iron ore in Austria, both crucial in wartime.

the military leaders who opposed his plans and surrounded himself instead with adventurers, gamblers, and ideologues like himself. It strains credulity that all this happened by coincidence.

The conference also shows that Hitler now thought Germany was strong enough that he no longer needed to exercise the kind of restraint he had hitherto displayed. He was also prepared to go beyond the simple removal of restrictions on German sovereignty, which had occupied his attention up to now, and implement his policy of gaining Lebensraum through the use or threat of force. The dramatic nature of this shift was masked, however, by Hitler's desire to conquer at first only German-speaking territory under the guise of self-determination.

Although Hitler mentioned Czechoslovakia as his first victim in the Hossbach Conference, it was actually Austria that he invaded first. The Alpine republic was an ideal target. Its population was almost purely German speaking, its economy had never fully recovered from the breakup of the multinational Habsburg Monarchy into mutually hostile nation-states, and it had a large and militant Nazi party. Hitler had learned a painful lesson in July 1934, when he had allowed the Austrian Nazis so much autonomy that they assassinated the Austrian chancellor, Engelbert Dollfuss, in a failed attempt to seize power and unite with Germany. Hitler was widely blamed around the world for instigating the putsch even though he had merely tolerated it. Thereafter he kept a firm hand not only on Austrian Nazis, but also on Nazis in such places as Czechoslovakia, Danzig, Lithuania, and Denmark, all of whom wanted their ethnic Germans to be annexed by Germany.

By March 1938, however, Hitler thought that restraint was no longer necessary in Austria and permitted local Nazis, especially in the southeastern province of Styria, to operate at will. In a desperate attempt to regain control of the situation, the Austrian Chancellor, Kurt von Schuschnigg, on March 9, called for a plebiscite on continued Austrian independence. To deny the Austrian Nazis a chance to campaign, the plebiscite was to be held only four days later. Fearing, with some justification, a rigged outcome, and claiming that Communists were threatening to take over Austria which was certainly not true, Hitler unleashed the German army. With an army of only 22,000 and abandoned by Mussolini, who had previously posed as the defender of Austrian independence, Austria offered no resistance and was quickly annexed.

In many ways Hitler's takeover of Austria resembled his reoccupation of the Rhineland. Both actions took place without prior negotiations and through the use of force. In both cases the Western Powers lodged formal protests in Berlin and Geneva (the latter being the headquarters of the League of Nations) but took no military counteractions. In both cases Hitler got what he wanted and Germany's strategic situation was improved. In both cases Hitler's popularity at home soared to new heights but his international standing declined. After both episodes the West decided to speed up its rearmament. One difference was that the Austrian annexation was improvised even though it was part of Hitler's strategic goals. Mussolini's response was also decidedly different. The annexation was a personal humiliation for the Duce even though he tried to be as gracious toward Hitler as possible. He had now lost the buffer between Italy and Germany and was more easily influenced by German pressure. Interestingly enough, Mussolini was able to regain some of his lost prestige both at home and abroad by serving as a peacemaker, not a warmonger, during the next diplomatic crisis.

That crisis, the biggest of the prewar era, and the one that brought Europe closest to war, involved well over 3 million German-speaking people of Czechoslovakia, who lived mostly along the borders of the country in a region the Nazis called the Sudetenland. These people had been awarded to the new Czechoslovak state at the Paris Peace Conference mostly to prevent the enlargement of Germany. The arguments advanced at the time to assign them to the Czechs were weak and contradictory. The Czechs sought to maintain the historic and geographic unity of the Bohemian crownlands that became the western part of Czechoslovakia, but they ignored history and geography when claiming the Slovaks who had been part of northern Hungary for a thousand years. Even economic arguments were questionable because the Sudetenland contained beer-, lace-, and glass-making industries, for which the Czechoslovak market was inadequate, whereas the more important steel industry was entirely within Czech-speaking areas.

All of these factors made it difficult either for the Czech government or for the West to use moral arguments when Hitler staked his claim to the Sudetenland on the basis of national self-determination. Had a European war broken out over the Sudetenland, the British and French governments would have been asking their soldiers to attack Germany—the only way the Third Reich could have been defeated—in order to prevent German-speaking people from uniting in one country. Throughout history, fear of negative public opinion has made most statesmen reluctant to bring their countries into war when they have not been attacked or when the issues are not clear. Complicating the problem for the West was the opposition of the British dominions (except for New Zealand) to war. French conservatives were also against war fearing that a German defeat would lead to the spread of Communism. Moreover, difficult as it is to remember in the early twenty-first century, Britain and France had been far more concerned about defending their worldwide empires since the end of World War I than they were about a revived German threat. Finally, the pursuit of national self-interest and balance-of-power politics, policies discredited by the World War, were still widely regarded as immoral, especially in Great Britain.

Although there were some legitimate or at least understandable reasons why the West hesitated to go to war against Germany in the fall of 1938, their actions are not immune from criticism. Not until September 16—less than two weeks before the Munich conference—did a British official think it was worthwhile to examine the implication of a peaceful German annexation of Czechoslovakia. Both British and French military "experts" wildly overestimated German strength while ignoring the value of the 750,000-man Czech army. The British worried about German bombing of British cities when no such possibility as yet existed. The reports simply made it easier for the British prime minister, Neville Chamberlain, to persuade his cabinet to abandon Czechoslovakia.

Nevertheless, at the end of September war seemed imminent over the relatively trivial issue of the timing of the occupation of the Sudeten districts. To head off the impending crisis, Chamberlain asked Mussolini to persuade Hitler to attend a four-power conference in Germany to partition Czechoslovakia. Mussolini was happy to oblige because he was painfully aware that Italy was not prepared to engage in still another war. (See figure 26.) The ensuing Munich conference on September 29–30 made everyone except the Czechs at least temporarily happy. Mussolini became a hero at home and abroad because he had helped prevent a war—not exactly the epitome of the Fascist ideology. The British and French as well as most Germans were relieved that they did not have to go to war over an unpopular issue. The Soviet Union, in the midst of its military purge, did not have to fulfill its treaty obligations to Czechoslovakia (although we know now that it had no intention of doing so unless the West also intervened). Hitler had once again proven his generals wrong because they had predicted that the West would go to war to defend Czechoslovakia. His popularity at home now rose to unprecedented heights.

Hitler had scored still another diplomatic victory, however, precisely because he had achieved a traditional and limited goal, annexation of the predominantly German-speaking Sudetenland, and he had obtained it without having to fire a shot. The Sudetenland was a region coveted not just by Nazis but by virtually all Germans as well, and his justification for the annexation, national "self-determination," was a concept first enunciated by the Allies, not the Nazis. Hitler had even submitted to negotiations at Munich. Had he been willing to stop his expansionism at this point, there is no doubt that he could have kept his recent gains.

Spectacular as Hitler's triumph was, it was not an unqualified success. Far from bluffing, as some post-Munich critics have suggested, Hitler was in fact angry that Czech concessions had deprived him of an easy military victory. More important, he had now exhausted the tolerance of the West. Chamberlain promised to guarantee the sovereignty of what was left of Czechoslovakia, the first such British commitment to a Central European state since 1756. After their initial feelings of relief, the British and French eventually stepped up their rearmament. Actually, British rearmament came in response to a public demand, and Chamberlain saw to it that rearmament was minimal. The British army envisioned in February 1939 was to be no larger than the Czech army sacrificed at Munich. When Kristallnacht occurred only six weeks after the Munich conference, Nazi Germany could no longer be considered a normal, albeit authoritarian, state. British and French public opinion now underwent a sea change. Germany was seen as a threat to world peace. The outcome at Munich was also dangerous for Hitler because it caused him to conclude that Chamberlain and the French premier, Edouard Daladier, were cowards who would back down when confronted by the threat of force. Furthermore, it convinced him that his own generals were weaklings whose advice could safely be ignored.

## THE APPROACH OF WAR

The real turning point in Hitler's foreign policy occurred in March 1939. Up to then he had focused first on removing those clauses of the Treaty of Versailles that restricted German sovereignty on military issues, and second on exploiting the principle of self-determination to annex nearby German-speaking areas. These goals, which were neither exclusively Nazi nor totalitarian, assured him a maximum of domestic support and a minimum of foreign opposition. By the end of 1938, however, these objectives had been almost completely fulfilled. Any new expansionism was likely to violate the principles he had been outwardly following and would unify his foreign opponents.

Such a step Hitler took in March 1939, when he ordered what has euphemistically been called the "occupation of Prague" but which in reality was the occupation of all the Czech-speaking areas of what was left of Czechoslovakia. The Führer, of course, had his pretexts. One was that the quarter of a million Germans remaining in Czechoslovakia after Munich had allegedly been mistreated. Besides, Bohemia and Moravia had belonged to the Holy Roman Empire and the Germanic Confederation and were therefore part of Germany's cultural sphere. This time, however, even the optimists and wishful thinkers in the West were not fooled by lame excuses, and many Germans were also unenthusiastic about this new acquisition. When the occupation of Prague was followed eight days later by the occupation of the Memelland, a district with a 60 percent German-speaking majority annexed by Lithuania after World War I, what was left of the British policy of appeasement was all but dead.

Hitler had not entirely abandoned traditional diplomacy—faits accomplis were hardly unprecedented in 1939—but he had abandoned his former high moral ground in favor of virtually undisguised aggression. His earlier diplomatic triumphs, though sometimes resented, had not precluded still more. Prague did exactly that. If Hitler had concluded after Munich that Chamberlain and Daladier were cowards, the Western leaders as well as most of their people now regarded Hitler as a liar, someone who certainly could not be trusted to uphold any further agreements. Chamberlain unilaterally offered to "guarantee" the independence of numerous Eastern European countries including Poland, and both Western powers once more greatly accelerated their rearmament programs; in April, Chamberlain, again bowing to British public opinion, introduced the first peacetime conscription law in its history. The road to World War II had been paved.

The seriousness of Hitler's miscalculation became obvious at the end of the last prewar diplomatic crisis, involving the Free City of Danzig. The city of 400,000 was 90 percent German speaking but had been severed from Germany in order to assure Poland free access to the Baltic Sea. Hitler wanted the city returned to German rule, along with a strip of land across the Polish Corridor, to permit the building of a railroad and an autobahn. Ironically, the demand was much less significant in terms of territory, population, and the balance of power than the annexation of Austria or the Sudetenland, and equally justifiable on the grounds of self-determination. Moreover, Poland was an authoritarian state with a strong anti-Semitic tradition and armed forces far weaker than those of Czechoslovakia were a year earlier. This time, however, the Western democracies had no confidence that Hitler's demand would be his last, and would not be followed by something far less reasonable. Besides, Chamberlain had already issued his guarantee to Poland, thus making the Polish government much less willing to negotiate.

Hitler thought he could intimidate the West into surrendering Poland by concluding a nonaggression pact with the Soviet Union. And the world was indeed astonished when the German government suddenly announced the signing of such a pact on August 23, following secret German-Russian negotiations. Historians have excoriated both the British for not concluding an alliance of their own with Russia, and Stalin for signing the agreement with Hitler. Actually, the actions of both the British and Stalin were rational based on what they knew at the time. Stalin had just completed his decimation of the Russian officer corps. Chamberlain had every reason to doubt the efficacy of the Russian armed forces as well the moral ramifications of allying with a dictatorship even more brutal than Nazi Germany. After Munich he also had no moral grounds for objecting to Soviet appeasement of Germany. However, he hoped that his very public courting of the Soviet Union would force Hitler to be more conciliatory about his demands on Poland. For his part, Stalin was reasonable in questioning the benefit of going to war against Germany, a war in which Russia would be likely to assume a disproportionate share of the fighting while not being compensated territorially. Hitler, on the other hand, had secretly promised him eastern Poland and the Baltic

States (Lithuania was included in the package only in mid-September) in exchange for merely remaining neutral.

Where Stalin himself miscalculated was in imagining that a war between Germany and the West would develop into a World War I–type of stalemate, which could then be exploited by the Soviet Union. In so reasoning, Stalin was blinded by doctrinaire Marxism that insisted that the fascists were the tools of monopoly capitalists struggling for markets. He completely ignored the Nazi ideology of agrarian expansionism. Stalin, in effect, also abandoned his many supporters in the West, particularly in France, by dropping the antifascist policy he had been pursuing since 1935. Stalin later tried to excuse the nonaggression pact by claiming that it had given him time to rearm. There is no evidence, however, that he speeded up Soviet rearmament after concluding the deal. In the meantime, his shipments of raw materials to Nazi Germany were invaluable for the Third Reich's war production. These exports effectively cancelled the effects of the British naval blockade of Germany, a strategy that had been valuable during World War I. Stalin could have rendered an enormous service to the West, and ultimately to the Soviet Union itself, if he had simply agreed to join a possible economic blockade against Germany. At most the pact gave Stalin time to repair some of the enormous damage he had done to his officer corps.

Hitler's expectation that the Nazi-Soviet Nonaggression Pact would neutralize the West turned out to be a disastrous illusion. He was at least correct, however, in thinking that the West would be unable to give effective assistance to Poland once war broke out. But he was fatally wrong in assuming that Chamberlain was bluffing when he warned Hitler that Britain would not make peace with him once the Polish campaign ended. Overriding the objections of both Goebbels and the leader of the German Air Force (*Luftwaffe*), Hermann Goering, as well as many of his generals, Hitler clung to the hope that British distractions with the independence movement in India would prevent Britain from declaring war and that France would not enter the fray without its British ally.

For Chamberlain and Daladier neither Poland nor Danzig were the real issues; it was Nazi expansionism and its threat to the worldwide status quo. Britain sent no money or arms to Poland in the summer of 1939. Although its military spending had doubled in 1939 over the previous year, it had no plans to bomb Germany in the event of war. Likewise, France, its promises to Poland notwithstanding, had no plans to invade Germany. Allied plans assumed that Germany would be defeated not in Poland, but only after a long war in which a blockade would play the critical role. Crucial for this strategy was the fresh support of Britain's dominions that had been lacking at Munich; for France it was the 76 percent of the population that favored war if Germany should attempt to take Danzig by force.

## THE BLITZKRIEG CAMPAIGNS

Historians are in general if not universal agreement that Hitler wanted a war with Poland in September 1939. Less apparent is whether he wanted a major European war at that time. A study of German armaments production in the year the war broke out does not give a conclusive answer. Between 1935 and 1939, military spending increased fivefold, from RM 6 billion to RM 30 billion. Meanwhile, the percentage of the gross national product devoted to armaments increased from 8 to 23. Other figures are especially impressive when compared to those of most other potential belligerents. For example, by 1938 Germany was devoting 52 percent of its national expenditures and 17 percent of its gross national product to arms. In that year of the Munich Conference, it spent more on arms than Britain, France, and the United States combined. Consumer goods production in Germany accounted for only 17 percent of total production in 1937–38, compared to 31 percent in 1928–29, although the former figure was still a much greater share than in the Soviet Union. The Four-Year Plan, inaugurated in 1936, was designed to make Germany capable of waging war in 1940, but not yet a general war.

On the other hand, armaments production still had serious shortcomings. None of the three armed services—army, navy, and air force—was adequately prepared in terms of research and development or the accumulation of munitions stockpiles. The *Luftwaffe* (air force), in particular, suffered from a dangerous shortage of construction factories, raw materials, and ammunition. There was not even a coherent program for the allocation of resources for the armed forces. The army was far from fully mechanized and was therefore still astonishingly dependent on horses for its mobility. Some historians have even suggested that Hitler went to war in order to gain raw materials, although this has remained a distinctly minority view. The army and the air force were preparing for a war they expected to begin in 1943, a date which Hitler mentioned at the Hossbach Conference in November 1937. As for the navy, Hitler ordered a major building program for it as late as January 1939, with a completion date set for 1946. However, Hitler expected to use it only after the Continent had been subdued. Hitler also paid little attention to the use of chemistry and physics in warfare. He was especially indifferent, until it was too late, to nuclear physics.

Nevertheless, Hitler was reasonably well prepared to fight the kind of war Germany actually pursued between 1939 and 1941. Even though Germany's rearmament program was unfinished, Hitler was well aware of the rapid, albeit belated, rearmament programs of Britain and France and reasoned that the balance of power would soon swing against Germany. But Germany's victories in the first two years of the war were not due primarily to its early arms buildup. The Führer, borrowing heavily from the British theorist B. H. Liddell Hart and the German Major Heinz Guderian, decided, against the overwhelming advice of his military experts, to create integrated, independently operating armored divisions and tank armies. These divisions, unencumbered by stocks of obsolete equipment, which hampered the British and French, were at the heart of Germany's brilliant *Blitzkriege*, or lightening wars, which it fought between the fall of 1939 and the fall of 1941. Their creation was Hitler's personal responsibility and his greatest military accomplishment.

The armored divisions and tank armies were only two aspects of a new German interest in mobile warfare. Interwar military planners in both Germany and the West were determined to avoid the war of attrition that had bled both sides white in World War I. Western military experts, with some notable exceptions, belatedly agreed with the early nineteenth-century German military theorist Carl von Clausewitz that defense was inherently stronger than offense. Such thinking led the French to rely heavily on the elaborate and expensive Maginot Line (a fortified, defensive line) near the German border, and the British to place still more emphasis on the use of a naval blockade. The Germans, on the other hand, decided that tanks, supported by infantry and airplanes, would restore mobility.

With its new tactics, tanks, and planes, Germany paraded through Poland in only about four weeks killing 70,000 Polish soldiers in the process while losing only 11,000 men of its own. Poland's defeat was certain if it remained isolated. The West made a desperate situation impossible for the Poles by begging them to stop their mobilization, in order to allow more time for negotiations, just before the Germans attacked on September 1. The result confirmed an old saying of Napoleon's: "Order, counter-order, disorder." Hitler's gamble that the West would not invade Germany proved to be all too shrewd. The French government and military had promised the Poles in May 1939 that they would begin an offensive no later than the fifteenth day after a German invasion of Poland. Nevertheless the French and British armies sat in their trenches assuming that Germany's Western Wall was impregnable. What they did not know was that only four fully trained and equipped German divisions were behind that only partially completed wall. All of Germany's tanks and planes were committed to the Polish campaign. By the end of the campaign, moreover, Germany had used up 80 percent of its ammunition supplies. Fifty percent of its motorized vehicles and tanks were unusable. The West had lost a golden opportunity to end the war almost before it had begun.

Hitler's success against Poland contrasted with the miserable performance of Stalin and the Russian army in its Winter War with Finland between November 1939 and March 1940. After the Finns rejected a Russian demand for a naval base on the southwest coast of Finland, the Soviets fomented some border incidents—much as Hitler had done with Poland—as a pretext for an invasion. Initially, at least, the attack was a humiliating failure. While the 200,000 Finnish soldiers used white camouflaged uniforms and ski troops to ambush Soviet columns with devastating effectiveness, the 1 million Russians suffered from supply problems, unimaginative leadership, and a lack of coordination between their armed services. The Russians finally broke through Finnish lines and imposed their original demands, but not before they had lost around 126,000 men—six times as many as the Finns—and the respect of the rest of the world, especially that of the Germans. The effect of the military purges was painfully obvious.

Bizarre as it sounds today, Stalin may have been willing to make an early and relatively lenient peace with the Finns because of fear of an Anglo-French intervention in the conflict, an intervention which the West hoped would impress isolationist Americans, especially in the Midwest with its large Scandinavian population. The early end of the Winter War prevented a Soviet war with the West with incalculable consequences for the war as a whole.

Nevertheless, Scandinavia became the center of military attention in April 1940 when Germany invaded Denmark and Norway. Scandinavia was not part of Hitler's original strategy. However, the German navy urged Hitler to invade Norway in order to gain the strategic port of Trondheim, from which it could easily attack British shipping. In addition, discussions in British newspapers about violating Norwegian neutrality in order to shut off supposedly vital shipments of Swedish iron ore to Germany by way of the Norwegian coastline finally persuaded Hitler to issue a directive for the invasion on March 1, 1940. Germany won another four-week campaign through the daring use of its air force and small navy. For Germany, however, the victory was a mixed blessing. On the one hand, Norway did provide Germany with submarine bases that were later used with devastating effectiveness to impede Allied convoys to Russia. On the other hand, Germany suffered serious naval losses and thereafter had as many as 400,000 troops tied down in occupation duty in Norway, troops that were badly needed elsewhere. Without intending to do so, the British already had succeeded in dispersing German troops into a secondary theater. Furthermore, isolationist sentiment in the United States did decline significantly as a result of the campaign.

Until the spring of 1940, World War II was hardly even a major European war, let alone war on a worldwide scale. No one was surprised by the quick defeat of industrially underdeveloped Poland, and the campaigns in Finland and Norway were regarded as mere sideshows. People in the West talked about the "Phony War" while the Germans said that the Blitzkrieg in Poland had been followed by a *Sitzkrieg*, or sitting war. All this suddenly changed on May 10, 1940, the day the Germans launched their attack on the West.

Even in the almost unthinkable event that Hitler had abandoned his dream of gaining Lebensraum in the East, it is hard to see how he could have avoided a western campaign. He was almost certainly right in believing that time was on the side of the West, which showed no sign of wanting to end the war. With their control of the world's waterways, the Western powers could draw on the resources of most of the world as well as the manpower of their still undiminished empires. Hitler also had reason to worry about the heavily industrialized Ruhr valley region, which was vulnerable to Allied bombing. Moreover, Hitler continued to fret that Germany's technological superiority would slip since the British and French had begun their rearmament later than the Germans. Moreover, he had good cause to doubt whether the Soviet Union would always be friendly and that Italy would remain helpful.

The campaign in the West in the spring of 1940 is one of the most remarkable in the annals of military history. Hitler and the Third Reich managed to accomplish in six weeks what the German emperor, Wilhelm II, had been unable to achieve in over four years: the defeat of France and the expulsion of British forces from the Continent. Much of the credit belongs personally to Hitler. The German dictator adopted a strategy, first conceived by General Erich von Manstein, for an initial, diversionary attack through central Belgium, followed by a larger attack through the dense Ardennes Forest in the southern part of the country. To succeed the plan required British and French troops to drive into previously neutral Belgium. Once they obligingly did so they were then cut off from retreat into France when German troops raced to the English Channel. Hitler was also responsible for the plan to seize the vital Belgian fortress of Eben Emael by using paratroopers who landed on the fort's roof and stuffed its air shafts with explosives.

On the other hand, Hitler was also to blame for not canceling the order of General Gerd von Rundstedt, who held back his tanks at Dunkirk in the mistaken belief that they would be needed later to defeat the main body of the French army. For once, Hitler was overly cautious, thus allowing the British to evacuate 338,000 Allied troops from Dunkirk. Whereas the British had expected to rescue no more than one-fifth of their forces they actually managed to save four in five. (See figure 27.) However, Germany now had three times as many divisions as the French army that was so demoralized that it surrendered three weeks later, on June 22. Hitler's popularity was now at its all time high. His judgment in economic, diplomatic, and military affairs seemed to be so infallible that no one dared to question it. Even this stupendous victory, however, was not cost free. Stalin used the German involvement in France to annex Estonia, Latvia, and Lithuania. In the United States, isolationism was again seriously undermined.

The subsequent Battle of Britain was a puzzle for Hitler at the time and has remained one for historians ever since. Was Hitler ever serious about invading Britain, and, if so, was an invasion likely to succeed? The issue of Hitler's intentions has arisen because of his earlier attitude toward Great Britain. He admired the sometimes ruthless way the British had built their world empire. He was also very critical of Kaiser Wilhelm II in *Mein Kampf* for alienating the British prior to World War I by building a large German navy. Hitler, by contrast, declared his intention to seek an alliance with the British. The Anglo-German Naval Agreement of 1935 and even the Munich accord encouraged him to think that such an alliance was possible. He failed to understand, however, that the British would never agree to his demand for a free hand on the Continent. Hitler's reluctance to invade and defeat Great Britain was also motivated by his fear that should the British Empire disintegrate, the Soviet Union would take over India, Japan would expand in East Asia, and the United States would acquire Canada.

Most historians now believe that Hitler was serious about invading the British Isles, at least between July and September 1940. This decision entailed both high risks and high rewards. A failed attack would encourage the United States to aid Britain and would destroy the myth of German invincibility. A German occupation of Britain, on the other hand, would make American intervention a virtual impossibility. Hitler was probably correct in thinking that the Luftwaffe could neutralize the British navy, thus allowing the German army to cross the English Channel, after which it would have faced only one fully equipped British division early in the summer. Luftwaffe chief Hermann Goering, however, failed to recognize the importance of bombing British radar stations and airplane manufacturing plants. But it was Hitler himself, over Goering's objections, who committed the fatal blunder of diverting the German air force from its critical goal of dominating the skies over southeastern England when he ordered the bombing of London in retaliation for the British bombing of Berlin. When it became clear that an invasion of Britain was no longer feasible in the fall of 1940, Hitler had no difficulty in abandoning "Operation Sea Lion" in favor of his ultimate dream of conquering the Soviet Union. The latter operation he thought was in any case the easier of the two objectives.

## THE ITALIAN INTERVENTION

In the meantime, the fall of France was accompanied by the belated entry of Italy into the war on the side of Germany on June 10, 1940. The intervention ultimately proved to be fatal for Mussolini and his

Fascist regime and arguably so for Hitler as well. The Axis alliance was born in October 1936, largely on the initiative of the Italian foreign minister, Count Ciano. The two governments simply pledged mutual cooperation on numerous issues. This agreement was then elevated to the status of a formal offensive alliance, "The Pact of Steel," in May 1939 even though Italy's generals were opposed to further dangerous commitments and Italian public opinion was anti-German. The Pact's only qualification was that it would not to go into force before 1943, by which time Mussolini hoped that Italy would have recovered from its recent wars.

It is a bit of a mystery why Hitler agreed to this alliance. He had earlier told a confidant, Otto Wagener, that "Italy has no war potential whatever. It has no coal, no wood, no iron, no ore. . . . And besides, the Italian is no soldier, neither on sea nor on land. There is not even a single battle in modern history in which an Italian army was victorious over another country's."[3] Hitler's assessment was exactly on target. Italy proved to be far more of a liability than an asset to Germany during World War II. It repeatedly forced Germany to commit troops to secondary theaters; Italy was ultimately invaded by the Allies because it was a partner of Germany.

So weak was Italy that the British chiefs of staff were actually divided as to whether it was preferable to have Italy as a neutral or as an enemy. Italy was not even prepared for a minor war in 1940 even though between one-third and one-fourth of government spending in 1939 had been on the military. Mussolini was aware of his country's lack of preparedness as were his military chiefs and the king. However, he was a victim of his own rhetoric. He had preached the glories of warfare for so long that he was practically forced to consider neutrality a humiliation, no matter how beneficial it might be for Italy. Besides, in the atmosphere of June 1940, when Germany appeared capable of ending the war in a matter of days, Mussolini feared that to delay intervention would cost Italy the return of Corsica, Savoy, and Nice, which France had acquired in the eighteenth and nineteenth centuries.

Italy's fundamental problem was that it was at best a second-rate industrial power. Its gross national product, which was less than half of Great Britain's per capita, was simply not capable of adequately

---

3 Quoted in Henry Ashby Turner, Jr., ed., *Hitler: Memoirs of a Confidant* (New Haven, 1985), 121.

supporting the weapons and ammunition needed to realize Mussolini's imperial ambitions. In fact, an Italian Commission on War Production had warned Mussolini in early 1940 that Italy would not be able to sustain a single year of warfare until 1949. Furthermore, it is all too easy to forget that Italy had nearly exhausted its meager supply of planes and tanks as well as ammunition between the beginning of the Ethiopian War in October 1935 and the end of the Spanish Civil War in late March 1939.

Consequently, the Italian army of 1940 was weaker in absolute terms than the Italian army of 1915. Its best guns had been captured from the Austro-Hungarians in 1918. Its air force, which had been the most modern in the world in 1934, was now obsolete. It had only 454 bombers and 129 fighters—nearly all were inferior in speed and equipment to British planes—hardly the 8,500 planes claimed by Mussolini. Its better planes had been designed to break speed and altitude records, not to fight wars. The navy was well supplied with battleships, but it lacked the necessary air cover that only aircraft carriers could have provided. In any case, the navy was reluctant to risk its expensive new toys in battle; many of them were sunk at their docks by British torpedo planes. Even more important, however, was Mussolini's unwillingness to create a genuine triservice general staff, because such an institution might have challenged his authority. Consequently, the armed services remained poorly coordinated. Moreover, the army, far from being Mussolini's compliant tool, frequently fought his wishes. Italy's most pressing problem, however, was its lack of strategic raw materials, fuel, and ammunition. Mussolini used these shortages as an excuse for not joining Hitler in war in the fall of 1939, rather than pointing out that the alliance was not supposed to be valid until 1943. Thus, he put himself in a servile position from the very beginning of the war.

A number of controversies surround the actual Italian declaration of war against France. The conventional view is that the Italian public was adamantly opposed to intervention. This was generally true prior to the German campaign in France and Belgium. However, the easy German victories created a widespread demand that Italy enter the war before it was "too late" for Italy to collect its fair share of French booty. The enthusiasm, however, which was especially strong among students, was predicated on the assumption that the war would be short and victorious. As mentioned earlier,

Mussolini's ambitions included not only the lost territories of Nice, Savoy, and Corsica, but also Tunisia, French Somaliland, and bases on the coasts of Algeria, Morocco, and Syria. Mussolini's imperial ambitions did not end there, however. He also had his eyes on Sudan, Uganda, Kenya, Aden, and Egypt. Historians are also divided as to whether Mussolini merely wanted to declare war or to actually fight one. The latter interpretation appears more likely, although Mussolini did not anticipate Italy's participation lasting more than a few months. Such a war would prove to the Italian people that they were truly a warrior nation, but the war would be over before anyone noticed Italy's lack of preparedness. Continued neutrality, on the other hand, might threaten the cohesion of the Fascist party, whose only source of unity had been its imperialistic and militaristic rhetoric. He had made his policy on war transparent in an essay written in 1932 in which he proclaimed that "Fascism . . . believes neither in the possibility nor the utility of perpetual peace. It thus repudiates the doctrine of Pacifism—born of a renunciation of the struggle and an act of cowardice in the face of sacrifice. War alone brings up to its highest tension all human energy and puts the stamp of nobility upon the peoples who have the courage to meet it."[4]

Mussolini further subordinated himself to Hitler in March 1940, when he promised to join the war at the opportune moment. Such a moment appeared to have arrived by June 10, the day the Duce declared war on the Allies. Although he now had nothing to fear from the nearly prostrate France, Mussolini forgot that Italy's security had long depended on good relations with Great Britain. The British, at this point, were no doubt down, but they were definitely not out. This fact, more than anything else, proved to be Mussolini's undoing.

Intervention was a failure from the very beginning. Italy's twenty-eight divisions gained only a few hundred yards before being stopped by France's four divisions. Its feeble effort went largely unrewarded, though there is some question as to the reason. Hitler's relatively lenient armistice terms for France may have been aimed at turning France into an eventual partner. Given the momentary anger that many French felt toward Britain in 1940 for having been allegedly left in the lurch, this expectation was not preposterous. Apparently both Hitler and Mussolini feared that harsh demands would cause

4 Quoted in Charles F. Delzell, ed., *Mediterranean Fascism, 1919–1945* (New York, 1970), 99.

the French navy to continue the fight alongside the British navy, thus threatening Hitler's plans for an invasion of Britain as well as endangering Italy's vulnerable coastal cities. As a result, Italy acquired none of the French territories Mussolini coveted, and Mussolini did not think to ask for the Tunisian port city of Bizerta, which might have secured his supply lines to Libya later in the war.

The outcome in France was an embarrassment for Mussolini, but not a catastrophe. The same cannot be said for his next adventure in Greece. For many years Mussolini had enjoyed playing the role of the senior fascist dictator. Indeed, for a time, Hitler was even inclined to concede him that status, as for example during their visit in Venice in June 1934. However, Italy's dependence on Germany during and after the Ethiopian War reversed their relationship. Consequently, Mussolini always eagerly sought to exploit any opportunity to assert his independence. When German forces occupied Prague in March 1939, Mussolini felt compelled to occupy Albania the next month. The tiny Balkan state would presumably make an excellent jumping off place for attacks on either Yugoslavia or Greece. When Hitler occupied Rumania in early October 1940, Mussolini thought it was time to get even by invading Greece.

The circumstances surrounding the invasion of Greece reveal a great deal about Mussolini's thinking or lack of it. Hitler had invaded Poland on September 1 of the previous year because he wanted to end the campaign before the fall rains turned Polish roads into mud holes. Mussolini launched the attack on Greece on October 28 at the beginning of the rainy season, without consulting Hitler and after just two weeks of preparation, simply because it was the eighteenth anniversary of the Fascist takeover. None of Hitler's campaigns thus far had been as unprovoked and treacherous as Mussolini's attack on Greece. At this time, the roads in Albania (where the invasion began) and northwestern Greece, when they existed at all, were often little more than cow paths. By comparison, Polish roads had been superhighways. Predictably, autumn rains quickly turned the Greek roads into quagmires. The cloudy weather also kept the Italian air force—Italy's only tactical advantage—grounded much of the time. Italy's 100,000-man army (about the size of the Greek army) was stopped almost immediately and was soon pushed back deep into Albania. Instead of regaining some of Italy's lost prestige, the fiasco lost what little prestige Mussolini and the Fascist regime still retained.

It marked the last time that Italy was capable of taking the initiative in the war and the beginning of the end of Fascism.

Greece was perfectly capable of handling Italy on its own, but Great Britain insisted on coming to its aid, starting in November 1940. Hitler was now confronted with the prospect of having his only important ally totally humiliated. The British air force sank half the Italian fleet at Taranto and threatened to gain a foothold in the Balkans from where it could attack oil fields in southern Rumania, vital to the German cause. On April 6, Hitler took matters into his own hands, invading both Greece and Yugoslavia and within three weeks driving the British—who had to transport their soldiers and equipment to Greece by ship rather than by rail—once more, off the Continent. Mussolini was rescued from defeat, but not from complete humiliation and dependence. His Greek fiasco earned him not only the contempt of the Allies, but also that of the Italians and Germans. Hitler had scored another quick and impressive victory, but now still more of his troops were tied down occupying much of the Balkans, where they were also soon faced with guerrilla warfare.

The campaign in Greece, which ended in early June 1941, with the German capture of Crete, marked the end of the first part of World War II in Europe. To a large extent it also marked the end of traditional warfare. The Greek campaign had been an old-fashioned war between gentlemen, with honor given and accepted by both sides. The Germans even insisted that Greek officers keep their swords after surrendering. Nothing of the sort was imaginable in the rapidly approaching war in Russia.

As long as diplomacy and warfare remained relatively traditional, both Axis powers were fairly successful. Hitler enjoyed not only success, but also goodwill in his early treaties with Russia, the Vatican, Poland, and Great Britain. He lost the goodwill but remained successful when he moved more aggressively to seize Austria and the Sudetenland, simply because the West regarded these goals as traditional, limited, and morally justified. However, he exhausted the patience of the West and provoked the acceleration of their armaments when he violated his own ostensive principle of self-determination by occupying Prague. Subsequently, the West was not prepared to make peace with Hitler after the Polish campaign. On the other hand, Hitler's conduct of the war well into 1941, with the partial exception of the seizure and occupation of Poland, was restrained enough to prevent the intervention of the United States and to discourage the appearance of resistance movements, as will be seen in the next chapter. Mussolini had not won any foreign friends for himself when he attacked Ethiopia in 1935, but the world could still see that conflict as a traditional colonial war, which did not merit military intervention by the great powers. However, Mussolini committed political suicide when he fell victim to his own Fascist propaganda about the virtues of warfare by involving himself in a war that he could not win. In June 1941, Hitler demonstrated that he had learned nothing from the Duce's criminal folly.

# 9 / TOTAL WAR, 1941–1945

## HITLER TURNS EAST

Until the fourth week of June 1941, World War II, for the most part, had been fought in a fairly conventional way. To be sure, Poland was an exception where the Nazis had already killed some of the Polish higher intelligentsia and by the spring of 1940 had deported 128,000 Poles and Polish Jews. But even these atrocities did not approach the genocidal character of the post–1941 period. German bombers had destroyed central Rotterdam in May 1940. British bombers had initiated the deliberate bombardment of German civilians in August 1940, but few German civilians were killed before 1942. The Luftwaffe destroyed much of Belgrade at the start of the German invasion of Yugoslavia in April 1941. Otherwise, however, for nearly twenty-two months the war had been "conventional" and relatively free of atrocities, especially the intentional killing of civilians. Traditional discipline had sufficed to keep German soldiers in line. When they occasionally crossed that line and engaged in looting or rape, they were punished by their officers.

Aside from Hitler's enormous miscalculation in starting the war to begin with, his management of the fighting had been rational—given his goals—and at times even brilliant. He had erred in letting so many Allied troops escape his grasp at Dunkirk and in allowing his emotions to get the better of him in retaliating against the bombing of Berlin. The failure of the Battle of Britain was a clear setback, but the foremost British military historian of the twentieth century, B. H. Liddell Hart, has admitted that without American assistance, Britain eventually would have been strangled by German submarines. Hitler undoubtedly acted rationally in making every effort to keep the United States out of the war, even tolerating U.S. aid to Great Britain and a number of deliberate American attacks on German submarines in the summer and fall of 1941.

Hitler's early successes rested on three foundations: Germany's early lead in rearming; its Blitzkrieg tactics; and Hitler's ability to fight on only one front at a time. Moreover, each of his campaigns had been followed by a long respite during which German industries were able to resupply the German army with stocks of new weapons and ammunition. Hitler also managed to acquire a number of small allies for Germany, including Hungary, Slovakia, Croatia, Bulgaria, Rumania, and Finland, by fulfilling their dreams of independence or by helping them to restore lost territories. Most important of all, by exercising self-restraint, he had managed to keep both the United States and the Soviet Union out of the war.

June 1940 to June 1941 was the last period in which Hitler was able to take the strategic initiative. It turned out to be a year of missed opportunities. Had he followed the advice of his famous general, Erwin Rommel, he could have easily taken North Africa and the Near East, where he would have encountered a friendly anti-British and anti-Jewish Arab population. The British would have been unable to intervene in Greece and there would have been no need for Germany's Balkan campaign and the subsequent disbursement of occupying forces. Germany also would have acquired all the oil that it needed. By extending his conquests into Iran he could have later threatened the Soviet Union's oil production in the Caucasus and cut off a supply route used by Russia's Western Allies after the German invasion of the Soviet Union. Hitler, however, was an extreme Eurocentrist. When he finally did send six new divisions to North Africa at the end of 1942, it was to rescue Mussolini and maintain the prestige of the Axis alliance, not because he suddenly realized the strategic significance of the area. For Hitler, Russia was the grand prize. It is unlikely that he ever considered other regions to be anything more than prerequisites or sideshows standing between himself and the acquisition of the fabled Lebensraum in the East.

For the last half-century and more it has appeared obvious to casual observers of the Russian campaign, code named Barbarossa, that Hitler's decision to invade was doomed to failure. The 183 million people of the Soviet Union were more than double the 80 million ethnic Germans of the enlarged Third Reich. More important, however, the size of the USSR was more than twenty times that of

Germany, even after its annexation of Austria, the Sudetenland, and large parts of Poland. European Russia alone was eight times the size of France. The front, which was 1,300 miles long at the start of the campaign, nearly doubled in length once the Germans had penetrated deep into the Soviet Union, thus thinning out the ranks of the Wehrmacht and lengthening supply lines. Blitzkrieg tactics that had worked so well in other parts of Europe where distances were finite and campaigns were brief, had allowed plenty of time for the maintenance of equipment, especially planes. The four-year war in Russia provided no such breathing spells. Furthermore, as Napoleon had already discovered, Russia's winters were bitterly cold and its roads were primitive. Moreover, its railroad tracks were of a wider gauge than those of Central and Western Europe, all factors which were impediments to an invader.

Nevertheless, Hitler's optimism about the German chances for victory in Russia was not as overly optimistic as is commonly supposed. Germany, after all, had defeated Russia in World War I even though it had been engaged in fighting simultaneously on several other fronts, especially in France. Shortly before the start of the German invasion in 1941, Stalin had virtually destroyed his officer corps, and the Russian army made a miserable showing in Finland, a country with about 2 percent of the Soviet population. Russian industries were more productive than they were in 1914, but so were Germany's. Russia's territory was vast, but it offered few natural barriers to an invader. Moreover, Hitler was far from alone in his optimism. His General Staff estimated that Germany would be able to occupy a line running from the lower Don River through the middle Volga to the Northern Dvina within nine to seventeen weeks. These areas contained so many of the factories and farm lands necessary for Russia's war economy that their capture would render further resistance impossible. Even this German prediction was conservative compared to the British estimate that the campaign would be over in ten days and the American expectation that it would last one to three months.

The trouble with Hitler's thinking was not his rational calculations, but his irrational prejudices. The Soviets' biggest weakness, according to the Führer, was their belonging to the inferior Slavic race. The Russians were "Redskins" who were dominated by the still more inferior Jewish-Bolsheviks. The only real state-building elements in Russia had been the Baltic Germans, and they had been driven from power by the Bolshevik Revolution. The present situation in Russia, therefore, represented a unique opportunity to gain Lebensraum at relatively little cost. In other words, it was primarily his Nazi ideology, especially its racism, which caused him to underestimate badly the resistance powers of the Soviets. Beyond that, the German General Staff lacked information on how many reserves the Russians were capable of calling up from the depths of their country. Hitler was so confident of victory that he made no effort to persuade the Japanese to attack eastern Siberia until January 1943 when Japan was heavily engaged in war with the United States. He also ordered the reduction of German armaments production on the eve of the attack; in July, when the campaign was far from won, he redirected armament production for an expected conflict with the United States. As a consequence, by December 1941, production was actually 29 percent less than it had been in July. Not until the spring of 1942, when his best chance for victory had already passed, did he make an all-out effort to speed up production.

Although Hitler's primary motivations for invading the Soviet Union were to gain Lebensraum for raw materials and to rid Europe of "Jewish Bolshevism," he had other reasons as well. The Führer managed to talk himself into believing that his invasion was really a preemptive strike. It is true that the Russians took advantage of the bulk of the German army being in France in June 1940 to militarily occupy and annex the Baltic States as well as northern Bucovina in Rumania. The Nazi-Soviet Non-Aggression Pact had merely assigned the Baltic States to the Soviet sphere of influence without defining exactly what that term meant. And it had not mentioned northern Bucovina at all. Moreover, Stalin concentrated Soviet troops in a menacing way on the Soviet-German demarcation line in central Poland, in spite of an earlier promise to Hitler that he would not do so. However, German military leaders learned of the Soviet buildup only in June, shortly before the German invasion and long after Germany had begun its own preparations for an offensive. The Russian foreign minister, Vyacheslav Molotov, also showed an indiscreet amount of interest in Finland, Rumania, Hungary, Bulgaria, and Turkey when he visited Berlin in November 1940.

Hitler also feared, or so he claimed, that Britain was fighting only in the hope of an eventual alliance with the Soviet Union. Ironically, it was the German invasion of Russia that brought about that very alliance. Hitler also disliked being dependent on the Soviet Union for many of Germany's imports of raw materials. Stalin had cut back shipments every time he thought the Germans were in trouble, as in early 1940, but had been punctual in the last few months before the German invasion in 1941. Overall, Germany benefited from this trade far more than the Soviet Union. It is again an irony that those supplies were cut off, rather than assured, by the German invasion. In one respect Hitler was probably right: if ever the Soviet Union were to be defeated, the time was in 1941. Its growing industrial and military strength would make such an adventure far more difficult if not impossible in the future.

Hitler kept the world's attention focused on the German bombing of Britain during the winter of 1940–41, while he began to shift troops to the east. By February, 680,000 German soldiers were stationed in Rumania and more were transferred to the East during the Greek campaign. By June, there were a little over 3 million Axis soldiers poised to invade Russia, but the number was at best only equal to the size of the Soviet army and may have actually been smaller. In any event, the German armed forces were less powerful than those that invaded France two years earlier. The ratio of German to Soviet forces contradicted military doctrine that assumes that an attacking army must be something like three times as numerous as the defenders.

## STALIN'S PREPARATIONS FOR WAR

If Hitler's preparations for the Russian campaign were slapdash and grounded on the illusion of Slavic inferiority, Stalin's efforts were based on outmoded weapons and tactics and a desperate desire to appease Hitler. Military spending in the USSR had increased from 3.5 percent of the national budget in 1932 to 32.5 percent in 1940 (a figure roughly comparable to Nazi Germany and far in excess to armament spending in either the United States or Great Britain) and its army had grown from 1.4 million in 1937 to 5.4 million in 1941. In the latter year the Soviets had 10,000 planes, twice as many as the Third Reich. During the Second Five-Year Plan, defense industries were enlarged two and one-half times faster than civilian industries. The problem, however, was not spending or quantity, but quality. Russia's most serious deficiency was its lack of trained officers and the timidity and lack of imagination of those who had survived Stalin's purge. In

the mid-1930s the Soviet Union had led the world in the mechaniza-
tion of its armed forces. However, the nation's foremost proponent of
motorized warfare, General Mikhail Tukhachevsky, had been the first
victim of the military purge, whereas Kliment Voroshilov and Semyon
Budenny, both firm believers in the continuing importance of horse
cavalry, had been spared. On the eve of the German invasion in June
1941, 75 percent of the army officers had been in active service for less
than a year. Stalin also refused to invest in computers or any technical
planning aids. Modern weapons, which had been designed and tested,
had not been put into mass production before the war broke out, and
few soldiers or pilots had been trained in their use.

Stalin had also committed an incredible blunder in dismantling
the so-called Stalin Line of fortifications, just east of the pre-1939
Soviet border. It had stretched for over 700 miles, from the Baltic to
the Black Sea, and had been built at a huge cost during the 1930s. It
was to be replaced by 2,500 fortifications along the new Soviet border.
But construction of the new fortifications began only in early 1941; by
June only about 1,000 of the new sites were fully equipped with heavy
artillery. The remainder had only machine guns. Stalin completely
ignored the advantages of a defense in depth. The old fortifications
could have been used as staging areas for a counteroffensive against
tired German troops. However, the very idea of deliberately giving
ground and utilizing the inherent advantages of defense never entered
Stalin's mind. Some historians have recently argued that Soviet forward
deployment suggests that Stalin was planning a preventative strike
or even an offensive of his own although there is no documentary
evidence to support this view. What can be said for sure is that Soviet
armed forces were prepared neither for a defensive nor an offensive
war on the eve of the campaign. In fact, they were not even as well
prepared for war as they had been in 1939, Stalin's claims to the
contrary notwithstanding.

For Stalin, even the suggestion of defensive plans and retreats was
tantamount to treason and defeatism, and those who proposed such
tactics were unceremoniously dealt with as traitors. Consequently,
there were not any contingency plans for strategic withdrawals, even
though they had been the traditional means by which Russia had
defeated earlier invaders. Soviet troops were not even equipped with
maps of their own terrain. In case of attack, Stalin, as well as his
High Command, thought only in nineteenth-century military terms
of immediately taking the offensive. Consequently, he stationed 170

of his 203 divisions and one-half the army's fuel reserves only a few miles from the new border. Soviet planes were parked wing tip to wing tip, making them easy targets for the German air force as were Soviet tanks which were painted in bright colors.

Like Mussolini and Hitler, Stalin was a captive of his own dogmatic ideology. A German attack on the homeland of socialism would necessarily be followed by uprisings of outraged proletarians in the rest of Europe. The fact that nothing of the sort happened in 1918 did not seem to faze Stalin. He was also blinded by his conviction that Hitler would not attack the Soviet Union in the immediate future. By May and June of 1941, his willingness to appease Hitler by continuing vital shipments of raw materials to Germany while ignoring the German military buildup on his western border, including the building of rafts and pontoon bridges within eyesight of Soviet soldiers, made Chamberlain and Daladier look hawkish.

Stalin's last and most grotesque blunder—an error of truly gargantuan and even criminal proportions—was ignoring innumerable and specific warnings of an impending German attack. Probably no leader in world history was so well informed of enemy plans as Stalin. One historian has calculated that the Soviet leader received no fewer than eighty-four separate warnings that came from: his own intelligence service; the British intelligence; the British prime minister Winston Churchill; President Roosevelt; and German Communists. On May 19, the German ambassador to Russia, Count von Schulenburg, who had previously tried to dissuade Hitler from the invasion, told the Soviet deputy foreign commissar, V. G. Dekanozov, the exact date of the German invasion. When the news reached Stalin he dismissed it as "disinformation." In some cases Stalin had people shot who brought him such unwelcome news. One hundred and eighty-five deep penetrations of Soviet air space by German reconnaissance planes—ninety-one of them in May and June—as well as reports of a massive buildup of German troops near the Soviet border were likewise ignored by the all-powerful and all-wise Russian leader. Stalin even refused to order the most basic steps for combat readiness to avoid "provoking" the Germans. If anyone in the Soviet Union was a "wrecker" and an "enemy of the people"—to use two of Stalin's favorite expressions—it was Stalin himself.

Stalin's refusal to believe the many warnings of an impending attack undoubtedly reveals his extreme mistrust of anyone's judgment except his own. It also shows his unwillingness to admit that his efforts

## World War II in Europe
### September 1939–June 1941

Axis nations and conquests to August 19th, 1939

Axis occupation and conquests to June 21, 1941

Vichy France and Vichy-controlled states

Annexed by U.S.S.R. prior to German invasion

Allied and Allied-controlled nations

Neutral nations

#### FURTHEST PENETRATION OF AXIS FORCES INTO RUSSIA

Axis Start Line Attack on USSR June 22, 1941

Axis Front Line November 12, 1941

Axis Front Line November 18, 1942

0        250 Mi
0      250 Km

to appease and indeed even to aid Hitler for nearly twenty-two months after the start of the war had been worse than useless because they had resulted in a relatively stronger Germany. Nevertheless, if we examine the military and diplomatic situation as it existed in the late spring of 1941 Stalin's actions become at least somewhat intelligible.

Stalin rejected the warnings—which he had been hearing since the summer of 1940—because he was convinced that they were an attempt, especially by Churchill, to drag him into a war with Hitler two years before he thought Russia would be prepared for such a conflict. A number of events lent at least some plausibility to this conclusion. June 1941 was one of the many low points in Britain's struggle with Germany. The British had been expelled from Norway, Belgium, and France in June 1940, from the Greek mainland in April 1941, and in mid-June from Crete. They had also already suffered numerous defeats in North Africa. Indeed, Churchill's survival as prime minister was in some doubt after the fiasco in Crete. Stalin was doubly suspicious of Churchill because the British leader provided no evidence of an impending German attack and obviously needed all the help against Hitler he could get. The more warnings Stalin received, therefore, the more the paranoid and Machiavellian dictator was convinced that they were phony. At worst, Stalin thought, Hitler was merely using a military buildup to make new diplomatic demands. Germany, he was convinced, would not attack Russia earlier than 1942.

## THE RUSSIAN CAMPAIGN IN 1941

At four o'clock on the morning of June 22, just after the last Soviet supply train had passed into German-held territory, the German army, or Wehrmacht, launched its massive invasion of the Soviet Union. The attack inaugurated a campaign that involved more soldiers on both sides than were engaged in all the other fronts of the war put together. Almost immediately, General (later Marshal) Georgi Zhukov phoned Stalin to inform him that the Germans were bombing Soviet cities. Two hours later Stalin finally gave the order to resist; another seven hours passed before a general Soviet mobilization began.

Stalin disappeared from public view for the first eleven days of the German invasion, emerging only on July 3 to deliver a radio address to the Soviet people. What Stalin was doing all this time has long remained a mystery to historians. The usual explanation is that he was immobilized by a deep depression or a nervous breakdown. Newly declassified documents, however, have revealed that even though he was depressed he was busy holding meetings from early in the morning until late at night. Hence Stalin's immediate reaction to the invasion was probably more one of embarrassment than depression.

Thanks to Stalin's refusal to take the strategic defensive in 1941, Soviet armies suffered some 4 million dead between June and the end of October, and at least another 2 million soldiers taken prisoner by the Germans, a half million of them at the Battle of Kiev in early September. By the end of the war 5.7 million Soviets had become POWs, of whom only 2 million survived, in part because the Wehrmacht had made no provisions for such huge numbers of prisoners. (See figure 28.) Within days, three-fourths of the Soviet air force were destroyed on the ground and many other planes were shot down in the air. So massive was the German destruction that the Luftwaffe commander called it "infanticide." In one week the German army was halfway to Moscow, being slowed only by rains and the inability of supplies to keep up with combat troops. By the end of July, the Russians had lost 17,000 tanks and 8,000 planes, equivalent to almost their entire inventory when the campaign began in June. However, the Germans had also suffered more casualties in one month than they had in all previous campaigns combined and were still far from their ultimate objectives.

Russian officers were shocked by Stalin's complete indifference to Soviet losses, which were nearly four times greater than German casualties for the whole war. If a Russian unit was surrounded and captured, but later escaped, Stalin regarded its members as deserters and had them either shot or consigned to labor camps. A similar fate awaited the roughly 2 million Russian prisoners of war who endured the horrendous conditions in German POW camps. Stalin regarded them as traitors and refused to allow the International Red Cross to help them. Only 15 to 20 percent of the survivors were allowed to return directly to their homes. As for unsuccessful generals, Stalin ordered them to return to Moscow where they were court-marshaled and shot on the same day, a practice to which not even Hitler resorted. Russian generals soon learned that it was better to attack again and again, even if they suffered huge losses, than to break off the attack and be considered lacking in determination.

Meanwhile, even when the German advance seemed to be progressing far better than expected, problems began to appear. For almost a month, from late July until August 23, Hitler and his generals wasted vital time debating their primary objectives while much of the German army was marching and countermarching. Such indecision was the result of not working out precise objectives before the campaign began. Hitler finally persuaded his generals to postpone the drive on Moscow until most of Ukraine was captured. However, when the attack on the Russian capital resumed in early September, Moscow had been reinforced and the Germans realized that they were about to face the Russian winter without proper uniforms or adequate amounts of antifreeze. This time the mistake was the Wehrmacht's, not Hitler's, because the Luftwaffe and the elite *Waffen SS* were well supplied with winter equipment. Good progress was nevertheless made by the Germans until fall rains turned Russian roads into pigpens.

However, the widespread belief, perpetuated by German generals after the war, that the failure to take Moscow was caused by the lateness of the German invasion in June, Hitler's hesitations in August, snowfalls in October—the earliest in living memory—and freezing temperatures in November and December are all based on the questionable assumption that Moscow could have been taken earlier in a matter of a few weeks, and, once taken, would have ended Russian resistance. However, a year later, the Germans failed to take Stalingrad after a five-month siege. Although Moscow, the political, industrial, and transportation hub of the Soviet Union would have been a wonderful prize for the Wehrmacht, there is also no reason to assume that the Russians would have simply quit if the city had fallen. They had certainly not done so when Napoleon conquered the city in 1812. Big cities were the fortresses of the twentieth century. Because the Germans reached within twelve miles of the Kremlin in early December does not mean that it was on the brink of falling.

Ultimately, of course, the Germans not only failed to capture Moscow but they were also pushed 50 to 150 miles back by a Russian counterattack. This action was made possible when Stalin, who had learned on October 4 that the Japanese intended to attack the United States, not the Soviet Union, transferred thirty-three divisions from the Manchurian border, where they had earlier clashed with Japanese troops, to Moscow. If ever there was a strictly military turning point in World War II it was on December 6, when the Russians began their counteroffensive, one day before the Japanese attacked Pearl Harbor.

Hitler himself had been well aware, before the Russian campaign began, that his best chance of victory was in 1941. With 23 percent of the German soldiers who had invaded Russia in June dead, wounded, or missing in action even before the beginning of the Soviet counter offensive, that chance had now been squandered.

### HITLER AND THE UNTERMENSCHEN

No greater mistake can be made by students of the Russo-German war than to imagine that it was won or lost because of purely military decisions. Hitler might well have lost the campaign even if he had chosen all the right targets. If the Russian army had not defeated him, the immense size of the Soviet Union, together with the implementation of guerrilla warfare, might well have done so. In the long run, however, it was a political decision, based on Nazi ideology, that proved to be Hitler's undoing, far more than any tactical mistakes he may have made.

Von Clausewitz had put it very succinctly in his book, *On War*, in which he wrote that "if we only require from the enemy a small sacrifice, then we content ourselves with aiming at a small equivalent by the War and we expect to attain that by moderate efforts."[1] Hitler did the exact opposite in Russia. Already in November 1940 Hitler had told his leading generals that the approaching war in the east would be a "war of annihilation." The Soviet Union would be turned into a vast colony that would enable the German population to grow to 250 million people in 70 to 80 years and would provide Germany with unlimited food and natural resources. Those Russians who survived the onslaught would be reduced to the status of slaves and would be taught just enough German to follow orders.

By demanding everything of the Soviets—the complete destruction of their country both politically and materially—Hitler achieved the near impossible: he turned Stalin into a hero and probably preserved the hated, corrupt, and inefficient Soviet system for another two generations. Simultaneously, he also created an ideologically improbable Anglo-Soviet alliance that was joined a few months later by the United States. Hitler wanted to create a great European if not a world empire. But he forgot that all the great and long-lasting empires of the past, including the Roman Empire, had offered the conquered and subject

1 Carl von Clausewitz, *On War* (Hamondsworth, UK, 1968), 400.

peoples political autonomy and a better life than they had known, especially in terms of prosperity and order. Hitler offered the Soviet people only slavery and death.

Hitler's decision to invade the Soviet Union was arguably the single most important one of the twentieth century. The irony is that Hitler had an opportunity to be the greatest liberator in world history. Many people in the Baltic States had frantically tried to pass themselves off as Germans in the summer of 1940 rather than fall under Soviet domination. Hundreds of thousands of Ukrainians actually did welcome German troops as liberators in the first few weeks after the invasion and several hundred thousand Soviets joined the Wehrmacht. No doubt tens of millions of Russian peasants would have joyfully embraced the opportunity to return to their confiscated private farms. Hitler could have dissolved the Communist party and created a band of dependent states running from Finland to the Caucasus, which would have willingly looked to Germany for protection against a possible revival of Soviet power. Hitler's top ideological adviser, Alfred Rosenberg, himself a Baltic German, in fact urged such a course on Hitler. The Führer never even considered doing so, except in the Baltic States themselves, where fairly moderate policies indeed enjoyed considerable success.

In keeping with his policy of annihilation, Hitler ordered the execution of all commissars and 100 Russians for every German soldier who was killed by partisans in the occupied territories. When the Soviet people, both soldiers and civilians, learned that their government's propaganda was actually true, and that the German invaders intended to abuse them even more cruelly than had Stalin, they reacted with a vengeance in order to defend their homeland, thus causing German soldiers to fight still more furiously. Thus, a vicious circle of mutual atrocities dragged on for nearly four years. In the meantime, Stalin became a national hero almost of necessity. He was the only person who could possibly lead the country to victory.

It may be objected that Hitler was merely being true to his philosophy in treating the Soviet people like *Untermenschen*, or "subhumans." To some extent, of course, this is true. Even his more moderate handling of the Baltic peoples occurred because they were not Slavs. On the other hand, he had been able to set his racial prejudices aside in treating the occupied Czechs with some moderation and in turning the Slavs of Slovakia and Croatia into allies. His occupation policies in Norway, Denmark, the Low Countries, and France were probably milder than Napoleon's and were restrained enough to prevent serious resistance movements from arising before 1943, when it was obvious that the war had turned against Germany. Therefore, one is left with the conclusion that it was Hitler's racism plus his growing belief, in the euphoric summer months of 1941, that restraint was no longer necessary as a tactical device that led him to discard all caution and pursue a policy of the utmost brutality.

The same thinking and timing pertained to the Jews. It was also about July 1941 that Hitler apparently ordered, or at least tolerated, the Holocaust of the Jews to enter its most lethal stage, with the construction of extermination camps in areas previously belonging to Poland. It is doubtful whether a single, comprehensive decision to kill the Jews was ever made. After the fall of France Nazi leaders had seriously considered deporting all European Jews under their control to Madagascar, a plan first conceived by the Poles before the war. Such a plan depended, however, on the total defeat of Britain and its navy. The picture had changed in 1941 when the Soviet Union's 2.4 million Jews were in German-occupied territory along with the majority of Europe's 11 million. The Nazis could also assume that the smoke and noise of battle would make it easier to camouflage their extermination policies since any news of the killings could be explained away as vicious rumors or justifiable retaliations for partisan resistance.

There was an inconsistency of logic in Hitler's decision, however. He argued before the invasion of Russia that the time was ripe to attack because Jews were a disintegrating factor in the Soviet state. If that were true, they should have been left to continue their supposedly subversive work. After the invasion began, Hitler argued that the Jews should be killed because they were the backbone of the Russian resistance. The Holocaust was also counterproductive because it killed many hundreds of thousands of Jews, such as metal workers, who had skills useful in war industries. Hitler was still careful to keep his role in the Holocaust a secret. The Holocaust itself was also pursued with as much deception as possible. An undisguised policy of mass murder would have given the Allies a propaganda gift and would have shocked most Germans.

By enslaving Soviets and exterminating Jews, Hitler was burning his own bridges and those of everyone associated with his atrocities. For all of these people, there was no turning back. Presumably, this knowledge would tie his followers ever closer to him and inspire them to keep fighting—for their very survival. A compromise peace with either Stalin or the Western powers was now impossible even in the unlikely event that Hitler might ever have been temperamentally so inclined.

## HITLER AND STALIN AS WAR LORDS

Deciding to carry out a ruthless war of extermination was not the only error Hitler committed in 1941, although it was probably the biggest. Hitler was just as stubborn about not taking the strategic defensive as Stalin. So when a hundred Soviet divisions, including the thirty-three transferred from Siberia, attacked German lines near Moscow in December, Hitler ordered his soldiers to fight in place. He finally did relent and allowed some retreats after January 15 that may have prevented the Soviets from achieving any decisive breakthroughs. Many historians credit Hitler's determination with preventing a rout, which might have driven the Germans out of the Soviet Union almost as quickly as they had invaded. Unfortunately, Hitler drew the conclusion that all Soviet offensives should be countered in the same inflexible way. As in the winter of 1941–42 he would eventually allow retreats, but only under less favorable conditions than would have been possible when first proposed by his generals. Victory, Hitler thought, was now no longer a matter of pragmatic calculation, but one of willpower and fanaticism.

More concretely, Hitler now made himself commander-in-chief of the army after becoming the minister of war in 1938. His new status put him in charge of both tactics and grand strategy. Like Mussolini, he had absurdly overloaded himself with responsibilities, but in the process had deprived himself of scapegoats in future defeats. His top officers became mere pawns, unable to take independent action based on their professional training. Instead they became much like Soviet generals had been up to this point. Hitler managed to retain their loyalty, however, partly through his magnetic personality, partly by intimidation, and partly with huge bribes. Those top generals who failed to reach his unrealistic expectations could expect to be dismissed, but not shot. On the other hand, Hitler did not hesitate to issue death warrants for junior officers.

Hitler's weakest features now became more obvious than ever: his grotesque overconfidence and his resentment of opposition by subordinates even when he knew these men were objective and correct. His armaments minister, Albert Speer, later wrote that the more catastrophic events became the more convinced Hitler was that everything he did was right. These characteristics grew ever more exaggerated with time. Furthermore, from this point on, none of these character traits was balanced by the professional judgment of his senior officers. During December and January 1941–42, Hitler had dismissed those generals who had objected to some of his earlier policies. By the war's end Hitler had dismissed half of all the officers who had been generals in 1939. They were usually replaced by men who told Hitler what the Führer wanted to hear, thus contributing to Hitler's unrealistic optimism in the second half of the war.

Modern technology almost conspired to make Hitler's control of the German army all the more total. With his headquarters usually in East Prussia, hundreds of miles from the front, he was able, by telephone, Teletype, and radio, to keep in constant communication with every front. Consequently, Hitler denied local commanders any initiative even though they, not Hitler, were fully aware of the terrain, roads, and weather conditions. All the Führer had were his maps and his determination. Although Hitler's constant interference was undoubtedly detrimental to the German army, his surviving generals in the postwar period also found it a useful alibi for their own mistakes.

Hitler still had some positive characteristics as a commander, which were all the more remarkable considering he had never attended a military academy or even so much as led a platoon in World War I. He had a subtle sense of surprise and was a master at psychological warfare. He was better informed about military history and weapons technology than many of the generals with whom he matched wits. Consequently, he wisely urged the development of several important new guns and tanks. His practical experience as a front-line soldier enabled him to understand military literature, which he continued to read during the war. He certainly had imagination, eloquence, dedication, willpower, and nerves of steel, all characteristics of successful commanders.

On the other hand, Hitler's negative qualities as a leader increasingly outweighed his positive ones. Like Stalin, he had no empathy for the suffering of the German soldiers on the front and never bothered to solicit the views of enlisted men. He was equally ignorant (or indifferent) to the plight of civilians—two other characteristics he shared with Stalin—because he never bothered to visit the ruins of bombed-

out cities, in part, at least, out of fear of assassination. More specifically, Hitler failed to follow two important rules of strategy starting in
1941: correctly selecting the primary target and deploying one's army
in such a way as to realize the first objective. The second rule could
hardly be followed as long as the German army was spread out from
western France to the steppes of Russia. By November 1943, there
were 177,000 German troops in Finland, 486,000 in Norway and
Denmark, 1,370,000 in France and Belgium, 612,000 in the Balkans,
and 412,000 in Italy, in addition to the 3.9 million on the Eastern Front
fighting 5.5 million Russians. By attempting to hold on to everything,
he ultimately lost everything.

Although Hitler's policies became more ideological and less pragmatic as the war progressed, his decision to declare war on the United
States on December 11, 1941—like Stalin's refusal to heed warnings of
an impending attack—was not the mad dog act it frequently has been
made out to be. For all practical purposes a state of war between the
United States and Germany already existed. In November 1939, two
months after the start of the war, Congress lifted its arms embargo that
had existed since the Neutrality Act of 1937 thereby permitting the
sale of war supplies to Britain and France. In March 1941, Congress
agreed to the "lend-lease" program in which the U.S. traded old ships
for British naval bases. On August 14, President Roosevelt and Winston
Churchill signed the "Atlantic Charter," a declaration of principles
for a future peace settlement that amounted to an informal alliance.
Then in September, Roosevelt announced that the U.S. would shoot
on sight Axis ships in waters considered essential for American defense.
Hitler was not naïve about potential American military strength as
has so often been suggested. He had bent over backwards to avoid a
conflict with the U.S. in 1941. However, he believed that a declaration of war against the United States would enable German U-boats
to cut off U.S. aid to Britain. He also hoped that Japan would keep
the United States busy in the Pacific in 1942 while he completed his
conquest of the Soviet Union. Thereafter, Germany would have the
resources to fight both the United States and Britain.

At almost exactly the same time that Hitler was abandoning his
earlier restraint and pragmatism and becoming more and more rigid
and doctrinaire, Stalin was gradually moving in the opposite direction.
He remained extremely indifferent to Soviet casualties throughout

the war. Consequently, the ratio of Soviet military casualties was 3.7 times greater than Germany's. As late as May 1942 Stalin insisted on an offensive near Kharkov that resulted in the loss of another 240,000 soldiers. Nevertheless, as early as 1941, he was beginning to show signs of realism and a willingness to listen to generals. When Hitler was cursing his generals and calling them idiots and cowards, Stalin was holding meetings, listening to battlefield reports, studying maps, asking difficult questions, and allowing his generals to argue among themselves before he made up his own mind. After having about twenty of them shot, the worst fate that the remainder might suffer was to be demoted, dismissed, or sent to a penal battalion. Stalin, unlike Hitler, was no military strategist, but in time he at least had enough sense to stop pretending to be one. The great Soviet victories at Stalingrad and Kursk in 1943 were planned and implemented by his generals. Stalin did, however, coordinate the strategies of others and allocated industrial and agricultural resources. For the first and only time in his career he paid more attention to the army than to the secret police. He also finally came to realize that "discipline" and "self-sacrifice" could not compensate for bad strategy and tactics.

Stalin soon moved to minimize the influence of Communist ideology. For example, in the early months of the campaign, Soviet propaganda already had replaced the theme of fighting for the Communist party with a nationalistic call to defend the motherland. From then on, and to this day, the Eastern Front is known in Russia as the "Great Patriotic War." In the name of efficiency, economic and military authorities were freed from political controls and allowed some initiative. By October 1942, political commissars were subordinated to commanders rather than the other way around, although Stalin continued to spy on his officers. Political speeches at workplaces were reduced or eliminated altogether. Stalin even allowed far more freedom of religion and received the head of the Russian Orthodox Church, Metropolitan Sergei. Antireligious propaganda ceased and antireligious organizations were dissolved in 1941. Clergy said prayers for Stalin, and churches, many of them previously closed, were renovated and filled for the duration of the war. All in all, Stalin tried to give the impression that the bad old tyrannical days were gone forever, and that victory would be the beginning of a new era. However, as soon as the fortunes of war began improving in 1943, the cult of Stalin was given a new emphasis, political controls were tightened, and journalists put back on shorter leashes. The appeal to nationalism and patriotism, on the other hand, continued.

In economic matters as well, Stalin showed that he could be a rationalist. He saw the necessity of removing more than 1,500 industrial plants along with 16 million workers to east of the Urals before they could be overrun by the Germans. Even so, total industrial production did not reach the 1940 level until 1944, but armaments production had already reached an index of 224, with 1940's equaling 100. Part of the reason for the economic recovery was that Stalin was not content with having women stay at home. By 1943, the percentage of the work force they comprised was 57, up from 38 in 1940. Over 1 million women, or 8 percent, also served in the Soviet armed forces by 1945.

The Battle of Stalingrad, which lasted from late August 1942 until the end of January 1943, perfectly illustrates Hitler's increasing dogmatism and Stalin's greater pragmatism. Stalingrad (today's Volgograd) was undoubtedly an important city, being the third-largest industrial center in Russia. Strategically, its capture by the Germans would have cut off rail and river traffic along the Volga between the oil fields of the Caucasus and the population and industrial centers of northwestern Russia. What Hitler did not seem to realize, however, was that the capture of any point along the Volga River in this region would have accomplished the same purpose—and at infinitely less cost. Hitler, however, was obsessed with conquering the city that bore his rival's name. His intentions were so obvious that he lost the element of surprise. Once German troops were in Stalingrad the Luftwaffe became almost useless as an offensive weapon because bombing and strafing would be as likely to kill German soldiers as Russians.

Hitler's greed and inability to decide on a primary target also worsened an already dangerous situation. His initial plan was to concentrate on Stalingrad, a dubious decision because the Russians would not have been able to reinforce the much more important Caucasus isthmus. Major successes early in the summer, however, caused Hitler to become overconfident and lose patience. On July 31, even before German troops reached Stalingrad, he ordered several divisions to drive directly into the Caucasus and sent still others north to aid in the siege of Leningrad. The fighting in Stalingrad, moreover, created a long exposed northern front defended weakly by Germany's poorly equipped Hungarian and Rumanian allies, who would have preferred fighting each other to fighting the Russians. On November 19, Stalin ordered a massive counterattack in the area, catching the Germans completely by surprise, cutting off their troops in Stalingrad, and causing their surrender two months later. When it was all over, the Axis forces had lost 150,000 men killed and another 90,000 who were taken prisoner. The Russians lost even more men—400,000 killed—but the German drive to the east had been stopped for good.

Stalingrad was not quite the decisive turning point it has been made out to be. Hitler's decision to annihilate the Russian people, the Soviet counteroffensive which began on December 6, 1941, and the United States' entry into the war the next day, were all more important. It is not even true that no more German victories followed Stalingrad. The Germans defeated the Americans at Kasserine Pass in Tunisia, in February 1943, and the Russians near Kharkov in March. The peak success of their submarine campaign also came during the first three weeks of March. The Germans even launched a major offensive against the Russians at Kursk in July, albeit with disastrous results. Stalingrad's importance was more psychological than military. After that (costly) victory, Stalin became more relaxed and benign toward his generals, loading them with honors. For the Germans, Stalingrad caused an enormous loss of popular confidence in the regime and its propaganda, in part because Hitler had made Stalingrad the symbol of the 1942 campaign and the Nazi press had predicted a great victory. German generals were also much less confident about the strategy they were ordered by Hitler to carry out.

Stalingrad and Kursk completed the role reversals of Stalin and Hitler. Kursk was the last time that the Nazis attempted to take the offensive in Russia. It also was the first time that Stalin was wise enough to deliberately go on the defensive even though his troops outnumbered the Germans by 1.9 million to 900,000. After Kursk, Hitler, like Stalin before him, committed German soldiers to the front before they were adequately trained. Moreover, it was now Hitler who hated to go over to the defense and stubbornly looked for ways to resume the offense. Liddell Hart believes that the German situation after Stalingrad need not have been hopeless if the Germans had fallen back to prepared defensive positions, for example, along the Dnieper River, and had Hitler allowed local commanders to use flexible defense techniques. Hitler actually did permit this tactic in the Baltic, where the Germans were able to hold their own until 1944 despite being outnumbered 6 to 1. But elsewhere Hitler was loathe to give up ground in 1943, even temporarily, every bit as much as Stalin had been in 1941. Therefore,

German losses in the last two years of the Eastern Front were unnecessarily high, even though they were still not as high as Russian casualties caused by costly frontal assaults.

Hitler followed the same philosophy on every front, rejecting the advice of his generals for timely withdrawals and consequently suffering needlessly heavy losses. In North Africa he denied Rommel the few divisions he needed in 1941 to conquer Egypt and the Near East. Then, when Rommel urged Hitler to pull out of the area altogether following the German defeat at El Alamein in the fall of 1942, Hitler instead increased the German contingent in a hopeless attempt to avoid an embarrassing defeat. The reinforcements simply meant a larger haul of prisoners for the Allies when the Germans were trapped in Tunisia in May 1943.

## THE FALL OF FASCISM

The capture of 130,000 Axis soldiers (60,000 of whom were Germans) in Tunisia hastened the downfall of Mussolini. His popularity had been declining ever since his intervention in Spain and then more rapidly after his disastrous invasion of Greece in October 1940. In the spring of 1941, Italian forces were driven out of East Africa including Ethiopia, which had been conquered with so much fanfare only five years earlier. That Italy had been able to stay in the war at all was due purely to repeated German assistance. Few people, however, appreciate being dependent and the Italians were no different. The meticulousness, strict discipline, and frequent lack of tact displayed by some German soldiers also did nothing to endear them to their Italian allies. Nor did German soldiers and civilians have much respect for Italy by 1943. Fascist propaganda, which attempted to convince the Italians that they were a militaristic people, fell flat.

As for Mussolini, he repeatedly asked Hitler to make peace with the Russians so that the Axis could concentrate elsewhere, but Hitler always refused. Most of the time, however, Mussolini, who was frequently depressed and in poor health, lost track of general policy and his duties as supreme commander and concentrated instead on minor details. Prior to several summit meetings with Hitler, he resolved to tell the Führer that Italy had to withdraw from the war, but each time the stronger willed Hitler convinced him that the war could still be won. Mussolini's pride was also a problem. In May 1943, he turned down

Hitler's offer of five divisions because he did not want the world to see how dependent on Germany he was, and also because he feared increased German domination.

Ultimately, however, it was the beginning of the Allied bombing of Italian cities, food shortages, casualties on the Russian Front, and finally, the loss of Sicily in July 1943, which brought down the Fascist regime, after nearly twenty-one years in power. The defeat in Tunisia had deprived the Axis of some of its most battle-hardened troops. Italy had 500,000 soldiers involved in occupation duty in the Balkans and almost a quarter of a million on the Russian front. These troops had never been used for an Italian attack on the British-held island of Malta, which, if successful, probably would have preserved Italy's oldest colony, Libya, at least for a time. Moreover, Italian industrial production had actually declined by 35 percent between 1940 and 1943 and, as mentioned, no general staff existed to coordinate the three military services and avoid competition between them. By late 1942, Mussolini publicly and privately said that the Italian people had failed him—not the other way around. Like Hitler, he could never admit having made a mistake.

The end came on the night of July 24–25, 1943. Under pressure from several moderate Fascist leaders who feared the consequences of a military defeat, Mussolini called a meeting of the Fascist Grand Council, which had not met since before Italy's entry into the war in 1940. No one could have guessed the outcome of the meeting and Dino Grandi, the former Italian ambassador to Great Britain, arrived at the meeting armed with grenades, in case the Duce ordered the arrest of his opponents. In a two-hour monologue he discussed the course of the war in great detail, taking credit for the few Italian successes and blaming defeats on his generals and the Italian people as a whole, who, he asserted, were unwilling to stand up and fight. After a nine-hour discussion the Council voted nineteen to seven to ask the king to restore the powers of the Parliament, the Grand Council, and those of the king himself. Although the vote did not mention Mussolini by name, it clearly showed that the Duce's own senior colleagues no longer had confidence in his dictatorship. It also demonstrated that, in contrast to Stalin, Mussolini had not taken the trouble to exterminate all his potential rivals. When he met with Victor Emannuel III at five o'clock on the afternoon of the 25th, the king informed him that the war was lost and that he, Mussolini, was being replaced by

Marshal Pietro Badoglio, a hero of the Ethiopian War. Upon leaving the palace, Mussolini was arrested and imprisoned. By midnight of the same day the entire Fascist party, along with its affiliate organizations, had disintegrated. Of the party's 4 million members, none made a serious attempt to resist the collapse. For two days the Italian people celebrated Mussolini's downfall with wild demonstrations and the destruction of his portraits and statues.

This account of Mussolini's overthrow clearly illustrates the difference between his regime and the totalitarian dictatorships in Germany and Russia. In Italy there were still two institutions, the Fascist Grand Council and the king, which, however shadowy they might have been, still existed and provided an alternate source of legitimacy once Mussolini had lost his popularity and even his will to rule. Hitler and Stalin had devoted much of their careers to making sure that no similar institutions existed in their countries.

Unfortunately for himself, Mussolini did not stay imprisoned for long. He would have preferred remaining retired for the rest of his life. However, in September, he was "rescued" from a supposedly secret prison at a ski lodge at Gran Sasso in the Abruzzi mountains by forty German paratroopers. He was put back in power, if it can be called that, by Hitler. The Führer threatened to treat Italy like an enemy and destroy the industrial north if he did not collaborate. For the next nineteen months Mussolini headed the phantom Italian Social Republic, better known unofficially as the "Salo Republic," for the village on Lake Garda in northern Italy where it was headquartered. Now even the pretense of equality with Hitler was gone. All of Mussolini's appointments to his own government had to be approved by the Germans. He claimed he was staying in power only to protect the Italian people from Germany, but he could not even prevent the Third Reich from annexing the German-speaking South Tyrol along with Trieste, both of which Italy had acquired from Austria in 1919. Nor could he prevent Italian workers from being shipped off to German factories, or over 7,000 Italian Jews from being deported to Nazi extermination camps. He was able to maintain his position only by the presence of German troops and 200,000 Italian soldiers, who spent most of their time fighting anti-Fascist partisans.

The Salo Republic, which controlled the ever-shrinking part of Italy not yet occupied by Allied armies, differed radically from Mussolini's earlier regime. For starters, it had no real capital, no constitution, and no diplomatic recognition, except by Germany and its few remaining allies. In many respects, Mussolini reverted—probably sincerely—to his early socialist philosophy, now that he no longer had to cater to the Roman Catholic Church, the monarchy, or industrialists. The Duce was also a changed man personally. Now over sixty, he was in poor health and visibly tired; he was also much more modest and courteous than before. He no longer wore gaudy uniforms or pretended to be infallible. On the other hand, because his regime enjoyed almost no popular support, he was forced to act ruthlessly against his many domestic opponents. Among the objects of his ruthlessness were those Fascist hierarchs, including his own son-in-law, Count Ciano, who had voted to oust him in July 1943. The five who remained in northern Italy were tried for treason and shot in January 1944.

Mussolini's dismissal as prime minister was followed by secret negotiations between the Allies and Marshal Badoglio's government, which resulted in Italy's unconditional surrender and subsequent "co-belligerency" alongside the Allies. Just as Hitler had predicted a dozen years before, Italy turned out to be more useful as an enemy than as an ally. For example, there was now no need to supply Italy with energy—that was the Allies' responsibility—and nearly 1 million Italian soldiers, who were taken prisoner by the Wehrmacht, were now available to work in German factories. The military campaign in Italy, which lasted from September 1943 until the end of April 1945, also tied down twice as many Allied troops as Germans because the narrow and mountainous Italian peninsula clearly favored the defense. Consequently, the Allied Italian campaign did not conclude until Germany itself was on the verge of total collapse. The end came for Mussolini on April 28, 1945, when he was captured and shot by Communist guerrillas as he was attempting to flee to the north in disguise.

## THE GERMAN HOME FRONT

During the war, Hitler's influence on the domestic scene in Germany was considerably less than his influence on military affairs simply because the latter consumed nearly all of his time after the start of the Russian campaign. Nevertheless, what he failed to do could often have as much import as what he did do. His attitude toward rearmament, for example, was far more relaxed than was assumed by the Allies at the time. Although Germany did clearly begin rearming sooner than Britain and France, not to mention the United States whose army ranked seventeenth in the world in 1939, it did not begin to convert to a full-fledged war economy until the spring of 1942. However, recent research has revealed that Germany was not as slow to mobilize its economy as historians once believed. For example, per capita production of consumer goods declined by 22 percent between 1938 and 1941, not the 3 percent claimed by Albert Speer, the former minister of armaments, in his memoirs. Meanwhile, "producer" goods used for armaments increased by 28 percent. That Germany did not convert to a full war economy even faster was due to its being able to stockpile supplies before each campaign and to recuperate its losses through the captured resources of its enemies. Hitler also hesitated to do anything that would lower civilian morale, which he saw as the decisive reason for Germany's defeat in 1918. Consequently, as late as 1943 the production of consumer goods was still 90 percent of the prewar level (although it declined another 18 percent in 1944), and the German people remained well fed until the very end of the war. Finally, relatively low production figures before 1942 also resulted from poor planning and overlapping jurisdictions that hindered policy implementation.

All of this changed in February 1942, if less dramatically than once supposed, when Hitler appointed his chief architect, Albert Speer, Reichsminister for Armaments and Munitions. Germany's armaments production had increased only slightly since 1938. Speer's selection proved to be inspired, but only because Speer was partially able to overcome Hitler's Social Darwinistic philosophy of giving the same task to several different people. As the ordnance minister, Speer borrowed, ironically, from the Jewish economist of World War I, Walter Rathenau, a system known as "organized improvisation." Civilian and military officials established branch committees to plan and develop new types of weapons and to discuss measures to speed up weapons production in general. At Hitler's insistence, the number of different armaments projects was also reduced in order to increase the production of the most-needed weapons. For example, the types of aircraft were reduced from 44 to just 5. The treatment of foreign workers also improved after 1941 as the military situation declined, with workers from western European countries receiving nearly as much pay as German workers. Eastern European workers, however, with the exception of Czechs, were still grossly underpaid and in the case of Russian POWs, badly underfed. Speer also could not overcome Hitler's prejudice against having large numbers of women working in factories, thinking it would be bad for the birth rate and the morale of front-line soldiers. However, this fact is less important than historians once believed because the number of females in the work force, already high in 1938, remained higher than in either Britain or the United States. Moreover, the 8 million foreign workers and prisoners of war in Germany who made up 58 percent of the work force in 1944 largely obviated the need for more female workers.

Thanks in part to the foreign workers, and incredibly long hours put in by German workers, the number of planes built in Germany increased from 11,000 in 1941 (up only slightly from 8,000 in 1938) to 39,600 in 1944. Tanks increased from 3,800 to 19,000, and artillery pieces from 7,800 to 62,300. Only the production of submarines remained basically unchanged because the Allies had won the Battle of the Atlantic by May 1943.

Armaments production would have been even more successful had it not been for the occasional interference of Hitler. Early in the war he had forbidden the development of any weapon that could not be manufactured within two years, on the theory that the war would be won or lost within that span of time. He changed his mind in 1942 when he belatedly realized that the war would be protracted, that is, the very type of war he had said in *Mein Kampf* that Germany should not fight. Even then, however, he was interested almost exclusively in offensive weapons with the exception of the atomic bomb whose development he opposed. The so-called vengeance weapons—the V-1 flying bomb, and the supersonic V-2 rocket—were scientific breakthroughs and caused a great deal of panic in Great Britain, but they were far from being decisive weapons. Although the famous V-2, the predecessor of the American moon rockets, was a sensational technological breakthrough against which there was no warning and no defense, it was highly inaccurate and carried relatively small warheads. Combined, the vengeance weapons dropped only 0.23 percent as many explosives on Britain as British and American planes dropped on Germany during the same period. In fact, compared with the results they produced the new weapons were a huge waste of money. On the other hand, the jet plane, first flown in 1939, but not mass produced until late 1944, could have made an enormous difference, particularly in defending German cities from Allied bombing raids. Instead it became available only after September 1944, when Germany was desperately short of fuel and pilots, and the war was hopelessly lost. That Hitler had so much faith in the new "miracle weapons" was no doubt due in part to his desperate grasping at straws. In part, however, it also resulted in his being told what his subordinates thought he wanted to hear, a structural flaw found in all three of the totalitarian dictatorships.

## THE WAR IN THE WEST

Hitler was not the only one to make serious mistakes during the war. The grand strategy of the Allies almost certainly prolonged the war, caused needless loss of life and property, and left a huge portion of Europe under Communist control when the war ended. If Hitler was wrong in committing several divisions to North Africa in 1943, the Allies were, to a substantial extent, wasting their time by remaining heavily committed to the Mediterranean theater after July, when the conquest of Sicily had been completed and Mussolini had been overthrown. To be sure, the reopening of the Suez Canal meant that shipments of lend-lease aid to the Soviet Union no longer had to go around South Africa. Aid to anti-Nazi partisans in Yugoslavia was also facilitated by the renewed use of the Mediterranean. There was also considerable psychological benefit to the Allies in knocking one of the major Axis Powers out of the war. The rapid conquest of southern Italy in September did enable the Allies to bomb German positions in the Balkans, southern France, northern Italy, and previously invulnerable cities in the Reich.

Further involvement in Italy after September 1943, however, was probably counterproductive. The campaign, especially the way it dragged on for nearly two years, was a long road to nowhere. It was fought mainly for political reasons. It demonstrated to public opinion in the United States and Great Britain as well as to Stalin, that the Western Powers were willing and able to take the offensive somewhere until such time as they were prepared to launch a major invasion of the Continent. Even if successful, it merely would have brought the Allies up to the Alps, an almost impossible barrier to Germany unless the Reich was already on the brink of defeat. The Allies' decision to seek the unconditional surrender of the Axis powers made at the Casablanca conference of January 1943—which was neither sought nor approved of by Stalin—along with their bombing campaign against

German cities, provided Josef Goebbels with more propaganda about the impossibility of surrendering than he possibly could have invented himself. The announcement also came as a relief to Hitler who was now freed of all pressure to seek a compromise end to the war.

Both the morality and the effectiveness of the bombing attacks have been called into question by historians. There is no doubt that they diverted 1.1 million people (which, however, included youths, men too physically disabled for military service, and prisoners of war) from war production to air-raid duty. Aircraft factories had to be dispersed, thereby reducing output. Much of the Luftwaffe had to be used to defend German cities instead of providing support in land combat.

On the other hand, the raids, especially those carried out by the British, were directed primarily at city centers with their civilian populations—consisting mostly of women, the very old and young and foreign workers—rather than bridges and oil refineries. This policy was followed by the British (but less so by the Americans) even after more accurate targeting methods were developed. More than one-third of British war production went into bombers, but the RAF long remained resistant to using bombers to search for German submarines. Consequently, even in the highly industrialized and geographically vulnerable Ruhr Valley of northwestern Germany only 10 to 15 percent of its productive capacity had been destroyed by the end of the war. And virtually no resources were spent on building landing craft, even though they were necessary for any invasion of Europe.

Germany's city centers contained cultural and residential buildings, and small, inefficient family-run stores, whereas factories were in the suburbs where they often escaped bombing altogether. Hence, German war production did not peak until September 1944, more than two years after the beginning of massive air raids. A case in point was Dresden in February 1945, when 30,000 civilians, mostly women, children and foreign workers, were killed, and some of the great architectural masterpieces of Western Civilization were destroyed. Even Josef Goebbels admitted in his diary that the bombing had seriously undermined civilian morale by March 1945, as it was intended to do. On the other hand, by that time Germany had hopelessly lost the war.

The cross Channel invasion of June 6, 1944, better known as D-Day, has been celebrated by politicians and the general public in the West as *the* turning point in World War II. Professional historians have been much more circumspect and have usually admitted only that the invasion was of decisive importance mainly in the Western Theater of the war. The popular view is rather self-congratulatory and assumes that the Russians had been doing little or nothing on the Eastern Front during the previous three years. Actually, as mentioned above, the decisive turning point in the war almost certainly came in 1941. The Channel crossing simply determined whether the Russians would defeat the Germans by themselves, or whether the West would share in that victory, and prevent the Communists from dominating the Eurasian continent from Vladivostok on the Pacific, to perhaps as far west as Brest in France, on the Atlantic.

The invasion was repeatedly postponed because the Allies had long been overestimating the Germans and because the United States was committed to taking the offensive against Japan in the Pacific. Churchill feared a repetition of casualties on the scale of World War I, and of those which the British and Canadians had suffered in the premature Dieppe raid on the northern coast of France in 1942. Much to the disgust of Stalin, and top American generals, Britain and the United States postponed a major invasion of the Continent in favor of sideshows in North Africa and Italy, while also imagining that the bombing of Germany alone might cause the Reich to surrender. Actually, the Germans may have been stronger in the west in 1944 than they were a year earlier. Their fortifications along the northern coast of France were certainly improved, and because the Eastern Front had in the meantime moved further west, it was easier for them to transfer troops between fronts. Nevertheless, the Germans were much weaker than the Allies feared. The concept of an "Atlantic Wall" was mostly a figment of Goebbels's propaganda.

On the other hand, Hitler also overestimated Allied strength. Although he correctly guessed that the Allies would land in Normandy, he and some of his generals thought that a still larger invasion would follow near Calais, in northeastern France, because it was much closer to Germany. Consequently, Hitler refused to allow von Rundstedt to move crack armored divisions to the presumed landing site because he wanted to save them for the "real" invasion, which was supposedly yet to come.

Hitler had predicted that if an Allied invasion succeeded, the war would be lost for Germany. Rather than acting on this sensible judgment, however, he kept the fighting going for almost another year, a year in which most of the destruction to German cities took place, a development to which Hitler was indifferent. Germany lost a half million men and most of its tanks in Normandy, in part because of Hitler's refusal to order a timely withdrawal. This delay also made it impossible to establish a defensive line along the Seine River in north central France. By September, the Allies enjoyed a twenty-to-one superiority in tanks and a twenty-five-to-one advantage in planes. However, they were slowed by a critical shortage of supplies, further exacerbated by the failure of British Field Marshal Bernard Montgomery promptly to clear the Scheldt estuary near Antwerp, Belgium. Some historians believe that the Western Powers missed an opportunity to end the war in 1944 because they pursued Eisenhower's "broad front" policy and experienced bad luck in their attempt to seize a strategic bridge across the Rhine at Arnhem in the Netherlands.

On December 15, Hitler launched what some have called his "last gamble" in Belgium. In reality, the subsequent Battle of the Bulge was no gamble at all on Hitler's part since, by this time, he had nothing to lose. His strategy, however, does tell us a great deal about his detachment from reality. Rather than saving his remaining strength for the defense of the German homeland and recalling hundreds of thousands of troops occupying Norway, Denmark, and parts of Latvia, he decided on yet another offensive, and not against the "subhuman" Russians, but against the West. Hoping to repeat his spectacular Ardennes offensive of May 1940, he imagined, at this late date, that if the Germans could capture Antwerp, it would destroy half the West's divisions, shatter its will, and cause a split between the Western powers and the Russians. In reality, all the momentary success of the offensive was made possible by stripping German defenses in the East, thus hastening a Russian breakthrough and ultimately the end of the war, with the Russians in possession of Berlin. It also placed the Western Allies in a poor bargaining position at the Yalta Conference in February, making it even more difficult than it otherwise would have been for them to resist Russian demands concerning Germany's eastern border with Poland. As for Hitler, he admitted to his confidant and minister of armaments, Albert Speer, that if Germany lost the Ardennes offensive the war itself would be lost. However, the subsequent defeat did not stop the Führer from continuing the hopeless struggle for another four months during which time German cities continued to be pummeled by Allied bombs.

## THE END OF THE THIRD REICH

If the successful Allied landings in Normandy on June 6, 1944, marked the final turning point in the military history of the Third Reich, the unsuccessful attempt to assassinate Hitler on July 20 marked the beginning of the last and most extreme phase of Nazi totalitarianism domestically. The plot was by no means the first attempt to kill Hitler, but it was the most carefully planned and biggest in terms of the number of conspirators involved, as well as the last. Several earlier attempts to assassinate the Führer, which had almost succeeded, merely confirmed Hitler's belief that he lived a charmed life and was destined for great things. The attempt in 1944 failed because a meeting, which Hitler was to attend in his headquarters in East Prussia, was moved from a concrete bunker to an above-ground wooden building, thus dissipating the effect of the bomb blast that was intended to kill Hitler. Whether the plot could have succeeded even if Hitler had been killed has been the subject of considerable debate.

What is more interesting is that both Nazi and Allied propaganda dismissed the plot as the work of a small clique of reactionary Prussian army officers. In reality, it involved a large number of people from many walks of life, including Social Democrats, trade unionists, theologians, scientists, and even disillusioned Nazis. To be sure, to have a chance of success the conspiracy had to be led by military officers. However belated the coup may have been, there was nothing comparable to it in the Soviet Union or Italy. It represents a tremendous act of moral as well as physical courage in view of Hitler's still considerable popularity and the fact that the conspirators had been given absolutely no encouragement from abroad.

The purge that followed the abortive coup plot was by far the largest in the history of Nazi Germany. Around 5,000 people, 2,000 of them army officers, were killed in the immediate aftermath of the plot, including 160 to 200 people who had been directly involved. But counting members of outlawed political parties, dissidents, and "defeatists," 11,448 people were executed between July 20 and the end of the war in May 1945.

These executions were merely one aspect of life in the Third Reich during its final ten months of existence. It was only now that the Nazi regime approached full totalitarianism. Almost all theaters and nightclubs were closed, along with universities and schools of domestic science and commerce. After July 1944, 140,000 Germans from the cultural sector and nearly 600,000 state and other public officials were reassigned to the Wehrmacht along with another 1 million workers. All military furloughs were canceled, and obligatory labor for women up to the age of fifty was introduced, but not fully implemented. Now, all men between the ages of fifteen and sixty were liable for conscription into the *Volkssturm* or "militia." Listening to foreign radio broadcasts or questioning the likelihood of victory became capital crimes. Goebbels's last success was to convince most Germans that defeat would be accompanied by starvation and annihilation which seemed plausible in light of Allied bombing and Soviet plundering and raping in eastern Germany.

Hitler's mental and physical condition in the last phase of the war has been the subject of considerable interest among historians. He apparently was convinced as early as 1937 that he did not have much longer to live. However, he still looked fairly healthy and vigorous in early 1942. But with the onset of the Russian campaign Hitler changed his old habits of sleeping late and indulging himself in plenty of relaxing entertainment. Constant meetings followed by short, drug-induced nights of sleep inevitably took their toll. By February 1945, he was starting to repeat himself, his limbs trembled, he walked stooped over, and his voice quavered, all symptoms of hardening of the arteries and Parkinson's disease. His crimes and errors were not caused by his illness; however, his physical decline and lack of sleep probably contributed to his moodiness.

Except for the very last weeks of his life when he became apathetic and untidy, Hitler's earlier character traits and political beliefs were simply exaggerated. He became even less tolerant, was convinced of being surrounded by traitors, complained that the courts were too lenient, was more prone to fits of rage, and was even more fanatical. He now lost all remnants of that pragmatism which had led to one political, economic, diplomatic, and military triumph after another between 1930 and 1941. His Social Darwinistic philosophy determined his final decisions. Like Mussolini, Hitler blamed the German people rather than himself for the catastrophe. They had proved to be less fit to survive than the Russians; therefore, they had lost the right to exist.

Hitler's seemingly inexplicable decisions after the summer of 1944 make a great deal more sense when seen in this nihilistic light. In September 1944, Hitler ordered a scorched-earth policy for all German territories that were about to be lost to the Allies. Germans were supposed to evacuate the areas; all who remained were to be denied the amenities of civilization including industrial plants and public utilities. Food supplies and farms were to be destroyed. Architectural monuments and works of art were all to be demolished. Such destruction, of course, would have reduced the fire power available to fight the Allies. The destruction of food and shelter would have had absolutely no impact on the amply provisioned British and Americans and not much even on the Russians, who by this time were being well supplied with food by the United States. Fortunately, not much German territory fell to the Allies before March 1945, when Albert Speer was able to trick Hitler into unknowingly signing an order countermanding it. In the end, Hitler failed in all his goals of conquering Lebensraum, exterminating all European Jews, and destroying Germany, although he came horrifyingly close in all three cases. He was completely successful only in killing himself on April 30, 1945, but not before issuing one final diatribe in his Political Testament against world Jewry and not before 4 million German soldiers and 3.2 million civilians had perished.

Meanwhile, Stalin's conduct of the war in its later stages, particularly his diplomacy, was a study in cold-blooded pragmatism. He had already used diplomacy to wring major territorial concessions from Hitler in the secret clauses of the Nazi-Soviet Nonaggression Pact. However, he never admitted that the Pact had helped precipitate World War II. He would not even allow it mentioned at the postwar Nuremberg Trials of major war criminals or in the postwar Soviet media. After the German invasion he made a virtue of his own weakness, just as Hitler had done between 1933 and 1935. In 1942, the Soviet Union was still in a precarious position and in need of all the help it could get from its new partners. This dependency, however, did not prevent Stalin from demanding, not just asking, for military aid and the opening of a second front that the Nazis would have to defend. He even suggested that cowardice could be the only reason for a delay, even though he realized that an invasion was completely impossible in 1942. After he had driven the Germans out of the Soviet Union in the summer of 1944, he sent part of his army into Rumania, Hungary, and Yugoslavia to extend his political influence, rather than immediately taking the most direct route through Poland to invade Germany. When his army did reach Warsaw in July 1944, he ordered it to pause and watch the Wehrmacht crush an uprising of anti-Communist resisters, in order to facilitate his postwar control of Poland.

Churchill and Roosevelt were anxious to please the Soviet dictator. If Stalin was dependent on them, they were equally dependent on him. That Germany suffered at least 75 percent of its casualties on the Russian Front undoubtedly enhanced Stalin's bargaining power. Nevertheless, Churchill, who had had an enormous distrust of Stalin before the war, now treated him like an insecure statesman whose trust had to be won through concessions. He started to refer to him as "Uncle Joe," a term also used by Roosevelt. At the Teheran Conference in November 1943, Roosevelt prepared to join Stalin's offer to toast the shooting of 50,000 German officers until the horrified Churchill objected. Although FDR probably considered the toast a joke, there is a good chance that Stalin did not, since he had ordered the execution of nearly as many Soviet officers only a few years before. At the Yalta Conference, the American president told an advisor that "Stalin does not want anything but security for his country, and I think that if I give him everything that I possibly can and ask nothing from him in return . . . he won't try to annex anything and will work for a world of democracy and peace."[2] That Roosevelt would expect a mass murderer of his own people to respect human rights in nations he had just conquered can only be explained by FDR's profound ignorance of Stalin's past.

Nevertheless, Western critics who have pilloried Roosevelt for "selling out" Eastern Europe at Yalta have been far off the mark. The Soviet domination of the East was virtually inevitable because of the fall of France and the belated entry of the United States into the war. Even a Western invasion of Europe in 1943 would have moved the East-West demarcation line only slightly further east, perhaps to the Oder river, Vienna, Prague, and Budapest, because a successful landing would have forced Hitler to transfer troops to the west to meet the new threat.

A fascinating thing took place in the course of the Russo-German campaign in 1941. Until then Hitler had managed to set much of his ideology aside. His campaigns were well calculated, pragmatic, and even marked with a certain restraint. The result had been a staggering

2 Quoted in M. K. Dziewanowski, *War at Any Price* (Englewood Cliffs, NJ, 1987), 321.

succession of victories. By contrast, soon after the beginning of the Russian campaign, the Führer cast all inhibitions aside and gave full vent to his most extreme ideological goals. This time an almost endless succession of defeats followed, which did not end until his suicide in a Berlin bunker in 1945.

Stalin, on the other hand, wore an ideological blindfold before and during most of the campaign in 1941. His distrust of everyone except Hitler and his refusal to take the strategic defensive, cost the Soviet Union literally millions of unnecessary casualties and allowed the invader to penetrate deep into the country. Before the end of 1941, however, he was starting to become a pragmatist. He turned the campaign into a war to save mother Russia and even enlisted the support of organized religion to complete this task. He began listening to his generals and accepting their advice. Diplomatically, he maneuvered the West into helping him defeat the Germans and conceding Eastern Europe as part of his sphere of influence. However, he disguised his political ambitions in Eastern Europe until after the war was safely won and he no longer needed the West. By the end of the war Stalin had secured for himself the position of infallible statesman. Shared dangers and accomplishments gave the Soviet regime the legitimacy it had never before had and would never enjoy again. (For one of the many monuments in Russia commemorating World War II, see figure 29.)

Meanwhile, Mussolini discovered that he had made a pact with the devil as soon as he entered the war in 1940. If Germany had won the war, Italy would have been at best a very junior partner. If Germany lost, the Fascist regime would be dragged down with it, as indeed it was. His militaristic ideology prevented him from staying on the sidelines the way General Franco did in Spain. (Franco remained in power until he died peacefully in 1975.) By comparison Mussolini and his mistress were shot and hung upside down in a gas station in Milan, in 1945, like two butchered pieces of meat.

# 10 / THE COLLAPSE OF SOVIET TOTALITARIANISM

*STALIN'S LAST YEARS, 1945-1953*

The relative moderation and pragmatism that marked Stalin's war years largely ended even before the war itself. An exception was the Russian Orthodox churches that had been reopened during the war that remained open after the conflict ended. Although he deported millions of ethnic minorities from their homelands to remote regions of the Soviet Union, he never again instigated anything so murderous as the Great Terror. As noted in the previous chapter, the cult of Stalin returned in 1943, after a two-year hiatus, and controls over journalists were also reapplied. Nevertheless, in his dealings with the West, he appeared to be the congenial, pipe-smoking "Uncle Joe" who, to be sure, was a hard bargainer when defending the interests of his country but was also a man who could compromise in the interests of world peace. At Yalta, he agreed to allow France to share in the occupation of Germany and to include democrats in the Polish government. At the Potsdam conference, held in July 1945, he also promised to join the war against Japan.

Even before the meeting at Potsdam, however, East-West relations began to sour as the common fear of Nazi Germany faded. In March 1945, President Roosevelt, growing alarmed at Soviet attempts to communize Poland, sent Stalin a strongly worded protest. However, neither Roosevelt, nor his successor, Harry Truman, was willing to risk war over Poland. Nevertheless, Stalin's relations with the West continued to deteriorate in the late 1940s until they reached a low point with the invasion of South Korea by Communist North Korea in 1950.

The causes of this East-West "Cold War" have been the subject of sometimes bitter disputes among historians. Contemporaries saw it resulting from Stalin's alleged imperialism and desire to communize as much of the world as possible. Some later historians claimed that the West, particularly the United States, overreacted to Stalin's legitimate desire for security in East Central Europe. Still other historians hold neither side entirely responsible and suggest that a confrontation was likely once the United States and the Soviet Union were left as the world's only superpowers. They point out that the traditional U.S. policy of seeking self-determination of nations, in this case in East Central Europe, was incompatible with Stalin's desire for security. With the temporary and partial exception of Czechoslovakia, freely elected governments in the areas occupied by Soviet troops at the end of the war were bound to be anti-Communist and, as such, would not fulfill Stalin's desire for security. On the other hand, Communist governments could only exist in East Central Europe with the support of Russian bayonets; and the presence of Russian troops as far west as the Elbe River in central Germany were bound to offend and frighten the West. In addition, there was a deep mutual suspicion which led both sides to construe the actions of their adversary in the most negative possible way.

Whatever view one favors, Stalin's highly suspicious personality should not be left out of the equation. These characteristics simply became more pronounced as he approached old age. Superficially, at least, there were some concrete grounds for that suspicion. The Anglo-French appeasement of Hitler before the war could easily be interpreted as a deliberate attempt to build up Nazi Germany as an enemy of the Soviet Union. The repeated delay in establishing a second major front in the West, especially in 1943 and early 1944, along with an interest Winston Churchill showed in a Balkan offensive, were also bound to arouse Stalin's distrust. However, to explain the origins of the Cold War by these actions alone is to ignore domestic considerations. One way of establishing social cohesion was through fear of a common outside enemy. In this effort Stalin was apparently so successful that the fear lasted until the 1980s. (See Figure 4.)

But Stalin also worried about internal enemies long before the cooling of diplomatic relations with the West. His paranoia and cruelty were exemplified by the rapid growth of *gulags*. These camps may have had 12 million inmates by the early 1950s, including thousands of former prisoners of war and civilians who, having been "infected" by the West, were transferred to Soviet camps as soon as the Germans released them. The maximum time served in these brutal labor camps rose from ten to twenty-five years. Consequently, it is probably naïve to believe that Stalin's treatment of his new subjects in East Central Europe would have been significantly different from his treatment of Soviet citizens if the West had pursued a more conciliatory policy.

Stalin's suspicious nature was probably also a factor in his rejecting Marshall Plan aid in 1947. Although the Marshall Plan is now seen as a quintessential Cold War measure, it was originally announced by Secretary of State George Marshall as an economic package that would aid all of Europe, including the Soviet Union. Such aid, however, if accepted, would have revealed to Western economists just how backward and weak the Soviet Union was and would have diluted Soviet dominance in its sphere of influence in East Central Europe. For example, the real wages of Soviet workers in 1948 were only 45 percent what they had been in 1928 and were still only 70 percent of the 1928 level in 1952. Accepting the foreign aid would also weaken Stalin's position at home by suggesting that Communist Russia needed the help of the capitalist West.

On the other hand, there is no evidence that Stalin had a timetable for taking over Europe any more than had Hitler. It is reasonable to assume that like Hitler, he took advantage of opportunities as they came along and was prepared to take control of as much territory as he safely could. However, the brutal tactics of Russian police organs in deporting democratic representatives from Poland and Hungary, together with a domestic Communist coup in Prague in March 1948, were no more unqualified successes than Hitler's takeover of Austria and the Sudetenland a decade earlier. In each instance, the opponents of totalitarianism were frightened enough to take countermeasures; in Stalin's case the West was provoked into forming the North Atlantic Treaty Organization (NATO) in 1949.

Stalin's foreign policy was no carbon copy of Hitler's, however. Even at his most aggressive, the Soviet leader would not push a confrontation to the point of war if only because the Soviet Union had been so weakened by the Second World War. He (and his successors) apparently also recognized the hopelessness of exporting their brand of Marxian socialism to the advanced countries of the West. When the West responded with an airlift to his cutting off of ground transportation to its zones of occupation in West Berlin in 1948, he did not interfere with the flights and eventually called off the Berlin blockade early the next year. When the North Koreans invaded South Korea in

1950 (with Stalin's support), he also avoided direct involvement. Nevertheless, his foreign policy was overly ambitious because the empire he created eventually strained the resources of the Soviet Union beyond the breaking point. If he had allowed in East Central Europe the kind of democratic neutrality he conceded to Finland (apparently to avoid pushing neutral Sweden into NATO) he almost certainly would have avoided an arms race that Russia could not afford.

Stalin kept himself just as isolated as he did the Soviet Union. During the last eight years of his life he made only two public speeches. He granted few interviews because he did not want journalists to see that he had grown old and thin and that his hair had become white. He also did not want them to know that his memory was not what it once had been. His rapid aging was at least partly due to his lifestyle. Like Hitler, he turned night into day by not going to bed until nearly dawn and like Hitler he was chronically sleep deprived during the war. Unlike Hitler, though, he smoked cigarettes and pipes and consumed large quantities of alcohol. Nevertheless, he maintained his grip on power by rarely allowing Communist party organs like the party Congress and the Central Committee to meet. For example, the party Congress met only twice between 1934 and Stalin's death in 1953. Like Hitler, he created great confusion (but also more loyal followers) by increasing the number of official positions and overlapping their responsibilities in a concerted effort to prevent any one person from accumulating too much power. Like Hitler and Mussolini as well as other dictators, Stalin was particularly careful not to groom a successor who might instead become a competitor.

Economically and culturally, the postwar years picked up where the prewar years left off. Stalin continued to regard peasants as enemies and consequently agriculture remained highly centralized, like the rest of the economy, but even more backward. The country produced less grain annually in the last four years of Stalin's rule than it had under Tsar Nicholas II in 1913! Culturally, the party continued to lay down the law in all fields, such as philosophy, linguistics, and mathematics. Stalin was particularly intrigued with the pseudoscience of the biologist Trofim Lysenko, who believed that plants could be permanently changed by their environment, an idea that the Soviet dictator believed could also be applied to human beings.

During the last five years of his life Stalin became almost as obsessed with Jews as Hitler had been, and he regarded them with much the same hostility as he had earlier the kulaks and his own generals.

If Hitler believed in a world conspiracy of Jewish Bolshevism, Stalin was convinced there was a world Jewish conspiracy of capitalism and Zionism (although he had supported the founding of Israel in 1948 as a way of weakening Great Britain in the Middle East). Stalin had thousands of elite Jewish doctors, intellectuals, and artists arrested and imprisoned as saboteurs, spies, or assassins. Dozens were executed, and thousands lost their jobs, especially if they were in the army or the secret police, now called the KGB, or if they were in party committees. Stalin's anti-Semitism struck close to home when he strongly objected to his older son, Yakov, marrying a Jew; his daughter, Svetlana, committed an unpardonable offense by falling in love with a Jew. Stalin broke up that romance by sending the paramour to a labor camp for ten years.

The last straw came when Golda Meir arrived in Moscow in the fall of 1948 as the Israeli ambassador. A big demonstration of Jews caused Stalin to inaugurate a campaign against Jewish culture and Zionism. "Rootless cosmopolitans" presumably threatened the Soviet Union. Jewish schools and publications were shut down and Nazi-like quotas were placed on Jewish students' admissions to universities and scientific institutes, as well as for the employment of Jews in the diplomatic corps and the legal profession. Stalin's anti-Jewish phobia and possibly his growing arteriosclerosis of the brain first diagnosed at this time finally convinced him that Jewish doctors throughout the country were secretly trying to kill their patients, so he had a large number of them arrested in the summer of 1952. In early 1953 he announced to his lieutenants that all Soviet Jews had to be deported to Siberia. There is also evidence that he was planning a new general terror in order to reestablish "discipline," which presumably had been impaired by the war.

## THE KHRUSHCHEV ERA

Soviet totalitarianism began disintegrating from the moment Stalin died on March 5, 1953. The process was painfully slow, however, and did not fully end until the Soviet Union itself dissolved in 1991, if indeed even then. Never again in Soviet history would there be a leader of Stalin's enormous power who so completely dominated his subordinates. And never again would state-mandated terror—one of the major elements of totalitarianism—be quite so ubiquitous and frightening. However, the fear of the secret police and gulags instilled by Stalin long outlasted his death. Its very memory was enough to keep most Soviet citizens firmly in line. The official Communist ideology also lost much of its rigidity and utopianism. However, it too, like fear, did not disappear and was at least passively accepted by the Soviet majority until the late 1980s.

Contrary to the fears of the Communist party's leadership, there was no popular revolt following Stalin's death, probably because there was too much fear and inertia. Astonishingly, there was even widespread grief when his death was announced. Stalin's autocracy was replaced by a collective leadership, and his power fragmented in many directions. Of decisive importance in reining in the terror was the overthrow of the chief of secret police, Lavrenti Beria. He was executed, along with his closest colleagues, at the end of 1953. His death, however, marked the last time that a major Soviet leader was executed. It also meant that the KGB was no longer a virtual state within the state but was subordinate to the party.

Beria had been one of just five men who had inherited the bulk of Stalin's vast powers. However, it was Nikita Khrushchev, born in 1894 the son of a Ukrainian miner, the general secretary of the Communist party, a title that Stalin had not used since 1934, who emerged victorious from the struggle for the succession in 1956. At a mere five feet and one inch the corpulent but gregarious Khrushchev seemed to his colleagues the least threatening of Stalin's possible successors, much like Stalin himself after the death of Lenin. Like Hitler and Stalin, Khrushchev's rivals badly underestimated him.

A process that later came to be known as "de-Stalinization" began immediately after the dictator's death. In the period between 1953 and 1955, party organs like the Congress and the Central Committee, which rarely had been called into session by Stalin and had no power when they did meet, regained the authority they had in Lenin's time. However, no thought was given to bringing the masses into the political process or to permitting an organized political opposition. By 1956, the extreme isolationism of the Soviet Union had also been abandoned.

Rather than withdrawing from the West, Khrushchev, wanted Russia to compete with it in industrial production, athletics, and cultural influence. Foreign travel and cultural exchanges with the West were encouraged, although travelers, both to and from the USSR, were closely monitored. Khrushchev himself traveled widely both at home and abroad exhorting local party officials and issuing both threats and appeals for coexistence. A considerable cultural thaw also took place during his rule as authors and artists were able to take up subjects that had been absolutely taboo under Stalin.

The most dramatic break with the past, however, and the high-water mark of de-Stalinization, was Secretary Khrushchev's four-hour "secret" speech to the XXth party Congress in 1956. The speech, entitled "On the Cult of Personality and its Consequences," was made to 1,500 delegates including some prominent foreign Communists. The speech could not remain secret for long and soon leaked out to the whole country. It was an attempt to cleanse the party and its ideology by separating them from the crimes of Stalin even though Khrushchev himself, as a member of the ruling Politburo, was complicit in many of these crimes. In an all-night session, Khrushchev enumerated the number of innocent party members and military officials who had been killed in the purges. He also blamed Stalin for all the failures of Communism after 1934; Stalin had been a megalomaniac who had eliminated all his rivals and afterwards a large portion of the Soviet people. Khrushchev, however, was careful to keep his attack personal. It was not an unambiguous critique of all of Stalin's deeds. The bureaucratic system, the highly centralized command economy, collectivization, and the monopoly position of the Communist party, along with its ideological infallibility, were all left unchallenged.

Khrushchev's speech, simultaneously brave and reckless, had enormous consequences, some intended and some not. It greatly reduced the pall of fear that had paralyzed society, and it increased the legitimacy of the regime. On the other hand, however much the general secretary may have wished to defend the principle of the party's infallibility, many Russians began wondering how an infallible party could have permitted a man like Stalin to attain power in the first place. In the West, the speech also had a shattering effect on Communist party members who had refused to believe rumors about Stalin's crimes. The speech, combined with the Soviet crushing of anti-Communist rebellions in Poland and Hungary (inspired in part by the official admission of Stalin's crimes), which took place a few months later, led many non-Soviet Communists to resign from the party.

Still more disillusionment with the regime resulted from revelations about Stalin's labor camps and collectivization. The publication of *One Day in the Life of Ivan Denisovich*, by Alexander Solzhenitsyn, made the general public aware of the horrors of life in a gulag. Even more information about the camps became available as a result of Khrushchev releasing most political prisoners. Disclosures about the involuntary nature and brutality of collectivization called into question the very legitimacy of the collective farms.

De-Stalinization involved much more than a simple denunciation of the past. Khrushchev was determined to increase the regime's stability by increasing the freedom of workers to choose their jobs and by catering to the popular desire for the availability of more and better consumer goods and housing. Wages, work hours, and pensions were also all improved. After 1955, peasants were no longer treated like enemies of the state. In April 1956, a decree abolished the fifteen-year prison sentences that had been given to peasants and industrial workers who had left their jobs. The slave labor of prison camps also became counterproductive in an increasingly technological era. Heavy industry, which had been the be-all and end-all of the Stalinist era, was now put on a par with light industry—in theory although not in practice. By 1960–61, Khrushchev was calling for some decentralization of industry and a larger role for the marketplace. However, any hope of significantly increasing the number of consumer goods was contradicted by the expansion of the space and military programs, which diverted capital, scientists, engineers, and managers into nonconsumer-oriented areas. There was also no overall concept, cohesion, or consistency to the general secretary's economic reforms. His ideas were later characterized by the Soviet ambassador to the United States, Anatoly Dobrynin, as ranging "from genuinely interesting to the impractical and bizarre."[1] An even greater problem was that Khrushchev raised unrealistic expectations in the people who were not satisfied with their standard of living only being modestly improved. His "Virgin Lands" project east of the Caspian Sea turned into an economic and ecological fiasco. By basing the legitimacy of the Soviet Union on economic performance, Khrushchev and his colleagues were endangering their own rule. His boast in 1961 that the Soviet Union would far surpass the West economically by 1970 turned out, in the long run, to be a bad joke. The general secretary also threatened the privileged positions of those party members whose jobs were tied to the status quo.

Khrushchev's foreign policy alternated wildly between attempts to improve relations with the West (détente) and threats of nuclear

1 Anatoly Dobrynin, *In Confidence* (New York, 1995), p. 47.

annihilation. Soviet relations with China also deteriorated, and the Cuban missile crisis of 1962 resulted in a Soviet humiliation that finally gave Khrushchev's enemies the excuses they needed to oust him. A speech he gave just two weeks before his removal, assigning a low priority to heavy industrial production and military strength, also threatened a great many vested interests in the USSR. However, when Khrushchev was overthrown by his enemies in the Politiburo in 1964 (the only time in the history of the Soviet Union when that body had exercised such power), he was accused of incompetence, not treason. After 1958 Khrushchev, like Stalin, had started surrounding himself with yes-men and did not bother to consult the Politbuoro before making important decisions. Though deposed, he was able to live out the rest of his life in peaceful retirement. Even those people close to him were merely demoted, not purged. Although Khrushchev's administration ended ignominiously, he can at least be credited with alleviating the worst aspects of Stalinism. A survey of young adults in 1998 placed Khrushchev behind only Nicholas II as the most respected Russian leader in the twentieth century.

## REACTION AND REFORM: FROM BREZHNEV TO GORBACHEV

Khrushchev's nine years of power were followed by the eighteen-year rule of Leonid Brezhnev (1964–82), the second longest in Soviet history. In general, Brezhnev's rule represents a conservative reaction to the reforms of his predecessor. The reputation of the KGB was restored and its 90,000 officers and 300,000 employees continued to run 900 labor camps containing over 1 million prisoners, although these numbers were sharply down from the Stalin era. By the early 1980s, even Stalin's memory had been largely rehabilitated. Although he was not the subject of virtual religious worship, he was again the great national leader whose devotion to the working class and selfless struggle for socialism was unquestionable. Serious criticism of his wartime leadership and collectivization was banned by the mass media that was still thoroughly controlled by the regime. What Khrushchev had called "crimes" were now called "mistakes." However, neither Stalinist terror nor rigid cultural orthodoxy returned, and there was even more emphasis on material incentives and individual rewards than under Khrushchev. This was a golden age for Soviet bureaucrats, the *nomenklatura*, who led comfortable lives without fear of being purged. However, all groups in Soviet society saw their standards of living rise fairly quickly until the late 1960s and then more slowly until the middle 1970s.

The improvement in the economy, however, especially in the early 1970s, was due largely to the increase in the international price of crude oil that greatly benefited an oil-exporting country like the Soviet Union. By the late 1970s, the Soviet economy stopped growing altogether. The reason for this stagnation is not entirely clear. Russia's successful but costly attempt to achieve military parity with the United States along with its aid to "liberation movements" in colonial territories are certainly partial reasons. Another explanation is the decline in the international price of crude oil in the late 1970s.

Perhaps the Soviet people were also simply morally and physically exhausted after sixty years of hard work and privation. Although there were more opportunities for plant managers to exercise initiative, the primacy of central planning remained unchanged. Drunkenness, slackness at work, and especially the corruption of state and party officials all became more common. Life expectancy declined and the infant mortality rate rose. Working conditions were bad, and the quality of goods produced was even worse. Productivity was also hurt by the 10 million inspectors—10 to 15 percent of the entire work force—whose sole job was to monitor and control the performance of other workers and the fulfillment of the quota system of production.

The political and economic situation of the Soviet Union did not improve after the death of Brezhnev in November 1982. His successor, Yuri Andropov, who had just completed fifteen years as chairman of the KGB, was already sixty-eight when he began his fifteen months as the general secretary of the Communist party. During that time he consolidated his power, the economy remained stagnant, and foreign relations actually deteriorated. His main accomplishment was reestablishing the KGB as the linchpin of the Soviet system and the interpreter of the party's will. His long-range goals (at least publicly) were still those of his predecessors going back to Lenin: to Sovietize the world and to create a new "Soviet man," which meant putting work ahead of one's material needs. Andropov carried out no reforms during his brief tenure in office, but he did recognize the need for change and dismissed some officials whose corruption went well beyond the norm.

When Andropov died in February 1983, he was succeeded by an even older man, the seventy-three-year-old Konstantin Chernenko. His chief asset seems to have been that he was about the same age as the other top leaders of the party and as such could be trusted not to make any drastic changes. He did not disappoint them. During his year in office he basically continued the policies of his predecessors, except perhaps for making the criminal code even harsher, and the use of torture more common. Chernenko was a nonentity who had no charisma or ideas and could not even read a speech effectively. He was simply an embarrassment to officials who had elected him.

It was perhaps for these reasons that Chernenko's death in March 1985 marked the end of the second generation of Soviet leaders who were born shortly before the First World War. The election of fifty-four-year-old Mikhail Gorbachev as general secretary by the Politburo represented as much of a generational change as the elections of presidents Kennedy and Clinton did in the United States. Born in 1931, Gorbachev belonged to a numerically large cohort that had escaped Stalin's purges and the ravages of World War II. He had had a model career in the Communist party, which he had joined when he was twenty. When he joined the Politburo in 1979, he became its youngest member.

Gorbachev's generation lacked the fanaticism of the first or even the second generation of Communist leaders. It was no longer satisfied with vague promises about a better life in the distant future. By the 1980s, the time had long passed when material privation could be legitimately blamed on the terrible destruction of World War II. This attitude was confirmed by information obtained from newly opened archives that revealed that the Soviet Union had defeated Nazi Germany *despite* the efforts of Stalin and the Communist Party, not because of them. This new generation was also much better educated than earlier ones, and in particular was well aware that the Soviet standard of living lagged far behind that in the West (and in some cases, as with East Germany, even its satellites) and was falling still further behind. What is perhaps most significant about Gorbachev's early career is that he reached his political maturity during the de-Stalinization of the 1950s, when the truth about Stalin's crimes and "exciting" new reforms abounded. He was the best-educated Soviet leader since Lenin, having earned a law degree from Moscow State University; he was also the most willing to experiment with new ideas. If Khrushchev had wanted to cleanse the Communist system, Gorbachev wanted it thoroughly reformed—but not abolished.

The attitudes held by Stalin's successors toward the memory of the Soviet dictator provide an excellent barometer for measuring the overall philosophy of their regime. Khrushchev had attacked Stalin for executing so many party members and military officers, but he did not actually claim that the purged officials had been innocent. Gorbachev condemned Stalin for both his punishments and his fantastic allegations. Gorbachev's policy of glasnost, or openness, made it possible to discuss many things in the press that previously had been taboo. Even the saintly Lenin was not completely exempt from criticism. Nevertheless, freedom of the press under glasnost fell far short of tsarist laws after 1865, which had exempted all books over 160 pages from censorship; after 1905, newspapers and pamphlets had been relatively free as well.

Gorbachev's other slogan was *perestroika*, or restructuring. It was a vague reference to the need for economic reforms. To carry out such reforms, however, he was dependent on the very people who had the most to lose by them: Communist hard-liners, the armed forces, and the KGB. Among the general public he also could not expect much sympathy from the older generation especially veterans of World War II and pensioners, who had a sentimental longing for the "good old days" of discipline and order.

## PROBLEMS OF THE SOVIET ECONOMY AND SOCIETY

Despite the tinkering done by Khrushchev and his successors, the Soviet economy and society during the Gorbachev years remained much as they were during the Stalinist era: all aspects of the Soviet Union were still highly centralized. Gorbachev revealed how difficult it was to make fundamental reforms when he asked in 1987: "How can we agree that 1917 was a mistake and all the seventy years of our life, work, effort and battles were also a complete mistake, that we were going in the 'wrong direction'?"[2] In the economy, the quantity of production, even if done by wasteful and obsolete means, was more important that the quality. Until Gorbachev, innovation was more often discouraged than encouraged. With regard to consumer goods

2 Mikhail Gorbachev, *Perestroika: New Thinking for Our Country and the World* (New York, 1987), p. 42.

the emphasis was still on annual increases in quantity. Qualitative improvements required innovations and new technology that in the short run would reduce production, and therefore they were seldom introduced.

The economy continued to be centrally planned, all farms were collectives (although peasants were still allowed to keep their relatively productive private plots of land), ordinary workers were denied real power in this workers' paradise, and a huge bureaucracy still enjoyed privileges undreamed of by the masses. All communications about resources and markets took place only "vertically," between factory managers and central planners in Moscow. No meaningful conversation took place "horizontally," between neighboring enterprises. The whole system was geared to satisfying the desires of the supervisory bureaucracy, not the consumers. Owing to corruption and a censored press, no managers or workers were laid off, and there were no bankruptcies resulting from the demand for a product not matching the supply. Actually, it is unlikely that central planners would even hear of such fiascoes, because factory managers would simply falsify their reports.

Much more serious in the long run than the low productivity of Soviet industries and the poor quality of the goods they produced was the damage done to the environment by the reckless drive for heavy industrialization. To create electricity, over 46,000 square miles of often-choice agricultural land was submerged by reservoirs. By the end of the 1970s, air pollution had reached dangerous levels in over 100 cities. Soviet rivers carried twenty times more pollutants than the Rhine, even though the latter traversed some of the most densely populated and highly industrialized areas in the world. Evaporation from irrigation caused the Aral Sea to lose about half its surface area, resulting in a tremendous loss of fish and the desertification of surrounding areas. Similar degradations to the environment took place in the Soviet satellites of East Central Europe. Damage to the forests of East Germany caused by air pollution was greater than anywhere else in the world. All of these environmental disasters were finally fully exposed in the Gorbachev era thanks to glasnost. However, glasnost could not prevent an even bigger catastrophe, namely the explosion at the nuclear power plant at Chernobyl in 1986.

The picture was no better in agriculture. Of course the Soviets faced some natural handicaps not often mentioned in the Western media. Much of their land was in areas that were either too cold or dry to be arable. Even in more naturally fertile areas, rainfall was erratic.

Nevertheless, most of the Soviet Union's agricultural wounds were self-inflicted. Stalin and his successors continued to insist that farms remain collectivized even though peasants produced one-third of the meat, 40 percent of the milk, and 55 percent of the nation's eggs on their private plots, which comprised only 3 percent of all agricultural land. On the other hand, the amount of grain grown on land belonging to the collectives could not even keep up with the needs of the growing population. And 10 to 15 percent of the grain and 50 to 60 percent of the fruits and vegetables rotted in the fields, ruined during the harvest, or spoiled on the way to the market. Beginning in 1963, and frequently thereafter, the Soviet Union imported much of its grain from the West. The shortfall was not due to a lack of investments. For years, about one-quarter of all governmental investments went into agriculture. Nevertheless, agricultural productivity remained at about 15 to 25 percent of U.S. levels.

The inefficiencies of the Soviet economy resulted in chronic shortages of basic foodstuffs, adequate housing, and consumer goods that people were willing to buy. In total calories, the diet of the average Soviet citizen was not far behind that of the average American. However, 70 percent of the Soviet diet in 1965 consisted of grains and potatoes, compared with 28 percent in the United States. Only 25 percent of the Soviet diet consisted of meat, vegetables, and fruits, and the diet did not markedly improve in the 1970s and 1980s. Even to obtain these meager foodstuffs and other necessities, Soviet housewives had to stand in line an average of three hours a day, as compared to two hours a day in 1930. For consumer goods, the problem was not availability, but the unwillingness of Soviet shoppers to buy what was for sale. For example, there was a shortage of decent shoes even though 800 million pairs were produced annually or nearly three pairs for every citizen. The same was true of clothing. Warehouses were full of clothes that no one would buy. In fact, on the eve of Gorbachev's rise to power, the accumulation of unsold goods was rising two to three times faster than the output of industry. Nothing else, not even the absence of civil liberties, caused so much dissatisfaction in the Soviet Union and its satellites as the lack of quality consumer goods. Yet it was central planning and state ownership of the means of production that were supposed to make the Soviet system superior to all others.

The increase in the level of education received by the average Soviet citizen only added to the general population's aggravation. By the 1980s, Soviet society no longer consisted of illiterate or semiliterate peasants and unskilled and poorly educated industrial workers. Even though it was far behind the most advanced Western countries, the Soviet Union was becoming to some extent a "high-tech" society. As late as 1959, 91 percent of the Soviet population had only an elementary education. By 1984 that percentage had dropped to 14. In 1941, only 2.4 million people had specialized or technical education. By 1960, there were 8 million such people. When the Soviet Union collapsed in 1991, 31.5 million citizens had this kind of advanced training. Moreover, whereas four-fifths of the population consisted of peasants on the eve of the Bolshevik Revolution, only one-fourth of the population was still comprised of farmers by the end of the 1980s. In Khrushchev's time only three Soviet cities had more than 1 million inhabitants. By the time of Gorbachev's administration that number had risen to twenty-two. Many of the country's intellectuals, especially in the late 1980s, traveled to professional meetings in the West or met with foreign colleagues in Russia. Despite Soviet propaganda, they were painfully aware of the Soviet Union's lack of consumer goods and general economic backwardness and were unwilling to tolerate it any longer. The indispensability of their scientific research also required a certain amount of intellectual freedom.

## SOVIET WOMEN IN THE LAST YEARS OF THE REGIME

Perhaps the most dissatisfied people in late Soviet society were women. Their social status had changed little since the 1920s. The issue of female inequality had been officially "solved" since 1930, so discussion of it was taboo in the Soviet press. Khrushchev did bemoan the small percentage of women in the Communist party in his famous "secret" speech of 1956, but the number continued to remain low. Somewhat surprisingly, it was the phlegmatic Brezhnev who reopened the issue of the proper status of women in communist society, but only because in the 1960s and 1970s the Soviet Union was suffering from falling economic productivity, labor shortages, and an exceedingly low birth rate. Even more discussion about women's issues took place during Gorbachev's tenure in office; but there were just as many voices supporting women's traditional status as there were calling for radical change. Deeper issues such as why so few contraceptives were available, why prostitution still existed in a socialist society, and why abortions took place under stressful conditions, remained off limits. In any event, even Gorbachev's famous glasnost and perestroika made very little difference in the day-to-day lives of Soviet women.

Women, along with men, did benefit from the Soviet Union being a more mechanized and technological society, so that after about 1960 they were a little less likely to be engaged in heavy manual labor than in earlier decades, and more likely to work in clerical or service positions. However, their jobs were still concentrated in less desirable or at least more poorly paid professions. During the 1980s, women comprised 98 percent of the nation's janitors, 90 percent of the conveyor-belt operators, and two-thirds of the highway construction crews. Women continued to be strongly represented in such traditional "women's" professions as teaching and medicine, where they made up 75 percent of the instructors and 70 percent of the physicians. Altogether, women held 51.5 percent of all nonagricultural jobs. As in the 1920s, they continued to earn only 60 to 70 percent as much as men did for the same work (about the same percentage as in the West), in part because few of them made it into the top ranks. Teachers received little more than half the income of skilled workers. Part of the reason for this differential was that schools encouraged boys to study difficult subjects like mathematics whereas girls were steered into the less prestigious and less lucrative humanities. Moreover, women lacked free time for study because they needed to work outside the home and were still responsible for all the housework with few labor-saving appliances. Consequently, it was difficult for women to upgrade their skills in night schools or through correspondence courses.

As indicated, women effectively held two nearly full-time jobs: one at the workplace and the other in the home, where they still spent at least thirty to forty hours a week on housework (forty-seven in East Germany) or about twice as many as their husbands. As a result, little time was left for bearing and raising children. Families continued to live in tiny, mostly two-room apartments where privacy was rare. The combination of these factors, along with increasing urbanization, meant that the birth rate steadily declined after the early postwar years, especially in the 1970s and 1980s, when it was barely above the replacement level. The demographic dilemma was aggravated by a shockingly high rate of infant morality, well above 20 per 1,000. One-time government grants given at a child's birth had little more impact than similar grants had had in Nazi Germany and Fascist

Italy. Only the prospect of getting a larger apartment seems to have had some effect on people's desire to have more children. Attempts by the government to increase births by denying women birth-control devices and information on contraception—again reminiscent of the fascist states—simply led to an enormous number of abortions, about five to eight for every live birth, giving the Soviet Union the highest abortion rate in the world. The procedure had been legalized again with little publicity in 1955 because so many illegal and dangerous abortions had been taking place.

Some Soviet women tried to cope with their hard and dreary lives by turning to alcohol; the rate of alcoholism among women became even higher than that for men, and for women it carried a much greater stigma. A more harmless coping device was fashion. Soviet women spent as much money as they could afford on clothes and cosmetics in order to bring some color into their lives. Here was one small way in which life for Soviet women had improved. In Stalin's time the wearing of unorthodox clothing could land a woman in prison.

In one other way Soviet women had changed by the 1980s. They were much less willing to tolerate their second-class status, and much more aware that women in the West were far better off. No doubt with some naïveté, Soviet women especially admired what they considered to be the comparative gentlemanliness and "casual elegance" of American men, who were also much better providers than Russian husbands. Soviet women contrasted this real or imagined American behavior with the lack of courtesy and even boorishness of Soviet men. Consequently, many Soviet women, by the late 1980s, were willing to state openly that Communist-style emancipation was a fraud that had merely turned them into beasts of burden working at the command of the government and their husbands.

## SOVIET SOCIETY IN THE 1980s: THE BALANCE SHEET

It would be neither accurate nor fair to end this discussion of Soviet society by suggesting that everyone was unhappy with the system and ardently favored radical change. Most Soviet citizens believed that very substantial improvements had been made in the educational system since the Bolshevik Revolution. The literacy rate for adults was close to 100 percent, and a fairly high percentage of the population had achieved advanced educations. Soviet schools had helped make the

USSR a world leader in some areas, such as space exploration. The country's standard of living, if far behind that of the West, was at least well above the level of the tsarist days as well as the early post–World War II period. By 1985, almost every Soviet family owned a television set and a refrigerator and two-thirds owned washing machines. Most people also appreciated the security provided by the cradle-to-grave state welfare system, including guaranteed employment, free (if poor) health care, low prices for food and housing, and safeguards against "internal anarchy." They also derived some satisfaction from the Soviet Union being one of the world's two superpowers, which enjoyed a very considerable influence around the world. At least as late as Mikhail Gorbachev's rise to power, the majority of the Soviet people would have been satisfied to return to something like the New Economic Policy of the 1920s with its mixture of free enterprise, state-run big industries, and social welfare programs.

What provided the system with its relative stability, however, were not those signs of progress that did benefit all citizens, but rather the very real privileges enjoyed by about 10 percent of the population. Party bosses, managers of factories and collective farms, senior military officers, research scientists, and world-class athletes lived in their own private and carefully guarded compounds. They used special hospitals having the best in medical technology, shopped in their own stores, which were well stocked with goods from the West, and had their own vacation homes (*dachas*). Whereas ordinary Soviets could expect to wait ten years to buy an automobile of very poor quality, the elite were whisked around in chauffeur-driven black limousines. In East Germany, where the fear of revolt was much greater than in the Soviet Union, the privileged classes also included doctors and teachers who had access to better housing than the rest of the population and who earned three times as much as common workers.

## THE REVOLT OF THE SATELLITES AND THE DISINTEGRATION OF THE SOVIET UNION

The Yale historian Paul Kennedy has identified what he calls "imperial overstretch" as the primary cause for the decline and fall of great powers. Such was almost certainly the case, at least in part, with the collapse of the Soviet Union. Although imperial powers hope to benefit economically as well as politically from their empires, the reverse is more likely to be the case, especially over the long run, and most especially if the subject nations derive few economic benefits from the empire. The Russians were able to provide the Eastern Europeans with some cheap raw materials from Siberia, and for a time the Soviets' military might was a welcome protection against a possibly resurgent West Germany. Otherwise, however, the satellite states were well aware that their forcible incorporation into the Soviet empire had cost them not only their freedom but was also a drain on their economies, because they were cut off from the markets and technology of the West. Many of the better-educated people, especially in East Germany, bitterly resented being denied the freedom to travel in the West. (See Figure 30.)

The empire was even more costly for the Soviet Union itself. To prop up the economies of their satellites, the Soviets sold them oil at half the world's market price. The satellites were also expensive militarily, because they required the presence of thirty-one combat-ready divisions equipped with the most modern weapons. In theory, at least, the satellites had to be protected from a possible attack by West Germany or from NATO as a whole. More realistically, however, the existence of the unpopular regimes could only be assured through the presence of Soviet tanks and bayonets. This critical fact was proven in an East German uprising in 1953, the Hungarian Revolution of 1956, and especially by the "Prague Spring" of 1968, when the Czechoslovak government of Alexander Dubček showed "dangerous" signs of wanting to liberalize the regime. Brezhnev feared these reforms might "contaminate" the other satellites and ultimately get completely out of control. To prevent this possibility, Brezhnev announced his doctrine that the Soviet Union and its European partners would forcibly intervene if the existence of a Communist government were in danger. By overthrowing the Dubcek government with troops from the Warsaw Pact (the Soviets' counterpart to NATO), Brezhnev in effect acknowledged that socialism in East Central Europe could be sustained only by force.

The Soviet Union, therefore, had to defend itself on five fronts: against NATO; China; militant Islam, especially in Afghanistan; dissidents in Eastern Europe; and dissidents in the Soviet Union itself. Even nonethnic Russians overwhelmingly did not identify themselves as Soviet citizens and felt a suppressed enmity toward the dominant

Russian majority, often disliking their non-Russian neighbors as well. The West, on the other hand, only had to defend itself against the Soviet Union and its very unreliable subject nations.

As the decades rolled past, the generation that had lived through the horrors of Nazi occupation was increasingly replaced by younger people who had grown up in the postwar world and knew only a peaceful and democratic West Germany. The détente policy of the 1970s pursued by the German Social Democratic chancellor, Willy Brandt, and the U.S. president, Richard Nixon, made it increasingly difficult for people living in Communist Eastern Europe to believe that they were in great danger of war. The siege mentality, one of the hallmarks of the Soviet ideology, became increasingly implausible in the era of coexistence and even more so under glasnost. For the Soviet Union, the possession of intercontinental ballistic missiles rendered the buffer status of its East Central European satellites largely obsolete. They had now become almost a pure liability. The same was even more true of far-away dependencies like Cuba and Angola, whose economies could only be maintained by massive Soviet assistance.

No one knows, of course, exactly what Mikhail Gorbachev was trying to accomplish in East Central Europe in the late 1980s, perhaps in part because, like Stalin and Khrushev, he did not even bother to consult the Politburo before making important decisions. The likelihood is, however, that he hoped to replace hard-line Communist leaders with popular reformers. Such a change would reduce the need for Soviet troops and expensive weapons and improve relations with the West. The declining Soviet economy of the early 1980s made it increasingly difficult for Russia to maintain its superpower status. Military expenditures absorbed no less than 30 to 40 percent of the country's gross national product. Improved relations with the West would enable the Soviet Union to reduce its military budget substantially, with the savings being invested in modernizing the Soviet economy and improving the standard of living. Gorbachev was encouraged in this belief by President Ronald Reagan, who was willing to abstain from his earlier virulent anti-Communism in order to end the arms race.

As a Marxist, however, even if a relatively enlightened one, Gorbachev believed that class differences were far more important than national ones. The Soviet state, he imagined, was a voluntary, multinational union, not the result of tsarist imperialism and Soviet conquests. Therefore, he badly underestimated nationalism as a centrifugal force, not only in the satellite states, but also within the Soviet Union itself. He believed the issue would fade away once the excesses of Stalin's nationality policy were replaced by a new tolerance. But nationalism proved to be a powerful force that he could not control. The new atmosphere of tolerance he created encouraged democratic elements and undermined the willpower of the ruling Communist parties in the satellite states. Furthermore, his open renunciation of the "Brezhnev Doctrine," and his unwillingness to support unpopular Communist governments in Eastern Europe, meant that their leaders were now emperors with no clothes. When demonstrations broke out in East Germany in the fall of 1989, revolutionary uprisings soon swept away hard-line and even the more moderate governments in all the Communist countries west of Russia.

## THE END OF SOVIET TOTALITARIANISM

The famous eighteenth-century historian and political commentator Alexis de Tocqueville wrote in his treatise on the French Revolution of 1789 that "the most perilous moment for a bad government is when it seeks to mend its ways. Only consummate statecraft can enable a king to save his throne when, after a long spell of oppressive rule, he sets to improving the lot of his subjects."[3] Soviet leaders, since at least Stalin, had been aware of this danger. None of them, including Gorbachev, had been elected to their office by a popular vote. They all relied on force, intimidation, or propaganda to push through most reforms.

It would be grossly inaccurate to assume, of course, that the Soviet Union of the late 1980s had exactly the same characteristics as the Soviet Union of the early 1950s. Stalinist terror had disappeared, but overt political opposition could still land a dissident in a work camp. Glasnost was clearly a step toward freedom of speech. However, until 1989 there remained, in the Soviet Union, many sacred cows, among them, the monopoly of power by the Communist party, central planning, and state-ownership of industries and property.

Only in 1989 did the fundamentals of Soviet totalitarianism, established by Lenin and entrenched by Stalin, begin to disappear. More open access to official archives revealed that the Baltic States had been occupied by the Soviet Union in 1940 as a result of a secret clause in the Nazi-Soviet Non-Aggression Pact of 1939. This revela-

3 Quoted in *Time*, January 1, 1990, 44.

tion completely undermined the legitimacy of the annexations and led to their secession in 1990. In March 1989, the first free elections were held in the Soviet Union since the elections of November 1917 for the ill-fated Constituent Assembly—which, it will be recalled, the Bolsheviks broke up after its first and only meeting. Thirty-seven key Communist bosses were voted out of office even though in most cases they ran unopposed but still could not garner 50 percent of the vote. In December of 1989, Gorbachev, an admirer of Lenin, attacked one of the most sacrosanct aspects of totalitarianism since Lenin himself, the infallibility of the ruling party, when he announced that "we no longer think that we are the best and are always right, that those who disagree with us are our enemies."[4] This radical change in policy was made official in February 1990 when the "leading role of the Communist Party" was removed from the Constitution and was followed by widespread defections from the party. An explosion of new non-Communist labor unions, cultural associations, and opposition political parties followed the party's loss of its monopoly of power. Meanwhile, glasnost caused the Soviet people to lose their fear of another pillar of the dictatorship, the secret police or KGB.

The election of the Communist party dissident, Boris Yeltsin, to the chairmanship of the Russian national parliament in 1990 proved to be the final blow to both to Gorbachev's leadership and the Soviet Union itself. Yeltsin proceeded to remove the Russian Federation from the Soviet Union and recognized the independence of the former Soviet republics. Gorbachev was now a man without a country to rule. He could have resisted Yeltsin's maneuvers only by force, something he was loathe to do.

The Communist party's problem was that even after monumental changes in its ideology and its lost monopoly of political power, it still had powerful assets. Although the party lost its property, every factory, office, and military regiment had a party cell, and party members continued to staff all important government and economic positions. Much like Stalin, the party had also destroyed, or prevented from arising, an alternative socioeconomic system. The combination of totalitarianism and bureaucracy had led to lethargy and inefficiency and had stultified the Soviet economy and culture. Seventy years of suppressing every form of private initiative had left most Soviets feeling that they were helpless and passive wards of the state who depended

4 Quoted in *Time*, February 19, 1990, 31.

on it for housing, health care, electricity, and a variety of subsidized prices. Moreover, the suppression of any organized opposition meant that there was no obvious alternative to totalitarian Communist rule. Throughout the Soviet period and for centuries before, work was what most Russians were compelled to do. With that compulsion removed there was no work ethic to take its place. Peasants, for example, when given the opportunity to own private farms, preferred to remain on collectives so they could collect their pensions. "Business," "profits," and "property" had become dirty words. The Communist system had succeeded not only in polluting the soil, water, and air; it had also polluted the mind.

At midnight on December 31, 1991, the flag of the Soviet Union came down for the last time over the Kremlin. Few countries in world history had ever collapsed so completely in wartime as the Soviets had in peacetime.

# 11 / LESSONS
# AND PROSPECTS

## THE TRIUMPH OF DOGMATISM

The totalitarian regimes are best known for their dogmatism and their doctrinaire fanaticism, and properly so. It was, for example, dogmatism that caused one disaster after another in the Soviet Union: War Communism; collectivization; an exaggerated emphasis on heavy industrialization; the purges; an unwillingness by Stalin to listen to the warnings of his advisors about a Nazi invasion; and a lack of freedom in education and the arts.

In contrast to the Soviet Union, where doctrinaire fanaticism was directed mostly at its own citizens, ideological rigidity in the fascist states was even greater in foreign policy. Italy's foreign policy objectives were grotesquely overambitious for what was still a largely underdeveloped country. Once Italy was confronted by a major military power like Great Britain, or even a minor power like Greece, its lack of realism and military strength were exposed almost immediately. In Germany, ideological dogmatism led to the expulsion of the country's most intellectually and commercially creative minority, the Jews, and a war of expansion that eventually united most of the world's major powers against it.

The totalitarian states were not always dogmatic. If necessary they could display a pragmatism that at times made them appear almost "normal." When the Soviet Union's industrial production dropped to 13 percent of the country's prewar level in 1920, Lenin realized that it was time to give up his radical War Communism, which had led to the confiscation of peasant foodstuffs and an overhasty nationalization of industries. Instead, he turned to a much more realistic New Economic Policy, which quickly restored the country's economy to prewar levels. With the country's very existence at stake following the

Nazi invasion in 1941, Stalin was capable of scrapping his utopian Marxism in favor of launching a "Great Patriotic War." Although he followed an expansionist foreign policy after the war, this policy was in his own mind at least in part defensive. He always respected the West's sphere of influence and never took steps that were likely to lead to a third world war.

Mussolini was shrewd enough to know that to retain power he needed the support, or at least the neutrality, of the king, the Church, and the middle and upper classes. Consequently, he was willing to sacrifice all of his earlier positions, even his anticlericalism, when the political climate changed, in order to gain support and to weaken opposition. The Concordat with the Vatican in 1929 was the best example of his pragmatism.

Even the supposed arch fanatic Adolf Hitler was perfectly capable of being pragmatic on any number of occasions. The failure of the Beer Hall Putsch caused him to abandon force in favor of legality in seeking the chancellorship. He renounced the German-speaking South Tyrol in order to win the friendship of Mussolini. He toned down his anti-Semitism in order not to frighten the more respectable elements of the middle class, and he even left Jewish businessmen alone for some time after he came to power in order not to disrupt the German economy. As chancellor, he posed for years as a simple veteran of World War I who wanted nothing more than to avoid a repetition of that bloodbath. Until 1939, his foreign policy was limited to relatively modest goals, which nearly all Germans enthusiastically supported, and which even the West felt moral qualms about opposing. Despite his bombastic espousal of Nordic racial superiority he had no problem allying with such "racially inferior" states as Japan, Croatia, and Slovakia. During the first two years of the war he tried repeatedly to make peace with Great Britain and to keep the United States out of the war.

Nevertheless, it would be very safe to say that pragmatism, no matter how successful and popular at home, was nothing more than a ploy for the totalitarian dictators, which they were eager to abandon at the very first opportunity. Exceptions were made only for things like entertainment, in which they had relatively little interest. Lenin and his followers considered the NEP to be a strictly temporary compromise of Bolshevik principles. Stalin backed off his collectivization policy and the Great Purges only when chaos had reached intolerable limits.

As soon as the tide of battle clearly shifted in 1943, he refurbished the cult of Stalin. After the war he restored prewar Stalinist orthodoxy in all areas of life and made sure that the Soviet people remained free from the contaminating influences of the liberal West. Stalin's successors, though lacking his incredible brutality and occasionally even making gestures toward improving the lot of long-suffering consumers, made sure that the essentials of Soviet totalitarianism remained intact. These vital components were the infallibility of Marxist ideology, the political monopoly of the Communist party, the command economy, and labor camps for anyone who got too far out of line.

Mussolini retained his pragmatism longer than the other dictators. Nevertheless, he used the balance of power between Hitler and the West to realize his imperialistic dreams beginning with Ethiopia. When it looked like the West was thoroughly defeated in June 1940, he again seized the opportunity to attack France. Likewise, when Greece appeared to be an easy target in 1940, he invaded, even though there was little to gain and a great deal to lose by the campaign.

Hitler also abandoned his pragmatism as soon as he thought it safe to do so. By 1938, he believed that German rearmament had progressed far enough that he could cease pretending to be a peace lover. He was also convinced that the German economy had fully recovered so that the expertise of Jewish businessmen was no longer essential. Therefore, he allowed "Aryanization" of Jewish property to accelerate. By the summer of 1941, when the war in Russia appeared to be won, Hitler no longer felt it necessary to show any restraint toward Soviet civilians, especially Jews. After successfully stopping a German retreat in the winter of 1941–42, he was more convinced than ever that the war could be won through sheer willpower.

## THE STRUCTURAL FLAWS
## OF TOTALITARIANISM

Aside from the dictators' willingness to surrender to their own ideologies, with fatal consequences, the very structure of the totalitarian dictatorships made their failures a near certainty. The most significant aspect of the totalitarian systems was the nearly limitless power it placed in the hands of the dictators. They could do almost anything they chose without fear of domestic, institutionalized restraints. This generalization applies most obviously to Stalin and least to Musso-lini. Stalin was able to ignore the passionate love 120 million Soviet peasants had for their private farms when he forced them onto hated collectives. He killed anyone he wished, no matter how high they were in the hierarchy of the Communist party or the military. He ignored countless warnings about an impending German invasion and left Russia inadequately defended when the awful moment arrived.

Mussolini ignored the opposition of the Catholic Church and of academicians when he rammed through anti-Semitic laws in 1938. It was he alone who decided that Italy should invade Ethiopia, aid Franco's rebels in Spain, attack France in 1940, invade Greece in the fall of the same year, and declare war on Yugoslavia in April 1941, the Soviet Union in June, and the United States in December.

Although Hitler enjoyed the support of a good many Germans in his anti-Semitic policy, the majority would have opposed his more extreme policies had they been fully informed of them. We still do not know Hitler's exact role in the Holocaust, but there is no question that he was always the driving force in the persecution of Jews. Hitler's prewar foreign policy was opposed by his senior military and diplomatic advisors almost every step of the way. It was he alone who decided on war in 1939, and it was he alone who had the power to keep it going long after it had become clear to any half-way rational person that the war was hopelessly lost.

Stalin, Mussolini, and Hitler also regarded loyalty to themselves to be a far higher virtue in others than competence. Corruption and incompetence could easily be tolerated as long as they did not become public scandals. All three men also liked to give overlapping respon-sibilities to their subordinates so that they alone could preside over the mess that they had created, and so none of their subordinates would emerge with the kind of clear-cut authority that might chal-lenge their own.

The monopoly status of the totalitarian parties, the infallibility of their ideologies, and their control over all forms of cultural expressions and public opinion, meant that they remained free of public criticism. This freedom from responsibility inevitably led to theft, corruption, nepotism, arrogance, bribery, graft, and a lack of accurate information about public sentiment. Spying and police reports were only partial solutions to this dilemma because informants were tempted to tell their superiors what they wanted to hear. With the brief exception of Stalin during the later stages of World War II, the dictators knew only what they wanted to know, not what they needed to know.

Spying was simply one way in which labor was wasted in the totalitarian dictatorships. In East Germany, at least 85,000 secret policemen (*Stasi*) were kept busy for forty years spying on 17 million people and writing 6 million documents (enough to fill 125 miles of shelves), most of which they regarded as worthless. (Not even the Third Reich had wasted so much manpower in spying on its own citizens.) However, total control of a country's population necessitated the creation of a huge bureaucracy. Bureaucracies were doubly useful to the dictators because they represented a form of patronage. Well-paid bureaucrats enjoying a host of privileges were not likely to lead a revolution, but they were also a tremendous drain on the economies of the states and created much popular cynicism.

All three totalitarian states tried to substitute propaganda for a free press, but with only mixed results. The general public was well aware that the news it received was censored and therefore was not inclined to believe it even when it was absolutely true. Wild rumors and secretly listening to foreign radio broadcasts filled the vacuum of reliable information. The dictators themselves became both the beneficiaries and the victims of their own propaganda. Totalitarian propaganda does appear to have convinced the Soviet, Italian, and German people that Stalin (and especially Lenin), Mussolini, and Hitler were no ordinary mortals. Whatever the faults of their political parties, which were often well known by the general public, the great dictators either did not know of them, or at least were not responsible for them. It was low-level Communist officials who were presumably to blame for the brutalities of collectivization and the purges, not Stalin, who once he became aware of the abuses intervened to stop them. (The Chinese held the same convictions with regard to Mao Tse-tung.) Fascist officials might be corrupt and grasping, but surely not Mussolini. Fanatical SA men might get carried away and burn down Jewish synagogues and wreck Jewish shops, but not with the approval of Hitler. Hermann Goering was responsible for the failures over Britain in 1940 and Stalingrad in 1942, but not Hitler. On the other hand, propaganda could not convince the Russians that they were better off materially than the West, could not make Germans lust for war in 1939, cajole the German people into believing that Italy was a powerful ally, and could not persuade the Italians that they were a warlike people. It could, however, convince the dictators that they were indeed infallible and that anyone who disagreed with them was at best wrongheaded if not an outright enemy.

Oddly enough, totalitarian propaganda for a long time was more effective abroad that it was at home. Many Westerners believed that Bolshevism was a noble experiment in socialism and that rumors of famine during collectivization were vicious lies. Britain and France were actually convinced that Italy was a truly great power at the time of the Ethiopian War and that to close the Suez Canal to Italian ships would entail great risks. The French believed in 1936 that by themselves they could not dislodge Germany from the recently remilitarized Rhineland, and both Britain and France felt that it would be far too costly to invade Germany while the Wehrmacht was off in the east obliterating Poland.

The totalitarian states also had mixed results with their economies. The abundance of cheap and forced labor in the Soviet Union encouraged wasteful labor-intensive methods. Soviet agriculture was a disaster from start to finish. Heavy industry made some impressive gains, and probably enabled the Soviet Union to survive the Nazi onslaught during World War II. On the other hand, the hell-bent drive toward industrialization left scars on the environment that will endure for decades, if not centuries. Soviet consumers were treated with virtual contempt, and housing was so flimsy that even relatively minor earthquakes in the 1990s brought scores of buildings down like houses of cards.

The Italian economy enjoyed moderate success during the 1920s, but was slower than Germany or Britain to recover from the Depression. Moreover, corporativism, far from destroying class divisions, exacerbated them. Germany enjoyed what at the time seemed like spectacular growth after Hitler came to power, but the recovery from the Depression actually began in 1932, and was not nearly as impressive as the German "economic miracle" after World War II.

The level of prosperity, or the lack of it, had a great deal to do with the overall popularity of the totalitarian regimes. Nothing enhanced Hitler's prestige so much as the rapid decline in the unemployment rate. Nothing was so detrimental to the reputation of the Soviet regime as its inability to produce high quality consumer goods and food.

The economic failures the totalitarian regimes suffered were often temporarily compensated by diplomatic and military victories, or by the need to defend the nation against invaders. Mussolini gave an enormous boost to the sagging popularity of the Fascist regime by conquering Ethiopia in 1935–36 and by persuading Hitler to attend the Munich conference in 1938. Germans who were lukewarm or even hostile toward the Nazis were thrilled by the bloodless takeover of Austria and the Sudetenland and by the easy military victories over Poland and especially France. By the time nearly all Germans were thoroughly disillusioned with the Nazi regime, following the defeat at Stalingrad, most of them felt they had no choice but to defend their country against the approaching Allies, especially in the face of the Allied demand for unconditional surrender. No matter how disgusted the Soviet people were with the terror and incompetence of Stalin's government, they were forced by Nazi barbarities to defend their country in 1941. The Soviet Union's growing military and political stature in the postwar world, together with the country's regular successes in the Olympic Games, also provided some vicarious pleasures for people whose lives were otherwise bleak and impoverished.

Whatever their temporary and partial economic, diplomatic, and military successes, the totalitarian states displayed a special talent for making enemies both at home and abroad. The Bolsheviks virtually declared war against the world and much of their own population when they came to power in 1917. They made no secret of their desire to overthrow the democratic and capitalistic governments of the West. They killed, deported, and sent to brutal labor camps the old aristocracy, the often highly educated bourgeoisie, the kulaks, and anyone else who did not toe the Marxist-Leninist-Stalinist line. The Soviet regime ultimately frightened most of the world and after World War II provoked the creation of the most enduring military alliance in world history, the North Atlantic Treaty Organization. The Nazis forced out two-thirds of some of their most creative and productive citizens, the Jews, and killed the remainder. After 1939 they declared war against most of the world. In so doing they brought about the most improbable of alliances, the coalition between the Soviet Union, Britain, and the United States. The Second World War not only brought the downfall of the Third Reich, but also ended centuries of European global domination. Mussolini, for a long time, was much more cautious, but even he eventually alienated the small, but highly productive, Italian Jewish community and then brought on the wrath of the West by allying himself with Germany.

## THE TOTALITARIAN LEGACY

The legacy of each of the totalitarian states differs substantially from the others. Because totalitarianism in Italy was only skin deep, its legacy has been undoubtedly the slightest. Until the mid-1990s the most obvious consequence of Fascism is the determination of most Italians not to have a strong executive authority. As a result, the country averaged about one prime minister per year since the overthrow of Mussolini. Nevertheless, the rejection of Fascism has not been complete. It is a startling fact that a married granddaughter of Mussolini, using her maiden name, was elected to the Italian Parliament in the early 1990s, a position she still held in 2002. It is hard to imagine a grandchild of Hitler suddenly appearing and using his grandfather's surname being elected to the *Bundestag* (federal parliament) of Germany. Moreover, a public opinion poll conducted in the late 1990s revealed that more than 60 percent of Italians believed that Fascism had been a "good regime" whereas only 0.2 percent described it as "brutal." Mussolini's name can also still be found etched in stone on many monuments around Rome and other Italian cities and even on the now Greek island of Rhodes.

The rise to the premiership of the richest man in Italy, the billionaire media magnate, Silvio Berlusconi, in 1994, 2001, and most recently in April 2008 can be seen as reflecting a growing disgust with its weak post-Mussolini governments. Italy's stagnant economy (making it the "sick man of Europe") and deteriorating education and health-care systems have created a growing desire to return to a strong leader and greater stability and prosperity. These feelings are perfectly understandable. What alarms some observers, however, is the prime minister's control of most of Italy's private television stations and his indirect control of state-run television, thus creating a conflict of interest. Corruption also remains a problem in Italy as does hostility toward illegal immigrants from Albania, North Africa, and the Middle East.

The Third Reich produced unexpected results after World War II, which would have astounded and infuriated the Führer. The catastrophic end to the war and horrifying revelations about the Holocaust thoroughly discredited racism, anti-Semitism, and extreme nationalism as respectable middle-class values, not only in Germany, but also in most of the rest of Europe and North America. They have survived only among radical fringe groups or in disguised forms. Authoritarianism and great power politics have been equally compromised among most Germans. Although extremist political parties have occasionally arisen in postwar Germany, their votes have remained small and they have disappeared within a few years. No one could have imagined in 1945 that a half-century later the United States and other countries would be practically begging Germany to play a larger role in world affairs.

For the sixty years of its postwar existence Germany has been ruled mainly by just two major parties, the Christian Democratic Union (the successor of the Center Party) and the Social Democratic Party, with two smaller parties often participating in coalition governments. This simplification of the multiparty system which existed in the Weimar Republic has produced political stability and social peace even during economic slumps. The ethnic Germans of East Central Europe, some of whom wished to be united with Germany, especially during the Depression, were either forced to emigrate to Germany after the war or have done so voluntarily since the collapse of the Soviet satellite system in 1989, thus settling, albeit ruthlessly, one of the troubling international issues of the late 1930s.

The only minority problem still facing Germany is the large and still not fully assimilated group of Turks who began coming to Germany as "guest workers" in the 1950s. The younger generation lacks good education and speaks neither German nor Turkish particularly well. Their relatively high crime and unemployment rates are occasionally fodder for right-wing parties who like the Nazis cannot imagine that Turks or other non-Europeans could ever be real Germans. However, this issue cannot be equated with the hysterical emotions created by the Jewish "problem" during the interwar period.

Some social and political benefits have also inadvertently arisen from the ashes of Hitler's Third Reich. His ruthless extermination of much of the German aristocracy following the failed July 20th assassination plot in 1944, the massive movement of population from the lost territories east of the Oder-Neisse Rivers, and the social demands of postwar reconstruction, have brought about a reduction of class and regional differences conducive to democracy. Hitler was also indirectly responsible in part for the establishment of the state of Israel in 1948, which resulted from the widespread sympathy for Jews created by the Holocaust. Finally, the corruption that was endemic in all the totalitarian states simply had less time to become rooted in German society because the Third Reich existed for a far shorter time than either Fascist Italy or Communist Russia.

On the other hand, it is much more challenging to think of anything positive arising from the Communist experiment in human engineering. Certainly the Soviet regime succeeded in spreading literacy and industrial skills to tens of millions of people. The more backward parts of the Soviet Union such as the Central Asian republics, began their existence as independent states with a much better educated populace, especially women, than lived in nearby Muslim states like Afghanistan, Iraq, Iran, and Pakistan. Women also derived some benefits in gaining access to jobs previously closed to them and child-care facilities. They paid a heavy price for these changes, however, by in effect having to hold two jobs: one at home and one in the marketplace. There is no doubt some pent-up hunger on the part of former citizens of Communist countries to read whatever they wish and to travel wherever they want. An intense reaction to tyrannical authority should help create a popular resistance against any party or government claiming monopolistic powers for itself. None of this is certain as of this writing (in 2008), however, and the electoral successes of Communist parties in East Central Europe, which have merely changed their names, are not encouraging. Even worse, however, are the consequences of expelling, or more often killing, the most hard-working and creative people of the former Communist countries: the old aristocracy (who at least served as patrons of the arts); the bourgeoisie; Jews; intellectuals; kulaks; and even leading Communist party members. The survivors learned that their best chance of staying alive was to avoid espousing unorthodox and creative ideas that might appear "subversive" and "dangerous." Instead, they waited passively for orders from far away bureaucrats who had little knowledge of local conditions.

The destruction of the environment in the former Communist states also finds no parallel in the former fascist states. The Nazis actually showed an enlightened attitude toward protecting the environment. Although they brought about a horrible destruction to the lives and property of other countries and ultimately to themselves, the property at least could often be repaired or replaced in a matter of a few years. The Communists have wrought degradation to the environment, for example at Chernobyl, which will take decades, at the very least, to repair. It may be even more difficult for them to root out the corruption, lying, and conformity that the Communist system encouraged. This task may be somewhat easier in the former satellite states where Communism was imposed from the outside and lasted for only about half as long as it did in the Soviet Union.

Looking to the future, the late and unlamented Taliban regime in Afghanistan is proof that totalitarianism is not simply a bygone curiosity of the twentieth century. However, of the three regimes examined in this book, totalitarianism is least likely to reappear in Germany. Democracy in Germany is no longer in its infancy. It now has a record of six decades of success and has been tested at times by considerable economic stress. Isolated pockets of racism still exist, but the Nazis so discredited racism that it is highly unlikely that any major political party will adopt it in the future as an integral part of its ideology. The German people have also learned both from the accomplishments and failures of the Weimar Republic. It is entirely possible, however, that a more nationalistic and assertive regime could appear in the not-too-distant future, but almost certainly not one with a racist or a militaristic ideology. Mussolini, however, was never quite so thoroughly discredited as Hitler, so Fascism, in some disguised form, has somewhat better prospects of re-emerging in Italy, especially if political corruption in that country continues unchecked.

The fate of the former Soviet Union is the biggest question mark. Unlike Germany and Italy, there is no democratic tradition in this part of Europe. The brief experiment in democracy between the two revolutions in 1917 was a miserable failure. Before and after 1917, there has only been a long and dismal history of autocracy and tyranny, frequently accompanied by brutality. Unlike Nazism in Germany and Fascism in Italy, Communism in the Soviet Union disappeared more with a whimper than a bang. Much of what the Communists created, such as collective farms, a highly centralized economy with far away "bosses," and even numerous statues of Lenin survived the overthrow of the regime. The privatization of property is progressing only slowly. (For an exception, see Figure 31.) To be sure, some Russians have already made fortunes, but they have created enormous envy in those people who are less fortunate. Unlike the fascist states, there has been no thorough purging of Communists from the government and the economy. There are also millions of Russians, especially pensioners and workers in state-owned factories whose salaries have plummeted, who still look on the relative stability of the regimes of Stalin, Khrushchev, and Brezhnev as "the good old days." For example, an opinion poll of 1,600 adults taken in 2003 revealed that 53 percent approved of Stalin whereas only 33 percent held a negative view of the dictator. New state textbooks "hail Stalin as 'the most successful Russian leader ever' and a state builder along the lines of Peter the Great and Bismarck."[1]

However, probably a majority of Russians would not embrace a party with a history of totalitarian control, corruption, terror, and concentration camps, as was illustrated by the defeat of the Communist candidate, Gennady Zyuganov (see figure 32), in the Russian presidential election of 1996. They will probably be less gullible to government lies in the future. Moreover, considerable economic progress was made under President Vladimir Putin who came to power at the end of 1999, but it is still too early to tell whether Russia is on a clear road to recovery. Another downturn in the economy, which is precariously dependent on the current high price of oil, together with a continuation of the high crime rate would make the emergence of an extreme nationalistic and authoritarian regime by no means unthinkable. However, the "good old days" that Russia now seems to be returning to are not to the days of Lenin and Stalin, with their purges, unrestrained terror, and hostility to free enterprise, but to the era of tsarist Russia. Not only have numerous Russian churches been rebuilt or refurbished, but the Russian Orthodox Church has also become a de facto state religion with other Christian denominations being barely tolerated if at all. Putin, who is the first Christian believer since the tsars, like Berlusconi represents a welcome return to political stability. With a 70 percent approval rating he appears to be retaining his hold on power in his new role as prime minister. He has eschewed the charismatic leadership of the totalitarian dictators—especially Hitler and Mussolini—in favor of a humorless, but pragmatic management style. However, like the dictators he has restored a sense of national pride and much of Russia's international influence. How he will share power with his forty-two-year-old hand-picked successor as president, Dmitri Medvedev, is an open question.

As in today's Italy, freedom of the press is threatened in Russia by the murder of several journalists who had been outspoken critics of

1 *Time*, December 31, 2007/January 7, 2008. p. 86.

the regime and by government-owned television stations which deliberately slant the news, although newspapers remain at least partially free. The judicial courts, which had been independent albeit corrupt under Putin's predecessor, Boris Yeltsin, have again become rubber stamps for dubious administrative decisions. Equally prone to use the rubber stamp has been the Russian parliament (Duma). The Russian Diaspora, the 25 million Russians who suddenly found themselves in foreign and often unfriendly countries after the breakup of the Soviet Union, could also become an issue for extreme Russian nationalists in the future. Corruption continues to be widespread as it is in many other former Communist states. Inflation and a widening gap between rich and poor are also problems although the poor have benefited to some degree by Russia's growing prosperity since the turn of the century.

None of these problems currently facing the former totalitarian dictatorships should be exaggerated, however. They do not begin to approach in intensity the economic and political problems of early post–World War I Central and Eastern Europe or the political extremism wrought by the Great Depression in the early 1930s. Nor should political success be necessarily measured in terms of conditions existing in the United States, Canada, Great Britain or other Western democracies.

The totalitarian regimes of twentieth-century Europe will be remembered, as long as history is studied, for their unprecedented brutality and destructiveness. Their few intended accomplishments ironically involved precisely those matters that were relatively nonpolitical. Their ultimate downfalls resulted from the implementation of their extreme, dogmatic ideologies. They will remain horrifying reminders of the consequences of placing dictatorial power in the hands of unscrupulous men.

# BIBLIOGRAPHICAL ESSAY

The number of books related to the three totalitarian dictatorships is enormous. Therefore, only the most useful of the standard works will be mentioned here. Books containing especially helpful bibliographies will be noted for readers who wish to investigate specialized topics.

Most of the books dealing specifically with the **concept of totalitarianism** were published in the 1950s and 1960s during the height of the Cold War. At that time it was fashionable to draw parallels between the Soviet Union and the fascist dictatorships; however, some have been published since the topic began to regain its popularity in the 1980s. A basic introductory text with a political science orientation is Leonard Schapiro, *Totalitarianism* (New York, 1972). One of the first books to deal with the subject and still a classic is Hannah Arendt, *The Origins of Totalitarianism* (New York, 1973), first published in 1951. Three other books which trace the origins and evolution of the concept are Jacob L. Talmon, *The Origins of Totalitarian Democracy* (New York, 1960); Stephen P. Soper, *Totalitarianism: A Conceptual Approach* (Lanham, MD, 1985); and most recently, Abbott Gleason, *Totalitarianism: The Inner History of the Cold War* (New York, 1995).

Carl J. Friedrich and Zbigniew K. Brzezinski described the **basic characteristics of totalitarianism** in their classic book, *Totalitarian Dictatorship and Autocracy*, rev. ed. (Cambridge, MA, 1965). Michael Curtis has written an excellent interpretive essay on various aspects of the subject in *Totalitarianism* (New Brunswick, NJ, 1979), as has Hans Buchheim in *Totalitarian Rule: Its Nature and Characteristics* (Middletown, CT, 1968). An interesting anthology on contrasting views on the subject is Paul T. Mason, ed., *Totalitarianism: Temporary Madness or Permanent Danger?* (Lexington, KY, 1967). A much more recent reappraisal of the subject is Ernest A. Menze, ed., *Totalitarianism Reconsidered* (Port Washington, NY, 1981).

A substantial number of books have systematically **compared totalitarianism with other systems or the different totalitarian**

**states** with each other. Good examples are Raymond Aron, *Democracy and Totalitarianism* (New York, 1969); Otis C. Mitchell, *Two Totalitarians: The Systems of Hitler and Stalin Compared* (Dubuque, IA, 1965); C. W. Cassinelli, *Total Revolution: A Comparative Study of Germany under Hitler, the Soviet Union under Stalin, and China under Mao* (Santa Barbara, CA, 1976); Aryeh L. Unger, *The Totalitarian Party: Party and People in Nazi Germany and Soviet Russia* (London, 1974); and William Ebenstein and Edwin Fogelman, *Today's Isms: Communism, Fascism, Capitalism, Socialism,* 9th ed. (Englewood Cliffs, NJ, 1985). A recent anthology is Ian Kershaw and Moshe Lewin, eds., *Stalinism and Nazism: Dictatorships in Comparison* (Cambridge, UK,1997). A work containing the original writings of people like Lenin, Stalin, Khrushchev, Mussolini, Goering, and Hitler is Carl Cohen, ed., *Communism, Fascism and Democracy: The Theoretical Foundations,* 3rd ed. (New York, 1996).

During the 1960s and 1970s the broad **concept of totalitarianism** temporarily gave way to the narrower theory of "fascism," which attained power only in Italy and Germany. However, fascism was also found, during its heyday in the 1930s, in less successful movements in nearly all countries west of the Soviet Union. The pioneering study of this subject was Ernst Nolte's *Three Faces of Fascism: Action Francaise, Italian Fascism, National Socialism* (New York, 1966), which was first published in German in 1963. The best of the newer books is Michael Mann, *Fascists* (New York, 2004). A rare new book on fascism is Roger Griffin, *The Nature of Fascism* (New York, 1991). Several theoretical studies of fascism have been written by A. James Gregor including *The Ideology of Fascism: The Rationale of Totalitarianism* (New York, 1969) and *Interpretations of Fascism* (Morristown, NJ, 1974), in which he discusses the social, psychological, and economic causes of fascism.

Most books on **fascism** are **anthologies** in large part because it is virtually impossible for scholars to be experts on fascism in more than one country. Probably the best of the group is Walter Laqueur, ed., *Fascism: A Reader's Guide: Analyses, Interpretations, Bibliography* (Berkeley, CA, 1976). Walter Laqueur has also edited *International Fascism, 1925–1945* (New York, 1966). See as well Stuart J. Woolf, ed., *European Fascism* (New York, 1968), which covers fascist movements in several countries, and, by the same editor, *The Nature of Fascism* (New York, 1969), which is more descriptive of the movement as a whole; and the massive tome, *Who were the Fascists?: Social Roots of European Fascism* (Bergen, Norway, 1980) edited by Stein U. Larsen, et al.

Other books **comparing various forms of fascism** include Alexander J. De Grand, *Fascist Italy and Nazi Germany: The "Fascist" Style of Rule* (London, 1995), Michael T. Florinsky, *Fascism and National Socialism: A Study of the Economic and Social Policies of the Totalitarian State* (New York, 1938) and Stanley G. Payne, *Fascism: Comparative Approach Toward a Definition* (Madison, WI, 1980). A very complete bibliography of works on fascism can be found in Philip Rees, *Fascism and Pre-fascism in Europe, 1890–1945: A Bibliography of the Extreme Right* (Sussex, UK,1984).

Turning specifically to **Italian Fascism**, the most recent general study is Philip Morgan, *Italian Fascism, 1919–1945* (New York, 1995). A very readable survey is R. J. B. Bosworth, *Mussolini's Italy: Life under the Dictatorship, 1915–1945* (New York, 2006). A brief general study is Alexander De Grand, *Italian Fascism: Its Origins & Development*, 3rd ed. (Lincoln, NE, 2000), which contains a superb bibliography. An invaluable reference work is Phillip V. Cannistraro, ed., *An Historical Dictionary of Fascist Italy* (London, 1975). Topically organized is the anthology edited by Roland Sarti, *The Ax Within: Italian Fascism in Action* (New York, 1974). For works published during the Fascist era, see William Ebenstein, *Fascist Italy* (New York, 1939), which covers all aspects of the regime, and the more political and popular *Mussolini's Italy* by Herman Finer (New York, 1965 [originally published in 1935]). An excellent book limited to the Fascist party is Dante C. Germino, *The Italian Fascist Party in Power: A Study in Totalitarian Rule* (Minneapolis, 1959). John P. Diggins reveals how popular Mussolini was in the United States up to the Ethiopian War in *Mussolini and Fascism: The View from America* (Princeton, NJ, 1972). This conclusion is also affirmed by Simonetta Falasca-Zamponi in *Fascist Spectacle* (Berkeley, CA, 1997). A recent historiographical study of Fascist Italy is R. J. B. Bosworth, *The Italian Dictatorship: Problems and Perspectives in the Interpretation of Mussolini and Fascism* (London, 1998).

On the broad range of **Soviet history** since the Bolshevik Revolution the newest work is Peter Kenez, *A History of the Soviet Union from the Beginning to the End* (Cambridge, UK,1999). Another excellent introduction is Adam B. Ulam, *A History of Soviet Russia* (Fort Worth, 1978). Much more detailed is the interesting interpretation by the "emigré" historians Mikhail Heller and Alexander Nekrich, *Utopia in Power: The History of the Soviet Union from 1917 to the Present* (New York, 1986). A good brief interpretative essay is Theodore H. Von Laue,

*Why Lenin? Why Stalin? Why Gorbachev?*, 3rd ed. (New York, 1993). Older and more specialized works which are still of value are John A. Armstrong, *The Politics of Totalitarianism: The Communist Party of the Soviet Union from 1934 to the Present* (New York, 1961); Herbert McClosky and John E. Turner, *The Soviet Dictatorship* (New York, 1960), which analyzes the distinguishing features of Soviet Communism; and Raymond A. Bauer, Alex Inkeles, and Clyde Kluckhohn, *How the Soviet System Works: Cultural, Psychological and Social Themes* (New York, 1960), which is based on extensive interviews with refugees who had recently escaped from the Soviet Union. Two much more recent works are the revisionist book by Stephen Cohen, *Rethinking the Soviet Experience* (Oxford, 1986) and Paul Dibb, *The Soviet Union: The Incomplete Superpower* (Urbana, IL, 1988), which concentrates on domestic and international problems faced by the Soviet Union in the 1980s.

The Nazi phenomenon can only be understood within the broad context of **modern German history.** Among the books with such a scope the most recent are Dietrich Orlow, *A History of Modern Germany, 1871 to the Present*, 3rd ed. (Upper Saddle River, NJ, 2002); and Holger H. Herwig, *Hammer or Anvil: Modern Germany 1648–Present* (Lexington, MA, 1994). Limited to the Second and Third Reich is Gordon A. Craig's *Germany, 1866–1945* (New York, 1980). Somewhat older, but still of value is Hajo Holborn, *A History of Modern Germany, 1840–1945* (New York, 1969). The impact of the Great War on German society is covered in Richard Bessel, *Germany after the First World War* (Oxford, UK, 1993). Good introductory textbooks on the Third Reich are Alan F. Wilt, *Nazi Germany* (Wheeling, IL, 1994), which has an excellent bibliography; Jackson J. Spielvogel, *Hitler and Nazi Germany: A History* (Englewood Cliffs, NJ, 2000), which also has a good list of suggested readings; K. Hildebrand, *The Third Reich* (London, 1984); Andreas Hillgruber, *Germany and the Two World Wars* (Cambridge, MA, 1981); and Robert E. Herzstein, *Adolf Hitler and the German Trauma, 1913–1945: An Interpretation of the Nazi Phenomenon* (New York, 1974). Two extremely well researched and detailed volumes on the Nazis by Richard J. Evans are *The Coming of the Third Reich* (London, 2003) and *The Third Reich in Power* (London, 2005).

Among the **textbooks** for more advanced students, the newest and most detailed is Michael Burleigh, *The Third Reich: A New History* (New York, 2000). Also new and comprehensive is Klaus P. Fischer, *Nazi Germany: A New History* (New York, 1998). Still excellent are Karl

D. Bracher, *The German Dictatorship: The Origins, Structure, and Effects of National Socialism* (New York, 1970), and Martin Broszat, *The Hitler State: The Foundations and Development of the Internal Structure of the Third Reich* (White Plains, NY, 1981), both of which have a strong political emphasis. For a colorful eyewitness account, see William L. Shirer, *The Nightmare Years, 1930–1940* (Toronto, 1984). How the Nazis' racial ideology affected German society can be seen in Michael Burleigh and Wolfgang Wippermann, *The Racial State: Germany 1933–1945* (Cambridge, UK, 1991). Excellent descriptions of daily life in Nazi Germany can be found in Bernt Engelmann, *Hitler's Germany: Everyday Life in the Third Reich* (New York, 1986); Richard Bessel, ed., *Life in the Third Reich* (Oxford, 2001); Pierre Aycoberry, *The Social History of the Third Reich, 1933–1936* (New York, 1999); and Timothy W. Mason, *Social Policy in the Third Reich* (Providence, 1993). Important documents related to Nazi Germany are found in Jeremy Noakes and Geoffrey Pridham, eds., *Nazism, 1919–1945: A History in Documents and Eyewitness Accounts*, Vol. I, *The Nazi Party, State and Society, 1919–1939* (New York, 1984); and Louis L. Snydor, ed., *Hitler's Third Reich: A Documentary History* (Chicago, 1981). An excellent bibliography of works published up to 1980 is Helen Kehr and Janet Langmaid, eds., *The Nazi Era, 1919–1945: A Select Bibliography of Published Works from the Early Roots to 1980* (London, 1982). A succinct historiographical study is Ian Kershaw, *The Nazi Dictatorship: Problems and Perspectives of Interpretation* (London, 1985).

**Nazi Germany** has been the subject of numerous **scholarly anthologies** since at least the 1950s. The most recent are Panikos Panayi, ed., *Weimar and Nazi Germany: Continuities and Discontinuities* (Harlow, UK, 2001) and Neil Gregor, ed., *Nazism* (New York, 2000). Other recently published works are David F. Crew, *Nazism and German Society, 1933–1945* (London, 1994), and Thomas Childers and Jane Caplan, eds., *Reevaluating the Third Reich* (New York, 1993). See also Hans Mommsen, ed., *From Weimar to Auschwitz* (Princeton, NJ, 1991); Henry Ashby Turner, Jr., *Nazism and the Third Reich* (New York, 1972); and Allan Mitchell, ed., *The Nazi Revolution* (Lexington, MA, 1990).

On the **ideological foundations of the three totalitarian states** described in this book, see J. Lucien Radel, *Roots of Totalitarianism: The Ideological Sources of Fascism, National Socialism, and Communism* (New York, 1975); Robert C. Tucker, ed., *Essays in Historical Interpretation* (New York, 1977), which has some excellent articles on Bolshevism and Stalinism; Renzo de Felice, *Fascism: An Informal Introduction to its Theory and Practice* (New Brunswick, NJ, 1976); and Eberhard Jäckl, ed., *Hitler's World View: A Blueprint for Power* (Cambridge, MA, 1987), in which the author argues that Nazism was intellectually coherent.

The literature on the **Russian revolutions of 1917** is immense and only a few of the more important works can be alluded to here. On the overthrow of the Romanovs see Leonard Schapiro, *The Russian Revolutions of 1917: The Origins of Modern Communism* (New York, 1984), who also shows how the Communists consolidated their power. On Lenin's role in the Bolshevik Revolution see Adam Ulam, *The Bolsheviks: The Intellectual, Personal and Political History of the Triumph of Communism in Russia* (Cambridge, MA, 1998); Bertram D. Wolfe, *Three Who Made a Revolution* (New York, 2001 [originally published in 1948]), which also covers Trotsky and Stalin; and Christopher Hill, *Lenin and the Russian Revolution* (London, 1971 [first published in 1947]).

**Lenin**, not surprisingly, has been the subject of numerous **biographies.** The most critical one, based on recently opened Russian archives, is Dmitri Volkogonov, *Lenin: A New Biography* (New York, 1994). Equally detailed, but older is Louis Fischer, *The Life of Lenin* (New York, 1964). A good brief introduction is Helene Carrere d'Encausse, *Lenin: Revolution and Power* (London, 1982). The Lenin cult is examined by Nina Tumarkin in *Lenin Lives! The Lenin Cult in Soviet Russia* (Cambridge, MA, 1983). Three books that examine Lenin's contribution to the formation of Soviet totalitarianism are Moshe Lewin, ed., *The Making of the Soviet System: Essays in the Social History of Interwar Russia* (New York, 1985); Samuel Farber, *Before Stalinism: The Rise and Fall of Soviet Democracy* (London, 1990); and Leonard Schapiro, *The Origin of the Communist Autocracy: Political Opposition in the Soviet State, First Phase, 1917–1922,* 2nd ed. (Cambridge, MA, 1977). A much more comprehensive and up-to-date biography of the Communist leader is Robert Service, *Lenin: A Biography* (Cambridge, MA, 2000) which depicts Lenin as both a Marxist ideologue and an opportunist.

Several books deal with the **establishment of the Fascist dictatorship,** but by far the most detailed, recent, and objective is Adrian Lyttelton, *The Seizure of Power: Fascism in Italy, 1919–1929,* 2nd ed. (Princeton, NJ, 1987). Other books on the subject were written by Italian contemporaries and include Gaetano Salvemini (edited and with an introduction by Roberto Vivarelli), *The Origins of Fascism in Italy* (New York, 1973), which is based on lectures delivered by the author in 1942, and Angelo Tasca, *The Rise of Italian Fascism* (New York, 1966 [originally published in 1938]).

The **Weimar Republic and the rise of the Nazis** have long attracted numerous historians. A bibliographical guide to the period is Peter D. Stachura, ed., *Weimar Era and Hitler, 1918–1933: A Critical Bibliography* (Oxford, 1979). A recent and thought-provoking survey is Detlev Peukert, *The Weimar Republic: The Crisis of Classical Modernity* (New York, 1992). Another brief survey is A. J. Nicholls, *Weimar and the Rise of Hitler,* rev. ed. (New York, 2000). Peter Fritsche in *Germans into Nazis* (Cambridge, MA, 1998) shows how the Nazis appealed to the Germans' desire for a sense of unity. *The Nazi Machtergreifung* (London, 1983), edited by Peter D. Stachura, is an anthology that examines the attitude of numerous groups such as women, the educated elite, the industrial elite, the army, and the churches toward the Weimar Republic and the rise of the Nazis. Jay W. Baird shows how the Nazis exploited the deaths of early Nazi "martyrs" in *To Die for Germany: Heroes in the Nazi Pantheon (*Bloomington, IN, 1990). Henry Ashby Turner, Jr., destroys the Marxist contention that big businessmen were responsible for the Nazi takeover in *German Big Business and the Rise of Hitler* (Oxford, 1985). The beginnings of the Nazi party are examined in the first volume of Dietrich Orlow's two-volume *History of the Nazi Party* (Pittsburgh, 1969). More biographical are Charles B. Flood, *Hitler: The Path to Power* (Boston, 1989); Otis C. Mitchell, *Hitler Over Germany: The Establishment of the Nazi Dictatorship (1918–1934)* (Philadelphia, 1983); and Konrad Heiden, *Der Fuehrer: Hitler's Rise to Power* (Boston, 1944), written by a journalist who followed Hitler from the beginning of his career. The Nazi takeover and consolidation of power is covered by Eliot Barculo Wheaton in *The Nazi Revolution 1933–1935: Prelude to Calamity* (Garden City, NY, 1969); and Henry Ashby Turner, Jr., *Hitler's Thirty Days to Power* (Cambridge, MA, 2000).

During the 1970s and 1980s historians devoted a great deal of attention to the **social origins of Nazi party members.** This effort had been initiated in 1934 when the Columbia University sociologist, Theodore Abel, sponsored an essay contest on why Nazis had joined the party, published as *Why Hitler Came Into Power* (Cambridge, MA, 1986 [originally published in 1938]). Peter Merkl further analyzed these essays in *Political Violence under the Swastika: 589 Early Nazis* (Princeton, NJ, 1975). The same scholar investigated why young men joined the SA in *The Making of a Stormtrooper* (Princeton, NJ, 1980). Other books of a sociological orientation are Thomas Childers, *The Nazi Voter: The Social Foundations of Fascism in Germany, 1919–1933* (Chapel Hill, NC, 1984); Richard F. Hamilton, *Who Voted for Hitler?* (Princeton, NJ, 1982); Michael H. Kater, *The Nazi Party: A Social Profile of Members and Leaders, 1919–1945* (Cambridge, MA, 1983); and Max H. Kele, *Nazis and Workers: National Socialist Appeals to German Labor, 1919–1933* (Chapel Hill, NC, 1972).

The **rise of the Nazis** has been examined not only at the national level, but **regionally** as well. Good local studies include Geoffrey Pridham, *Hitler's Rise to Power: The Nazi Movement in Bavaria, 1923–1933* (New York, 1973); Johnpeter Horst Grill, *The Nazi Movement in Baden, 1920–1945* (Chapel Hill, NC, 1983); Bruce F. Pauley, *Hitler and the Forgotten Nazis: A History of Austrian National Socialism* (Chapel Hill, NC, 1981); the classic work by William Sheridan Allen, *The Nazi Seizure of Power: The Experience of a Single German Town*, rev. ed. (New York, 1984); and Jeremy Noakes, *The Nazi Party in Lower Saxony, 1921–1933* (London, 1971).

**Stalin, Mussolini, and Hitler** have all been the subject of numerous **biographies.** A book that compares the stages in life of Stalin and Hitler is Alan Bullock, *Hitler and Stalin: Parallel Lives* (New York, 1992). Two recent comparative studies are Robert Gellately, *Lenin, Stalin, and Hitler: The Age of Social Catastrophe* (New York, 2007) and Richard J. Overy, *The Dictators: Hitler's Germany and Stalin's Russia* (New York, 2004). The newest study of Stalin is Robert Service, *Stalin: A Biography* (Cambridge, MA, 2004). Another relatively new study devoted to all aspects of Stalin's rule is *Stalin's Russia* by Chris Ward, 2nd ed. (London, 1993). Four brief, but more reliable, analytical, and up-to-date biographies are Robert Conquest, *Stalin: Breaker of Nations* (New York, 1991); Albert Marrin's popular *Stalin: Russia's Man of Steel* (New York, 1988); Jonathan Lewis and Phillip Whitehead, *Stalin: A Time for Judgment* (New York, 1990); and Hélène Carrère d'Encausse, *Stalin: Order through Terror* (London, 1981). Much more detailed are Dmitri Volkogonov, *Stalin: Triumph and Tragedy* (New York, 1991); Alex de Jonge, *Stalin and the Shaping of the Soviet Union* (New York, 1986); and Adam B. Ulam, *Stalin: The Man and his Era* (New York, 1973). Probably the best biography of Stalin is the (to date) two-volume work by Robert C. Tucker, *Stalin as a Revolutionary, 1879–1929*, and *Stalin in Power: The Revolution from Above, 1928–1941* (New York, 1973, 1992). Taking advantage of newly accessible sources, especially as they pertain to the purges is Walter Laqueur, *Stalin: The Glasnost Revelations* (New York, 1990). Stalin's own views on various political and economic issues as seen in his speeches can be found in his *Problems of Leninism* (Moscow, 1953). Arguing that Stalin could be a revolutionary, realist, and cynic all at one is Hiroaki Kuromiya, *Stalin* (New York, 2005). Good anthologies with contrasting views of Stalin are contained in all three editions of Robert V. Daniels, ed., *The Stalin Revolution*, 3rd ed. (Lexington, MA, 1990); G. R. Urban, ed., *Stalinism: Its Impact on Russia and the World* (New York, 1982); and T. H. Rigby, ed., *Stalin* (Englewood Cliffs, NJ, 1966).

The volume of literature on the **life of Mussolini** is much more limited than for the other totalitarian dictators. The new and most complete is R. J. B. Bosworth, *Mussolini* (London, 2002). More controversial but highly readable is Denis Mack Smith, *Mussolini: A Biography* (New York, 1982). A more recent and more popular work is Jasper Ridley, *Mussolini: A Biography* (New York, 1997). Another strictly popular account is Anthony James Joes, *Mussolini* (New York, 1982). Somewhat older works are Laura Fermi, *Mussolini* (Chicago, 1966); Christopher Hibbert, *Benito Mussolini: The Rise and Fall of Il Duce* (Harmondsworth, UK, 1965); and Ivone Kirkpatrick, *Mussolini: A Study in Power* (New York, 1964). Two standard works on Mussolini's early years are Gaudens Megaro, *Mussolini in the Making* (Boston, 1938) and A. James Gregor, *Young Mussolini and the Intellectual Origins of Fascism* (Berkeley, CA, 1979). Although not a full-fledged biography, *Talks with Mussolini* (Boston, 1933), by the German journalist Emil Ludwig, still has interesting revelations about Mussolini's views on a wide range of topics when he was near the top of his popularity.

The **literature on Hitler** is staggering although the number of first-rate, comprehensive biographies is surprisingly small. The newest and most complete study in the massive two-volume work by Ian Kershaw, *Hitler, 1889–1936, Hubris* and *Hitler, 1936–1945, Nemesis* (New York, 1998, 2000), which, however, contains no dramatic new thesis. Kershaw has also written a brief introduction to the Nazi leader in his book *Hitler* (London, 1991). Joachim C. Fest, *Hitler* (New York, 1975) is still probably the most readable one-volume biography. Alan Bullock, *Hitler: A Study in Tyranny*, rev. ed. (New York, 1961) remains a standard work even though it was first published more than forty years ago. Strictly popular and anecdotal is John Toland, *Adolf Hitler* (New York, 1976). Two psychoanalytical studies of Hitler which have been criticized for being founded on much guesswork are Robert G. L. Waite, *The Psychopathic God: Adolf Hitler* (New York, 1977) and Rudolph Binion, *Hitler among the Germans* (New York, 1976). The latest psychological study is *Hitler: Diagnosis of a Destructive Prophet* by Fritz Redlich, M.D. (Oxford, 1998), which contains some interesting information on Hitler's health after 1941. A historiographical account of the literature on Hitler that also corrects many myths is *The Hitler of History* by John Lukacs (New York, 1998).

A fascinating, but frequently unreliable way to trace **Hitler's career** is to read **books by people who knew him best,** starting with Hitler's own semiautobiography, *Mein Kampf* (Boston, 1943 [originally published in 1925, 1927]). *Hitler's Table Talk, 1941–1944: His Private Conversations* (New York, 2000) reveals the Führer's opinion on an almost infinite variety of subjects. His only close teenage friend, August Kubizek, wrote *Young Hitler: The Story of our Friendship* (London, 1954). The Harvard educated Ernst Hanfstaengl discussed their close association between 1921 and the parting of their ways in 1934 in *Hitler: The Missing Years* (New York, 1994). Otto Wagener wrote about their relationship in the late 1920s and early 1930s in *Hitler: Memoirs of a Confidant* (New Haven, CT, 1985), which has been edited by Henry Ashby Turner, Jr. For Hitler's years in power the best eyewitness account is Albert Speer, *Inside the Third Reich* (Old Tappen, NJ, 1997 [originally published in German in 1969]). A recently published work emphasizing Soviet interests in Nazi Germany is Henrik Eberle and Matthias Uhl, eds., *The Hitler Book: The Secret Dossier Prepared for Stalin from the Interrogation of Hitler's Personal Aides* (New York, 2007). For verbatim texts of Hitler's speeches, see Max Domarus, ed., *Hitler: Speeches and Proclamations 1932–1945*, 4 vols. (Wauconda, IL, 1990–92).

**Secondary sources** are, of course, also indispensable for the study of **Hitler.** The most recent work is Brigitte Hamaan, *Hitler's Vienna: A Dictator's Apprenticeship* (New York, 1999) which has relatively little new information about Hitler himself, but presents a fascinating picture of the Habsburg capital during Hitler's sojourn there. On his youth and early career up to 1933, see Bradley F. Smith, *Adolf Hitler: His Family, Childhood & Youth* (Stanford, CA, 1967) in which the author rejects the theory that the young Hitler could be identified as a monster in the making; Helm Stierlin, *Adolf Hitler: A Family Perspective* (New York, 1976); Werner Maser, *Hitler: Legend, Myth & Reality* (New York, 1971); and Eugene Davidson, *The Making of Adolf Hitler* (New

York, 1977). Excellent interpretive essays on wide-ranging aspects of Hitler's life include Sebastian Haffner, *The Meaning of Hitler* (Cambridge, MA, 1978); and Eberhard Jäckl, *Hitler in History* (Hanover, NH, 1984). Two books which show both the limitations of Hitler's power and his indispensability to the Nazi movement are Edward N. Peterson, *The Limits of Hitler's Power* (Princeton, NJ, 1969); and Joseph L. Nyomarkay, *Charisma and Factionalism in the Nazi Party* (Minneapolis, 1967). Hitler's career as well as other top Nazi leaders are covered in Ronald Smelser and Rainer Zitelmann, eds., *The Nazi Elite: 22 Biographical Sketches* (London, 1993); and Joachim C. Fest, *The Face of the Third Reich: Portraits of the Nazi Leadership* (New York, 1999).

The **economic aspects of the Soviet Union** have been one of the most carefully analyzed aspects of the regime. A recent general study is Alec Nove, *An Economic History of the USSR, 1917–1991* (Harmondsworth, UK, 1992). The principles of the Soviet economy have been described by Robert W. Campbell, *The Soviet Type Economies: Performance and Evolution* (Boston, 1973). The most important economic institutions and problems are covered by Marshall Goldman in *The Soviet Economy: Myth and Reality* (Englewood Cliffs, NJ, 1968). Books that describe the consequences of Stalin's collectivization of Soviet farms are Robert Conquest, *The Harvest of Sorrow: Soviet Collectivization and the Terror-Famine* (New York, 1986); Sheila Fitzpatrick, *Stalin's Peasants: Resistance and Survival in the Russian Village after Collectivization* (New York, 1994); the gripping first-hand account of Miron Dolot, *Execution by Hunger: The Hidden Holocaust* (New York, 1985); and M. Wayne Morris, *Stalin's Famine and Roosevelt's Recognition of Russia* (Lanham, MD, 1994).

The **economies of the fascist dictatorships** have attracted far less attention from historians than almost any other aspects of life. On Fascist economic policies, see A. James Gregor, *Italian Fascism and Developmental Dictatorship* (Princeton, NJ, 1979); and Roland Sarti, *Fascism and the Industrial Leadership in Italy* (Berkeley, CA, 1971). Two recent studies which both argue that the Nazi economic recovery preceded accelerated rearmament are Dan P. Silverman, *Hitler's Economy: Nazi Work Creation Programs, 1933–1936* (Cambridge, MA, 1998); and *Nazi Economics: Ideology, Theory, and Policy* by Avraham Barkai, translated by Ruth Hodass-Vaschitz (New York, 1996). A brief, but new overview of Germany's economic revival can be seen in R. J. Overy, *The Nazi Economic Recovery, 1932–1938* (London, 1982). On the relationship between big business and the Nazi regime see Arthur Schweitzer, *Big Business in the Third Reich* (London, 1964). A personal approach is Ronald Smelser's excellent biography of Robert Ley: *Hitler's Labor Leader* (New York, 1988). A long section on Nazi economic policies can also be found in Franz Neumann, *Behemoth: The Structure and Practice of National Socialism, 1933–1944*, 3rd ed. (New York, 1966).

On **propaganda, Nazi Germany** has nearly monopolized the attention of historians. Most general histories of the Soviet Union do not even list the topic in their indices although Adam Ulam, *A History of Soviet Russia* (Fort Worth, 1978) is an exception. However, propaganda in the early years of the Soviet Union has been well covered in *The Commissariat of Enlightenment: Soviet Organization of Education and the Arts under Lunarchsky, October 1917–1921* by Sheila Fitzpatrick (Cambridge, MA, 1970); and Peter Kenez, *The Birth of the Propaganda State* (Cambridge, MA, 1985). The propagandistic uses of Soviet film can be seen in Richard Taylor, *The Politics of Soviet Cinema, 1917–29* (Cambridge, UK, 1979). Peter Kenez, in *Cinema and Soviet Society from the Revolution to the Death of Stalin* (London, 2001), argues that Soviet films failed in their attempt to get Soviet citizens to work harder. In "Mussolini: Artist in Propaganda," *History Today* 9 (1959): 223–32, Denis Mack Smith argues that Mussolini was so successful a propagandist that he convinced himself that Italy was truly a great power. Edward R. Tannenbaum, *The Fascist Experience: Italian Society and Culture, 1922–1945* (New York, 1972) has a chapter entitled "Popular Culture and Propaganda" (pp. 213–47). By contrast, the titles related to Nazi propaganda are almost endless. Two good introductions are Z. A. B. Zeman, *Nazi Propaganda*, 2nd ed. (London, 1973); and Ernest K. Bramsted, *Goebbels and National Socialist Propaganda* (East Lansing, MI, 1965). David Welch has published several works on Nazi propaganda including *The Third Reich: Politics and Propaganda* (London, 1993) and two edited works, *Propaganda and the German Cinema, 1933–1945* (Oxford, 1983) and *Nazi Propaganda: The Power and the Limitations* (Totowa, NJ, 1983). Another study of Nazi films is Hilmer Hoffman, *The Triumph of Propaganda: Film and National Socialism, 1933–1945* (Providence, 1996), which argues that newsreels and documentaries were the most important aspects of film propaganda. Oron J. Hale has described *The Captive Press in the Third Reich* (Princeton, NJ, 1964); and Ian Kershaw examines the *Führermythos* in *The Hitler Myth: Image and Reality in the Third Reich* (Oxford, 1987).

Works on the **fine arts in the Soviet Union** are scarce. However, an excellent book that compares art and architecture in all three totalitarian states is Igor Golomstock, *Totalitarian Art in the Soviet Union, Nazi Germany and Fascist Italy* (New York, 1990). On Soviet literature there are Edward J. Brown, *Russian Literature since the Revolution*, 3rd ed. (Cambridge, MA, 1982); and Gleb Struve, *Russian Literature under Lenin and Stalin, 1917–1953* (Norman, OK, 1971). For Italy there is Victoria De Grazia, *The Culture of Consent: Mass Organization of Leisure in Fascist Italy* (Cambridge, UK, 1981); Edward Tannenbaum's *The Fascist Experience*, op cit; and Marcia Landy, *Fascism in Film: The Italian Commercial Cinema, 1931–1943* (Princeton, NJ, 1986).

For **culture and society in Nazi Germany** there are George L. Mosse, ed., *Nazi Culture: Intellectual, Cultural and Social Life in the Third Reich* (New York, 1966); David Schoenbaum, *Hitler's Social Revolution: Class and Status in Nazi Germany, 1933–1939* (New York, 1997); Richard Grunberger, *The 12-Year Reich: A Social History of Nazi Germany, 1933–1945* (New York, 1971); *Art in the Third Reich* (New York, 1979) by Berthold Hinz; and Barbara Miller Lane, *Architecture and Politics in Germany, 1918–1945*, 2nd ed. (Cambridge, MA, 1985). Alan E. Steinweis shows the attempt of the German government to influence artists and entertainers in *Art, Ideology, & Economics in Nazi Germany: The Reich Chambers of Music, Theater, and the Visual Arts* (Chapel Hill, NC, 1993). See also Glenn R. Cuomo, ed., National Socialist Cultural Policy (New York, 1995). The ambiguous attitudes of the Nazis toward music are revealed by Erik Levi in *Music in the Third Reich* (New York, 1994), and Michael H. Kater, *Composers of the Nazi Era: Eight Portraits* (New York, 2002).

On **education and youth in the Soviet Union,** see George S. Counts, *The Challenge of Soviet Education* (New York, 1957). George Kline, ed., *Soviet Education* (New York, 1957) a collection of reports by former teachers and students in the Soviet Union. See also James Riorden, *Sport, Politics and Communism* (New York, 1991). For Italy there are Tracy H. Koon, *Believe, Obey, Fight: Political Socialization of Youth in Fascist Italy, 1922–43* (Chapel Hill, NC, 1985) and the older, but still useful L. Minio-Paluello, *Education in Fascist Italy* (London, 1946).

Books on **education and youth in Nazi Germany** are plentiful. A general work on education is Gilnier W. Blackburn, *Education in the Third Reich* (Albany, NY, 1985). Geoffrey J. Giles, *Students and National Socialism in Germany* (Princeton, NJ, 1985) focuses on German universities. Alan D. Beyerchen, *Scientists under Hitler: Politics and the Physics Community in the Third Reich* (New Haven, CT, 1977) looks at how scientists were affected by the regime. On the youth movement in general see Walter Z. Laqueur, *Young Germany: A History of the German Youth Movement* (New York, 1962). On the Hitler Youth there are Peter D. Stachura, *Nazi Youth in the Weimar Republic* (Santa Barbara, CA, 1975); Gerhard Rempel, *Hitler's Children: The Hitler Youth and the SS* (Chapel Hill, NC, 1989); and Michael H. Kater, *Hitler Youth* (Cambridge, MA, 2004). Two personal accounts are Alfons Heck, *A Child of Hitler: Germany in the Days when God wore a Swastika* (Frederick, CO, 1985); and Horst Kruger, *A Crack in the Wall: Growing Up under Hitler* (New York, 1982).

The status of **women in the totalitarian dictatorships** was badly neglected by historians prior to the 1980s. Thereafter, however, a substantial number of books have appeared. On Soviet women, see Barbara Evans Clements, *Daughters of Revolution: A History of Women in the USSR* (Wheeling, IL, 1994); Mary Buckley, *Women and Ideology in the Soviet Union* (Ann Arbor, MI, 1989); Wendy Z. Goldman, *Women, the State and Revolution: Soviet Family Policy and Social Life, 1917–1936* (New York, 1993); and Francine Plessix, *Soviet Women: Walking the Tightrope* (New York, 1990). Marcelline Hutton argues in *Russian and West European Women, 1860–1939* (Lanham, MD, 2001) that Soviet women gained equal educational and job opportunities, but still suffered from low pay. On women in Fascist Italy, the only good book in English is Victoria de Grazia, *How Fascism Ruled Women: Italy, 1922–1945* (Berkeley, CA, 1992). Jill Stephenson pioneered the study of women in the Third Reich with her *Women in Nazi Society* (New York, 1975) followed by her *Nazi Organization of Women* (Totowa, NJ, 1981). A prize-winning book in the field is Claudia Koonz, *Mothers in the Fatherland: Women, the Family, and Nazi Politics* (New York, 1981). A more recent book on a similar topic is Lisa Pine, *Nazi Family Policy, 1933–1945* (Oxford, 1997). Brief biographies of famous Nazi women can be found in *Women of the Third Reich* by Anna Maria Sigmund (Richmond Hill, Ont., 2000). On women's fashions see Irene Guenther, *Nazi Chic? Fashioning Women in the Third Reich* (New York, 2004).

The area of **health in totalitarian societies** has been virtually monopolized by historians of Nazi Germany, no doubt in large measure because of the Nazis' interest in biology. Several excellent works have appeared recently on Nazi health policies and doctors. By far the most fascinating is Robert N. Proctor, *The Nazi War on Cancer* (Princeton, NJ, 1999), which shows that the Nazis were decades ahead of other countries in fighting the disease. Proctor has also written *Racial Hygiene: Medicine under the Nazis* (Cambridge, MA, 1988). Also of interest are Michael Kater, *Doctors under Hitler* (Chapel Hill, NC, 1989); and R. J. Lifton, *The Nazi Doctors: Medical Killing and the Psychology of Genocide* (New York, 1986). Stefan Kühl has shown the affinity between eugenics in Nazi Germany and the United States in *The Nazi Connection: Eugenics, American Racism and German National Socialism* (New York, 1994).Various aspects of the Nazi appeal to the masses is covered by Shelley Baranowski, *Strength through Joy: Consumerism and Mass Tourism in the Third Reich* (New York, 2004).

**Religion in the totalitarian states** has also attracted a number of scholars. A brief introduction on *Religion in the USSR* has been written by Robert Conquest (London, 1968). The difficult life of the Russian Orthodox Church under Communism has been examined by John S. Curtiss in *The Russian Church and the Soviet State, 1917–1950* (Boston, 1953). Other religious groups are studied by Walter Kolarz in *Religion in the Soviet Union* (London, 1961). On church-state relations in Italy see Daniel A. Binchy, *Church and State in Fascist Italy* (London, 1941, reprinted, New York, 1970, with a new preface); Richard A. Webster, *The Cross and the Fasces: Christian Democracy and Fascism in Italy* (Stanford, 1961); and Anthony Rhodes, *The Vatican in the Age of the Dictators, 1922–45* (London, 1973). For Germany, see Victoria Barnett, *For the Soul of the People: Protestant Protest against Hitler* (Oxford, 1992); John S. Conway, *The Nazi Persecution of the Churches* (New York, 1968); and Guenter Lewy, *The Catholic Church and Nazi Germany* (New York, 1964).

The literature on **terror** in the totalitarian states is huge especially for the **Soviet Union and Nazi Germany** where it was the most common. A broad survey of the secret police in the USSR is Boris Levytsky, *The Uses of Terror: The Soviet Secret Police, 1917–1970* (New York, 1972). The secret police in both the Soviet Union and its satellites is covered by Jonathan R. Adelman, *Terror and Communist Politics: The Role of the Secret Police in Communist States* (Boulder, CO, 1984). Conquest has described the Soviet purges in *The Great Terror: A Reassessment* (New York, 1990). Robert W. Thurston maintains that the Soviet population actually believed that there were numerous "enemies of the people" during the *Terror in Life and Terror in Stalin's Russia, 1934–1941* (New Haven, 1996). The background to the purges can be studied in J. Arch

Getty, *Origins of the Great Purges: The Soviet Communist Party Reconsidered* (Cambridge, UK, 1985). How Soviet citizens responded to the terror can be seen in Sheila Fitzpatrick, *Everyday Stalinism, Ordinary Life in Extraordinary Times: Soviet Russia in the 1930s* (New York, 1999). A wide-ranging anthology on various aspects of terror during the 1930s is J. Arch Getty and Robert T. Manning, eds., *Stalinist Terror: New Perspectives* (Cambridge, UK, 1993). A gripping story of life in a Russian labor camp by an author who survived eight years in one is Alexander Solzhenitsyn's novel, *One Day in the Life of Ivan Denisovich* (New York, 1963, 2001). The same author has also written about *The Gulag Archipelago* (London, 1976–78). The depths of Stalin's anti-Semitism is explored in Arkady Vaksberg's *Stalin against the Jews* (New York, 1994).

Books in English dealing exclusively with **Fascist terror** are few. There are, however, Meir Michaelis, *Mussolini and the Jews: German-Italian Relations and the Jewish Question in Italy, 1922–1945* (London, 1978) and Susan Zuccotti, *The Italians and the Holocaust: Persecution, Rescue, Survival* (New York, 1987). Resistance to the Fascist regime is discussed by Charles F. Delzell, *Mussolini's Enemies: The Italian Anti-Fascist Resistance* (Princeton, NJ, 1961); Aaron Gilette, *Racial Theories in Fascist Italy* (New York, 2002); and most recently, Michele Sarfatti, *The Jews of Mussolini's Italy: From Equality to Persecution* (Madison, WI, 2006). Sarfatti believes that Mussolini was anti-Semitic from the early 1920s.

Books related to **Nazi terror** are once again practically limitless. The more subtle aspects of terror are described by Detlev K. Peukert, *Inside Nazi Germany: Conformity, Opposition, and Racism in Everyday Life* (New Haven, CT, 1987). John M. Steiner, *Power Politics and Social Change in National Socialist Germany: A Process of Escalation into Mass Destruction* (Atlantic Highland, NJ, 1976) is a brilliant analysis of the impact of how Nazism controlled individual patterns of thought and behavior by a survivor of Auschwitz. On the many instruments of terror see George C. Browder, *Foundations of the Nazi Police State: The Formation of Sipo and SD* (Lexington, KY, 1990); Helmut Krausnick, Hans Buchheim, Martin Broszat, and Hans-Adolf Jacobsen, *Anatomy of the SS State* (London, 1968), which covers the varied activities of the SS; and Jacques DeLarue, *The Gestapo: A History of Horror* (New York, 1964). Another work on the Gestapo is Eric A. Johnson, *Nazi Terror: The Gestapo, Jews, and Ordinary Germans* (New York, 1999). Robert Gellately shows that the German people did not always disapprove of concentration camps and were frequently informers in *Backing Hitler: Consent and Coercion in Nazi Germany* (Oxford, 2001).

**Nazi racism and anti-Semitism** are huge subtopics within Nazi terror. The background of Nazi racism is covered by George L. Mosse in *Toward the Final Solution: A History of European Racism* (New York, 1978). Two general surveys of the Nazi persecution of German Jews that emphasize the peacetime years are Saul Friedländer, *Nazi Germany and the Jews,* Vol. I, *The Years of Persecution, 1933–1939* (New York, 1997); and Hermann Graml, *Anti-semitism in the Third Reich* (Cambridge, UK,1992). Karl A. Schleunes, in his classic work, *The Twisted Road to Auschwitz: Nazi Policy toward German Jews, 1933–1939* (Champaign, IL, 1990), shows that the Nazis did not have a blueprint for the "Jewish Question" when they came to power. Ingo Muller, *Hitler's Justice: The Courts of the Third Reich* (Cambridge, MA, 1991) proves that German courts merely helped enforce Nazi barbarities. On the November Pogrom of 1938 there are the popular accounts of Anthony Read and David Fischer, *Kristallnacht: The Unleashing of the Holocaust* (New York, 1989); and Gerald Schwab, *The Day the Holocaust Began: The Odyssey of Herschel Grynszpan* (New York, 1990).

There are several good books dealing with the **opposition to the Nazis.** Leonard B. Schapiro, *Political Opposition in One-Party States* (London, 1972) is a broad, comparative survey. *Contending with Hitler: Varieties of German Resistance in the Third Reich* (Washington, DC, 1991) is an excellent anthology edited by David Clay Large. Another valuable scholarly study is Ian Kershaw, *Popular Opinion & Political Dissent in the Third Reich: Bavaria 1933–1945* (Oxford, 1983).

The **origins of World War II** have never attracted the tremendous volume of literature that has been devoted to the causes of the First World War. Nevertheless, A. J. P. Taylor, *The Origins of the Second World War* (Old Tappan, NJ, 1997; [first published in 1961]) provoked a considerable debate, which is still continuing, by arguing that there was much in Hitler's diplomacy that was traditional and unplanned. The controversy surrounding this path-breaking book has been reviewed in the anthology edited by Gordon Martel, *The Origins of the Second World War Reconsidered: The A. J. P. Taylor Debate after Twenty-five Years* (Boston, 1986). Gerhard Weinberg's two-volume study of Hitler's diplomacy comes closest to being definitive: *Volume I, The Foreign Policy of Hitler's Germany: Diplomatic Revolution in Europe 1933–1936* (Chicago, 1970), covers Hitler's early diplomacy; *Volume II, Starting World War II* (Chicago, 1980) is devoted to the immediate origins of the war. A very recently updated study by Richard and Andrew Wheatcroft is *The Road to War,* 2nd ed. (London, 1999), which points out that for most of the interwar period Britain and France were more concerned about defending their worldwide empires than they were in stopping Hitler. There are also several excellent shorter works on the diplomatic prelude to the war. The best synthesis is probably Keith Eubank, *The Origins of World War II,* 2nd ed. (Wheeling, IL, 1990). Eubank has also edited an anthology of contrasting views in his *World War II: Roots and Causes,* 2nd ed. (Lexington, MA, 1992), which contains a six-page bibliographical essay. See also P. M. B. Bell, *The Origins of the Second World War in Europe,* 2nd ed. (London, 1997). An interesting interpretive essay which argues that Hitler had a *Stufenplan,* or foreign policy based on planned stages, is Klaus Hildebrand, *The Foreign Policy of the Third Reich* (Berkeley, CA, 1973). On Soviet attitudes toward the Munich crisis see Hugh Ragsdale, *The Soviets, the Munich Crisis, and the Coming of World War II* (New York, 2004). The immediate prelude to the war is studied in Williamson Murray's excellent work, *The Change in the European Balance of Power, 1938–1939: The Path to Ruin* (Princeton, NJ, 1984).

**World War II** is another area that has produced a staggering number of publications, albeit by no means all of great scholarly value. A timeless classic about warfare in general is Anatol Rapoport, ed., *Clausewitz On War* (Harmondsworth, UK, 1968). On World War II itself we now have the massive and comprehensive work of Gerhard L. Weinberg, *A World at Arms: A Global History of World War II* (Cambridge, UK, 1994). The same author has put together his wide-ranging studies of the war in *Germany, Hitler, and World War II: Essays in Modern German in World History* (Cambridge, UK, 1995). The most recent one-volume history of World War II is Williamson Murray and Allan R. Millett, *A War to be Won: Fighting the Second World War* (Cambridge, MA, 2000). A large, outstanding, although by now somewhat dated book is Henri Michel, *The Second World War,* translated by Douglas Parmele (London, 1975). Another older, but slightly less detailed work is Peter Calvocoressi and Guy Wint, *Total War: Causes and Courses of the Second World War* (New York, 1983). B. H. Liddell Hart's two-volume *History of the Second World War* (New York, 1972) is also still of value although it tends to emphasize the British role in the war. His earlier work, *The German Generals Talk* (New York, 1948), based on his postwar interviews, must be used with caution. Somewhat sympathetic descriptions of Germany's leading generals can be found in Correlli, Barnett, eds., *Hitler's Generals: Authoritative Portraits of the Men Who Waged Hitler's War*

(New York, 1989). There are likewise many shorter introductions to the war. Among these are John Keegan, *The Second World War* (New York, 1989); M. K. Dziewanowski, *War at any Price* (Englewood Cliffs, NJ, 1997); and James L. Stokesbury, *A Short History of World War II* (New York, 1991). Hitler's talents as a military leader have been explored in Percy Ernst Schramm, *Hitler: The Man and the Military Leader* (New York, 1978); and John Strawson, *Hitler as Military Commander* (London, 1971). Hitler's overall strategy is explained by Norman Rich in *Hitler's War Aims: Ideology, the Nazi State, and the Course of Expansion* (New York, 1973). The early stages of the war are studied in John Lukacs's superb book, *The Last European War, September 1939/December 1941* (Garden City, NY, 1976). Hitler's blunders are clearly delineated by Ronald Lewin in *Hitler's Mistakes: New Insights into What Made Hitler Tick* (New York, 1984); and *How Hitler Could Have Won World War II: The Fatal Errors that Led to Nazi Defeat* by Bevin Alexander (New York, 2000). Looking at the war from the opposite perspective is Richard Overy, *Why the Allies Won* (New York, 1995). Very insightful is Heinz Magenheimer, *Hitler's War: Germany's Key Strategic Decisions, 1940–1995* (London, 1998). How the German people reacted to the course of events during the war is found in Marlis G. Steinert, *Hitler's War and the Germans: Public Mood and Attitude during the Second World War* (Athens, OH, 1977).

Somewhat more **specialized works about World War II** include Geoffrey Roberts, *Stalin's Wars: From World War to Cold War, 1939–1953* (New Haven, CT, 2006), which is an excellent survey based on original documents; and Constantine Pleshakov's detailed exposé of the critical first days of the Russian campaign, *Stalin's Folly: The Tragic First Ten Days of World War II on the Eastern Front* (Boston, 2006). Another brief but highly readable work on the same subject is John Lukacs, *June 1941: Hitler and Stalin* (New Haven, CT, 2006). On other specialized subjects see also the economic studies of Alan S. Milward, *War, Economy and Society, 1939–1945* (Berkeley, CA, 1977); and William Carr, *Arms, Autarky and Aggression: A Study in German Foreign Policy, 1933–1939* (New York, 1972). Comparisons between German and British strategies can be found in Alan F. Wilt, *War from the Top: German and British Military Decision Making during World War II* (Bloomington, IN, 1990). Denis Mack Smith ridicules the Duce's naïve prewar and wartime foreign policy ambitions in *Mussolini's Roman Empire* (New York, 1977). By far the best work on Italy's early participation in the war is MacGregor Knox, *Mussolini Unleashed, 1939–1941: Politics and*

*Strategy in Fascist Italy's Last War* (New York, 1982). The last phase of the war is covered by a British army officer who fought in Italy, Richard Lamb, in *War in Italy, 1943–1945: A Brutal Story* (New York, 1993). The ultimate consequences of Mussolini's intervention are seen in Frederick W. Deakin, *The Brutal Friendship: Mussolini, Hitler and the Fall of Fascism* (New York, 1962). The fate of Fascist leaders is discussed in Roy Palmer Domenico, *Italian Fascists on Trial, 1943–1948* (Chapel Hill, NC, 1991).

Works confined to the **Eastern Front** are also plentiful. Stalin's catastrophic misjudgment of Hitler's intention to invade is explored in Gabriel Gorodetsky, *Grand Illusion: Stalin and the German Invasion of Russia* (New Haven, CT, 1999). The most recent work on the fighting itself is David M. Glantz and Jonathan House, *When Titans Clashed: How the Red Army Stopped Hitler* (Lawrence, KS, 1995). A good, brief introduction is James Lucas, *War on the Eastern Front, 1941–1945: The German Soldier in Russia* (New York, 1982). Somewhat older, but still a standard work is Alexander Werth, *Russia at War, 1941–1945* (London, 2001). Far more detailed accounts of the campaign are the three volumes by John Erickson, *The Soviet High Command* (New York, 1962); *The Road to Stalingrad* (London, 1975); and *The Road to Berlin* (Boulder, CO, 1983). The self-defeating nature of the war waged by the Nazis is seen in Alexander Dallin's scholarly *German Rule in Russia, 1941–1945: A Study of Occupation Policies* (New York, 1957). Close-up views of Hitler during the Russian campaign can be found in H. R. Trevor-Roper, *Blitzkrieg to Defeat—Hitler's War Directives, 1939–1945* (New York, 1964). Albert Speer's *Inside the Third Reich*, op cit., is a riveting narrative of Hitler and the late war years by a man who became Hitler's armaments minister in 1942. On Stalin's military leadership, see Severyn Bialer, ed., *Stalin and His Generals* (New York, 1969). On Nazi wartime propaganda consult Jay W. Baird, *The Mythical World of Nazi War Propaganda, 1939–1945* (Minneapolis, 1974). On resistance movements during the war, the best works are Jorgen Haestrup, *European Resistance Movements, 1939–1945* (London, 1985); and M. R. D. Foot, *Resistance: European Resistance to Nazism 1940–1945* (London, 1976).

Only three major works were published on the **Holocaust** prior to the mid-1970s. These are Gerald Reitlinger's *The Final Solution: The Attempt to Exterminate the Jews of Europe, 1939–1945* (Dunmove, PA, 1981), first published in 1953; Leon Poliakov, *Harvest of Hate: The Nazi Program for the Destruction of the Jews in Europe* (Syracuse, NY,

1954); and Raul Hilberg, *The Destruction of the European Jews,* rev. ed. (New York, 1985). Since the 1970s, however, there has been a veritable deluge of publications, only the most important of which can be mentioned here. A good, basic survey is Yehuda Bauer, et al., *A History of the Holocaust* (New York, 2001). More detailed are Leni Yahl, *The Holocaust: The Fate of European Jewry* (Oxford, 1990); Martin Gilbert, *The Holocaust: History of Jews in Europe During the Second World War* (New York, 1985); and Benno Muller-Hill, *Murderous Science: Elimination by Scientific Selection of Jews, Gypsies, and Others, Germany, 1933–1945* (New York, 1988). A relatively new book on the Holocaust is Daniel Jonah Goldhagen, *Hitler's Willing Executioners: Ordinary Germans and the Holocaust* (New York, 1996), which makes the very controversial allegation that most Germans had been waiting since the mid-nineteenth century for the right moment to exterminate Jews. A broad, popular account of the Holocaust including the increase in anti-Semitism during the interwar years is Deborah Dwork and Robert Ian van Pelt, *Holocaust: A History* (New York, 2002). On the central figure in the Holocaust, see Richard Breitman, *The Architect of Genocide: Himmler and the Final Solution* (New York, 1991). A wide-ranging anthology on anti-Semitism and various aspects of the Holocaust is Francois Furet, ed., *Unanswered Questions: Nazi Germany and the Genocide of the Jews* (New York, 1989). On the German response to the persecution of the German Jews both before and during the war, see Sarah Gordon, *Hitler, Germans and the "Jewish Question"* (Princeton, NJ, 1984).

The literature on the **Soviet Union since 1945** has also been late in coming, but since the emergence of Gorbachev in 1985, and especially since the disintegration of the country in 1991, it has quickly multiplied. A brief survey is Alec Nove, *Stalinism and After: The Road to Gorbachev* (Boston, 1989). A popular study by an American foreign service officer which concentrates on the decline of Communism in Eastern Europe after 1945 is Jay Taylor, *The Rise and Fall of Totalitarianism in the Twentieth Century* (New York, 1993). On the development of the Soviet government during and after Stalin's rule see Jerry Hough and Merle Fainsod, *How the Soviet Union is Governed* (Cambridge, MA, 1979). A general view of Soviet society is D. K. Shipler, *Russia: Broken Idols, Solemn Dreams* (New York, 1983). Secret government operations are revealed by a former agent in *Special Tasks* (Boston, 1994) by Pavel Anatolii Sudoplatov. On the Khrushchev years, see the general secretary's own memoirs, *Khrushchev Remembers: The Last Testament* (Boston, 1974) as well as Roy and Zhores Medvedev, *Khrushchev: The Years in Power* (New York, 1975), and Martin McCauley, *Khrushchev and the Development of Soviet Agriculture* (London, 1976). A superbly written and scholarly biography is William Taubman, *Khrushchev: The Man and His Era* (New York, 2003). The status of the Soviet economy at the end of the Khrushchev era is described in *The Soviet Economy since Stalin: Goals, Accomplishments, Failures* (Philadelphia, 1965). On the Brezhnev years, see John Dornberg, *Brezhnev: The Masks of Power* (London, 1974). The corruption endemic to Soviet society has been explored in Milovan Djilas in *The New Class: An Analysis of the Communist System* (New York, 1957), in which he argues that a new privileged group of party officials was reaping the benefits of Communism; and Konstantin M. Simis, *USSR: The Corrupt Society* (New York, 1982). An insider's look at the Cold War is provided by Anatoly Dobrynin, the Soviet ambassador to the United States from 1962 to 1986, in his memoirs, *In Confidence* (New York, 1995).

The six-year rule of **Mikhail Gorbachev** and the collapse of Communism in the Soviet Union and East-Central Europe not surprisingly produced an avalanche of books. Gorbachev himself outlined his program of reform in his book *Perestroika: New Thinking for Our Country and the World* (New York, 1987). A good explanation of Gorbachev's rise to power is Robert Kaiser, *Why Gorbachev Happened* (New York, 1992). Moshe Lewin argues in *The Gorbachev Phenomenon: A Historical Interpretation*, exp. ed. (Berkeley, CA, 1991) that Gorbachev was the product of long-term changes in the professional and intellectual classes which recognized the need for political reform. In *A Normal Totalitarian Society: How the Soviet Union Functioned and How it Collapsed* (Armonk, NY, 2001), Vladimir Shlapentokh, a former citizen of the Soviet Union, argues that the USSR was still a viable, if backward, state until Gorbachev unintentionally brought about its dissolution. Robert V. Daniels maintains in *The End of the Communist Revolution* (London, 1993) that the Soviet Union disintegrated because of the incompatibility of democracy and the nationality problem. The same issue is discussed by Ronald Grigor Suny in *The Revenge of the Past: Nationalism and the Collapse of the Soviet Union* (Stanford, 1993). A journalist's eyewitness account of the Gorbachev years and immediately thereafter is found in David Remnick's *Lenin's Tomb: The Last Days of the Soviet Empire* (New York, 1994). Geoffrey Stern, *The Rise and Decline of International Communism* (Hants, UK, 1990) includes a third and final section on the decline of Communism in the Soviet Union and its satellite states. Two anthologies on Soviet internal and foreign problems on the eve of the collapse of Communism are Rajan Menon and Daniel N. Nelson, eds., *Limits to Soviet Power* (Lexington, MA, 1989), and the more philosophical *Totalitarianism at the Crossroads*, edited by Ellen Frankel Paul (New Brunswick, NJ, 1990). On the overthrow of Communism in the Soviet dependencies, see the anthology by Ivo Banac, *Eastern Europe in Revolution* (Ithaca, NY, 1992). The daily events which led to the downfall of the Communist system are recounted from articles which appeared in *The New York Times* in Bernard Gwertzman and Michael T. Kaufman, eds., *The Collapse of Communism* (New York, 1991).

For those who wish to examine the **East German Democratic Republic** as an example of totalitarianism there are several excellent and recently published books from which to choose. Henry Ashby Turner, Jr., surveys the entire history of both East and West Germany in *Germany from Partition to Reunification* (New Haven, CT, 1992). Two books which analyzed the German Democratic Republic shortly before its demise are C. Bradley Scharf, *Politics and Change in East Germany: An Evaluation of Socialist Democracy* (Boulder, CO, 1984); and Mike Dennis, *German Democratic Republic: Politics, Economics and Society* (London, 1988). A revealing first-hand look at the GDR by an American is Paul Gleye, *Behind the Wall: An American in East Germany, 1988–89* (Carbondale, IL, 1991). The collapse itself is covered in Melvin J. Lasky, *Voices in a Revolution: The Collapse of East German Communism* (New Brunswick, NJ, 1992).

The fate of the **Nazi war criminals** is revealed by Bradley Smith in *Reaching Judgment at Nuremberg* (New York, 1977); and Robert E. Conot, *Justice at Nuremberg* (New York, 1983). The insights of a prison psychologist who interviewed the top Nazis at Nuremberg are found in G. H. Gilbert, *The Psychology of Dictatorship* (Westport, CT, 1950). The impact of the Nazi regime for the future of German democracy is discussed in Ralf Dahrendorf, *Society and Democracy* (Garden City, NY, 1967).

# INDEX

abortions
    in Germany, 132, 140
    in Italy, 126, 127, 138
    in Soviet Union, 120, 121, 122, 123,
       248, 249
agriculture
    under Bolshevik rule, 14, 68–69
    collectivization of in Russia, 69–76,
       89, 92, 113, 145, 148, 239, 240,
       256, 259
    in Fascist Italy, 82
    Hitler's goals for, 8, 167–68
    in Nazi Germany, 86
    in Soviet Union, 4–5, 5, 17, 68–69,
       236, 239, 240, 245–46, 261
Albania, 194
Alexander III (tsar of Russia), 13
Allied Powers, 209
Allies
    bombing in Italy, 219
    bombing of Germany, 197, 223,
       224–26, 227
    D-Day and, 225–26
    events precipitating alliance, 200–
       201, 262
    Italy's declaration of war on, 194
    North African campaign, 218
    strategy of, 224
    surrender of Italy, 221
    *See also* France; Great Britain; Soviet
       Union; United States; World
       War II
Alliluyeva, Nadezhda, 48
Andropov, Yuri, 242–43
Anglo-German Naval Agreement, 171,
    190

Anglo-Soviet alliance, 200–01, 209,
    231, 262
Angola, 252
anticapitalism, 24, 79, 83–84
anticlericalism, 24, 26, 53, 54, 257
antifeminism, 112, 124–28, 129
anti-intellectualism, 48, 111
antimilitarism, 53, 149
antimiscegenation laws, 158–59, 162,
    163
antimonarchism, 24, 26
anti-Semitism
    in Austria, 59–60, 159
    Catholic Church and, 139, 140
    discrediting of, 263–64
    fascism and, 7–8
    in Germany, 105–06, 111–12, 115,
       119, 130, 134, 154–62, 164,
       211, 266
    of Hitler, 37–38, 40–41, 60, 61,
       230, 257, 259, 262
    in Italy, 25, 111, 112, 139, 143,
       162–63, 262
    Lenin and, 13
    in Poland, 183
    results of, 154–63
    of Stalin, 236–37
    United States and, 135, 158
"April Theses" (Lenin), 14
*Arbeitsbuch*, 85–86
armistice (1918), 32, 33, 37
arms race, 236, 252
arts/architecture. *See* culture
Aryan race, 7–8
atheism, 16, 18, 52,
    137–38

*Hitler, Stalin, and Mussolini:*
*Totalitarianism in the Twentieth Century,* Third Edition
Developmental editor: Andrew J. Davidson
Copy and Production editors: Lucy Herz, Linda Gaio
Proofreader: Claudia Siler
Indexer: Pat Rimmer
Printer: Versa Press